This book analyses the structure and motive forces that shape the global arms transfer and production system. The author distinguishes three tiers of arms producers, defined by such factors as defence production base, military research and development capabilities and dependence upon arms exports. These factors interact with underlying political, economic and military motivations to drive states to produce and export arms, and provide the force which directs the international trade in arms. The author discusses the United States and the Soviet Union, the European arms suppliers and the emerging arms producers of the developing world. Although it concentrates on the contemporary period, the book covers a wide historical span, from the development of military technologies in the fifteenth and sixteenth centuries to twentieth-century revolutions in weaponry. By focusing on the processes of technological innovation and diffusion, the author shows the evolutionary nature of the spread of military technologies, and situates the current arms transfer system in a broad historical context.

CAMBRIDGE STUDIES IN INTERNATIONAL RELATIONS: 22

# Arms and the State: Patterns of Military Production and Trade

*Cambridge Studies in International Relations* is a joint initiative of Cambridge University Press and the British International Studies Association (BISA). The series will include a wide range of material, from undergraduate textbooks and surveys to research-based monographs and collaborative volumes. The aim of the series is to publish the best new scholarship in International Studies from Europe, North America and the rest of the world.

## CAMBRIDGE STUDIES IN INTERNATIONAL RELATIONS

# ARMS AND THE STATE: PATTERNS OF MILITARY PRODUCTION AND TRADE

## KEITH KRAUSE

*Graduate Institute of International Studies, Geneva*

CAMBRIDGE
UNIVERSITY PRESS

Published by the Press Syndicate of the University of Cambridge
The Pitt Building, Trumpington Street, Cambridge CB2 1RP
40 West 20th Street, New York, NY 10011–4211, USA
10 Stamford Road, Oakleigh, Melbourne 3166, Australia

First published 1992
First paperback edition 1995

Printed in Great Britain by Woolnough Bookbinding, Irthlingborough, Northants.

*A catalogue record for this book is available from the British Library*

*Library of Congress cataloguing in publication data*
Krause, Keith,
  Arms and the state: patterns of military production and trade /
Keith Krause.
      p.      cm. – (Cambridge studies in international relations: 22)
  Includes bibliographical references and index.
ISBN 0 521 39446 5
1. Defense industries. 2. Arms transfers. 3. Military assistance.
I. Title. II. Series.
HD9743.A2K73 1992
338.4'7623–dc20   91–5025   CIP

ISBN 0 521 39446 5 hardback
ISBN 0 521 55866 2 paperback

CE

*To my parents*

# CONTENTS

# FIGURES

# TABLES

# ACKNOWLEDGEMENTS

This project began as a doctoral dissertation. The final product bears little resemblance to the original conception, however, and for that I have to thank many teachers, friends and colleagues along the way who influenced my thinking on the discipline of International Relations and the proper place of any study of arms transfers within it. I began, as do many initiates to International Relations, with a practical and political interest in the control of the arms trade, and I reflected all the worst biases of our discipline: a narrow focus on current events, great power relations and foreign policy outputs. My intellectual evolution towards a recognition of the need for a more historical and systemic understanding of the underlying forces of change and evolution at work in the modern international system was the consequence of working in an environment in which the importance of the historical dimension of any question was taken as a given. The results of this evolution are reflected in this book.

Initial stimulus was provided by the late Professor Hedley Bull, who exercised a subtle, yet profound, influence on my thinking about this topic and about International Relations. Professor Adam Roberts supervised the original doctoral dissertation, and together with Lawrence Freedman, Wilfred Knapp and the anonymous reviewers of Cambridge University Press, pointed the way forward to the final typescript. Along the way, many other colleagues commented on my ideas as they were presented in various forums.

I am grateful for the professional assistance and courtesies offered by Agnès Allebeck, Ian Anthony, Judith Frey, Dan Gallick and Herbert Wulf. The manuscript benefited tremendously from the diligent and dedicated work of my research assistant, Ken Boutin. Tom Quiggan also provided material for some of the tables, and Kirsten Semple word-processed several chapters and tables to perfection. Michael Bryans, Andrew Ross, Michael Slack and Wanda Taylor read and commented upon portions of the typescript. Finally, research support over the past three years was provided by the Faculty of Arts and the Centre for International and Strategic Studies at York University, and by the Canadian Social Sciences and Humanities Research Council.

Responsibility for errors of fact or judgement is, of course, ultimately mine alone.

# INTRODUCTION

The arms trade is a ubiquitous aspect of international relations. Today it involves up to 50 states as suppliers and 120 as recipients, and its annual volume exceeds $48,000 million.[1] But although its current scope and magnitude are unprecedented, arms transfers have been used at least since the Peloponnesian Wars to achieve the political, military and economic goals of states and rulers.[2] The invention of the cannon in the fourteenth century, and the 'Military Revolution' of which it was a catalyst, ushered in the modern global arms transfer and production system, as leading suppliers of that time such as Liège and Venice shipped their products to customers across Europe.[3] But over the following six centuries, suppliers ascended and disappeared and the trade, then as now, had an impact on the direction of international politics and the evolution of the modern state system.

The patterns of change and continuity in the modern state system are complex, multi-dimensional and ill understood.[4] On the broad canvas, different writers have highlighted crucial turning points in the legal, economic, technological, military and political spheres. These include the crystallisation of the modern state system after the Peace of Westphalia, the emergence of market economics, the transition from mercantilism to capitalism, the technological transformation of the Industrial Revolution, the rise of modern nation-states, the changing nature of warfare and the rise and fall of empires.[5] Although the links between arms transfer relationships and these spheres of international politics are equally ill defined, each of these dimensions of change can be connected, in one fashion or another, to changes in arms transfers and production. In particular, states' perceptions of the role of arms production and the arms trade in guaranteeing wealth, power and victory in warfare changed as a result of these transformations. Thus an exploration of the emergence and evolution of the international arms transfer and production system could be seen as a sort of prism through which these deeper changes could be viewed.

But my central concern is the obverse: to situate changes in the arms transfer and production system against this broader backdrop. Then one can make sense of the pattern of evolution and change one finds and draw out the implications of this for the present and future. This book thus explores how the structure of the global arms transfer and production system – the geographical locations of centres of innovation and production, the pattern of arms transfers and the diffusion of military technology – evolves. A simple tracing of who sold what to whom would not help us understand this underlying structure, and existing knowledge does not tell us if arms transfers have always played the same, or even a similar, role in international politics.

To be more specific, the arms transfer and production system is located at the intersection of three important sets of concerns (or sets of forces for change) in international relations that are seldom considered together. These can be called 'wealth', 'power' and 'war'. The first concerns those economic forces in the modern (post-feudal) world that shape the production and distribution of goods within and between states. To some degree, the production and trade in weapons are subject to the same pressures and evolutionary dynamic as are commodities such as bananas and televisions. The second set of forces, the pursuit of power by states, often results in attempts by states to change their position in the arms transfer and production system, attempts which accurately reflected shifts in the international hierarchy of power. As pointed out by Paul Kennedy and Robert Gilpin, what determines paramouncy is in part the ability of a state to capture the process of military innovation and production. The third set of forces (which is almost a subset of the second) is the often dramatic catalyst to military innovation and production (and social and political organisation for warfare) that war provides. Historical and contemporary examples abound of redoubled efforts for military production and innovation before, during and after major conflicts, and of the dramatic societal impact of the introduction of new military technologies.

None of these three sets of forces has absolute primacy over the others (at least over the medium term), and all have played a role at one point or another in shaping the patterns of military innovation and production, and the subsequent transfers of arms and know-how that result in the diffusion of military technology. In addition, the nature of the forces themselves has changed, as illustrated by the evolution from the mercenary wars of the fifteenth century to the total wars of the twentieth, or the transformation from mercantilist to capitalist trading in the nineteenth century. But it is critical for our understanding of the workings of the contemporary system to gain some insight into how these forces interact, and which of them may be more, or most, important over the longer term in shaping the structure of the arms transfer and production system.

This large topic contains many more specific questions, which are tackled in two distinct, but connected, parts. Chapters 1–3 discuss the historical evolution of the international arms transfer system, roughly from the Military Revolution of the fifteenth century to the early twentieth century. It presents a *longue durée* historical view of the arms trade that restores perspective to a subject too often seen only in the light of day-to-day transactions. As Fernand Braudel points out, 'the social sciences, by taste, by deep-seated instinct, perhaps by training, have a constant tendency to evade historical explanation ... by concentrating overmuch on the "current event"'.[6] Few students of the arms trade have asked if historical parallels to the present situation exist, caught up as they are in the latest controversies over American sales to Saudi Arabia or Soviet shipments to Ethiopia. A *longue durée* viewpoint also presents the dynamic motive forces driving the arms transfer system and demonstrates that it possesses a 'life cycle' initiated primarily by the motor of technological change. A state's position in the cycle, and the progress of the cycle itself, crucially affects the options states possess for using arms transfers and arms production as a tool of foreign policy. Finally, this historical perspective establishes that a greater continuity in the relationship of state power to military innovation exists than is commonly supposed.

This historical-structural examination prepares the ground for a comprehensive picture to be drawn in chapter 4 onwards of the contemporary (post-1945) arms transfer and production system, which will locate it with reference to the evolutionary scheme sketched in chapters 1–3. With the present system located in its historical context, and with a better understanding of the motive forces of change in the system, this snapshot can be extended, and the outlines of the likely future shape of the arms transfer system (and its impact on the relations between states) can be traced. Readers interested only in contemporary developments will be tempted to skip the historical material in chapters 1–3, and it can only be stressed that, in the arms trade as elsewhere, the historical dimension of contemporary developments can be ignored only with peril.

The intention is not, however, to build a model of the international arms transfer system and provide a scientific predictive account of its role in the relations between states. Such models are too often static structuralist presentations of a ceaselessly repeating timeless monotony that robs individual actors of what little freedom they possess to shape their world. Equally important, one must not simply project the current system back into time, automatically finding the causal roots of contemporary developments. No one with a sensitive understanding of contemporary politics can escape noting the contingency of events; it is wise to keep this in perspective when evaluating the opportunities and projects of a Henry VIII or Gustav Adolphus.

Thus my more modest goal is to explore and articulate how the forces that affect the international arms transfer system worked themselves out from the Military Revolution of the 1500s until today and, more specifically, in the three periods following episodes of rapid technological innovation (the cannon/gunpowder revolution, the Industrial Revolution and the 'revolution in mobility'). This weighing of the various forces in the global arms transfer system will provide a better guide with which to make more specific judgements on the ability of any actor to manipulate its role in the system and achieve its policy goals. An understanding of the way in which the structure constrains the options of actors, and of the relevance of past constraints to current developments, is a much more important tool for assessing the future of the arms transfer system than the stated plans of decision makers.

These issues are of interest to various groups in addition to historians. States and individual decision makers always operate within structures that dictate the limits of their agency, but the role played by these structures is seldom understood, except in its vaguest outlines. Any assessment of the possibilities for success or failure of the specific changes which states or decision makers attempt to work on the world, however, depends critically on an understanding of these structures, their evolutionary processes and the types of change they allow. Since these structures only unfold and evolve slowly, a long historical perspective is essential.

To put this in concrete terms I can offer here two examples, one analytic and one practical, of the confusion created when scholars lack an understanding of the structural evolution of the global arms transfer and production system. As Aaron Karp observes in a summary of recent developments in the arms trade:

> Since academic analysis of the international trade in arms and military equipment began in the mid-1960s, a weighty literature has emerged. Much has been done to illuminate basic facts, trends and relationships. None the less, understanding remains far from complete. Events in 1987 helped show the limits of insights about the arms trade [and] ... made it apparent that the international arms trade is evolving in ways that had not been anticipated ... Old

4

assumptions can no longer be taken for granted. Basic relationships are not as clear as they seemed to be just a few years ago.[7]

A weighty literature capable of having its assumptions and understanding of basic relationships overturned by the developments of only a few years is unable to distinguish ephemeral from durable change. If it is true, as Karp later argues, that 'in retrospect, the arms trade patterns of the 1960s and 1970s may come to be seen as anomalies in the history of international relations', one wonders why, since the history of international relations is not a dark secret, this anomaly became apparent so late.[8]

The second example concerns the renewed attention being paid to the problem of controlling arms transfers. On the policy level, this interest is reflected in the creation of the Missile Technology Control Regime and the United Nations-sponsored expert-group study, Transparency in International Arms Transfers. On the analytic level, several scholars have recently addressed various specific problems of arms transfer control.[9] Yet as Thomas Ohlson points out:

> arms transfers are essentially a *systemic* phenomenon ... [that] result[s] from national political, military and economic motivations and considerations in both supplier and recipient countries ... Arms transfers can neither be understood nor judged without insight into the dynamics of this complex web of system interaction between and within interest groups and states.[10]

Because it generally fails to treat arms transfers within their systemic context, the existing literature offers a poor guide to addressing specific concerns such as control of the arms trade.

Before I present the structure of the book more clearly, it will be useful to sketch the three distinct phases the literature on the arms trade has passed through. The first phase, which spanned the interwar period, was distinguished by polemical, partisan and prescriptive analyses of the evils of the arms merchants, who were held partly responsible for the First World War and the lesser conflicts that preceded it. A quotation from an article of the period captures the flavour of the analysis:

> In 1899 British soldiers were shot down by British guns that British armaments firms had sold to the Boers ... in 1914 ... German soldiers were killed by German guns manned by the armies of King Albert and Czar Nicholas II ... Bulgarian troops turned French 75s on French poilus [and] ... China has been pleased to use excellent Japanese guns for the purpose of killing excellent Japanese soldiers.[11]

Titles such as *Merchants of Death: A Study of the International Armaments Industry; Iron, Blood and Profits: An Exposure of the World-Wide Munitions Racket; Der Blutige Internationale der Rüstingsindustrie* and *Le Creusot: Terre féodale* made up the backbone of the literature, the corpus of which was filled by pamphlets and exposés distributed widely throughout America, Britain, France and (to a lesser extent) Germany.[12] The central argument was that 'governments driven by the economic crisis work hand in hand with armament manufacturers in preparing for the next war', and the main prescription was for arms industries to be nationalised.[13] The literature accorded arms transfers great influence over the policies and destinies of states, and individuals great (even conspiratorial) control over arms transfer policies. Although this was an understandable reaction to the horrors of modern total war, the writing was anecdotal and unsystematic. The evidence did not support its conclusion that 'armaments makers apply the two axioms of their business: when there are wars, prolong them; when there is peace, disturb it', and only rarely can one find any hint that the solution to the problem was more complex than simple nationalisation of the international arms firms.[14]

This literature did spawn slightly more sophisticated efforts to understand the international arms trade with the establishment in Britain and the United States of government commissions to investigate the arms industry. But the United States Senate's Nye Committee became a precursor of the McCarthy hearings, with grandstanding, scapegoating and evidence-stretching being the order of the day.[15] Britain's 1934 Royal Commission on 'The Private Manufacture of and Trading in Arms' was a more sedate affair. Although 'the tide of popular feeling was [now] running fiercely against private manufacture' of arms, the Commission did not advocate any concrete action against private arms dealers.[16] The League of Nations, which had enshrined in its charter its grave objection to the private manufacture of 'implements of war', also studied the arms trade. Its *Statistical Yearbook*, published annually between 1924 and 1938, was the first systematic attempt to collect data on the extent and structure of the international arms transfer system, but was hampered by the reluctance of governments to release potentially damaging information.[17] The various League Disarmament conferences of the 1920s and early 1930s did little but stonewall arms control efforts.

The study of the arms trade had advanced little by 1945. The Cold War period, with its intellectually oppressive ideological climate and its massive transfers of weapons to the new alliances, was not conducive to dispassionate analysis, and the requisite data were not public. But a number of trends converged in the late 1950s and early 1960s to alter this, including:

> the growing number of arms consumers;
> the belief that arms transfers to new states in Africa, Asia and the Middle East would facilitate more intense partnerships and alliances;
> fears of a nuclear and conventional arms build-up that spurred peace research and data collection;
> the emergence of the Soviet Union as an arms supplier;
> the rebuilding of European arms industries.

These changes triggered the second phase (covering roughly 1965–73), which saw the first systematic and rigorous analyses of arms transfers. In 1970, the Stockholm International Peace Research Institute began publishing the *World Armaments and Disarmament Yearbook* (including data on arms transfers) and the Massachusetts Institute of Technology Arms Control Project published its study *Arms Transfers to Less Developed Countries*.[18] The International Institute for Strategic Studies' new publication, the *Military Balance*, also contained detailed information on global military arsenals. Individual studies by Harold Hovey (1966), Lewis Frank (1969), Geoffrey Kemp (1970–1) and John Stanley and Maurice Pearton (1972) also emerged. This work concentrated on case studies of specific suppliers and industries or on transfers to specific clients or regions, and relied on anecdotal or *ad hoc* data. None the less, these studies posed the questions that have concerned scholars since. It was in this period that the consensus emerged, buttressed by the behaviour of policy makers, that arms transfers were an important tool of foreign policy that supplier states could use to gain influence over clients.[19]

The third phase, covering the period from 1973 to the present, witnessed an explosion of studies that paralleled the growth in the arms trade itself. Much of this material also used a case-study approach, and few attempts were made to situate arms transfers in the broader fabric of relations between states. Two notable exceptions were Robert Harkavy's *The Arms Trade and International Systems* and Stephanie Neuman and Robert Harkavy's *Arms Transfers in the Modern World*. At the risk of oversimplification, this recent literature can be grouped into three categories. The first (and largest) is the 'American foreign policy' literature, represented by such authors as Paul Hammond, David Louscher, Anthony Cordesman, Anne Cahn, Andrew Pierre and Michael Klare. These authors focused on foreign policy and the political motives and effects of arms transfers (and occasionally on their military implications), and generally left aside purely economic or economic/structural considerations. Consequently, their stress on the policy aspects of arms transfer relationships and on specific bilateral relationships such as the American–Saudi Arabian or American–Israeli led to an emphasis on agency and the actions of decision makers. This applies across the American political spectrum, whether or not the issue is the manipulation of arms transfers as 'a valuable foreign policy instrument for use in a wide variety of circumstances' or proposals for restraint on arms transfers, justified as enlightened self-interest.[20] Only occasionally have attempts been made to fit arms transfers into a broader international relations framework and to give a dynamic account of the factors affecting the evolution of the arms transfer system.[21]

The second group, working in a 'European political economy' tradition, includes authors such as Wolfgang Mallmann, Herbert Wulf, Michael Brzoska, Thomas Ohlson and Mary Kaldor. Here one finds the strongest emphasis on a structural account of persistent features of the arms transfer system and an approach that integrates the economic, political and military motivations driving arms suppliers and recipients. On the one hand, their account of dependency and imperialism in relations between states led to a reliance on a strong variant of the 'arms transfers provide political influence' thesis.[22] On the other, they possessed a commitment to reducing the arms trade, or at least recipients' dependence on the superpowers.[23]

Finally, there are the iconoclasts who specialise in one aspect of the arms transfer system as regional specialists (David Pollock or William Quandt on the Middle East, Anne Gilks on China), or as economists (James Katz on developing world industries), or as analysts of the policy of a specific non-American supplier (Roger Pajak for the Soviet Union, Edward Kolodziej for France, Aaron Klieman for Israel). The detailed nature of the scholarship, and the limited scope of the conclusions drawn, does generate much wisdom on the arms trade. The scholarship is, however, neither systematic nor integrated, and by emphasising idiosyncratic factors it obscures structural constraints and recurring patterns operating on all participants in the arms transfer system.

There are five general weaknesses in the arms transfer literature. First, it is ahistorical, in two senses. It makes virtually no reference to arms transfers before the Second World War, and it seldom situates the changes discussed within the overall context of the evolution of international political relationships. While this would be defensible if the current epoch were unique, much can be learned about likely future patterns of transfers from past arms transfer systems. Second, it is Americo-centric and policy-orientated: with few exceptions much of the material is concerned with generating specific policy prescriptions for the United States. This may again be defensible, but not if the analysis is narrowed to current popular subjects that add little to our understanding of the role of arms transfers in international relations. Third, there is little discussion of recipients' motivations to purchase arms, and of the impact transfers have on them. This is doubtless because what is at hand is information about suppliers, but again, recipients' attitudes and expectations affect the conclusions that can be drawn about the future evolution of the arms transfer system. Fourth, few writers integrate economic, military and political perspectives, with the result that the interaction of the different motivations for producing, supplying or receiving arms is neglected. Finally, the literature is largely atheoretical and fails to analyse arms transfers against the backdrop of the interactions of states in the international system:

> Students interested in the international traffic in arms tend to make a series of assumptions about the international behaviour of national systems ... the larger theoretical questions and broader analytic perspective ... remain[ing], for the most part, unexplored.[24]

Running as a thread through all these weaknesses is one major flaw: little or no analysis (with the exception of the European political economists) of the structure of the arms transfer and production system. Direct analysis of the structural aspects of the current system is evident in the work of only a few authors, although many more make passing reference to the structure of the system without subjecting it to searching examination. A good example is the division of the arms market into different tiers of producers or suppliers. There has been little detailed work on how to divide the tiers or on what would determine membership in them (other than an *ad hoc* evaluation based on market share), no systematic attempt to relate this to the structure of the defence industry in various states, no attempt to determine if this structure is historically aberrant, and little attempt to assess the possibilities of movement between tiers.[25]

Although this book does not avoid all these weaknesses, it does examine some of the neglected aspects. It begins with the historical account of the development and structure of the international arms transfer system, with chapter 1 outlining the argument and providing the organising principles for the historical evidence. The key argument is that there have been a series of technological revolutions in armaments which, when married with the pursuit of wealth, power and victory in war that motivated state policy, resulted in the emergence of several foci of innovation that were the source of increased arms transfer activity. The role of technological innovation as an exogenous variable catalysing the waves of the arms transfer and production system is detailed, and a life cycle of the international arms transfer system is sketched. It is argued that rapid innovation is followed by a period of levelling during which military technology is diffused, secondary and tertiary producers emerge and the arms transfer system manifests its traditional three-tiered structure. Finally, the structure of the three tiers, and of relations between actors in different tiers, is outlined.

Chapters 2 and 3 then detail the evolution of the arms transfer and production system from the European emergence from feudalism to the Second World War. This survey is necessarily fragmentary because of the scanty evidence and absence of work to draw upon, but it supplies evidence for the argument presented in chapter 1. It is broken into two periods: chapter 2 deals with the period leading up to the Military Revolution of the sixteenth century, and chapter 3 with the period of the Industrial Revolution and the revolution in mobility of the early twentieth century.

The second half of the work turns to the contemporary system. The greater information available allows an examination not only of the long-term evolutionary dynamic of the contemporary system, but also of the short- and medium-term forces at work, such as the acquisition cycle of weapons, the impact of decolonisation, and the debt load of Third World recipients. Chapter 4 presents as the starting point a descriptive and statistical snapshot of the emergence of the contemporary arms transfer system. Chapters 5, 6 and 7 examine the three tiers of producers identified (which can be characterised as the core, the semi-periphery and the periphery) in terms of the structure of arms industries within each tier, the mechanisms for arms sales decision making, and the differing economic, political and military driving forces that direct their participation in the arms trade. Chapter 8 discusses the role of recipients in the system, and highlights the range of clients' responses to their subordinate status in the arms transfer and production system that one finds below the threshold of an attempt at indigenous arms production.

Finally, the conclusion compares and contrasts the contemporary arms transfer system with previous epochs, drawing out the persistence of such features as tiers of producers or the rise of indigenous industries in major customers, and differences such as the current use of arms transfers as positive tools of foreign policy rather than negative instruments that must be controlled, or the emergence of genuinely transnational arms production. It also projects current trends into the future, assesses the impact these developments will have on the future evolution of the international system, and examines the conclusions found in the current literature in the light of this work.

A study of such wide-ranging scope undoubtedly has many shortcomings. Since the main thrust is to provide a better understanding of the motive forces in the arms transfer and production system, its main contribution is *not* in shining a light into some dusty corner and uncovering new information. It relies extensively on secondary sources, especially from the specialist literature on arms production in various states. The drawback is that a reliance on secondary sources cannot confirm their conclusions against primary documents and hence is beholden to their weaknesses. But such an endeavour would produce a very different book. There are also some aspects of the arms trade and arms production that are treated in less detail in this book. The most important of these is the purely domestic procurement aspects of arms production decisions, which for the United States and Soviet Union accounts for the bulk of production. I am concerned with production only in so far as it helps explain the existence or shape of the arms market or the imperative to trade weapons (either as an exporter or importer), for technological or other reasons. Second, I do not examine (except indirectly) the proliferation of nuclear, biological or chemical weapons technologies, although the diffusion of nuclear technology may well be the fourth technological revolution. Third, the focus on technological innovation and diffusion gives this book a 'high-tech bias' that should not be taken for ignorance of the destructive impact of the introduction or use of unsophisticated weapons in a conflict. Fourth, readers looking for an exposé of the sensationalist aspects of arms deals – the bribery, influence-peddling and covert deals – will be disappointed, as these subjects do not lend themselves to scholarly study. As a final caveat, given the uncertainty and secrecy surrounding arms production and sales, and the poor quality of the data one must work with, it is worth underlining the tentative nature of some of the evidence (and hence conclusions) presented in what follows.

# 1 MOTIVE FORCES IN THE EVOLUTION OF THE ARMS TRANSFER AND PRODUCTION SYSTEM

To understand the evolutionary dynamic of the global arms transfer and production system, one must first untangle the forces that generate the demand for the production and trade in weapons and second, explain the way in which this demand may change over time. Thus this chapter will begin by expanding upon the motive forces briefly outlined in the introduction – the pursuit of wealth, power and victory in war – to sketch the way in which these may shape the emergence and evolution of the global arms transfer and production system. The second section will focus on the processes of technological innovation and diffusion in the arms transfer system. The final section will outline the structure of the arms transfer system this analysis suggests. This chapter thus both presents the argument in skeletal form to be measured against the evidence to follow and provides some organising principles for that evidence.

Two important difficulties with this approach should be acknowledged at the outset: a wide gulf separates the scholarship that concentrates on different sets of forces identified here as fundamental, and there is no consensus on the process of change in the international system on which one could easily erect an analysis of the evolution of arms transfers and production. In a sense, the three motive forces distinguish the intellectual foci of different disciplines: the 'pursuit of wealth', that of economics and economic history; the 'pursuit of power', that of international relations; and the 'pursuit of victory in war', that of military history. What follows thus runs the risk of simplifying the analysis of complex historical processes to reductionist single-factor (or sets of factors) explanations, but it is justified since the goal is not to analyse changes in arms transfers and production to illuminate the evolution of the modern international system, but rather to situate the changing patterns of the arms trade against this broader historical backdrop.

12

## Motive forces in the production and transfer of arms

### *The pursuit of wealth*

The pursuit of wealth is a shorthand to describe the economic forces governing the production and distribution of goods within and between states. Although arms are unlikely to be traded like other commodities, arms production is an industrial process that depends to a degree on various inputs and factor endowments in an economy. These include the overall level of industrialisation, the existence of an adequate economic infrastructure, the supply of skilled labour, the existence of backward and forward linkages with other industries (for the supply of raw materials, subcontracting, and the marketing of spin-off products), the level of state support and protection, and the existence of a market for the goods.[1] The success or failure of arms production depends in the long run as much (if not more) on these factors as on the political will (pursuit of power) that may have spurred the initiation of arms production. Economic factors essentially limit the geographical extent of arms production in a given period, depending on the distribution of factor endowments.

But the distribution (and relative importance) of these factors is not static, and many economists have pointed out that the global economy 'has developed in waves, each wave associated with a different technology and a different location'.[2] One would expect the focal points of the arms transfer system to track (at least loosely) shifts in the productive centres and dominant processes in the global economy. The ability of a state to adopt new productive processes would be more important for the long-run success of weapons manufacture (and exports) than the simple ability to reproduce weapons technology at the existing technological frontier. The speed at which these processes (mechanised production, for example) are adopted will depend upon a combination of political and economic stimuli.

The economic dimension of arms production is also not a one-way street. An arms industry not only depends on a particular level of industrial development to succeed, but in turn can be regarded as a potential catalyst or leading sector for industrialisation, capable of stimulating economic development through its backward and forward linkages. As Clive Trebilcock, in his study of nineteenth-century European arms industries, put it:

> if a high-quality armament sector could produce a battery of stimulating effects within an advanced manufacturing economy ... would it not *a fortiori* exert an even more powerful influence within the

13

European economies classed as developing or less developed at that time?[3]

Advanced arms production has been variously associated with dominant sectors such as metal-working, naval engineering, iron- and steel-making, heavy industrial machinery manufacture, transportation and electronics, which has made it a clear adjunct to civilian technological advancement. While the historical and contemporary evidence on the spin-off benefits of arms production is mixed, the issue is significant for the evolution of the arms transfer system.[4] One can imagine two opposite possibilities. At one pole arms industrialisation is a strong catalyst of industrial development, the success or failure of specific initiatives depends little on the initial factor endowments of a state, and military production has a relatively open-ended global expansion. At the other pole, investment in armament industries has a negative impact on economic development and growth, depends entirely on factor endowments, and the global diffusion of military production is limited. Reality, of course, corresponds to neither alternative, and these two forces interact in a complex and dynamic way. Certainly the belief that an arms industry will catalyse industrial development (or is an essential attribute of a modern economy) can help explain many state-sponsored arms production initiatives, while the limits of arms production may still be dictated by somewhat dynamic factor endowments. Where one finds oneself between these two poles, however, is an empirically and theoretically important issue.

Finally, state policies towards the arms trade depend not only on political factors but on prevailing economic and political beliefs. For example, in the sixteenth to eighteenth centuries, the mirror image of 'military self-sufficiency [as] . . . an aspect of autarchy in the mercantilistic sense' would be the belief that weapons, being the source of power (analogous to specie), should not be traded except for strictly political reasons.[5] This would result in direct intervention in (or control of) the arms trade. With the shift from mercantilist to *laissez-faire* thought, however, trade is seen as the source of wealth and power and the engine of growth for sustained and enhanced productive capacity; this would logically result in fewer direct restrictions on arms transfers. A shift to indirect political intervention in the market also follows from this, and objections to the trade in technology may even diminish, as long as the wellsprings of technological innovation are not directly threatened. But if these wellsprings are threatened (as some argue they are today by the internationalisation of industrial

14

production and the freer flow of technology), one could anticipate a resurgence of neo-mercantilist concern over the diffusion of technology via arms transfers.

## The pursuit of power

The primary driving force behind the large-scale production of arms is the existence of states in potentially conflictive relationships operating under the security dilemma in a self-help system. As Thomas Esper's study of military self-sufficiency in early-modern Russia noted:

> a state's power, indeed its very survival, is closely related to the adequacy of its military organization to meet foreign policy needs. Not only is this adequacy dependent upon manpower and other economic resources, plus efficiency, training and morale factors; it is also greatly affected by weapons technology.[6]

The first consequence is that large-scale arms production should emerge wherever a state system exists, and more specifically as a simultaneous accompaniment to the birth of the modern state system out of the European feudal order. Weapons, like any other commodity, require a market demand to stimulate production, and as long as the primary consumers are individual soldiers 'required to furnish their own arms and equipment ... it is bootless to inquire into the industry – which must generally have been local – that provided the armor and weapons ... before the stage when governments were prepared to equip their troops'.[7] Of course, arms production and trade existed prior to the advent of the modern state system, and patterns of trade should help explain where and why centres of innovation and production appear. But the emergence of the modern state system should mark a major discontinuity in arms production, and similar discontinuities in the pattern of arms production should appear whenever the state system undergoes rapid and far-reaching change.

The pursuit of power by states serves to explain more than just the *appearance* of large-scale arms production, as the possession of advanced military technology (and the ability to reproduce it or to innovate) is a crucial dimension of the relative capabilities of states. Prominent analyses of change in the international system concentrate on the uneven distribution of economic and technological capabilities and the forces that generate a decline in the military and economic capabilities of states.[8] If shifts in the distribution of relative capabilities are one of the indices of change in the international system, and if

15

military technology is one of the basic capabilities of states, then the pursuit of power will also drive states to attempt to capture the process of military innovation and production.

If the existence of states in competition is sufficient to explain arms production, only a small extension of logic is required to explain the arms trade. All states in a self-help system, if they could, would produce arms. The uneven distribution of economic, social and technological capabilities means, however, that differences exist in states' abilities to produce arms, and arms transfers are then a logical result of the quest to acquire modern means of warfare. This simple point highlights the link between arms transfers, arms production and the structure of the international system: transfers are only the result of an inability to produce weapons, itself a desire produced by the self-help nature of the international system. Hence one must track shifts in patterns of production to make sense of patterns of trade (and, ipso facto, change the system to eliminate the trade). This makes weapons critically different in at least one respect from other commodities, in which patterns of production and trade may follow the dictates of comparative advantage. Hence also changes in the structure of the arms transfer and production system ought to mirror changes in the international system as a whole.

One expectation that follows from this would be that the trade in arms (and key inputs in arms production) would be ceaselessly subject to restrictions and manipulations, as states attempt to aid friends, hinder foes and protect advantages they possess. If this is so, it is unlikely that 'up until the 1930s, arms were normally exported as freely as any civil item' or that 'political considerations with regard to international arms trade were of secondary importance'.[9] A second, more important, expectation is that because acquiring weapons is second best to producing them, the arms transfer system is likely to be not only a trade in goods, but also a vehicle for the transmission and diffusion of military technology. This would take the form of attempts to acquire the means to *reproduce*, to *adapt*, and eventually to *produce* weapons. Thus an understanding of the dynamic of the arms transfer system requires an analysis of the process of diffusion of military technology, a problem explored in greater detail below.

### Victory in war, arms production and arms transfers

In Leon Trotsky's provocative words, 'war is the locomotive of history'. War is the proving ground of military technology, and the pursuit of victory in war provides a stimulus to arms transfers, arms

16

production and military innovation. Although war is in some sense merely the concrete manifestation of the pursuit of power, the demands generated before, during and after war can have direct and indirect effects on the arms transfer and production system distinct from the effects caused by the overarching pursuit of power by states.[10] The most immediate direct consequence of war is increased demand for arms (either imported or indigenously produced), but this potentially ephemeral demand does not necessarily affect the structure of the arms transfer system. A prolonged conflict that is punctuated by wars, however, creates increased demands for the transfer of military technology and the development of indigenous arms industries and has a potentially more lasting impact on the arms transfer sytem. As Esper notes with respect to Muscovite Russia, 'the requirements of external war compelled Russia to seek the most advanced military techniques even though it lacked a comparable level of economic and technological developments'.[11]

The indirect impact of war may also be significant. War has been argued by some analysts (beginning with Werner Sombart's *War and Capitalism*) to have played 'a prominent part . . . in the rise of modern capitalism during the sixteenth, seventeenth and eighteenth centuries'.[12] As A. H. John points out: 'in all wars, the demands of government fall mainly on the heavy metal industries, the allied manufacture of munitions, shipbuilding and on certain sections of the textile industries'.[13] The stimulus to production and innovation in these sectors, or the organisational changes precipitated by war, can perhaps catalyse or accelerate economic development. On the other side, war has been indicted as hindering capital accumulation and investment, permitting the deterioration of capital stock, distorting investment priorities, squandering labour resources, and wreaking general mayhem on orderly economic development.[14] Whatever the macro-economic consequences, these distortions are likely to have a more pronounced impact on the armaments sector, and hence are relevant factors in the evolution of the arms transfer and production system. Finally, analysts have argued that the demands of war stimulated the development of the modern nation-state by increasing the need for central organisation and taxation.[15] This too has an indirect impact on the arms transfer system, for if the optimum scale of the nation-state is partly determined by its ability to mobilise for war, then the international hierarchy will be reflected in the arms transfer and production system, and changes in it will track against the backdrop of changes wrought by the pursuit of victory in warfare. Even the global dominance of European powers can be explained as a consequence of the political and military entity forged through European warfare, but at this point the pursuit of victory in war and the pursuit of power merge.

### The dynamic role of technology

These disparate threads can be woven into a more coherent tapestry with the unifying idea of technological change. Scholars working within each of the traditions identified have pointed to the dynamic role of technology in the process of change. Within the pursuit of wealth tradition Immanuel Wallerstein has noted that:

> the physical locus of the most 'dynamic' sectors has also regularly changed – both within state boundaries and across state boundaries . . . in this way, technological advance has created a situation of constant geopolitical restructuring of the world-system.[16]

Within the pursuit of power tradition, Robert Gilpin has argued that:

> the diffusion of military and economic technology from more advanced societies to less advanced societies is a key element in the international redistribution of power.[17]

Within the pursuit of victory in war tradition, Martin van Creveld has pointed out that:

> war is completely permeated by technology and governed by it. The causes that lead to wars . . . the blows with which campaigns open . . . the relationship between the armed forces and the societies that they serve . . . even the very conceptual frameworks employed . . . in order to think about war and its conduct – not one of these is immune to the impact that technology has had.[18]

By extension, if one narrows the analysis to the arms transfer and production system, one expects changes in the distribution of military technology (as a subset of technology writ large) to be a key element in determining patterns of arms production and trade.

Since our focus is on the diffusion and reproduction of military technology, including both the science of making weapons and the art of producing and operating them in a particular socio-cultural, economic and political context, one must clarify and distinguish the different meanings associated with the term 'military technology'. Figure 1 displays schematically four types of military technology by successive levels of complexity, with the least complex having the widest geographical distribution and the most complex being relatively scarce. Technology I, the most basic and common, refers to the

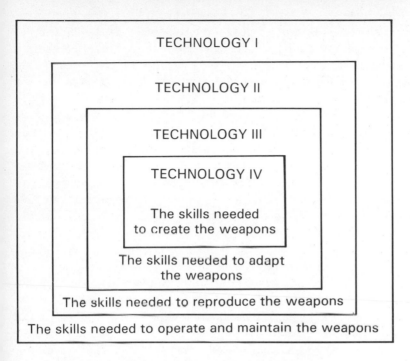

Figure 1 Different types of military technology

skills needed simply to operate the weapons (or weapons systems) and their related technological artifacts. Technology II describes the basic scientific and engineering skills needed to reproduce (or copy) technology I. Technology III refers to the forms of military and economic organisation needed to use, adapt or refine the weapons for particular battlefield or marketplace conditions.[19] Technology IV covers the social, political and economic organisation (or motivation) needed to produce new forms of technology and to advance the production frontier. This is the least widely distributed skill, possessed by only a few states in any historical epoch. These distinctions will reappear in the general description of the global distribution of arms production capabilities (and hence arms transfer patterns), for the degree of mastery of technologies I–IV is the limiting condition that dictates the structure of the arms transfer and production system.

### Technology as an exogenous variable

There is broad agreement that possession of modern weapons is a key element in determining the international hierarchy of power, but less consensus on the dynamic aspect of this process. However, scholars are examining more closely the relationship between technological change and change in the international system, and asking if technological innovation and diffusion in the military realm is an exogenous variable introduced into the international system via the arms transfer and production system, or a purely endogenous phenomenon. The construction of cause and effect in this argument (not restricted to military technology) has spawned a great debate that can only be sketched here. On one hand, if military innovation (as a specific case of technological innovation) is an exogenous process, then the emergence of the modern state system (and a great deal else) is a *consequence* of technological innovations that provided advantages in warfare to states possessing modern weapons systems that could only be afforded (and used) by states with a certain threshold wealth and social organisation. Thus, for example, William McNeill explains the demise of the Italian city-states by arguing that 'as soon as guns became critical weapons in war, Italian technological primacy in the armaments industry decayed . . . the major effect of the new weaponry was to dwarf the Italian city-states'.[20] This is also the argument advanced by Lynn White to explain the rise of feudalism as a consequence of the successful introduction of the stirrup in warfare, and by Carlo Cipolla and Daniel Headrick in explaining various phases of European imperialism.[21] As Edward Kolodziej summarises it, 'modernization . . . is mediated through the nation-state system . . . [and] military technology is viewed as a key, if not the only, motor force of this complex process'.[22]

On the other hand, one can view technological change and innovation itself as a product of a particular concatenation of social and economic forces that result in the capture of the process of technological innovation by certain states. 'Invention', as Michael Polanyi noted, 'is a drama enacted on a crowded stage', and the basic technologies that underlie specific seemingly revolutionary innovations are usually widely diffused and known.[23] In the early modern period, for example, the technologies required for cannon-founding and gunpowder-making were available to the Chinese, Europeans, Byzantines and Muslims.[24] The explanation of why Europeans were first to apply these technologies to warfare in a systematic and successful fashion is rooted in the social and economic environment, and is not dependent upon radical technological innovations. As Lynn White notes, 'the acceptance or rejection of an invention, or the extent to which its implications are realized if it is accepted, depends quite as much upon the condition of a society, and upon the imagin-

20

ation of its leaders, as upon the nature of the technological item itself'.[25]

Ultimately the two processes are inextricably intertwined, and some writers argue that the process may have run in different directions in different epochs. The most common formulation of this argument is that the process of technological innovation was more purely exogenous until the Industrial Revolution, when the state began to take an increasingly active role in the research and development aspect of modern industrial technologies. Robert Gilpin presents the general case: 'In the premodern world, the diffusion of military techniques ... was a principal factor in the rise of new powers ... in the modern world, on the other hand, an advanced economic and scientific base on which to build is a much more important precondition.'[26] Authors such as Mary Kaldor and Maurice Pearton have applied this specifically to military technology, arguing that state intervention in the process of military technological innovation created a modern 'military-industrial complex' only in the late stages of the Industrial Revolution, and perhaps not until after the Second World War.[27] It is beyond the scope of this book to try to break the Gordian knot of cause and effect, but one of my theses is that although a distinctively modern military industrial complex can be identified, a much greater continuity in its evolution is evident when one examines the links between state power and the earlier stages of military innovation. Although direct state support may not have been provided to innovation, it is an oversimplification to argue that 'knowledge (construed either as pure or applied science, or an industrial network, or as the content of education) ... and the traditional power of the state for war or peace ... have [historically] been separate and remained so, though with diminishing force, till the middle of this century'.[28]

## Technological innovation and technological revolutions

If military technology had been static since the invention of the crossbow, the evolutionary dynamic of the arms transfer and production system would involve a linear diffusion of weapons and associated skills (technology I), followed by the techniques for reproducing them (technology II), with limited adaptation to different environments and no fundamental innovation. But the process of change from 'the crossbow to the H-bomb' has not been linear, or the focal points of innovation constant. Again, as arms exports are tied to limitations on the ability of states to produce arms, innovations or revolutions in military technology will transform the arms transfer system in their wake.

The first distinction to draw is between incremental innovation and revolutionary change. For economists, the concept of technological innovation has a precise meaning: it is an outward shift of the production function that increases output for any given combination of capital and labour.[29] With a slight redefinition of the terms, innovation in the military sphere can be defined as changes in weapons systems that supply greater (or more efficient) destructive power within a given combination of labour and weaponry. The shift from the matchlock to the flintlock, from powdered to corned gunpowder, and from the Little Willie tank of the First World War to the Centurion all represent greater or lesser incremental innovations in military technology. Most importantly these innovations, dramatic as their impact may have been on the battlefield, do not require any fundamental restructuring of strategy and organisation for warfare (although tactics were certainly affected).

Occasionally, however, innovations break out of a given production function and so alter the character of military strategy, organisation and planning as to qualify as revolutionary. These 'military revolutions' are not the sole product of technological changes, or the pursuit of power (changes in state organisation), or revolutions in economic foundations (or thought). Rather, they require a convergence of all three forces to compel a radical restructuring of most (if not all) of the dimensions of organisation for warfare. This reorganisation, seen as a sort of environmental change, condemns certain types of organisation for warfare (or even of social organisation) to extinction and favours others. The application of gunpowder and advances in metallurgy to military technology in the fifteenth and sixteenth centuries marks one such environmental change, which will be explored more fully in the next chapter.

The pace of both revolutionary change and incremental innovation is unpredictable and probably ungeneralisable. Only four truly revolutionary changes in military technology can be identified: the cannon/gunpowder revolution of the fifteenth and sixteenth century; the application of steel and steam to warfare associated with the Industrial Revolution of the nineteenth century; the mobility revolution catalysed by the marriage of the internal combustion engine and modern electronics in the twentieth century; and nuclear weapons.[30] To date, the first three of these revolutions in military technology can be associated with a specific cycle of change of arms transfers and production patterns.

22

What happens after the technological revolution is crucial, as the continuing 'process of developing a modern technology ... involv[es] not only scientific discovery and invention, but also innovation, technical improvement and the spread of the innovation through extensive imitation'.[31] This incremental innovation is not purely linear, and within a given framework of technological knowledge there are two processes at work that shape the distribution of production and exports. The first is declining returns to investment in innovation: in economic terms, the production frontier becomes increasingly difficult to move outward. The second is the process associated with Raymond Vernon's product cycle, in which new products are first made and sold in domestic markets, then exported directly to foreign markets, then manufactured within foreign markets (direct foreign investment), and finally exported to the home market from foreign markets.[32] Both of these phenomena have direct consequences for arms production and transfers, although neither has been explored in great detail.[33]

### The diffusion of military technology

In an economist's perfect model, the migration of technologies can be explained as:

> a simple utilitarian process: a technique, having proved its value in one place, is adopted by people in another place who think it may be useful to them as well. In a perfectly free market with perfect access to information, the spread of innovations would result from calculations of expected marginal returns.[34]

Such a pattern of diffusion would result in a division of production corresponding to the distribution of factor endowments and comparative advantage, with relatively passive acceptance of this by non-producers. In the military realm, the pursuit of power would result in a wide distribution of arms production. Of course, these perfect economic conditions do not hold for civilian goods, let alone military innovations, and technological diffusions occur in a political, economic and socio-cultural context that determines whether or not a specific technology will be grafted on to its new environment. In fact:

> one of the most compelling facts of history is that there have been enormous differences in the capacity of different societies to generate technical innovations that are suitable to their economic needs. Moreover, there has also been extreme variability in the willingness and ease with which societies have adopted and utilized technological innovations developed elsewhere. And, in addition, individual societies have themselves changed markedly over the course

of their own separate histories in the extent and intensity of their technological dynamism. Clearly, the reasons for these differences, which are not understood, are tied in numerous complex and subtle ways to the functioning of the larger social systems, their institutions, values, and incentive structures.[35]

In the literature on technological diffusion there exists no all-encompassing theory of how technology is diffused. One can, however, follow Melvin Kranzberg and divide technology transfers into three categories:

(a) material transfer (the simple diffusion of machines and materials)
(b) design transfer (the transmission of blueprints, formulas, books, etc.)
(c) capacity transfer (the transfer of basic scientific knowledge and technical expertise).[36]

These can be applied to military technology by tying Kranzberg's transfer processes to the types of military technology defined above. The transfer of:

technology I is *material* transfer;
technology II is *design* transfer;
technology III is *capacity* transfer.

With technology I, the correspondence is straightforward; with the others some clarification is required. The transfer of designs, blueprints and basic engineering know-how allows the recipients to reproduce the technology, and the transfer of scientific knowledge and technical expertise is closely linked to the ability to adapt the technology to specific local needs (of the battlefield or the marketplace).[37] Technology IV, the ability to innovate, remains on this account somewhat independent of the transfer process.

The factors that determine the outer limits of the diffusion or transfer of any of these types of technology are many, and apply equally to military and civilian production. These factor endowments include the existence of local demand for the products, local investment capital, research and development (R&D) investment, the availability of raw material inputs, the local cost of labour and its level of expertise, the importance of returns of scale, the level of infrastructure support, and cultural, social and linguistic barriers.[38] In the case of military production, we can add another factor necessary for successful diffusion: political will. Given the nature of the military market, arms production will seldom (if ever) be undertaken and sustained without the support and participation of the state.[39]

The arms trade will include all three types of transfer, and it is unlikely that there will be a smooth linear progression between them. One would rather expect an uneven or step-wise distribution of production capabilities, with different production thresholds based on the different basket of factor endowments required. The transfer of technology I requires little or no local capital and labour expertise, but some infrastructure support, whereas the shift to technology II calls into play significant capital and labour resources, as well as scale-of-production factors. Moving from the transfer of technology II to III involves the surmounting of socio-cultural and financial barriers (R&D investment) that may discourage innovation or adaptive behaviour.[40] Delineating what these thresholds are and where they may be located is a primary task of what follows.

An equally large gap should exist between states able to adapt weapons and those that have successfully captured the process of innovation itself, and here the problems of technological diffusion and innovation become linked. Technological innovation also requires available basic knowledge (experts and methods) and a social, cultural and political environment that discriminates in favour of the innovator. In the case of gunpowder, for example, the basic knowledge was widely available, but only in early modern Europe was this knowledge combined with existing metallurgical techniques to address a specific military problem. After this initial step, production becomes further localised based on other determinants of diffusion and innovation. In any case, however poorly we understand the social and economic forces behind technological change, what must be emphasised is the crucial role played by technological innovation and its subsequent diffusion in catalysing and fuelling the arms trade. As one writer notes: 'il est certain que la dissemination et le commerce des armes ont été intimement liés aux progrès réalises par la technologie militaire'.[41]

### Military technology and social change

Mention should be made of the relationship between military technology and social change, for as Gerald Berg notes, 'the introduction of a new weapon changes warfare on a vast scale only when the values and structures of society enhance its use'.[42] A discussion of the impact of military technological change on social organisation takes one far beyond the ambit of this book, into cultural anthropology

25

and social history. It is worth noting this impact, however, for two reasons. First, it highlights the dynamic interaction between technology and society, with the adaptive capacity of both (as a response to the changes wrought or dictated by the other) coming into play over time for the well-being and even, perhaps, survival of a social order. There are numerous examples of the demise of societies and states that were unable to adopt new technologies. Examples include the already-mentioned decline of the Italian city-states, the defeat of the Mamluks by the Ottomans (discussed in chapter 2) and the retreat of the Africans in the face of the nineteenth-century European onslaught.[43] Second, the inability to adopt the techniques of social and military organisation required to use the new weapons effectively (technology I) is only a more extreme case of an inability to adopt the techniques needed for the reproduction and adaptation of military technology itself (technologies II and III). As some social systems may founder on technology I, others may founder on technology II or III. Hence there is a conceptual continuity between states that cannot use modern military technology, those that use it but cannot reproduce it, those that can reproduce it but not adapt it, and those that can adapt it but not innovate.

## The arms transfer system: characteristics

The analysis can now be brought directly to bear to describe the structure and evolutionary dynamic of the global arms transfer and production system as it is generated by the interplay of the forces described above. This presentation points towards the discussion to come and presents the central theses of the book, by outlining thematically the *structural features* and *evolutionary dynamic* (phases) of an 'ideal type' arms transfer and production system. Although it would be preferable to present the two separately, the cyclical or wave-like nature of the evolutionary process makes an integrated sketch more appropriate (I use 'wave' in preference to 'cycle' because strictly speaking the end of one cycle must contain within it the seeds of the next one, which is not necessarily the case with waves that can be exogenously induced by technological innovation).

The starting point (for illustrative purposes) is an arms transfer and production system in which arms production capacity is unevenly distributed, the existing technology has diffused as widely as possible, and arms are transferred from the productive focal points (at the technological frontier) to the periphery. Innovation is costly and perhaps even exhausted, and weapons themselves may have become 'baroque'.[44] The basic knowledge required for a revolution in military technology is widely distributed, but not yet applied to the demands of warfare. Phase one then corresponds to the relatively exogenous introduction ('relatively' because it depends in part on existing social and political structures) of revolutionary military-technological change that will (ultimately) transform the strategy and organisation required for warfare. The enduring structural characteristics of the arms transfer system emerge, however, only long after this transformation begins.

The new motors of technical innovation are unevenly distributed, and as a consequence leading centres of production and innovation emerge (the first structural feature of the system). Innovation and production will first be driven by the pursuit of victory in warfare and the pursuit of power. But the forces of technological change play themselves out on a larger canvas, with new technologies demanding different raw materials, levels of skill, combinations of labour and capital, and socio-cultural environments than may be present in existing centres of production. Thus certain producers become vulnerable, new centres of production emerge and others are condemned to inferiority. The new centres are the foci for the emergent arms transfer system, and become what can be called 'first-tier' arms producers. They are able not only to innovate and advance the technological frontier, but also to produce weapons systems for all military applications.

The result of this, as phase two begins, is the existence of technological gaps in the weaponry possessed by different states. Since state power is often equated with military power, and since possession of the most powerful weapons available has long been a driving influence behind foreign policy, demand from states that do not possess weapons based on the new technologies will produce a rapid expansion of the arms trade. On the supply side, the relatively great profits to be realised in the early stages of the product cycle result in increased capacity and rapid incremental innovation. This, plus the chance to lower unit costs (by realising economies of scale and spreading R&D costs), will drive producers to export arms, especially if local demand cannot absorb all increases in output. As a consequence of these demand-pull and supply-push factors the arms transfer pipeline is filled with technology I transfers of weaponry and associated skills. Thus relatively feverish international arms transfer activity accompanies a period of rapid technological change.

The second structural feature of the arms transfer system is a consequence of the political (pursuit of power) salience of the new military technologies, which dictates that states will attempt to exercise control over the arms trade through restriction or regulation of politically sensitive exports. How extreme these restrictions become depends on the prevailing economic ideology of trade and the nature of the perceived threat. First-tier producers will either attempt to stem the haemorrhage of their monopoly on new weapons, or will use export policies to sell off their short-term monopoly but ensure the maintenance of their R&D capacity (and hence ability to innovate). In either case the state, conscious of the political implications of the arms trade, takes steps to monitor or control it. This perception of the political significance of arms transfers will not just be manifest negatively via interdictions on arms transfers, but arms transfers will also be used positively as tools of foreign policy to buttress or win an ally, to arm 'the enemy of my enemy' or to strengthen alliances.

As the system evolves into phase three, restrictions on weapons transfers and the overarching pursuit of power will create demands for the transfer of the techniques for producing arms, in addition to the weapons themselves. The strongest clients, not satisfied with purchasing weapons, will attempt to produce a range of weapons based on the new technologies (and some may for a time be successful) and begin the process of technology transfer by importing technologies II and III. The reasons for this are both political and economic. On the political level, the pursuit of power makes possession of a technologically advanced arms industry one of the first goals of major arms purchasers and the prerequisite to a claim to great power status. An indigenous arms industry may not quite be the *sine qua non* of a great power, as the ability to support a modern arms industry reflects underlying capabilities that also support a claim to great power status, but in so far as arms production is the product of political decisions and not spontaneous developments dictated by factor endowments, its existence contributes to the ability of states to attain great power status. Without an indigenous arms industry, one could not ultimately act independently on the world stage.

Thus both technology II and technology III enter the transfer pipeline during this phase, with major arms recipients attempting to import skilled workers, training, patents, machinery or entire factories through licensed production and co-production deals, with or without the cooperation of first-tier suppliers. But, as with civilian technologies, the diffusion of military technology will be imperfect. Even with strong political will behind the effort, the unequal distribution of the factor endowments needed to capture technological processes means many technological transplants will fail to bear fruit in their new soil, as states discover that the requirements for participating in the technological revolution are stringent.

With determination and over time, however, some states will succeed in capturing the basic scientific knowledge and technical expertise associated with arms production (technology III). They will produce a variety of weapons at or near the technological frontier, and may even advance with it, but will rarely be able to innovate (because, among other things, of lesser resources for R&D investment). These producers will also be limited in other ways by their overall lower factor endowment base, and will become 'second-tier' suppliers (another structural feature of the system). One of the key elements of this lesser endowment base will likely (although not necessarily) be a lower level of domestic demand for arms, and wherever domestic demand is limited great pressure will exist to export arms (if production is not already limited by other factors). More importantly, these economic pressures on the industry make it more likely that power political considerations will be overridden, and the export of technology II through licensed and co-production arrangements with clients lower on the technological ladder will be prominent.

The fourth phase witnesses an acceleration of the process of technological diffusion via an expansion of the number of producers and consumers and the emergence of second-tier suppliers who satisfy some of their needs and begin to sell arms to the next lower level of participants. This has two consequences. First, the heightened supply competition reduces the ability of first-tier states to reap political benefits from arms transfers because some of the most important clients have become fellow producers and because second-tier producers, driven more intensely by the need to maintain and expand a fragile productive base, are wont to export more promiscuously. The ultimate advantage of innovation remains with first-tier suppliers, however, providing them with a greater latitude to override economic considerations with political ones and some advantage in the range or quality of weapons systems they can supply. Second, a 'third tier' of arms producers who also attempt to create an indigenous arms industry with technological imports emerges. Their progress, however, is based only upon the successful capture of technology II: the blueprints, formulae, patents or machines needed to reproduce a given artifact. Although the motivation behind attempts to build indigenous arms industries is again both political and economic, it differs slightly from the second tier. Political motivations will be less closely linked to the pursuit of great power status in the international system (since production at the frontier is out of the question) and

29

more closely tied to claims to regional hegemony or desire to reduce dependence on potentially fickle suppliers. The specific requirements of warfare also play a lesser role, since alliance with a great power would almost certainly guarantee more advanced weapons than can be produced indigenously. The dominant economic motivation will be to use arms production as a leading sector in economic development. Although success may be rare, the *potential* for realising such enduring economic benefits (which itself has political implications) will motivate great initial efforts. One consequence, however, of such enclave industrial development is that the export market will be much more important than the almost-certainly limited domestic demand. This further increases competition between suppliers and decreases the political utility of arms transfers. Another consequence is that arms production will be concentrated in a few weapons systems, rather than spread across the board.

While new military technologies are progressively diffusing throughout the system, continued incremental innovation occurs in first-tier states (and to a much lesser extent in the second tier). If the processes of diffusion and innovation proceeded at the same pace, the technological lead of first-tier states would never decline. The progress of the product cycle, however, results in declining marginal returns to R&D investment and increased unit costs, and hence the process of innovation slows. It may even halt completely with mature technologies, for which incremental innovations can become dysfunctional. One example of this would be the current ability of aircraft manufacturers to build planes too fast and manoeuvrable for pilots to fly! Thus instead of growing or remaining constant, the gap between the sophistication of the weapons possessed by first-tier states and by simple consumers slowly narrows. On a different level, the structure of production and trade begins to approximate more closely the pure economic model in which production is distributed according to factor endowments and comparative advantage.

In theory, the eventual result would be all states possessing all modern weapons systems (even if they could not produce them) with victory in warfare depending solely on relative numbers. But just as the ability to produce advanced weapons is unevenly distributed, so too is the ability to use them. Below the threshold of second- and third-tier producers (who also acquire arms), two types of arms recipients exist. Neither can produce weapons, and both obtain the tools of modern war via transfers of technology I, but one group is able to use the weapons effectively and integrate them successfully into an existing socio-cultural and technological social order. The others, whatever their purchasing power, are unable to make even the minimal adaptations necessary to use new technologies, and become the true dinosaurs of the evolutionary process. The historical fate of such states was political extinction; today, given the inviolability of state boundaries, a more likely fate is the near-complete surrender of effective sovereignty to stronger regional or extra-regional powers.

The final phase of the wave is marked by a slow settling of the previously active arms transfer system. The process of technological diffusion is completed (as far as it will be), and the motors of innovation either grow dormant or begin to migrate (based on new technologies). A clear international hierarchy becomes established, and those states who failed to compete in armaments production (among other things) fall from or do not reach great power status. The political utility of manipulations of the arms transfer pipeline also declines: enough suppliers exist to make it a buyers' market, more states are capable of satisfying their own military needs, and influence becomes an idiosyncratic product of involvement in evanescent and unpredictable conflicts, rather than a systemic characteristic. The system awaits a new cycle of technological innovation.

The structural elements of the arms transfer and production system will not be evident in the early stages of a wave for two reasons. First, the fundamentally political nature of weapons production results in many more attempts to manufacture arms than would be the case with other commodities. Second, ephemeral factors (such as wars, economic difficulties or political leadership) have much greater scope to obscure the underlying structure of the system during the period when innovation and diffusion are proceeding rapidly. But in the mature phases of a wave the arms transfer system will manifest its coherent structure: a primary division between producers and consumers and a three-tiered division within the rank of producers.

Using the categories introduced above to describe technology transfer, the structure of the arms transfer system can be summarised as follows:

> first-tier suppliers innovate at the technological frontier
> second-tier suppliers produce (via the transfer of *capacities*) weapons at the technological frontier and adapt them to specific market needs
> third-tier suppliers copy and reproduce existing technologies (via transfer of *design*), but do not capture the underlying process of innovation or adaptation

strong customers obtain (via *material* transfers) and use modern weapons

weak customers either obtain modern weapons and cannot use them, or do not even obtain them.

What does this tell us about the relationships between different groups of producers and consumers in the arms market? First-tier states, with the largest R&D investments and domestic markets, will produce the entire range of modern weapons systems at the technological frontier and be the dominant arms producers. The well-being of their arms industries will not depend on exports, although the demand for their arms will be likely to make them prominent exporters. They will concentrate on exports of weapons, however, conscious of the long-term potential loss of their technological and market advantages through the transfer of weapons technology via licensed and co-production arrangements. Second-tier states will have a much lower overall R&D, domestic procurement and production base, and will depend more heavily on exports or state subsidies. Their export share will be limited by their inability to produce arms at the technological frontier for the same cost as first-tier states. It is possible that a sustained capacity to export weapons across the board can be maintained, but some product specialisation will be anticipated. The greater economic pressures on second-tier suppliers will also mean a greater willingness to export the knowledge and skills required to make weapons, in addition to the weapons themselves. Third-tier suppliers will be even more heavily dependent upon exports, and will find their comparative advantage in a competitive market in specialised niches for low-cost and unsophisticated or easy-to-operate weapons based on low R&D investments. Their share of global production and exports will also be relatively limited. Only a major domestic commitment to override economic considerations and procure weapons locally will keep second- and third-tier industries healthy, and even then the domestic market may not guarantee their survival.

## Concluding comments

Ideal types are only suggestive, and reality will not correspond to this sketch of the evolutionary dynamic and structure of the international arms transfer system. Also omitted from it are any unique elements that may vary from epoch to epoch: since history is not a ceaselessly monotonous cyclical repetition, one would expect transformation as well as repetition, as each epoch may share a similar evolution, but build on previous changes. The most obvious (but not the only) transformation is the progressively increasing destructiveness of weapons. Another would be the progressive capture of the process of technological innovation by state policy, which as it ceases to be an exogenous variable marginalises all but those states that can mobilise vast amounts of capital, draw upon a pool of skilled innovators and offer a large market. Such factors as these can only be explored in their specific historical context.

To determine decisively how well this sketch of the global arms transfer system fits the historical reality would require detailed data on the volume, value and sophistication of arms transfers in all phases of the waves; a full description of clients and the distribution of their purchases; and complete information on the structure of domestic arms industries (the level of R&D spending, the proportion of production that is exported and so forth). This information is available (partially) only for the post-1945 period. Thus the assessment of the pre-1945 arms transfer system that follows can only be suggestive, but by placing the brief history of the contemporary arms transfer system within a historical context of evolution and change, it can at least shine some light on the impact of these deeper motive forces on current and future developments.

# 2 THE EMERGENCE OF A GLOBAL ARMS TRANSFER AND PRODUCTION SYSTEM

## Arms transfers in the pre-modern period

Arms transfers and arms production have appeared as an inevitable concomitant to war and military preparations throughout human history. Although from our vantage point the technologies of warfare in the pre-modern period were primitive, important technological advances and sources of innovation created even then a diffusion of techniques for (and possibly a trade in) arms and armour between Greece, Central Europe and Asia.[1] The significance of improved weaponry was not lost on early rulers, who supported and encouraged military innovation: 'Hellenistic mechanicians earned their livelihood as military engineers. War industry was lavishly supported ... [and] kingdoms and cities competed keenly for the services of the most able engineers, whose rewards, in terms both of money and prestige, were great.'[2] The first major technology that required such investments was the catapult, which emerged around 399 BC in Syracuse and was soon diffused throughout the Mediterranean. Its impact on war and society may have been great, as 'improvements in siege craft that promoted the equality or ascendancy of the besieger played a part in the establishment of larger political units' and the decline of Greek city-states.[3]

The first recorded arms transfers are probably those found in Thucydides' *Peloponnesian War*. What was transferred, however, was usually not only arms, but men, weapons, supplies and ships. Athens, for example, demanded the supply of specified numbers of ships and men as part of membership in the Delian League.[4] Transfers were part of alliance systems and treaties, and it is likely that little autonomous commercial weapons trade existed, as the prerequisites for a production monopoly or oligopoly did not exist. The technology, materials and skills necessary to build ships and arm men were relatively evenly distributed and widely known, and although not all states were equally endowed, the ability to arm themselves depended only upon their wealth, population and taxation base, and not upon the import of key factors of production.

During the Roman period, the production and distribution of strategic goods was controlled by the state, and the Empire procured arms for its soldiers in scattered 'factories' near raw materials and major garrisons, with major production centres in the fourth and fifth centuries located in northern Italy and Gaul (France).[5] No 'inter-state' arms trade existed, as 'les lois d'Empire romain interdisaient toute fourniture d'armes aux barbares', and there is no evidence that state factories produced for the domestic market.[6] In any case, trade in general was a marginal and subordinate activity before AD 1000, but wherever technological gaps and a basis for trade existed, arms were one of the commodities bought and sold. The evidence for this is derivative but solid in four cases in which restrictions on the arms trade by rulers of states were imposed. Documents from Charlemagne's capitularies (768–814) prohibited the export of Frankish armour, which was much in demand, from his territories.[7] In 971, the Doge of Venice forbade the sale of arms to the Saracens against whom the 'Orientals' (Balkan peoples) were fighting.[8] Beginning in 1179, the Church also forbade the sale 'aux Sarrasins des armes, du fer, des bois, de construction navale ou des bateaux', on pain of excommunication or imprisonment, repeating this interdiction in 1215, 1245, 1304 and 1454. Also at the Church's insistence, 'les doges de Venèse et les consuls de Gênes défendirent à leurs sujets de transporter les armes vers Alexandrie en Egypte, qui était à cette époque une véritable plaque tournant du commerce entre les chrétiens et les infidèles'. Venice and Genoa were noted at this time for the quality of their armour and the skill of their metal-workers. Finally, in 1370 Edward III 'concluait un traité avec le comte de Flandre et les villes de Gand, Bruges et Ypres, stipulant l'interdiction de fourniture d'armes et d'autres marchandises aux ennemis d'Angleterre'.

In all cases the political implications of arms transfers are clear, and the existence of these ordinances suggests a trade significant enough to pose a threat. With uniform military technology spanning Europe, arms exports diminished one's potential arsenal and augmented that of likely (or actual) enemies. Since the output of a good armourer was not large, this could be a serious drain when no surplus production existed. The political hazards of arms exports to potential enemies was thus recognised early, along with the general prohibition against trade with an opponent in wartime. But most of the trade of this period remained passive, responding to orders from specific princes or magistrates rather than actively seeking markets for already-manufactured wares.[9]

## Technological change and the 'Military Revolution'

According to the historian Michael Roberts, the 'Military Revolution' that occurred between 1560 and 1660 'stands as a great divide separating mediaeval society from the modern world'.[10] The revolution involved new military battlefield tactics, the emergence of standing armies, new types of fortifications, and a dramatic increase in army size. But underlying and in some ways preceding these specific developments was a series of social and technological changes in the period between 1450 and 1650 that created the conditions for the emergence of a genuinely global arms transfer and production system in the fifteenth and sixteenth centuries. The first of these underlying socio-economic changes was the commercialisation of war, which made mercenaries and weapons available to any ruler with sufficient financial resources, a process that took root in Italy in the fourteenth century. This 'commercialization of military service depended upon, and simultaneously helped to sustain, the commercialization of weapons manufacture and supply', in which rulers began to insist upon standardised weapons calibres, gunpowder and supplies.[11] This was coupled with the second change, the emergence of European states and princes with sufficient control over their territories to raise the necessary revenue to purchase arms and men. The result was, however, that 'only rich states were capable of bearing the enormous cost of the new warfare. They were eventually to eliminate the independent cities.'[12] The third change was the qualitative increase in trade that permitted a wide exchange of goods across the continent and around the globe. This growth of a market economy stimulated arms production, as some centres were able to generate the surplus production without which no large-scale arms trade could have emerged. Thus the trade shifted from the local peddling of arms from fair to fair to a 'situation in which, during the 1600s, government orders began to make up the bulk of arms trade activity'.[13]

Within this ferment, technological changes were revolutionising the business not only of making war, but of ruling states, in part by the harnessing of science to warfare. The key innovations were developments in gunpowder, cannon and firearms; the net effect of these innovations was to catalyse and accelerate the shift for providing weapons of war from the individual to the state and to consolidate the power of the state. As Fernand Braudel notes, 'artillery and firearms quite transformed inter-state warfare, economic life and the capitalist organization of arms production'.[14] Gunpowder can be traced to ninth-century China, but it did not emerge in Europe in a militarily usable form until the fourteenth century.[15] Cannon followed soon after (in both Europe and China), and they were in regular use in European warfare from the beginning of the Hundred Years War (1337–1453). Primitive muskets and arquebuses emerged somewhat later, at the end of the fifteenth or early in the sixteenth century.

The military use of gunpowder and cannon created a technological gap between those states and rulers who possessed the materials, skills and techniques for manufacturing them, and those who had to purchase the means to guarantee their security. A premium was also placed on incremental innovations, for a potentially decisive advantage could be gained with lighter, more accurate or more powerful weapons. Cannon, which began as vase-shaped vessels firing arrows and stones, transformed themselves by 1400 into tubes of iron rods welded together with hoops. By the late fifteenth century, state-of-the-art metallurgy had made these weapons more accurate and less apt to burst: the welded tubes had progressed to brass and bronze cannon (between 1450 and 1471), followed by much cheaper (but somewhat inferior) cast-iron guns (perfected around 1543).[16] After 1420 gunpowder was made more effective by 'corning' rather than powdering, and shot shifted from stone to iron after 1467 (giving smaller guns more destructive power). Around 1450, muskets and handguns were invented; uniform calibres were implemented around 1544; rifling was discovered around 1630. The possibility and process of technical change was itself a catalyst for the arms transfer system, for the rapid diffusion of innovations was essential for military effectiveness.

## The emergence of new centres of production and the decline of traditional centres

The most prominent centre of arms production and transfers in the early and mid fifteenth century was Italy. Secondary centres of production existed in Germany and the Low Countries, but arms were produced wherever sufficient concentrations of ore, markets and skilled craftsmen could be found, generally to serve local demand.[17] The early technologies were relatively widely distributed, and perhaps the original dominance of Italy can be explained by its then wide trading network. The operation of the forces discussed above in the fifteenth to seventeenth centuries, however, made Italian producers vulnerable, allowed new centres of production to emerge and condemned other states to inferiority. As we shall see, by the middle of the seventeenth century the loci of military innovation and production had decisively shifted to the Low Countries, Britain and Sweden.

Post-Renaissance Italian arms production was centered around Milan, Venice, Genoa and Brescia, and was built on an older contraband trade network that stretched to Egypt and beyond. Already:

> au XIIIe siècle, on en trouvait déjà de traces, non seulement dans les sources locales mais aussi dans les documents étrangers, qui commencent des lors à témoigner de la pénétration des produits italiens d'importation. L'apogée de ce mouvement se situe vers 1450, moment où les armes d'Italie, surtout les armures, sont répandues dans toute l'Europe.[18]

Competition between Italian city-states to 'assurer leur propre approvisionnement militaire en créant des centres armuriers sur leur territoire ou en encourageant les activités de ceux qui s'y étaient développés spontanément' stimulated production and innovation.[19] The best example of this was the Arsenal of Venice, which at its mid-sixteenth-century zenith brought together in one establishment (employing up to 1,500 craftsmen) naval and artillery construction and military stockpiles for the large Venetian fleet.[20] When this type of stimulus (for the Venetian Arsenal was not unique) was coupled with the well-developed Italian trading network, an arms trade with virtually all of Europe and the Mediterranean followed. It appears that Venice in particular played a primary role as producer and diffuser of cannon and firearms to the Balkans and Ottoman Turkey in the late 1300s.[21]

But the Italian city-states were the first victims of economic and technological changes. Overall, Italian industry faced great competition, and 'in Milan and neighboring Brescia the manufacture of arms and other metalcrafts suffered'.[22] As William McNeill points out:

> As long as the race lay between ever more efficient crossbows and more and more elaborate plate armour, Italian workshops and artisan designers kept the lead ... [but because Italy had to import metal, and] ... because European guns quickly became giant tubes ... weighing more than a ton ... as soon as guns became critical weapons in war, Italian technical primacy in the armaments industry decayed.[23]

By 1500, Milan was importing German cannon; by 1606 half of the Venetian fleet was constructed abroad; and in 1684 Venice sent its gunsmiths to England to learn new guncasting techniques.[24] Although Italian city-states quickly developed siege defences that were the envy of Europe (the *trace italienne*), 'the major effect of the new weaponry was to dwarf the Italian city-states'.[25] But although Italy was no longer at the forefront, it remained at least a centre for firearms production and exports. In 1542, at least 7,600 muskets were exported, and in 1562, 25,000 guns were sold abroad. This trade was from 1537 only permitted under government licence, and the gunmakers' output was occasionally used for political ends: in 1564, for example, 'the Signoria of Venice granted a whole consignment of arms [including firearms and armour] to an agent of the Polish crown'.[26]

By the late sixteenth and early seventeenth century, however, the centres of production and innovation had shifted to England and the Low Countries. The volume and sophistication of arms production in, and exports from, these centres classify them as first-tier producers and exporters. The experience of the most prominent centre in the Low Countries, Liège, is representative: until 1492, Liège was one of many local production centres that traded with England, Scotland and the Iberian peninsula, but it was not sufficiently developed to compete directly with Italian (and German) production.[27] Its arms were sought after and technically advanced, however, and seen by some as a political threat, by others as a political tool. Philip II of Burgundy made a gift to James III of Scotland in 1457 of two Flemish cannon, but his son, Charles the Bold, besieged and sacked Liège in 1467–8 after it refused to submit to his edict forbidding the manufacture of arms.[28]

When Liège declared its neutrality and disarmed in 1492, its arms industry blossomed. During the sixteenth century, merchants needed simple sellers' permits to export their arms, and their neutrality 'enabled them to work in peace while so many other nations were seeking the means of waging war among themselves'.[29] The vast trading network of the region meant that its export-based industry flourished, and Liège supplied a large part of the weapons used by both the Spanish and the Dutch during the wars of 1568–1609. By the seventeenth century, Liège guns were arguably 'the best and cheapest of Europe and the world', and some sense of the volume of trade can be gained from the following figures: in 1575, 300 cannon were shipped to Spain, in 1632, 4,000 muskets were sold to Louis XIII in France, in 1689, 10,000 went to William III in England, and in 1713, 18,000 rifles were sold to the Prussian king.[30] The denouement of the Liège story is illustrative, however, of the impact of the vicissitudes of political and technological change in this period. Liège was annexed by France during the French Revolution, and in 1797 a ban was placed on weapons exports (except to occupied Holland). In 1804, civilian exports (sporting arms) were also banned, and although this ban was subsequently relaxed slightly, it was a disaster for the industry. Although Liège's ability to trade was restored after 1815, by then its productive base had disintegrated sufficiently to remove it from the ranks of the producers who emerged in the early stages of the Industrial Revolution.

England, with its relative political stability and large trading network, became the prototype first-tier state as it captured the process of innovation and large-scale arms production of cast-iron cannon. As John Nef notes:

> Cannon made of cast iron appeared before the middle of the fifteenth century in the dominion of the powerful and enterprising dukes of Burgundy, and somewhat later in Italy. These cannon were clumsy, ineffective pieces. It was not until after the Reformation that cast iron cannon ... were turned out in any number, and then they were manufactured not on the continent but in south-eastern England.[31]

The expansion of England's arms industry paralleled its rise in military and political power, and the perfection of cast-iron artillery was a consequence of the high demand for lower-cost artillery (cast iron was cheaper than bronze, and England had to import its copper). In the late 1300s, a large proportion of English ordnance was imported, mainly from Italy, the Low Countries and France, and as late as 1450, James II was importing Flemish artillery.[32] Domestic supply was divided between workshops at the Tower of London and private founders' output. England also imported virtually all its powder, but a vigorous countertrade continually depleted government stores, and its export was forbidden in 1414.[33] Henry V (1413–22) imported gunmasters from Germany to build cannon; a century later Henry VIII's (1509–47) continuing military entanglements precipitated 'the importation of ... foreign armourers and gun founders from France and the Low Countries to form schools for the production of war material in England about the year 1515', and by the 1520s England was no longer dependent upon foreign weapons.[34] But although Henry's first solution to his military needs was to import weapons and technologies, the search for cheaper alternatives in the later years of his reign led to the most important development of this period: the perfection of the technology for founding cast-iron guns, which were subsequently diffused throughout Europe.[35] Whatever England's early mastery of the techniques for cannon-making amounted to, the locus of technical innovation shifted decisively towards it sometime in the first half of the sixteenth century, a product of both the acquisition of knowledge via the migration of iron-workers (some of whom probably specialised in cannon-founding) and economic pressures.

The evolution from importer to exporter was completed by the late sixteenth century, when 'English guns were eagerly sought after throughout the continent', and exported to Denmark, Holland, France, Flanders and Spain.[36] As A. Rupert Hall notes, 'England enjoyed a quasi-monopoly of cast-iron artillery, a product . . . that owed much originally to immigrant iron-founders, from about 1540 until 1620, when the rising Swedish ironmasters began to market cannon through Amsterdam.'[37] England produced annually more than 500 tons of iron artillery by 1575, and more than 1,000 tons by 1600; by comparison the best estimate for the artillery in the French arsenal in 1544 is fewer than 1,000 tons.[38] But the prevailing sixteenth-century economic ideologies of mercantilism and autarky meant that this trade was inevitably viewed suspiciously: after it was pointed out to the Privy Council that the export of guns from England ensured that 'yor enimie is better fourneshed with them than or own country ships ar [sic]', Elizabeth I in 1574 ordered gun production to be limited to the amount needed 'for the only use of the realm', and heavy fines were imposed for unauthorised exports.[39] This was a novel development, for previous restrictions on the arms trade in France, Spain and Portugal had been designed, in the face of insufficient domestic production, to preserve available supplies for the state or ruler (one exception to this being the Church's edicts against trade with the infidel). In the English case, however, it was *surplus* production that could strengthen opponents that motivated draconian measures.

The result of restricting production to domestic demand, however, coupled with the declining demand for cannon as a result of the peace between England and Spain (1604), was that there was insufficient work to preserve the pool of skilled workers. By 1613, founder John Browne was testifying that exports were needed to preserve his business in the light of falling government orders (between 1613 and 1618 half of Browne's production of 1,200 cannon were sold to the Dutch). His plea was not successful, and in 1619 further restrictions were imposed: all sales and testing had to take place in London, and all exports 'were to be shipped exclusively from the Tower wharf'.[40] Some exports were maintained through the 1620s and 1630s, though the licensing system ensured that they flowed almost exclusively to the United Provinces in the Thirty Years War.[41] In 1660, restrictions on exports were further reinforced, as the Tonnage and Poundage Act gave the sovereign the power 'to prohibit the transportation of gunpowder, arms and ammunition out of the Kingdom whenever he should see cause to do so, and for such time as should be specified'.[42] These laws were reinforced in 1756 and 1793, with bans on the export of saltpeter and naval material, which were directed at restricting exports in times of crisis. By the late seventeenth century, England again depended almost entirely on imports of European arms, in part because of the restrictions placed on the industry during the previous century.[43]

The evolution of Sweden from consumer to producer of arms, and its ephemeral membership in the first tier, reinforces the observation that political will and the pursuit of victory in war were essential ingredients in building a successful arms industry, but that it could not be maintained without an adequate socio-economic base. Until the reign of Gustav Adolphus (1611–32), Sweden depended primarily on English arms. Gustav hired Louis de Geer, a Dutch founder, to create an arms industry in the Swedish forests by shipping Flemish iron-workers and blast furnace technology to Sweden and by bringing new financial and technical methods into this relative backwater of Europe.[44] Unlike the skilled workers of previous migrations, de Geer remained a Dutch resident, only hired on a contractual basis to do business in Sweden. Two results obtained: on the one hand, de Geer spawned new competition for the foundries around Liège; on the other, he 'seems to have always had cannon to spare for the Netherlands. He shipped some four hundred great guns from Swedish ports to the United Provinces by 1627, on the eve of battles which were to drive back over the Rhine–Meuse delta the Spanish armies.'[45]

By the Thirty Years War, cannon and other high-technology weapons had become crucially important, and arms transfers were beginning to be used systematically in a *positive* way by states to influence alliances and the outcome of battles. As de Geer was aiding the United Provinces, the English were shipping cannon in the same direction. The result was that 'as long as . . . England, Sweden and the United Provinces could keep peace among themselves, avoid strife and ship cannon and other firearms to each other and to their friends on the Continent, they possessed a force of resistance . . . which it was increasingly difficult for the large continental states . . . once so much wealthier, to match'.[46] With the decline of the English arms industry in the early 1600s, Sweden dominated the international market for cast-iron cannon until the late eighteenth century.

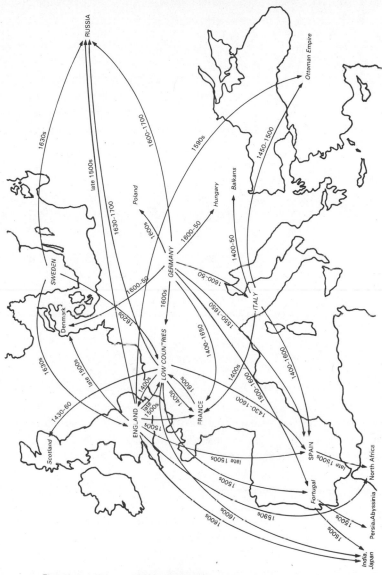

First-tier states: *ITALY, ENGLAND, LOW COUNTRIES, SWEDEN, GERMANY*

Second-tier states: *FRANCE, RUSSIA, SPAIN*

Third-tier states: *Portugal, Ottoman Empire, Scotland, Hungary, India, Japan, Poland, Balkans*

Recipients: *Denmark, North Africa, Persia, Abyssinia*

Figure 2 Patterns of arms transfers, 1400–1700

## The diffusion of weapons technology and the emergence of second-tier producers

Virtually all European states and principalities purchased weapons from the two first-tier producers at some point in the period from 1450 to 1650, the most prominent customers being France, Spain, Italy, Russia and the Ottoman Empire. The overall pattern of armaments flow (as well as it can be pieced together) is presented schematically in figure 2, which highlights major customers and centres of production. From the dates indicated the shift from Italy to England and the Low Countries is abundantly evident. One anomalous feature of the map, however, is the position of arms production in Germany. Although less information is available on arms production in this region, the technological sophistication of the weapons is well attested to. By

> the first half of the seventeenth century, the only large manufacture of guns in Central Europe, aflame with war, was that at Suhl, in Saxony ... its gun factory not only produced arms for Germany; pieces were exported to Hungary, Italy, Spain, Switzerland, Russia, Poland, Denmark and France.[47]

This, and the fact that German gun-founders were in high demand across Europe, suggests that Germany should perhaps be considered as a first-tier producer. But for all its technological achievement, political disunity and fragmentation kept centralised state investment low and occasionally resulted in setbacks. The great arsenal in Suhl, for example, was the most important arms production centre in Europe, but was destroyed in 1634 during the Thirty Years War.[48] This, coupled with difficult access to markets, meant that Germany did not play as central a role in the early arms trade as it probably could have, given its endowments.

Major customers of this period, however, were not content just to buy arms, or to restrict the flow of weapons out of their country. Cognisant of the importance of an arms industry to guarantee national independence and power, they attempted to foster indigenous arms industries by acquiring the necessary technologies and infrastructure. Technological diffusion primarily took the form of the migration of skilled workers, and the Swedish, Russian, French, Spanish and Ottoman arms industries all enjoyed significant boosts from such migrations, which were encouraged by state policies.[49] But only where the new technologies fell on fertile ground did an arms industry take root, and only France, Russia and Spain successfully became second-tier producers, although their successes were virtually all ultimately

44

ephemeral or limited. The failure of other states, such as Portugal and the Ottoman Empire, to reach even this level condemned them to the status of third-tier producers.

From the beginning of the modern period France could not meet its armaments needs, and the evidence suggests that domestic production could meet only a small percentage of the demand during the Hundred Years War. France suffered from this shortage in armaments until the seventeenth century, despite repeated efforts to create a self-sustaining arms industry.[50] German and Italian armourers supplied the French market, and the French government imposed severe restrictions on the export of arms:

> Much earlier legislation was summed up in a French ordinance published in 1572: 'because the founding of cannon and ball and the gathering and manufacture of the materials for gunpowder are a sovereign right, belonging to the King alone for the safeguard and defence of the realm', no subject whatsoever was to make or seek to sell such war material without licence from those deputed to act 'in the interest of the prince and of the public good'.[51]

To cope with this, the French kings between 1422 and 1498 'deliberately built up Tours as an ... arms centre by encouraging foreign armourers and gun-founders, chiefly Italian, to settle there'.[52] Technicians from Liège were also encouraged to migrate, and Charles VIII even attempted to convince the Milanese to waive legislation prohibiting the emigration of skilled craftsmen. Milan was not the only centre worried about the loss of its technological edge: 'in the second half of the eighteenth century, the [Liège] authorities tried time and again to prohibit the emigration of fire-arms workers [even with threats of imprisonment] ... to no avail'.[53] What is interesting to note is how dominant centres of production reacted against the loss of their technological monopoly (in the form of skilled workers) and the power this conferred on them. In addition, the French instituted an embargo on the *import* of arms (without licence), in an attempt to support the indigenous industry.

The results were, for a time, impressive: Philippe Contamine notes that 'du milieu du XVe siècle au milieu du XVIe siècle ... l'artillerie a connu une très sensible croissance ainsi que des améliorations techniques à certains égards décisives'.[54] Arms production was sustained throughout France by conscious state policies, but this success did not last. By the 1660s Louis XIV's advisor Colbert was still importing Liège technicians to establish an industry to supply guns to his new navy.[55] His successes, despite the renewed mustering of state resources, were again temporary, not because France lacked the technological base, but more likely because the commercial infrastructure (credit, internal transport) was underdeveloped. Although a relatively advanced level of arms production was reached, in general the French failed to catalyse a large-scale domestic arms industry and remained partially dependent upon foreign supplies throughout this period.

Russia's ambitious efforts to found an indigenous industry, also fully backed by the state, enjoyed similar mixed success. In the fourteenth century Muscovite Russia was largely self-sufficient in armaments, but it rapidly fell behind Western European advances in military technology. In the early fifteenth century Russia was importing all its cannon, but Ivan III (1462–1505) began importing foreign (mostly Italian) craftsmen to train Russians in the new techniques for manufacturing bronze cannon, which arrived in Russia roughly some twenty-five years after their development in Western Europe.[56] The manufacture of armaments was a state monopoly (direct or indirect) from the outset and by the mid 1500s production was well established, although some weapons were still imported. Russia remained, however, a classic second-tier producer, able to reproduce and adapt technology but not to innovate. As Thomas Esper argues:

> there is no evidence that Russia was responsible for any important technological innovation in this area of production. Quite the contrary, it seems obvious that while the Russian economy could sustain a rather high level of weapons manufacture, the technology employed had been developed elsewhere.[57]

Thus in the early seventeenth century, as Western technology advanced, foreign help was again required and Russia became a major importer of both Western arms and technology, with the clear goal of reducing or eliminating dependence upon uncertain foreign supply in an era of protracted warfare. In 1632 a Dutch-run arms plant was established near Tula to manufacture the new cast-iron guns (which had appeared in England roughly fifty years previously) and to train Russian workers. Although imports were still needed throughout the seventeenth century, production was sufficiently advanced for some of the cannon to be exported: roughly 1,000 pieces were exported in 1636–7.[58] Peter the Great (1682–1725) made another concerted effort to improve the technological level of arms production with foreign help, and by 1720, more than 13,000 cannon had been produced in his factories.[59] Reducing dependence upon imported firearms was also a major goal of Peter's efforts, and some sense of the volume of imports can be gained from the following figures: Russia imported 10,000 Swedish firearms in 1631, 40,000 from Holland between 1653 and 1655,

37,000 (source unknown) between 1659 and 1662, and 30,000 (source unknown) between 1708 and 1712. The army had about 100,000 men at this time.[60] By 1720, however, the annual production of Tula's gunsmiths had reached about 20,000 (equal to French production), and the ratio of imports to domestic production, which had stood at about 2.5 to 1 in the mid 1600s, had essentially been reversed. But although a high degree of military self-sufficiency had been achieved by the early eighteenth century, Russia's

> metallurgical and armaments industries had been purposefully fostered by the state for political reasons, and did not at all reflect the country's general economic level. Its condition of military self-sufficiency could endure into the nineteenth century only because no significant advances in weapons technology were made until then, when a new cycle of military innovation began.[61]

Spain experienced similar difficulties in producing and obtaining adequate quantities of arms as did France and Russia, but enjoyed less success in creating a durable arms industry. In the mid sixteenth century, Spain was 'almost totally dependent upon foreign artillery supplies' from Germany, Italy and the Netherlands, and was technologically behind the first-tier states, being incapable of producing cast-iron cannon until the 1600s.[62] But a series of reforms in the 1570s attempted to stimulate arms production in order to reduce dependence upon foreign supplies. The mechanism for this was again the importation of armourers and founders from Italy, Germany and the Netherlands, but Spain did not possess a sufficiently well-developed economy for imports of skilled workers and other inputs to take root. Factories often closed temporarily for lack of foreign or local expertise, and the ebb of state support (and its penury) was a constant problem.[63] Some success was achieved, but by 1590 only three-quarters of Spanish demand for cannon could be met with indigenous production, imported weapons continued to be cheaper (and better), and in general, Philip II's (1555–98) 'repeated efforts to establish factories producing cannon . . . always failed to flourish'.[64]

After 1570 the Spanish also attempted to license all exports (and to permit them only if no royal orders were pending) and launched 'frantic efforts to secure imports of English cannon' through extralegal channels in the face of a leaky English prohibition.[65] By the end of the century, Sir Walter Raleigh was protesting in the House of Commons against this loss of England's technological lead: 'I am sure heretofore one ship of Her Majesty's was able to beat ten Spaniards, but now, by reason of our own ordnance, we are hardly matched one to one.'[66] But Raleigh need not have worried, for the flow of weapons

47

was not matched by a diffusion of military technology, and Spain's failure to create a modern armaments industry on the level of other first-tier states, or to compete in the new technological realm, merely hastened its decline.

One should note that the political significance of arms transfers was demonstrated by the various actions states took to restrict them. Although efforts at control were often ineffective because of the uncertain writ of rulers in their territories, governments became actively involved in the arms trade soon after the technological, social and economic revolutions made large-scale production possible. Four patterns of involvement manifest themselves. The first reaction was to protect one's limited resources, as in the French and Spanish cases. The second, manifest by leading producers such as Milan, Liège and England, was the desire to protect one's technological lead. The third, which appeared in virtually all states at one time or another, was the desire not to arm a potential or actual enemy. The fourth (and less frequent) pattern was the use of arms transfers as a positive tool of influence to aid friends. This characterised the behaviour of England and Sweden, Italy to the Poles and the Burgundians towards Scotland, but was not generally characteristic of the arms trade of the period.

## The emergence of third-tier producers and extra-European technology and arms transfers

The last feature of the international arms transfer system during this period was the extra-European diffusion of new weapons and the emergence of a third tier of producers within and outside Europe. Within Europe, in addition to the first-tier producers at the forefront of technology who met most of their own needs and second-tier producers who strove to create a modern industry with some modest results, one could also find peripheral producers such as Portugal, Scotland and Hungary. Outside Europe, the radically different social and cultural factors, economic base, and pressures for military development also meant that third-tier producers such as Turkey, India, China and Japan were able only to emulate with much effort the successes of European states. Behind these states lay a group of states that found themselves consigned to the role of passive consumers or even victims of changes in military technology.

Within Europe, the smaller peripheral states quickly fell behind in the new military technologies, developing only the weak or enclave arms industries characteristic of third-tier production. The first European state to decline from great power status, Portugal, was importing large quantities of Flemish and German cannon by the late 1400s. Despite the stimulus provided to local production by the rapid expansion of its commerce and overseas trade, Portugal

> remained largely dependent on foreign guns ... [and] the inherent weakness of the situation became obvious in the course of the second half of the sixteenth century ... When Portugal severed connections with Spain in 1640, she was forced to turn to Holland, her traditional foe, for guns and ammunition ... when war broke out between Portugal and Holland in 1656, Portugal had to import ammunition from Hamburg.[67]

In the early sixteenth century Scotland was also acquiring the techniques of bronze gun-founding from French founders, but although a foundry was established, throughout the 1500s most of Scotland's ordnance was imported. There was quite simply neither the know-how, materials, state support, nor economic infrastructure necessary for an arms industry, and 'the many foreigners employed suggest the difficulty in obtaining native expertise and ... [the] technical difficulties'.[68] Poland had similar difficulties in responding to the threat posed by Gustav Adolphus: although technology was imported and gun-casting commenced in the 1630s, the decentralised nature of the state and lack of firearms and soldiers trained with them meant defeat by the Swedes in 1655.[69] Somewhat later, Hungary was using cannon forged in the 1640s in its war of independence (1703–11) against the Habsburgs, and managed to establish two primitive cannon foundries during the war.[70] Firearms production was similarly primitive, and imports (which would have come from Poland) were difficult because the Great Northern War (between Russia and Sweden) created high demands for arms. Elsewhere in Europe similar arms production efforts could be found, but these never managed to generate either large-scale production or the arms exports that could have ensured survival.

In principle Europeans were opposed to trading away their technological monopoly outside Europe. But the general prohibition on trade with 'infidels' and 'barbarians' did little to preserve the European arms monopoly: a portion of Spain's and Portugal's purchases, and Italian production, always found itself in Ottoman Turkey, North Africa or further afield in Asia. Its proximity meant that the Ottoman Empire was quick to acquire new military technologies, but, typical of a third-tier state, it relied heavily on imported weapons or technologies. Cannon appeared in the Balkans as early as 1378 (less than fifty years after their appearance in Western Europe) and primitive bombards were produced in Dubrovnik soon after, with the help of Italian,

German and Hungarian founders.[71] By the mid 1400s cannon were being cast throughout the Balkans, and probably passed to the Turks via this route: the cannon used by the Turks to capture Constantinople in 1453 (which demonstrated the decisive value of large siege artillery) were cast by renegade Hungarians. Some indigenous production followed in the sixteenth and seventeenth centuries, but this appears to have depended upon foreigners; as late as 1550 the Turks had 40 or 50 German technicians manufacturing artillery in Istanbul and acquired much of their arsenal as war spoils.[72] Indigenous production none the less enabled the Ottomans to exercise their claim to great power status, both through force of arms in Europe and the Middle East and the dispatching of arms and artillery experts throughout the sixteenth century to Muslim (or friendly) rulers from Turkestan and Uzbekistan to India and Sumatra to aid in the struggle against the Europeans.

Portugal, with the most extensive trade network, was the prime diffuser of new weaponry to Asia and Africa, despite its third-tier status. In the early sixteenth century, for example, it supplied both the Persians and the Abyssinians with firearms or cannon in their battles against the Turks.[73] Firearms and cannon appear to have been introduced to India by the Portuguese soon after their arrival, and by the late 1500s the port of Hormuz played a central role as a clearing house for Portuguese and Italian weapons destined for India.[74] Firearms were introduced to Japan in 1543, and cannon around 1551.[75] China was a somewhat different case, having used gunpowder for military purposes (primitive bombs, grenades and fire lances) for several centuries prior to the introduction of European weapons. China was casting primitive bronze 'eruptor' artillery as early as the thirteenth century, and may in fact be where modern cannon originated.[76] But by the time of the European arrival, Western armaments were technologically superior, and either adopted or imitated.

Arms production in Asia soon followed, and by the end of the sixteenth century cannon were being produced in China, Japan, Korea, India, Java, Burma and Afghanistan. As early as 1505 Milanese and Venetian workers were casting iron guns in Calicut for use against the Portuguese, although this early production is not duplicated elsewhere in India, where reports of Dutch and English founders appear only in the latter half of the seventeenth century.[77] This suggests that advanced artillery production in India developed 50–100 years behind Europe, and is confirmed by the dependence of Indian rulers upon the Dutch and English for cannon between 1618 and 1666. Further afield, the Dutch attempted in the late sixteenth century to increase their influence in Asia by building foundries in Japan, although they were much more concerned with preventing locals from learning the new techniques. Nevertheless, the Japanese were soon casting their own firearms (with European technical assistance): by 1556 there were reportedly 300,000 firearms in Japan. They experienced greater difficulties with cannon-founding, but by the late 1500s indigenously produced cannon were in wide use in siege warfare. But the consolidation of Japan and China under a central administration meant that arms production was closely controlled and even curtailed, and that arms were confined either to government arsenals or to frontier areas.

The Europeans, it turned out, had little to fear from the simple diffusion of technology, as what mattered ultimately was not the technology itself, but the uses to which it was put. All third-tier states had difficulty in using new weapons, which required new military skills and forms of organisation and were ill adapted to other socio-cultural milieux, but differences in the ability of states or cultures to adapt did appear:

> the native peoples of America, Siberia, Black Africa and Southeast Asia lost their independence to the Europeans because they seemed unable to *adopt* Western military technology, [while] those of the Muslim world apparently succumbed because they could not successfully *adapt* it to their existing military system. But the peoples of East Asia, by contrast, were able to keep the West at bay throughout the early modern period because, as it were, they already knew the rules of the game.[78]

Both the Turks and the Indians, for example, lagged behind not only in production, but also in the adoption of new techniques required by the weapons they obtained. On land, in the battles of 1548, Turkish troops failed to use their pistols effectively; at sea, until the seventeenth century they relied upon archers rather than musketeers for their attacks.[79] The fact that many arms were acquired as war booty and not by purchase or local production also hindered the integration of armaments and arms industries into military life. As Geoffrey Parker notes, 'although Turkish craftsmen could copy any new Western weapon that they found on a battlefield or that a renegade brought to them, it usually took them a long time; and . . . even then, they only seemed able to deploy them within the traditional military framework'.[80] In India, contemporary descriptions attest to the 'timid and unskillful' firing of Indian gunners with both firearms and cannon.[81]

Further, the engine of technological change remained firmly rooted in Europe. As Carlo Cipolla explains, 'despite the fact that the "know-how" was broadcast by renegades, Jesuits and official missions of "technical assistance", non-European countries never succeeded in filling the vast technological gap that separated them from Europe'.[82] Although the skill often existed to copy imported weapons, the critical mass necessary for innovation never developed. In India, for example, the artillery of the late eighteenth century had not advanced upon the technologies of the fifteenth and was of poor quality. In part because the stimulus to innovation declined with a decline in warfare, the technological sophistication of weapons also lagged somewhat behind that of the West. China was supplementing its cannon production with purchases of superior European weaponry by 1600, and in Japan, political circumstances (the unification of the country under the Tokugawa shogunate in 1603) dictated an almost complete cessation of military innovation.

But the failure to rise above third-tier status was irrelevant in the establishment of regional dominance, for there were always states less able to adapt which were passive consumers of weapons. The example of the Ottoman Empire is instructive, for it adapted far better to the new weapons than its neighbours in Persia, the Mamluk kingdom and Islamic North Africa, who acquired new weapons but were unable to adopt new methods of war-fighting and hence suffered grave military and political defeats. As Halil Inalcik notes, 'The use of fire-arms was considered, in these traditional societies, to be something "common" and not compatible with the traditional ethics and symbolism of the established military class or with feudal and tribal organization.'[83] The Mamluks acquired guns as early as 1400, forty years after they appeared in Europe, yet in contrast to the use of cannon in Europe, they consistently refused to use firearms on the battlefield.[84] Between 1500 and 1516 they even cast cannon in large quantities, but these were dispatched to Mediterranean and Red Sea coastal outposts and played almost no role in the clash with the Ottomans. The resistance of the Mamluk military to stooping to using battlefield firearms was so strong that it sealed their defeat by the Ottoman Janissaries. Safavid Iran used guns only reluctantly at first; the consequence was defeat by the Ottomans in 1514.[85] And the North African tribal dynasties of the sixteenth century suffered defeat at the hands of both the Ottomans and the Portuguese when they were unable (or slow) to develop new military formations to incorporate new weapons.[86] The Ottomans may not have been good fighters by European standards, but their superiority in firearms was the main factor that enabled them to bring West Asia and Egypt under their control.

# Conclusion

Although this survey of global arms production and transfers in the early modern period is sketchy, the main outlines serve to confirm the thrust of the argument presented in chapter 1: arms production is hierarchically stratified into three tiers (albeit loosely defined in this period), and the mechanisms of military technological innovation and diffusion appear to give the system a clear structure and evolutionary dynamic that promotes some states or regions and condemns others to inferiority. The precise limits of technological diffusion (and the consequent tiers into which different states fall) are also conditioned by the motive forces that underlie international politics: the pursuit of power (which signals the rise and fall of states such as Spain, Portugal, England or the Netherlands); the pursuit of victory in war or its absence (which conditions the actions of leaders such as Gustav Adolphus, Peter the Great or the Tokugawa shogunate); and the pursuit of wealth (in determining the socio-economic foundations of arms production). The interplay of these forces plays a major role in determining membership in the tiers of arms production during the period of the Military Revolution.

What is missing from the picture is an active state-sanctioned (or accepted) arms trade that would have made this period correspond more tightly to the ideal type life cycle sketched in chapter 1. Arms are widely traded, but this represents more a triumph of primitive capitalism and the prestige and power of modern technology than a triumph of conscious state policies. The dominant mercantilist ethos that controlled or throttled down arms production in many states, coupled with the drive for autarky inherent in the self-help system, limited the expansion of arms production in states in all three tiers, and perhaps even slowed the pace of technological innovation. But these similarities and differences will become more clear when the second and third cycles of the system are examined in equal detail.

# 3 FROM THE MILITARY REVOLUTION TO THE INDUSTRIAL REVOLUTION

The first wave of the arms transfer and production system, which had been triggered by the introduction of the revolutionary military technologies of gunpowder, cannon and firearms in the early fifteenth century, played itself out through the imperfect process of technological diffusion in the sixteenth and seventeenth centuries. The period that followed, from roughly the late seventeenth to the early nineteenth century, was, by contrast, relatively quiescent. The high degree of state control of arms production and exports (directly or via licensing) had the effect, as the English case demonstrated, of keeping production at or near the level needed to supply domestic needs only; thus the pace of technological change was almost consciously slowed.[1] The weapons themselves continued to spread, diffused by empire-builders and traders, but the diffusion of the techniques to produce and utilise them properly was much slower. No new centres of production arose, and the structure of the system that had manifest itself by the late 1600s was not fundamentally altered.

The most important reason for the stability of the international arms transfer system between 1650 and 1850 was the relatively slow pace of technological change compared to the preceding and following periods. The armament of soldiers, armies and navies changed little in this period: in Britain, the 'Brown Bess' was the standard firearm from 1690 to 1840, 'the field gun of the 1840s was only a slightly more sophisticated version of the gun the soldiers of the sixteenth or seventeenth centuries would have recognized', and 'the *Sovereign of the Seas*, launched in 1637, was similar in all but detail to every English capital ship built until 1860'.[2] Some important changes in weaponry did occur, but these all fell into the category of incremental innovations that did not fundamentally call into question the strategy or organisation of warfare. The most notable changes were the development of cannon-boring (as opposed to casting on a mould), the replacement of matchlock firing mechanisms with flintlocks, and the lightening of field guns and their carriages.[3]

54

Technological change was slowed partly as a result of deliberate state policy: once weapons had been standardised within armies, innovation required a costly re-equipping of one's own forces. As no direct benefits from the exploitation of technological improvement could be realised, only far-sighted rulers would embark on a reform campaign that would (and did) clash with the conservative resistance of the military to change.[4] As a consequence, 'by [the 1840s] armaments had become a backwater, an exceptionally stagnant pool in an otherwise swiftly flowing current of technology'.[5] Thus until the locus of innovation passed to private industry during the Industrial Revolution, the international arms transfer system passed through a period of relative stability.

Of course, arms were still traded in this period, and numerous examples testify to the political importance of what were primarily state-to-state transfers. The French supplied large quantities of arms to the United States during the Revolutionary War; according to one estimate, about 100,000 muskets were transferred between 1778 and 1783.[6] On the other side, in 1775 the European powers (under English pressure) prohibited the export of arms and ammunition to the same insurgents, with little success. In 1814 the British undertook to prevent the sale of arms to Spain's rebellious American colonies. Sweden continued to export iron for military purposes throughout Europe, and Prussia exported some finished weapons to neighbouring Poland, Denmark, Russia and Austria. All European arms industries were given a tremendous boost by the mobilisation and equipping of the vast armies that accompanied the Napoleonic Wars. French cannon production rose from 900 to 13,000 a year, and Britain assumed the role of primary supplier for the anti-Napoleonic forces, sending arms to Prussia, Russia and Austria and subsidising these purchases to the tune of £65.8 million.[7] The British arms industry also revived somewhat in the eighteenth century around cannon production at the Carron works in Scotland to equip the ascendant Royal Navy.[8] But although trade and production were closely controlled and conducted at the behest of the state, Europe was undergoing a shift in the underlying economic ideology of trade from mercantilism to capitalism that would soon transform the arms trade.

Beyond Europe arms and arms technology continued to be imperfectly diffused, depending upon local conditions and external influences. Russia, in its competition with the West, had still not achieved technological self-sufficiency, and in 1779 the manager of the Carron works emigrated to Russia to build a cannon factory for Catherine the Great. The same process of diffusion occurred with the incremental innovation of cannon-boring, which was transferred (somewhat involuntarily) to second-tier states (the Prussians and Russians) by the Dutch.[9] But in Japan and China military technology remained unchanged until the middle of the nineteenth century: contact with the West was strictly regulated (and hence military technology was not transferred), relative political tranquillity meant firearms and cannon remained auxiliary elements of Asian armies, and naval skills in both Japan and China declined as both turned away from seaborne commerce and conquest.[10] Although both China and Japan were casting cannon during the Opium War (1839–42) and when Perry landed in 1853, the level of sophistication was inferior to that of European weapons, as would be expected in third-tier producers.

In Africa, colonial competition and local demand resulted in massive firearms imports (but few cannon) from the mid seventeenth century and defeated efforts to restrict the small arms trade until the late 1800s. Up to 180,000 guns a year were delivered to the continent between 1658 and 1750, the number rising to 300,000 a year in the second half of the century. The import of firearms appears to have had a decisive impact on slave gathering and the consolidation of the slave-exporting African states (and defeat of lesser states), thus dramatically changing the nature of warfare and statecraft.[11] The most powerful recipients were quick to realise the advantages conveyed by modern weapons: the diffusion of weapons throughout North Africa from the sixteenth to the nineteenth century was slow, 'because the various North African and Egyptian rulers tried to prevent the trade in guns to the central and Eastern Sudan because they planned to bring these areas under their own ... authority'.[12] The same effect was manifested in sub-Saharan Africa, where during the eighteenth century, 'the bulk of the firearms taken into Asante and Dahomey was not carried further afield, because both states imposed restrictions on the distributions of guns in the lands to their north'.[13]

## The Industrial Revolution and the re-emergence of leading producers

The Industrial Revolution applied new technologies in metallurgy and steam power to warfare and had a profound impact on the arms transfer system and the international distribution of power. Between 1858 and 1888, the whole nature of armaments underwent its greatest period of revolutionary innovation since the development of gunpowder and cannon. Ships evolved from wind to steam power and wooden to iron (and later steel) construction. Rifled, breech-loading, steel cannon were perfected, which increased their accurate range three-fold. Breech-loading rifled firearms with an accurate range of 600 to 1,000 metres (double or triple previous ranges) also became the norm.[14] The impact of these developments was summarised by Maurice Pearton:

> Henceforth, the international order was divided into those states which possessed the materials, skills and facilities to manufacture the improved weapons and techniques and those which did not. Industrial states had many more options, they could bring their power to bear or influence the policies of other states either more quickly or more intensively. Non-industrial states could either develop their own capacity or become dependent on those who had it.[15]

Pearton's only misjudgement was that this was not the first time such a development had occurred! Of course, the Industrial Revolution did not occur in a vacuum, and its impact on military technology and organisation was conditioned and channelled by a previous societal change in the scale of preparation for warfare that accompanied the Napoleonic period, which saw armies and military spending double or triple in scale.[16] This underlying change was a precondition for the revolution in military technology, for it provided the state with mobilised resources on the scale that was necessary in order for new technologies to be applied successfully. The direction of flow between civilian and military technology was also not always one way, a fact that assumed great importance for second-tier producers. Two crucial early civilian innovations, Henry Cort's (1784) puddling process for iron-founding and John Wilkinson's (1774) piston lathe (which allowed effective steam engines to be built), were both spin-offs from military contracting experience.[17]

The military advantages accruing from industrial development ensured that Britain, Germany and (to a lesser extent) France, the three giants of the Industrial Revolution, became first-tier arms producers and ascendant military and political great powers. Eighteenth-century innovations in metallurgy quickly found military applications in these three states (indicating their nascent first-tier status), but it took key events or policies in the nineteenth century to catalyse weapons development: the Crimean War for Britain, expansion in the 1860s in Prussia, and the defeat of 1870 in France. It must be noted that the impetus for weapons development was the pursuit of victory in war, although it was the underlying economic endowments associated with the pursuit of wealth that positioned these three states to take advantage of existing technological innovations. An examination of the development of arms industries in each of these states will clarify the reasons for the upsurge of arms trading and production in the late nineteenth century. In each case, new relationships between the state, industry and technology were developed that built upon but substantially altered the control and direction of arms production of previous periods.

The British arms industry was given a decisive push in 1854, when a Newcastle engineer, William Armstrong, after reading of the difficulties British soldiers had with their weapons at the battle of Inkerman, applied modern engineering techniques to gun design to construct a lighter and more accurate breech-loading rifled cannon.[18] Until then British forces had been supplied by the Crown's Royal Ordnance Factories and Dockyards. The government accepted Armstrong's designs, offered him a post (in return for his patents) and began purchasing his guns. But by 1862, difficulties with the new breech-loaders and cries from other manufacturers for open competition precipitated a crisis, the result of which was that the government, after having renewed private interest in the manufacture and sale of arms, retreated to procurement from state arsenals. They also purchased a gun design from the French, and approached the German firm of Krupp in 1862–3 for naval guns.[19] The other major pillar of British arms production was Vickers, which, although it began as a heavy industrial concern, by 1888 had turned towards naval defence construction.[20] It too relied on the state to fill its order books, but from the beginning also exported arms. Between 1903 and 1912, 33.9 per cent of Vickers' naval production was exported, and it was the pre-eminent international naval producer.

The British government's attitude to its arms producers was a curious one. In the case of Armstrong and his main competitor, Joseph Whitworth (until their 1897 merger), their partial exclusion from the domestic market (as state arsenals were favoured until 1887, when state policy gave half its procurement orders to private firms) meant that they vigorously pursued export sales. In Armstrong's words, 'the firm had no alternative but to commence a new career, based on foreign support'.[21] Whitworth made his first sales to Brazil; Armstrong was by the late 1860s selling to Italy, Egypt, Turkey, Chile, Peru, Denmark, Austria, Spain, Holland and both sides in the American Civil War.[22] The relatively permanent overcapacity that private British arms producers found themselves with in the late nineteenth and early twentieth century meant that exports were an integral requirement for all firms' well-being. In fact, 'the government always assumed, down to 1914, that the private armament trade was well-placed to secure alternative support, if not from commercial work, then at least from the export sale of its specialities'.[23] But it should be noted that before 1862, British firms were *not* exporting arms on a *laissez-faire* basis. The international free-trading arms market of the late nineteenth century was a major departure from previous practice and a product (if inadvertent) of government decisions.

Armstrong's and Vickers' main competition in the international arms market was the German steel firm of Krupp, which had been experimenting with muskets and larger pieces as early as 1836.[24] But despite earlier Prussian efforts to reduce its dependence upon Swedish military iron by fostering small-scale indigenous production in Spandau and Potsdam, interest in the new weapons was low: in 1847, Krupp offered his new steel cannon to the Prussian government, where it languished for two years before being rejected. Krupp cannon were tested by the French in 1855 and presented as gifts to the Swiss, Austrians and Russians, but remained unsold until Egypt bought 26 in 1855.[25] The Prussian breakthrough occurred in 1859, with an order for 312 large guns. But by then Krupp had already solicited an international market, for much the same reason as Armstrong: steel guns were expensive to produce and design, and R&D and unit costs had to be spread as widely as possible. For engineering firms with international clients foreign orders were commonplace and Krupp cannon were soon in Egypt, Russia, Belgium, Holland, Spain, Switzerland, Austria and England. Krupp's biggest customer, outstripping Prussia five-fold, was Russia: the Tsars were so intent on participating in the Industrial/Military Revolution that they even asked Krupp to relocate his entire plant to Russia![26]

Despite the *laissez-faire* ethic of the era, Krupp did offer frequent assurances that he 'would never peddle a gun "which might some day be turned against Prussia"'.[27] But his customer list expanded so rapidly that it was difficult to see how his promise could be kept: by 1877 Krupp had more than twenty customers and had produced 24,576 cannon, of which 13,910 (57 per cent) had been exported. By 1914, the firm had supplied arms to fifty-two states, and 51 per cent of its 53,000 cannon had gone abroad.[28] Between 1875 and 1891, only 18 per cent of Krupp's production stayed in Germany. As in the British case, one sees a strong (although not exclusive) reliance on exports to ensure the health of the concern, a reliance that appears to have been passively accepted by the state for the advantages it created in domestic procurement.

France was a more reluctant entrant in the international arms market, either because it was more cognisant of the political implications of such trade or because it was a late industrialiser and convert to *laissez-faire* economics. As one contemporary English writer observed:

> For nearly four centuries the manufacture of ordnance in France was carried on exclusively in the arsenals of the Government, all private enterprise in this direction having been checked, while . . . the French government only exceptionally availed itself of the opportunities afforded . . . to obtain some ordnance from abroad . . . Not only had private enterprise been always fettered by a total prohibition from supplying the needs of the country . . . it was . . . stifled by regulations that prohibited any French industrialist from furnishing ordnance to foreign governments.[29]

Until 1870, cannon and naval production was concentrated exclusively in government arsenals, and exports were small and irregular, usually concentrated around wars when arms were transferred to friends and allies such as Egypt, Italy or Turkey.[30] But the defeat of 1870, the French equivalent of the Crimean experience, led successive French governments to modernise and expand arms production, which *doubled* between 1874 and 1885 and doubled again by 1914. More significantly, private firms were also involved for the first time: the dominant French heavy engineering firms of Schneider and Forges et Chantiers de la Méditerranée (F. et C.) were asked to participate (against a certain amount of military resistance) in the rearming, receiving their first orders for 250 and 340 cannon respectively.[31] No significant foreign sales could be made, though, until the law prohibiting exports was repealed; this occurred, after repeated attempts, in 1885.[32] By 1890–1900, twenty-three states had adopted French weapons, among them Russia, Spain, Sweden, Greece, Bulgaria, Serbia, Mexico, Chile, Japan and the Transvaal. As one critic noted, however: 'parmi ces pays, deux, la Bulgarie et la Turquie, devaient se trouver en guerre contre la France en 1914–1918, d'autres part, Le Creusot armait des ennemis héréditaires, la Turquie et les pays balkaniques, le Japon et la Chine', as well as virtually all potential rivals in South America.[33] Both Schneider and F. et C. grew also to rely heavily upon exports: between 1885 and 1914, about half of Schneider's 90,000 cannon were exported; between 1856 and 1899 about 44 per cent of F. et C.'s military production was exported.[34] Still, it should be noted that exports as a percentage of total arms production in France were unlikely to have exceeded 10 per cent, as state arsenals did not export their production.[35]

These three producers dominated the first stage of the industrialisation of warfare and 'nearly all the other powers . . . [were] frankly beholden to England, France or Germany for the essential parts of their naval [and other] armaments'.[36] But it is important to grasp that this period of relatively free trade in arms was a historical aberration; it was not the case, as many later writers argued, that 'up until the 1930s, arms were normally exported as freely as any civil item'.[37] From the outset of the industrial revolution in armaments, the British and Prussian governments permitted extensive exports. State resistance to allowing exports was strongest in France, and the explanation offered by one analyst for why France finally adopted a *laissez-faire* policy is instructive:

> Dans le motifs de la loi, on avait mis en avant l'esprit de liberalisme et de libre entreprise, qui régissait alors l'économie, l'exemple des pays étrangers, qui permettaient le commerce des armes de guerre, ce qui n'était donc pas nuisible à la défense nationale et enfin, l'idée qu'il ne fallait pas leur laisser le bénéfice d'un tel commerce et que la libération de cette industrie permettrait d'ouvrir de nouvelles usines et de faire de nouvelles exportations.[38]

The relationship between state and private production was some-what curious because, as Clive Trebilcock points out in the case of Britain, the government 'maintain[ed] the Royal Ordnance Factories in relatively steady employment while forcing the private trade to carry the full burden of the "armament cycle"'.[39] As a result, individual firms such as Schneider or Vickers were more dependent upon exports than the industry as a whole, but were also crucial to the process of technological innovation. Governments realised that the locus of technical innovation rested with the private firm, that decisive (if temporary) advantages could be gained by a state possessing a new weapon or technique, and that the irregularities of government procurement necessitated exports to maintain plant and research and development expertise. In Britain, liberal politicians even 'advocated giving more orders to private firms on the grounds that this would stimulate competition among inventors and producers', and naval construction policies encouraged firms to sell arms abroad to preserve their capacity.[40] Altogether, this reflected a somewhat casual approach to military technological superiority that could not be afforded by the second- and third-tier states that rapidly attempted to acquire the new weapons. First-tier 'governments, in short, encouraged the export trade because they considered ... they had more to gain than to lose by it'.[41] Britain's previous experience in the seventeenth century, and Liège's dominant role in the market in the sixteenth and seventeenth, suggested that this logic was correct.

## The political consequences of the new arms transfer system

What were the political consequences of these developments, and in what ways did the dominant supplier states manipulate their status? To answer this question, one must first assemble the scattered information on the structure of the market: this has been done in table 1, which lists recipient states according to the number of first-tier producers from whom they purchased arms. This table understates the degree of market overlap, for it only lists major customers of first-tier supplier states; in the case of Krupp, only half of its fifty-two customers have been included. None the less, this only reinforces the main point: there was such a large degree of overlap that virtually no state, save a colony or dependency, needed to depend on a single supplier for arms, and thus it was not possible to deduce the political orientation of a state from its arms purchases. Table 1 does not reveal, however, which states were predominantly dependent on one supplier, or what changes (if any) in orientation occurred between 1865 and 1914.

At the outset, first-tier suppliers were reluctant to interfere in the free trade in weapons even during crises: when in July 1870 the Prussians attempted to divert two cannon ready to be delivered to Russia, Krupp responded that he would have to ask the Tsar first! To put a peacetime ban on the export of arms to another state would also have been tantamount to a declaration of war. The clearest example of this was Prussia's (and Krupp's) dilemma on the eve of the 1866 Austro-Hungarian War. Instead of banning exports, the Prussian War Minister sent a timid dispatch to Krupp: 'I venture to ask whether you are willing, out of patriotic regard to present political conditions, to undertake not to supply any guns to Austria without the consent of the king's government.'[42] Krupp's response was an evasive 'no'. Even after this near-collision, a curious competition ensued: in 1868 Krupp almost sold Napoleon III 300 cannon, and the Prussian navy entertained Armstrong's sales team. In both cases, however, political wisdom trumped economic advantage, and a 'buy locally' policy followed.

States, however, rapidly found other ways than direct interference to manipulate arms transfers to their political advantage, and the largest contracts and most intense relationships tended to follow the developing alliance networks. For example, Russian co-production deals (discussed below), although internationalist, leaned heavily on Britain and France. The French parliament authorised much of the

Table 1. *Suppliers of major arms recipients, 1860–1914*

| All major suppliers | Two of the three major suppliers | One of the three major suppliers |
| --- | --- | --- |
| *(Britain, France, Germany)* | *(Britain and France)* | *(France)* |
| Chile | Peru | Mexico |
| Denmark | United States | Uruguay |
| Spain | Norway | Persia |
| Holland | | Bolivia |
| South Africa | | Haiti |
| Russia | *(Britain and Germany)* | Serbia |
| Japan | | Dominican Republic |
| China | Austria-Hungary | |
| Romania | Egypt | *(Germany)* |
| Argentina | | |
| Portugal | *(France and Germany)* | Switzerland |
| Belgium | | Siam |
| Italy | Morocco | Montenegro |
| Greece | England | Cuba |
| Brazil | Sweden | |
| Turkey | Bulgaria | *(Britain)* |
| | | Canada |

*Note:* This table only includes the major clients of the three dominant suppliers. If all weapons were included, some states in the 'Two of three' and 'One of three' categories would certainly have more diversified acquisitions patterns.
*Sources:* from text.

credit needed for these projects, and also arranged for Russian engineers to study the newest production techniques.[43] The motivation for this was clear: French policy required the Russians to be able to respond rapidly against the technologically superior Prussian army. After 1903, as the competition took on a keener political edge, Krupp was no longer allowed to raise loans on the Paris Bourse to finance Russian weapons purchases.[44] As exports grew, governments also reasserted their authority: in 1880 the British government prevented the sale of advanced ships to China during its conflict with Russia, and in 1900 it passed the Exportation of Arms Act, enabling it to prohibit arms exports to specific countries (although this power was not used until 1914).[45]

The main forum for this competition was the Balkans (although competition in China was also intense). The new and usually poor Balkan states depended on loans from the great powers to finance their military and industrial purchases, providing an entrée for a new form of complex arms transfer competition. As Pearton explains:

> Every project for modernizing the economy, which would help define the state more clearly, was looked at in military terms . . . in

> the existing conditions [the arms firms rivalry] could not be merely commercial, and their successes and failures were registered by their own governments as evidence of the progress of national policy in the area ... Where political conflicts were acute ... the firms, even though legally and financially separate from the state, became adjuncts to its foreign policy.[46]

The result was the projection of greater European conflicts into the region: the Greeks and Bulgarians were armed by the French, while the Turks and Romanians used predominantly German weapons. The Germans propped up the Ottoman Empire with massive investments; and Prussian–Ottoman military cooperation, which had originated in the 1830s, extended far beyond the supply of weapons: 'the German model was adopted en bloc and in the long run brought a political return in the form of adherence to the German structure of alliances'.[47] Bulgaria was permitted by the French government to float a loan on the Paris Bourse for weapons purchases only if it bought French arms.[48] Another form of competition was the provision of military advisors to clients: Turkey received German assistance; Bulgaria and other Balkan states received Russian help; France aided Greece. But because the overlap in markets was only in part due to different areas of expertise (the British in naval armaments, the French in small cannon, the Germans in heavy weapons), and because most clients followed a conscious policy of diversification to avoid becoming beholden to one supplier, the efforts of the French, Germans and British to manipulate the arms transfer system reaped few long-term political benefits. Proof of this manifested itself in the First World War, when British and French transfers to Turkey failed to keep it out of the war, when French soldiers were fired upon by Bulgarian troops using French weapons, when German weapons in Russian hands were turned against German soldiers, and when the French arming of Italy produced no conspicuous political benefits.

## Export-driven technological diffusion and second- and third-tier arms production

A large international market for arms meant (as table 1 suggests) a rapid diffusion of advanced weapons and techniques, but, as in the Renaissance, this was not accompanied by a rapid diffusion of the skills needed to innovate. Nevertheless, after an initial period of passive consumption, many states attempted to create indigenous arms industries, the four most noteworthy ones being Italy, Austria-Hungary, Russia and Spain. Each of these states was a late industrialiser that by the outbreak of the First World War had managed to create a significant modern industrial base with a leading-sector arms industry. In all cases (with the possible exception of Austria-Hungary), reliance on foreign technology or capital was great, and the arms production effort was state-driven rather than spontaneously generated by private efforts. The key mechanism for technological diffusion was no longer the migration of skilled personnel, but the licence or co-production deal, by which entire factories and production processes were transferred as branch plants.[49] It is worth quoting at length one economic historian's analysis of these developments:

> By 1900 . . . foreign capital and expertise had combined to place upon international offer a 'package' of weaponry technology very much more sophisticated than the conventional manufacturing practice of the developing economies. Exporters were increasingly willing to supply complete production systems as well as hardware items, and importers were increasingly anxious . . . to secure domestic sources of armament production . . . The 'gap' between the imported weaponry technology and the resident manufacturing technology could be so disposed as to encourage important transfers of practice, machines, and materials from the 'military' to the 'civilian' sectors. Effectively then, pre-war armament development generated an overseas transmission of high-quality engineering practice . . . [and] Tsarist Russia – alongside colleagues in underdevelopment such as Italy, Spain and Austria-Hungary – was a natural recipient for this transmission.[50]

Aside from the traditional motive of securing themselves from uncertain foreign supply that might be embargoed in time of war (the pursuit of victory in war), or attempting to render credible a claim to great power status (the pursuit of power), a new economic motive (with great contemporary resonance!) began to drive arms production. If an industrial-based armaments industry stimulated technological and industrial advances, and if industrialisation was the hallmark of a great power, possession of an armaments industry for the economic spin-offs it might generate could be a step to achieving or maintaining that status, irrespective of its military implications. Such benefits might not be inconsequential in second- and third-tier states, as Trebilcock argues:

> the international diffusion of high-quality armament manufacture should be ranked in developmental effectiveness alongside the major technological transfers brought about by the railway and agricultural machinery workshops which sprang up across Europe in the half-century after 1850.[51]

Exports also often forced the pace of technological development and pushed first-tier producers to upgrade their own weaponry. For example, the Armstrong-built Chilean cruiser *Esmeralda* (1882) was faster than, and outgunned, anything the Royal Navy possessed in that class.[52] Armstrong repeated the whipsaw in 1890 by providing its most advanced eight-inch guns to the Russians, and in 1902 the British government was forced to buy two cruisers destined for Chile, out of concern for the export of such advanced samples. Krupp went as far as to convince the Russians in 1861 to experiment with new breech-loading mechanisms and suggest improvements.

The pattern of development in the four second-tier states was remarkably similar. In 1884 the Italians, having decided that 'relying on a foreign supplier . . . was potentially dangerous', induced Britain's Armstrong to establish a joint venture by threatening to cut off ship-building contracts. In 1904 and 1906 the process was repeated with both Armstrong and Vickers '[binding] themselves to give the new companies the full benefit of their experience and design'; the result was some of the largest engineering works in Europe.[53] According to Trebilcock, 'the possibility even exists that the military-industrial complex provided the *main* stem of Italian industrialization, that the development of the capital goods sector relied almost entirely on defence contracts'.[54] The Spanish repeated the Italian experience although on a smaller scale and with less success. In the 1880s, Spain imported 97 per cent of its shipping, and the laws of the Construction of the Fleet of 1887 and 1908 were specifically intended to strengthen the indigenous heavy industry and reduce dependence upon foreign ship-building. This was accomplished (to a limited extent) with co-production technology transfers: major British armaments firms (most notably Vickers) refurbished dockyards and arsenals, and were bound by contract to 'encourage the national industries as far as possible' in their efforts. These efforts involved the transfers of the most advanced patents and designs, intensive training for local personnel, and a deliberate encouragement of local economic linkages.[55]

Russian efforts to catch up with first-tier producers were on a grand scale and catalysed by the Crimean experience. At the outset (in the 1850s and 1860s) they concentrated on indigenous private firms which obtained critical equipment or materials abroad.[56] But these efforts were unable to keep pace with technological developments abroad, and by the turn of the century (after the failure of attempts to buy Krupp's and Armstrong's plant outright), deals were signed between 1900 and 1913 for the direct transfer of production techniques with eight firms from all three major producers. These deals resulted in a gun foundry, an armour plate foundry, a shell factory, battleship construction facilities and a steel-casting works being established. One ship-builder promised the Tsar 'a private factory such as no other nation possesses, excepting England ... the most recent, the most modern, and the most effective which could be provided'.[57] The Russians were careful to conserve the benefits of imports through direct transfers of patents and technology, local subcontracting, or the direct transfer of skills (training Russian engineers in England or France). But although their efforts to create an indigenous arms industry enjoyed some success, the limitations of Russia's level of economic development and overall socio-economic system meant that it was unable to acquire the ability to innovate (and rise to first-tier status). As one observer noted, 'impulses to invent or to propagate new inventions were sporadic at best. Harassed administrators were almost always sure to decide that it was better to meet their superiors' instructions by adhering to familiar methods of work.'[58]

The Austro-Hungarian case is the only one in which a relatively successful indigenous industry was created without significant help from first-tier producers. One reason for this was the Hungarian War of Independence of 1848–9, which gave a great boost to indigenous arms production under difficult circumstances and created a base of skills and factories that was later expanded.[59] Whatever the reasons, between 1890 and 1914, the two largest arms enterprises, Skoda and Steyr, grew to compete effectively at the level of first-tier technology. Arms production may have been (as in Italy) the leading sector of the Austrian economy in the post-1903 period, but the overall economic and political difficulties of the Habsburg monarchy prevented what would otherwise have been a logical rise to first-tier status.[60]

These four states all enjoyed varying degrees of success in developing indigenous arms production capabilities, the main determining factor appearing to be their overall level of heavy industrialisation. They had little success in penetrating the export market, however, which remained dominated by the three first-tier producers. Table 2 gives some impression of this dominance, but because it only deals with naval weaponry it understates French and German export activity and overstates that of Italy and the United States (both of which produced few land armaments). The export activity of Spain and Russia appears to have been negligible. This dependence upon domestic contracts persisted until early in the twentieth century, when a less concentrated distribution of exports emerged.

Other states lower in the international hierarchy attempted by

Table 2. *Market shares for naval warships and ordnance, 1900–14*

| Producer | Market share |
| --- | --- |
| Britain | 63 |
| France | 9 |
| Germany | 8 |
| Italy | 9 |
| United States | 9 |
| Austria | 2 |

*Source:* Clive Trebilcock, *The Vickers Brothers: Armaments and Enterprise 1854–1914* (London: Europa Publications, 1977), 123.

similar methods to acquire modern arms industries via the transfer of European technologies, but these third-tier efforts were more clearly enclave industries that had few backward or forward linkages in the local economy. The most noteworthy efforts took place in Turkey, Japan and China, although arms production on a limited scale appeared wherever a sufficient combination of political will and military and economic circumstance dictated, such as in Iran or Egypt. Cannon and muskets based upon European technology and of relatively high quality were produced in Egypt in the 1820s and 1830s, as part of Muhammad Ali's drive to stimulate industrial development and reduce dependence upon arms imports, and in Iran in the 1850s.[61]

Arms production in the nineteenth-century Ottoman Empire relied primarily upon imports of German arms and technology and was part of a broader movement of military and economic reform. Under the sultans Mahmud II and Abdulmecit, foreign machines and technicians were imported to produce artillery, muskets and other equipment and uniforms in state factories at Tophane, Dolmabahce and elsewhere near Istanbul. Although ambitious, in general 'these [factories] were poorly run and failed to meet the needs of the state', and the effort to compete in advanced arms production, while 'not impossibly far beyond the Empire's technical capacities', was abandoned for political and technical reasons.[62] Two other factors also played a role in the failure of an indigenous arms industry to take root: first, 'by mid-century the pace of European technological progress had made it increasingly difficult to contemplate the local production of hand guns, artillery or ships'; second, as foreign loans stimulated imports in the late nineteenth century, reliance on European armaments increased.[63]

Japan's military response to Perry's arrival in 1853 (and the Chinese defeat in the Opium Wars) was swift, despite the preceding two centuries of neglect of its firearms and ship-building industries. Although limited arms importing and cannon casting had taken place before 1853, in the 1860s and 1870s the import of weapons and foreign experts (first Dutch, then French and British) became widespread, and arms production and military ship-building were the first Western industries introduced into modern Japan. By the 1870s two arsenals and three ship-building complexes had been established, 18 per cent of Japanese warships were domestically produced (with 52 per cent being British- and 22 per cent American-built), and limited exports of small arms and artillery had occurred.[64] But although arms production continued to expand, it remained (until 1911) the exclusive preserve of state arsenals, demonstrating a qualitatively different level of state involvement from that in second-tier producers of this epoch.

What also placed Japan squarely in the third tier was the fact that (unlike second-tier states) it was unlikely to be able to sustain indigenous innovation, as even the successful incorporation of Western arms required a radical restructuring of military (and to a lesser extent political) organisation. As David Ralston notes, 'the men of the new ruling elite in Japan were conscious practically from the start of the ramifications the reforms might have . . . Recognizing that the military power of the European states depended on the existence of a strong economy and an educated, vigorous populace'.[65] In the military realm, this restructuring was illustrated by the hiring of Westerners to establish and teach in Japan's military academies and by continued imports of new weapons and weapons technologies. The victories in the Sino-Japanese (1894–5) and Russo-Japanese Wars (both of which were fought mainly with imported weapons) at least partly demonstrated the success of Japanese efforts to compete with the West in military matters, and the Western embargo implemented during the latter conflict led to a redoubling of its pursuit of foreign arms technologies. One result was that the nascent arms industry was such an engine of industrial growth for the entire economy that 'nearly all the mechanical industries which apply modern science and arts found their origin in military industry, or developed under its influence'.[66]

Attempts to acquire and produce new land and naval arms were catalysed in China by the twin external and internal shocks of the Opium War (1839–42) with Britain and the Taiping Rebellion (1850–64). Development was slow, the main problems being conservative official attitudes that hindered innovation in weaponry and tactics and a decentralised state structure that prevented effective organisation.[67] By 1875, however, under the impact of the policy of 'self-strengthening', state arsenals and dockyards using modern Western machinery had been established at Shanghai, Foochow, Soochow and Tientsin, and some progress had been made in reducing direct dependence upon skilled foreign managers.[68] But despite the desire to avoid dependence upon foreigners, production was ultimately based upon either copies of foreign designs or indirect foreign expertise (of British, French, German or American provenance) and lagged technically behind contemporary European developments.[69] This slow progress relative to advances in Europe called state support into question, the consequence being that ships and arms were bought simultaneously with efforts at indigenous production. In 1884, about half of the modern ships in the Chinese navy were domestically built, and the majority of the rest, British built. Unlike the Japanese case, however, these developments did not produce military victories, and the Empire lost major wars to both France (1884–5) and Japan (1894–5). Also unlike Japan, Chinese arms production was 'always an isolated activity, dependent upon imports with no effect on the life of the country surrounding', and it went into serious decline in the 1890s.[70]

In all these cases, adaptation and the acquisition of new technologies was triggered by the pursuit of victory (or avoidance of future defeats) in warfare. The pursuit of great power status played a role somewhat later, as did (in the Japanese case) the realisation that modern arms industries were integral parts of advanced industrial economies. In all three cases, however, the ability both to use the weapons and to produce them was restricted by indigenous economic, social and political factors, ranging from suspicion of Western influences and technologies to inadequate economic infrastructures to insufficient state financial support, making them again classic third-tier producers. Although in theory arms exports (which were prohibited by law in China, and government controlled in Japan) from these producers might have enhanced their productive capabilities, the relatively low quality of production and poor development of the international market would probably have prevented exports from being profitable. In the end, the independence sought was a chimera, as Thomas Kennedy notes in the case of China:

> after thirty years of arsenal operation, China still had to look abroad for most of the technology and all of the specialized machinery needed to update production. The introduction of new technology and the maintenance of modernized production still required foreign technical assistance. Even raw materials and fuels in many instances continued to come from abroad ... In short, the environment of foreign dependency in which the industry developed forced the arsenals to rely on China's potential enemies for the elements necessary to maintain modernized production.[71]

Below these third-tier producers were simple consumers for arms (mostly in Africa and smaller Asian states) who attempted to obtain modern weapons in the face of European attempts to slow or prevent the diffusion of technology. Although European states attempted to preserve the benefits they enjoyed from monopolising international arms transfers, they were generally incapable of acting in concert. In addition to the already-noted competition for markets that allowed second- and third-tier producers to acquire the technologies to manufacture arms (thus somewhat reducing their dependence upon first-tier states), first-tier producers were unable to control the flow of arms to clients that had little or no bargaining power. In Africa, for example, the 1890 Brussels treaty, which attempted to control arms imports to Africa, was not generally successful. The treaty prohibited imports of firearms, powder, balls and cartridges except under certain conditions, and was designed to 'avoid the development and pacification of this great continent ... [being] carried out in the face of an enormous population, the majority of whom will probably be armed with first-class breech-loading rifles'.[72] Arms continued to be widely sold beyond colonial frontiers wherever the commercial and political advantages outweighed immediate concerns, and recipients of these weapons used them to consolidate their hold over neighbouring territories and states.[73]

One final feature of the arms transfer system during this period, noteworthy because of the later conspiracy theories that sprang from it, was the tendency of firms to form cartels and other monopoly arrangements. Armstrong and Vickers shared contracts and fixed prices, and Vickers bought Krupp fuses for its shells and licensed its 37mm gun to another German firm. Krupp licensed its armour plate production to Britain, France and the United States; this was only part of a larger arrangement between all major engineering/armaments firms that cartelised nickel production and marketing. As these examples suggest, 'it was a period of cartelization, of the forming of trade associations, price fixing syndicates and patent pools'.[74] But one does not have to adopt a conspiracy theory to explain these developments. During this time orders were irregular and unpredictable, barriers to entry were high, and government support not forthcoming. The result was that:

> a few large businesses, faced with unpredictable demand, will *naturally* tend to combine ... agreements between firms will develop easily, they will become especially necessary if there is a single customer ... a laissez-faire government recognizing few responsibilities to industry.[75]

71

The important feature of the arms industry was the specific characteristics of its market, not the behaviour of firms. The main conclusion to
draw is *not* that the behaviour of firms created a market in which
intervention by governments of supplier states for political benefits
was impossible, but rather that the firms' behaviour was conditioned
by a *prior* government decision (explicit or implicit) to permit a
*laissez-faire* market to emerge in the hope that the benefits of rapid
innovation could be most fully realised through stimulation of competition in domestic industry.

## Continuity and change in the interwar arms transfer and production system

By the First World War the same structure that had manifested
itself during the Renaissance had emerged: a dominant tier of sellers
who, by virtue of their mastery of new techniques, were the pre-
eminent powers; a second tier of states (Russia, Italy, Austria-
Hungary and Spain) that, cognisant of the risks of dependence on
foreign suppliers and of the benefits of possession of an arms industry, attempted to emulate first-tier producers' success; and a growing
number of third-tier states (most prominent among them China, Japan
and Turkey) that possessed limited capabilities to produce arms based
on technologies diffused from first-tier states. Between 1860 and 1914
the international arms transfer system evolved from a hegemonic
state in which the first tier monopolised modern weapons supplies to
one in which modern armaments were diffused throughout the globe.

Although the First World War marked a decisive historical discontinuity in many realms, the interwar international arms transfer system
was characterised more by the continued evolution of the existing
system, albeit distorted by the appearance of novel factors. Elements of
continuity were found in the policies and productive capacity of France
and Britain, in their increasing sensitivity to the political implications of
arms transfers, and in a stabilisation of the number of arms producers
in the second and third tiers.[76] A temporary discontinuity was the disappearance of Germany from the arms transfer system until the 1930s,
and new forces included the advent of the Soviet Union and United
States as major suppliers (which was to have a decisive impact in the
next cycle) and the increased role of public opinion as a factor shaping
the behaviour of governments and international political institutions.
In general, however, this period corresponded to the later stages of the
evolution of a 'wave' of the international arms transfer system.

In France and Britain, the arms industry languished in the 1920s and early 1930s as a result of the dramatic drop in domestic procurement that followed the war. Schneider experienced a near collapse in production between 1920 and 1935, and in 1927 the two dominant British firms, Armstrong and Vickers, merged to avert the collapse of the former. By 1930, even Armstrong–Vickers had gone out of the arms export business, save for the construction of naval vessels.[77] But new firms with new products (aircraft and tanks), stimulated by their wartime mobilisation and production experience, kept these two states temporarily in the first tier of weapons exporters. Britain and France, in the 1930–9 period, controlled 17 and 16 per cent respectively of the export market in combat aircraft, 26 and 28 per cent in tanks, and 59 and 10 per cent in warships. Overall, they controlled 25 and 11 per cent of the arms market between 1929 and 1938 (using a data base that excludes naval and aircraft transfers).

Table 3 summarises the available data on the structure of the interwar arms trade, and it suggests a high degree of continuity with the pre-1914 period: Britain, France and Germany remained dominant suppliers; Italy and Austria-Hungary (Czechoslovakia) remained second-tier suppliers, and Japan successfully ascended to this level. A multitude of lesser states (Belgium, Sweden and Poland) became third-tier suppliers. The United States also emerges as a major force for the first time.

National political control over the arms trade continued to encroach on the *laissez-faire* system of the prewar period. Britain in 1921 established a comprehensive licensing system for arms exports (which excluded aircraft) and embargoed exports to China (until 1929), the Soviet Union, Africa and ex-enemy states.[78] These regulations were strengthened after 1931 and embargoes were applied to the Sino-Japanese, Chaco, Italo-Ethiopian and Spanish Wars. By 1939 Whitehall directly conducted arms and aircraft sales to certain countries. France participated in the Ethiopian embargo, discouraged exports during the 1920s and nationalised its arms industry in 1936, so that 'aucune livraison d'armes à l'étranger n'était faite sans l'accord du Quai d'Orsay'.[79] The arms market profile also roughly reflected the prevailing alliances. Vickers–Armstrong continued its cooperative ventures with Japan, Spain and Italy until 1930, and new projects were started, for political reasons (and in cooperation with the French), with Poland, Romania and Yugoslavia. French arms transfers followed efforts in the 1920s to replace the lapsed British and American security guarantee with a series of treaties dubbed the 'Little Entente'. Schneider became part-owner of the Czechoslovak Skoda factory in a government-sponsored deal, special arrangements were made with

73

Table 3. *The international arms trade, market shares by supplier, 1920–39*

| Country | League of Nations[a] 1920–8 | 1929–37 | Sloutzki[a] 1929–38 | Combat aircraft | Tanks | 1930–9 Sub-marines | Warships |
|---|---|---|---|---|---|---|---|
| Britain | 28.6 | 27.0 | 25.0 | 17.3 | 26.1 | 36.0 | 58.9 |
| France | 22.0 | 16.3 | 10.7 | 15.6 | 27.9 | 10.0 | 10.1 |
| Germany | — | 4.0[b] | 10.9 | 9.5 | 4.1 | 8.0 | — |
| US | 27.9[c] | 10.5 | 9.9 | 22.8 | 14.7 | 8.0 | 2.3 |
| Italy | 1.8 | 3.9 | 3.7 | 12.7 | 10.9 | 24.0 | 17.8 |
| Czech. | 4.3 | 12.1 | 12.6 | — | 6.9 | — | — |
| Sweden | 3.5 | 8.0 | 8.1 | — | 3.1 | — | — |
| USSR | — | — | — | 5.6 | 5.6 | — | — |
| Poland | — | 0.1 | — | 2.2 | 0.7 | — | — |
| Japan | 0.3 | 5.8 | — | — | — | 8.0 | 3.9 |
| Holland | 2.2 | 3.1 | — | 3.0 | — | 3.0[d] | — |
| Spain | 3.7 | 1.5 | — | — | — | 3.0[d] | 3.9 |
| Belgium | 1.7 | 4.7 | 5.0 | — | — | — | — |
| Other | 4.0 | 3.0 | 14.1 | 11.3 | — | — | 3.1 |

*Notes:* [a] Sloutzki's and the League's data include heavy equipment and small weapons, and exclude naval and aircraft transfers.

[b] The League data include only Germany for 1935–7, during which time its real share of arms transfers was 11 per cent, as noted by Sloutzki.

[c] The American share for transfers in 1920–8 is inflated by the inclusion of transfers for 1920, when the US accounted for 52.1 per cent of global totals. This may be a statistical artifact. For the period 1921–8, the US share was 20.2 per cent.

[d] Dutch and Spanish shares for submarine sales have been estimated: between them they accounted for 6 per cent of the market.

*Sources:* Columns 1–2: League of Nations, *Statistical Yearbook of the Trade in Arms and Ammunition* (Geneva: League of Nations, annual, 1924–38).

Column 3: Nokhim Sloutzki, *The World Armaments Race, 1919–1939* (Geneva: Geneva Research Centre, 1941), 71.

Columns 4–7: Robert Harkavy, *The Arms Trade and International Systems* (Cambridge, Mass.: Ballinger, 1975), 61, 69, 73, 74.

Romania, and Polish purchases of French arms were subsidised.[80] Every major seller took advantage of the chaos in China to sell weapons there, in spite of a 1919 Arms Embargo Agreement nominally adhered to by most suppliers.[81]

The third major element of continuity in the interwar arms transfer system was the continued evolution and rise of second-tier producers who had successfully industrialised and who subsequently entered the arms export market to spread the costs of research and development in their industries. The main actors were Czechoslovakia, Sweden and Italy (as indicated in table 3). For Czechoslovakia, 'export sales of arms took on a new justification in that they secured ... an income in currency which (unlike the Czech crown) was convertible', and thus the state played a large role in encouraging and promoting its nascent arms industry.[82] Roughly 40 per cent of Skoda's production was exported, and Czechoslovakia garnered more than 10 per cent of the world market, selling arms to China, Japan, Ethiopia, and both sides in the Spanish Civil War. The experience of other second-tier suppliers was similar, if on a lesser scale: arms transfers were undertaken commercially, and were not controlled or manipulated for political purposes. The main impact of the rise of second-tier sellers, however, was to reduce the dominance of the market by first-tier sellers. This in part explains the problems experienced by Schneider and Vickers–Armstrong in the 1920s and 1930s, as they were forced to compete for customers with and within former client states.

Better information for this period allows a more accurate picture of the overall structure of supplier–client relationships to be drawn up. Table 4 summarises the market structure: it points out that few states depended upon one supplier for more than 60 per cent of their arms acquisitions. What this table does not show, however, is when the states that had multiple suppliers diversified their supply, or which producers played a large role in this process. Germany's role in the interwar arms transfer system will be discussed below, but it is clear that before 1933, most states that had diversified supply sources in the interwar period obtained the bulk of their arms from the 'Western' bloc. As table 5, which lists the states that shifted from dependence on 'Western' arms to a multiple supplier pattern, suggests, the majority of these states diversified their supplies after 1933, Nazi Germany being the main beneficiary. What is most interesting is how quickly these states diversified when Germany began making large-scale arms transfers in the late 1930s: even states that did not become Axis allies in the Second World War found it prudent to diversify their arms supplies. The German effort also had political ambitions, and in Latin America transfers were apparently facilitated with offers of military aid, concessionary loans and barter deals.[83] This attempt to woo allies was not without its successes, at least in keeping some states out of the early war effort, but although political considerations played a part in sales and purchases, ideological competition was not so intense as to make purchases from rival blocs unthinkable. This limited the foreign policy leverage which a supplier state could gain from an arms transfer relationship.

These elements of continuity with the previous arms transfer system were accompanied by a temporary discontinuity and two relatively durable changes. The discontinuity was the disappearance of Germany as a first-tier supplier. Under the Versailles settlement, Germany was forbidden to manufacture armaments over the amount

Table 4. *Suppliers of major arms recipients, 1918–39*

| Multiple suppliers | Predominantly one supplier | Sole supplier |
|---|---|---|
| Guatemala | *(Britain)* | *(United States)* |
| Loyalist Spain (to 1936) | | |
| Belgium | Australia | Cuba |
| Czechoslovakia | Canada | Honduras |
| Argentina | Ireland | Haiti |
| Austria | Estonia | |
| Bolivia | Greece | *(Britain)* |
| Brazil | Iraq | |
| Chile | Latvia | Saudi Arabia |
| China | | New Zealand |
| Denmark | *(United States)* | Egypt |
| Ethiopia | | |
| Finland | Colombia | *(Italy)* |
| Iran | Dominican Republic | |
| Japan | Mexico | Albania |
| Lithuania | Nicaragua | |
| Norway | Philippines | |
| Peru | | |
| Romania | *(France)* | |
| El Salvador | | |
| Sweden | Poland | |
| Switzerland | Costa Rica | |
| Thailand | | |
| Turkey | *(Italy)* | |
| Uruguay | | |
| Venezuela | Afghanistan | |
| Yugoslavia | Ecuador | |
| Netherlands | Hungary | |
| South Africa | Paraguay | |
| | Nationalist Spain (from 1936) | |
| | | |
| | *(Czechoslovakia)* | |
| | | |
| | Soviet Union | |
| | | |
| | *(Germany)* | |
| | | |
| | Bulgaria | |
| | Portugal | |

*Note:* The dominant supplier state is listed in brackets. A 'sole' supplier provides all of a client's arms, a 'predominant' supplier more than 60 per cent of them, and 'multiple' suppliers up to 59 per cent for any one supplier.
*Source:* Harkavy, 115, with additional information from Sloutzki, 73–96.

Table 5. *States that diversified suppliers from the Western to Axis bloc*

| 1934 | 1935 | 1936 | 1937 | 1938 |
|---|---|---|---|---|
| Peru | Lithuania | Chile | Argentina | Finland |
| Romania | | Iran | Bolivia | Brazil |
| Austria | | Yugoslavia | Venezuela | Thailand |
| Uruguay | | Denmark | Norway | El Salvador |

*Source:* Harkavy, 119.

needed to maintain Weimar's small naval fleet, plus four large guns a year.[84] Like other features of the Versailles settlement, however, this had only ephemeral impact. Although Krupp did not resume large-scale arms production until 1933, secret research, development and production were conducted much earlier. This involved a steady flow of money from the Weimar government, the establishment of research teams, and the 'frequent departures of key ordnance technicians for countries which had been neutral during the war'.[85] Between 1918 and 1921, Krupp filed eighty-four patents for heavy cannon, field guns, shells and fire-control devices. The growing Soviet arms industry also employed Krupp engineers and directors (under the Rapallo treaty), in return for which facilities for training future Luftwaffe pilots and testing artillery were provided.

The most audacious German efforts were conducted in Holland and Sweden: cannon were built by the German-owned Swedish firm Bofors, and in Holland, German-owned firms researched, designed and constructed U-boats for Japan, Finland, Spain, Turkey and Holland itself.[86] Manufacturing equipment was also exported to the Balkans and Latin America, and manufacturing subcontracted to Belgium, Switzerland and Spain. This explains in part the relatively large role played by these states in the interwar arms transfer system. The results of this research into design and construction went directly to Germany, and beginning in 1928 hidden production of tanks in Germany itself was also undertaken. But the weapons and knowledge thus generated were intended primarily for rearmament, not export, thus explaining the relatively small German market share in the 1930s. German exports of arms actually declined in most categories between 1935 and 1940.[87]

The second novel feature of the interwar international arms transfer system was the public outcry against the arms trade that followed the First World War. British Prime Minister David Lloyd George captured the spirit of the era when he said, 'there was a feeling . . . that Krupp's in Germany had a very pernicious influence upon the war spirit in Germany . . . there was not one [at Versailles] who did not agree that if you wanted to preserve peace in the world you must eliminate the idea of profit . . . in the manufacture of armaments'.[88] This sentiment was embodied in the League of Nations Covenant, which stated that 'the manufacture by private enterprise of munitions and implements of war is open to grave objections'. The 1919 Saint Germain Convention (which never came into effect) would have prohibited arms exports, except in exceptional cases and by means of export licences, and in 1921, the League renewed its efforts in this direction by proposing a similar convention on arms sales.[89]

The public outcry was fuelled by the inflammatory (and often inaccurate) publications mentioned in the introduction. The argument was that 'detail upon detail, incident upon incident, illustrate how well the armaments makers apply the two axioms of their business: when there are wars, prolong them; when there is peace, disturb it'.[90] In the early 1930s, public agitation successfully created the Senate Nye Committee in the United States and the Royal Commission on the Private Manufacture of and Trading in Arms in Britain.[91] Although the findings of the committees are not important here (the Nye Committee was narrowly in favour of nationalisation; the Royal Commission against it), one should note that these developments reinforced the already-established trend towards government control of arms exports. Even if the arms industry was not to be nationalised, the political implications of its output no longer escaped notice.

The final major discontinuity, which had great future import, was the changing role of the Soviet Union and the United States. From the beginning, the Soviet Union regarded the transfer of arms as a political act, and there was no question but that all aspects of production and exports would be carefully controlled. Although the Soviet economy was too weak for it to become a major actor in the international arms market, Soviet leaders were not ignorant of the possible political benefits to be derived from arms transfers: supplies were passed to Ataturk in Turkey, the Chinese Kuomintang, Iran, Afghanistan and the nascent Reichwehr.[92] More important was the dramatic expansion of the Soviet Union's domestic production base, which positioned it for a major role after 1945. In the late 1920s, 'the Soviet Union had virtually no tank industry, little or no warship production, and low artillery and ammunition production; the aircraft industry was the brightest spot in an otherwise gloomy picture'.[93] In the 1930s some foreign weapons were acquired in limited quantities to be copied as the basis for Soviet production, and by 1940 this had conspicuous results: annual aircraft production rose from 860 (1930–1) to 8,805 (1938–40), tank production from 740 to 2,672 and artillery production from 1,911 to 14,996.

The United States experienced a similar revolution of its productive base (doubling its GNP during the First World War), and although this expansion was not explicitly orientated around military industries, arms exports did rise from $40 million in 1914 to $1,290 million in 1916 to $2,295 million in the nineteen months before the Armistice.[94] Prior to 1914, only six government arsenals and two private firms were producing weapons; by the end about 8,000 firms had some arms production experience. The number of heavy gun factories rose from four to nineteen. The rapid increase in production during the war was based, however, almost entirely on British- and French-supplied designs for ordnance, guns, aircraft and tanks (although an Anglo-American-designed tank was built by the end of the war). After the war American producers, especially in the aircraft industry, relied heavily on exports, much as had the great cannon makers of the 1860s. Up to 75 per cent of aeronautical production was exported, and in small arms the industry leader (Remington) exported 40 per cent of its sales.[95] But what was to be of decisive future importance was the marriage of European technologies to American manufacturing methods, which involved capital-intensive assembly-line production to produce high volumes of standardised weapons at relatively lower costs. This development was a harbinger of the technological lead that the United States was to take in the next wave of the arms transfer and production system.[96]

Unlike the Soviet Union, however, American exports were at first not subject to government supervision or control. From roughly 1793 until 1917, private exports were not regulated; from 1905 to 1912, exports to Latin America and China were regulated to 'promote stability and discourage revolution'; and from 1934 to 1939, exports were regulated to keep the United States out of the coming European war.[97] But the 1926–7 Burton Resolution, which would have embargoed arms sales either to aggressors or to belligerents in general, was opposed by the War and Navy Departments on 'the grounds that it would weaken the private armaments industry of the United States on which the government relied heavily for national defence in times of emergency', discriminate against non-producing states, encourage the growth of other indigenous arms industries, and allow other states to supply what the Americans refused to.[98] This rationale, once widely adopted by other states, was the foundation for the full-blown evolution of the arms transfer system into its contemporary epoch after 1945.

## Conclusion

The evolution of the second wave of the arms transfer system from its genesis in the 1840s to maturity in the early twentieth century corresponded in several ways to the ideal type described in chapter 2. The pattern of rapid diffusion of new technologies throughout the system was evident, as was the emerging stratification of the system into three tiers. The attempt by second- and third-tier states to reproduce the new weapons also led to efforts (especially as the gap

79

between first-tier and other producers narrowed in the latter stages) to control or manipulate the flow of weapons and technologies, in recognition of their political significance. But the second wave was not simply a repetition of the first. The changed underlying ideology (and conditions) of economics and trade led to large-scale arms exports and a dramatically altered state–industry relationship. Exports and production were at first relatively unregulated in first-tier states, and exports were permitted because they facilitated the maintenance of innovative capabilities and the productive base. Private production was also considered to be a key element encouraging innovation, although the hand of the state in encouraging and supporting innovation was large. Second- and third-tier states, however, responded much more like Alexander Gerschenkron's 'late industrialisers', which attempted to accelerate the process of development with high levels of direct state involvement and regulation. One significant lacuna, however, was the relative absence of third-tier arms exports, although the emergence of significant second-tier exports in the interwar period suggests this may have developed had the system continued to evolve.

But the relative exhaustion of the military potential of the Industrial Revolution and the acceleration of military research and development in the years leading to the Second World War had already sown the seeds of another technological revolution. Although Britain, France and Germany were able to remain at the forefront of technical developments (in the German case by the adoption of a consciously subversive and revisionist policy) in this period, the marriage of the mobility offered by the internal combustion engine to the possibilities of modern electronics that occurred during and after the Second World War meant that military research and development and arms production would be conducted on a scale that excluded all but the very largest states from being innovators. Existing second-tier states such as Spain, Czechoslovakia and Italy were not destined to play leading roles in this new system; despite their large volume of sales they never became innovators, and usually remained dependent upon first-tier producers for crucial new high-technology items such as aircraft engines.[99] The American and Soviet concentration on aircraft and tank production in the 1930s and the Soviet mobilisation of the entire productive process foreshadowed the decisive roles that these weapons and states would play in future warfare and in the post-1945 international arms transfer system.

# 4 AN OVERVIEW OF THE POST-1945 GLOBAL ARMS TRANSFER SYSTEM

The volume of information available on the post-1945 (and especially the post-1960) period allows a much more complete picture to be drawn of the evolution of the arms transfer and production system. Despite some suggestive indications presented in the historical chapters above, the evidence is insufficient for one to draw definitive conclusions on the motive forces driving the system and its evolutionary dynamic. But an unfocused history of arms transfers since 1945 would not be sufficient either, and the historical backdrop is essential to an understanding of contemporary developments in the arms transfer and production system. What follows is a sketch of the post-1945 international arms transfer system that illuminates its outlines and current structure based on the factors that have already been highlighted as critical: technological innovation, the transfer and diffusion of technology and the relationship between production and exports. It concentrates on producers and suppliers; chapter 8 will integrate this discussion with an examination of the role of arms recipients. Chapters 5–7 will present in detail the policies, practices and motivations of the different tiers of producers or suppliers. This will allow the evolution of the contemporary global arms transfer and production system to be placed against the backdrop of historical precedent and account for some of the distinctive features of the current system. Although the historical chapters emphasised arms production and arms transfers almost equally, the emphasis in what follows will be placed on transfers, with arms production only figuring prominently in so far as it helps explain a producer's participation in the transfer system.

## The post-1945 setting

The Second World War accelerated the evolution of the arms transfer and production system, compressing what would have been the later phases of the second wave with the ascendance of the new technologies and producers that marked the beginning of the third wave. What was of greatest long-term significance was the decisive transformation of military technologies that occurred during and after the Second World War. The technologies associated with such items as radar, jet aircraft or ballistic missiles required research and development (R&D) funds and procurement budgets that were qualitatively larger than ever before. They made the relationship between the state and basic research even closer, further blurred the line between military and civil technologies (as exemplified in the computer chip), and tied greater numbers of researchers and firms into a web of military research. An illustration of this is the estimated one-fourth to one-third of American scientists and engineers whose jobs depend directly or indirectly on military research. The marriage of new technological imperatives to vast sums of state funds also resulted in rapid increases in the unit cost of weapons systems: an American M–1 tank costs triple what an M–60 did (in constant dollars), a British Harrier jet is almost quadruple the cost of a Hunter, a French Mirage F1 triple the cost of a Mystère. Most other weapons systems have doubled or quadrupled in real unit cost over the past thirty years.[1] This development is characteristic of a period of revolutionary technological change that spawns a new arms transfer system. Table 6 below gives some idea of the specific changes in military technologies that the post-1945 period has witnessed and the current or future state-of-the-art systems possessed by the United States or the Soviet Union.

Given this technological sea change, the arms transfer system of the period from 1945 to 1955 immediately stands out as aberrant on four counts. First, the industrial infrastructure to support arms production in most of Europe was virtually destroyed, and several expected participants in the arms transfer system were temporarily absent from it. These included most notably Germany (East and West) and France, but also lesser suppliers such as Italy and Czechoslovakia, all of whom depended until the early 1950s on either American or Soviet arms. The division of Germany, the moral and legal injunction initially established against West German arms production and exports, and the subservience of East Germany and Czechoslovakia to the Soviet Union also limited the role played by these states in the arms transfer system. When these producers re-emerged as major players, they were consigned to second-tier status. Britain was somewhat of an exception, as it emerged from the war with its arms industries intact and in the first postwar decade was second only to the United States as an arms exporter.[2] But it was also (as the Italian city-states were) the first victim of the new system, and was unable to remain at the frontier as a

Table 6. *The evolution of military technologies in the post-1945 period*

| Second World War vintage technologies | First-generation technologies | State-of-the-art technologies | Futuristic technologies |
|---|---|---|---|
| piston engine fighters and bombers | jet engines; turbo prop/fan/shaft engines | high-bypass turbofan fighters; 'stealth' aircraft | hypersonic and composite material aircraft |
| V–1 and V–2 rockets; unguided rockets | short-range cruise missiles; guided rockets | precision-guided missiles; long-range cruise missiles | 'smart' missiles; hypervelocity guided missiles |
| pulse radars | doppler and scan radars | pulse-doppler and over-horizon radars | back-scatter techniques |
| optical gun systems | radar fire-control gun systems | laser range-finders | rail guns |
| steel and aluminium alloys | titanium and magnesium alloys | composite materials, plastics and silicone | ceramics and heat-resistant plastics |
| portable radios and encryption | data links; satellite transmission | real-time satellite and television images | real-time battlefield command and control |

*Sources:* I am grateful to Tom Quiggan for his assistance in preparing this material. Portions of it are derived from Stockholm International Peace Research Institute (SIPRI), *SIPRI Yearbook of World Armaments and Disarmament 1990* (London: Oxford University Press), 323.

technological innovator with the United States by the 1970s and 1980s (although it was capable of producing advanced weapons).

Second, the Soviet Union remained generally aloof from the system, although it held third place as an arms exporter during this early period and was perhaps even second to the United States if arms transfers to Eastern Europe are included. But despite the volume of arms it transferred, prevailing economic and political imperatives (the desire for rapid economic recovery, the need to consolidate gains in Eastern Europe, and the 'two camp' theory of global conflict) meant that the Soviet Union played a smaller role than would have been otherwise expected, given its industrial and economic base and international political stature. It was not a truly global supplier until its 1955 arms deal with Egypt.

Third, defence spending in the NATO and Warsaw Pact states was inflated to near-wartime levels during the Cold War (in value, not in percentage of Gross National Product). The United States occupied the leading role as arms producer and supplier, in part because of the prostration and/or absence of major competitors, in part because wartime mobilisation provided a tremendous boost to military industries. But the most important factor in its rapid ascendance was its decision to offer extensive military aid and equipment to the European allies, a decision that boosted defence procurement and accelerated the pace of military technological change. As a side effect, it also encouraged or facilitated high levels of arms production in otherwise marginal producers such as Canada or Belgium.

Finally, the logical new third-tier suppliers – those states with a sufficiently high level of industrial development, a large enough resource base, and political will – were (with the exception of the Latin American states) restrained by the legacy of colonialism and the inward focus of post-independence (or post-revolutionary) politics from actively developing military industries. Although states such as Egypt, Argentina and Brazil had developed small military production bases in the 1930s or earlier, these producers fell behind as production shifted to new technologies. Other logical early third-tier producers that had not yet emerged were India, China, Iran and South Africa.

These deviations from a more traditional structure obscured the natural outlines of the new system for a considerable time. Thus the norm on which most analyses of change were based was in reality an artificially distorted oligopolistic system built on American dominance (and rising Soviet participation). But a longer historical perspective would have immediately suggested that the post-1945 situation was an aberration that was likely to change as the pace of technological change slowed, new technologies were diffused throughout the system, and something resembling a traditional structure emerged. This is what occurred roughly between 1965 and 1990, and it reflected not so much idiosyncratic decisions on the part of the Soviet Union, France, Germany, Brazil or India, as the expected response of states to the pressures of the pursuit of power, wealth and victory in war in international politics.

By the early 1960s, the outlines and evolutionary dynamic of the new system were already becoming more clear. The Soviet Union's 1955 decision to supply arms to Egypt opened the way for a series of agreements in the Middle East and elsewhere; the French, German, Czech and Italian arms industries began to supply their domestic needs and seek international markets; other states such as Sweden, the Netherlands and Switzerland assumed their small (but not inconsequential) role; and American dominance continued. The locus of political competition shifted to the developing world, and the acceleration of the decolonisation process in the 1960s provided new arms customers. An evaluation of how well the subsequent evolution of the arms transfer and production system corresponded to the model sketched in chapter 1 will have to wait until the conclusion; what is required at this point is a statistical sketch of the outlines of the arms transfer and production system that will lay the groundwork for the discussion of supplier tiers that follows.

## A statistical sketch

Reliable data on arms transfers begin to emerge in the early 1960s, by which time the traditional evolutionary pattern was in evidence. Tables 7 and 8 outline the market shares of the major suppliers from 1963 to 1988, in constant dollars and percentage shares. The most striking feature of table 7 is the tremendous increase in arms transfers: between 1963 and 1988 they more than *quadrupled* in real terms, the most rapid periods of increase occurring around 1972 and 1978. There was also a relatively linear increase in transfers between 1950 and 1962, although much of this could be explained by postwar rearmament and the need for armed forces to catch up with the technological changes that occurred during the Second World War.

The second point to note is that by 1963 the three tiers had begun to re-establish themselves in the distribution of market shares. Although there is no mechanistic inevitability to the timing or emergence of a traditional arms transfer system (there was nothing predictable about the Soviet 1955 decision to supply Egypt with arms, for example), the unexpected and radical nature of certain developments (whether it be the rise of Soviet arms transfers, the decline of Britain, or alleged commercial amorality of France) can be discounted to a great degree. In addition, underneath these stratified export shares lay a more profound qualitative gap between tiers, based upon distinct policies, motivations and industry structures. Since the percentage of arms production that is exported differs between the tiers (as is noted in table 10 below), the difference between the military industrial bases of different tiers is even more pronounced than table 7 suggests, with the United States and the Soviet Union far ahead of any rivals in total arms production. Although the primary focus is on weapons traded between states, it is a mistake to ignore domestic procurement and to treat the 'arms market' as equivalent to interstate transfers.[3]

The United States and the Soviet Union, as first-tier producers, held a huge but slowly declining share of the market, which dropped from a high of more than 75 per cent to a low of about 60 per cent in the mid 1980s, with an apparent subsequent recovery. The second-tier producers (East and West European and other industrial producers) had

Table 7. *Global arms deliveries, 1963–88, four-year averages (million constant 1988 US dollars)*

| Country | 1963–6 | 1967–70 | 1971–4 | 1975–8 | 1979–82 | 1983–6 | 1987–8[a] |
|---|---|---|---|---|---|---|---|
| United States | 4,842 | 8,575 | 10,751 | 11,039 | 10,099 | 11,885 | 14,536 |
| Soviet Union | 4,415 | 4,614 | 8,312 | 12,951 | 23,978 | 21,339 | 22,219 |
| France | 481 | 507 | 1,450 | 2,512 | 4,202 | 4,833 | 2,340 |
| Britain | 557 | 402 | 1,071 | 1,613 | 2,707 | 1,705 | 1,447 |
| West Germany | 360 | 329 | 475 | 1,373 | 1,730 | 1,838 | 1,125 |
| Italy | 74 | 76 | 295 | 817 | 1,284 | 1,067 | 381 |
| Czechoslovakia | 449 | 379 | 531 | 1,161 | 1,167 | 1,250 | 1,045 |
| Poland | 412 | 445 | 443 | 856 | 1,125 | 1,304 | 957 |
| Other industrial | 444 | 565 | 1,010 | 1,859 | 2,369 | 2,538 | 1,762 |
| Other East European | 22 | 46 | 240 | 370 | 997 | 1,634 | 1,242 |
| China | 223 | 491 | 916 | 280 | 680 | 1,535 | 2,738 |
| Developing | 310 | 48 | 156 | 1,448 | 2,961 | 3,044 | 2,543 |
| World | 12,589 | 16,475 | 25,649 | 36,282 | 53,297 | 53,972 | 52,333 |

*Notes:* These data cover arms *deliveries*, not *agreements*. For a brief discussion of problems with arms transfer data, see the appendix.
[a] Average for the two-year period 1987–8 only.
*Source:* United States, Arms Control and Disarmament Agency, *World Military Expenditures and Arms Transfers* (Washington: Arms Control and Disarmament Agency, various years). Hereafter cited as ACDA, *WMEAT.*

by the 1970s rebuilt their arms industries and occupied a secure position in the global market. Overall, the second-tier proportion of total supply rose from about 17 per cent in the mid 1960s to 30 per cent in the late 1970s and early 1980s, only to suffer a decline to about 20 per cent in the late 1980s. The pressures pushing second-tier suppliers to increase their exports (and hence their market share), notably the need to spread R&D costs and realise economies of scale, will be discussed in chapter 6. But the considerable variation evident within this tier is noteworthy, especially the declining share of Britain relative to other suppliers and the increased status of states such as Italy. This will be elaborated upon in chapter 6. It is in the third tier, though, that the most important gains have been registered, the share covered by states in the developing world (including China) rising from about 4 to more than 10 per cent. Most of this increase was concentrated in the 1980s; as late as 1979 third-tier states captured only 5 per cent of the export market.[4] This development (which will be discussed in chapter 7) is well predicted within the wave model: as lesser states harness some of the industrial and technological requirements for arms production, they evolve from being passive consumers, to acquiring new military technologies (via licensing and co-production arrangements),

Table 8. *Global arms deliveries, 1963–88, four-year averages (percentage shares)*

| Country | 1963–6 | 1967–70 | 1971–4 | 1975–8 | 1979–82 | 1983–6 | 1987–8[a] |
|---|---|---|---|---|---|---|---|
| United States | 38.5 | 52.0 | 41.9 | 30.4 | 18.9 | 22.0 | 27.8 |
| Soviet Union | 35.1 | 28.0 | 32.4 | 35.7 | 45.0 | 39.5 | 42.5 |
| France | 3.8 | 3.1 | 5.7 | 6.9 | 7.9 | 9.0 | 4.5 |
| Britain | 4.4 | 2.4 | 4.2 | 4.4 | 5.1 | 3.2 | 2.8 |
| West Germany | 2.9 | 2.0 | 1.9 | 3.8 | 3.2 | 3.4 | 2.2 |
| Italy | 0.6 | 0.5 | 1.1 | 2.3 | 2.4 | 2.0 | 0.7 |
| Czechoslovakia | 3.6 | 2.3 | 2.1 | 3.2 | 2.2 | 2.3 | 2.0 |
| Poland | 3.3 | 2.7 | 1.7 | 2.4 | 2.1 | 2.4 | 1.8 |
| Other industrial | 3.5 | 3.4 | 3.9 | 5.1 | 4.4 | 4.7 | 3.4 |
| Other East European | 0.2 | 0.3 | 0.9 | 1.0 | 1.9 | 3.0 | 2.4 |
| China | 1.8 | 3.0 | 3.6 | 0.8 | 1.3 | 2.8 | 5.2 |
| Developing | 2.5 | 0.3 | 0.6 | 4.0 | 5.6 | 5.6 | 4.9 |
| World | 100.0 | 100.0 | 100.0 | 100.0 | 100.0 | 100.0 | 100.0 |

*Note:* [a] Covers the two-year period 1987–8 only.
*Source:* ACDA, *WMEAT* (various years).

to entering the market as sellers. The most notable successes in this regard have been Israel, South Korea, Brazil, India and China.

One feature that should be noted is the relatively large share held by Warsaw Pact states, most prominently Poland, Czechoslovakia and Romania. In the first two cases, the industries were built on pre-1945 experience and skills, and under other conditions one would expect these states to behave like small second-tier suppliers. This is also reflected in their military R&D effort (see table 9 below). None of their sales or production (until recently) was determined freely, though, as decisions were made within the framework of Comecon economic planning and Warsaw Pact military policy. At least until 1989, 'the Eastern bloc arms industries [were] integrated extensions of those of the Soviet Union'.[5] These states have often also been used as simple conduits for Soviet-sponsored deals, as Czechoslovakia was used in the 1955 Egyptian deal, and Romania with respect to Iraq more recently.[6]

Some analysts have argued that 'unless they change their attitudes (an inheritance from the first phase in international arms transfers after World War II) and cease to attach strings to arms transfers, the USA and the USSR will continue to lose market shares to other suppliers'.[7] The model sketched in chapter 1 suggests, however, that the market shares of table 8 will stabilise at or near their present distribution, for several reasons. First, the rate of decline of the American and Soviet shares appears to have slowed, and has perhaps come close to the floor market share for first-tier suppliers. Second, the locus of military technological innovation (as noted below in table 9) still rests with the United States and the Soviet Union. The most sophisticated components and weapons, such as jet engines and precision-guided missiles, are still monopolised by a few states, and new technologies such as radar-invisible aircraft, one-shot one-kill weapons, or any hypothetical spin-offs of research into ballistic missile defences will also come from first-tier states. Third, second-tier producers are squeezed by numerous factors that will impede their future expansion: they are forced to sacrifice their technological lead through co-production and licensed production projects, they have had to work together to develop new generations of weapons as R&D costs escalate, and they are unlikely to be able to mobilise greater amounts of resources (unless this is done cooperatively). Finally, third-tier producers' arms industries generally depend on first- or second-tier suppliers for one or more crucial inputs, and a truly autonomous and technologically advanced arms industry does not exist outside the first or second tier. Many existing third-tier industries have also not been accompanied by the rising level of industrialisation that would be necessary to advance with the technological frontier or cross the threshold to second-tier status.

As was noted in chapter 1, the stratification into tiers of arms suppliers is not based only upon export market shares, but also upon underlying factor and technological endowments in military production and innovation, with first-tier states being centres of innovation, second-tier states managing to stay near the technological production frontier, and third-tier states merely producing weapons. This by itself explains nothing of the arms *transfer* system. But the more complete information available on contemporary defence industries can help us better understand the motives driving (and limitations upon) the export policies of producers in the three tiers. Although all exporters are governed by a combination of military, economic and political motivations, the varied defence industrial profiles of the three tiers gives each a different mix of motivations for exporting weapons, and fuels the evolution of the system in a slightly different way.

One way of discerning the structure of global arms production is to assess shares of military R&D spending. Such figures are notoriously difficult to obtain or compare (and are likely not very reliable), but table 9 summarises the best available information, based primarily on data from the Stockholm International Peace Research Institute and the incomplete United Nations study of military R&D. Both sources estimate world military R&D spending at approximately $100,000 million annually, or about 25 per cent of world R&D spending and 10 per cent of world military spending.[8] Table 9 clearly indicates the dominance of the United States and the Soviet Union in military research, and their consequent influence on the speed with which (and direction in which) the frontier of military technology advances. As one analyst has noted:

> The amounts spent on research are important determinants of its results, even though they do not lead directly to measures of research output. It is clear that the USA, spending about seven times as much as ... the UK, would have to be enormously inefficient not to get more results.[9]

The figures in table 9 suggest that the Americans and Soviets account for about three-quarters of world military R&D; these figures accord well with other estimates that range from 75 to 85 per cent.[10] Below them second-tier producers, Britain, France, Germany and Czechoslovakia, play prominent roles, but at a level roughly one order of magnitude smaller than the first-tier producers' efforts. Japan is an anomaly, and it should be noted that wildly different estimates exist for Japanese military R&D, primarily because most of it is done in the private sector without direct state support. The estimate given appears to be too high (or, rather, is probably much more comprehensive than the estimate for other producers); other available estimates (which are much too low) range from $175 million to $300 million.[11] The next grouping, which includes India, Israel, China and other producers in the developing world (as well as the smaller industrialised producers), follows with an R&D effort ranging from one-half to one-sixth (or less) that of the second-tier states. This more or less conforms to the three-tiered structure elaborated in chapter 1, although there are, of course, some aberrations at this level too (notably China, whose spending seems to bridge the second and third tiers).

Of perhaps equal significance is the proportion of defence spending that is devoted to R&D, either by states or by individual firms. In the United States, Research, Development, Test and Evaluation (RDT&E) spending has averaged about 10 per cent of military spending, and one should add to this the R&D undertaken by firms that is not directly covered by Department of Defense allocations.[12] The Soviet Union has been estimated (allowing for great uncertainty in this figure) to spend up to 25 per cent of its military budget on research and development.[13] Britain, France, Czechoslovakia and China spend up to 15 per cent on

Table 9. *Estimated military research and development expenditures, 1984 (or nearest available year)*

| Country | million US dollars | % of military spending |
|---|---|---|
| United States | 37,300[a] | 12.9 |
| Soviet Union | (55,000–75,000)[b] | (20–8)[b] |
| Japan | 7,430[c] (1987) | 1.0 |
| Britain | 3,700 | 14.3 |
| France | 3,300 | 11.4 |
| Czechoslovakia | 1,290* | 15.1 |
| West Germany | 1,260[d] | 3.9 |
| China | (750–1,250) | (15.0) |
| East Germany | 580* | 4.8 |
| Poland | 525* | 3.3 |
| Sweden | 360 | 5.6 |
| Israel | 300* (1980) | 5.8 |
| Italy | 600[e] | 3.6 |
| India | 250 | 2.0 |
| South Korea | 70[f] | 1.6 |
| Argentina | 30* | 1.2 |
| Thailand | 2 | 0.2 |
| Turkey | 1 | — |
| Total | (113,000–133,000) | 12.0 |

*Notes:* [a] Figure from Organization of Economic Cooperation and Development, *Science and Technology Indicators: Basic Statistical Series, Recent Results, Selected S&T Indicators 1981–86* (Paris: OECD, 1986). SIPRI, *Yearbook 1987*, gives a figure of $23,670; the International Institute for Strategic Studies, *The Military Balance, 1987–88* (London: IISS, 1987), 239, gives a figure of $43,000 million (and its totals for Britain and France are $3,430 and $3,610 respectively). I have thus used the OECD figure.

[b] Albrecht's percentage of military spending devoted to R&D for the Soviet Union is 25; the 20–8 per cent ranges are given in SIPRI, *Yearbook 1990*, 164–5. The dollar figures correspond to the 20–8 per cent range.

[c] The estimate for Japan is derived from a 1990 Office of Technology Assessment report that suggests up to 19 per cent of total Japanese R&D is defence-related, which gives the figure above. United States, Office of Technology Assessment, *Arming our Allies: Cooperation and Competition in Defense Technology* (Washington: Office of Technology Assessment, May 1990), 106.

[d] Estimate for West Germany derived from Rainer Rilling, 'Military R&D in the Federal Republic of Germany', *Bulletin of Peace Proposals*, 19:3–4 (1988), 323.

[e] Figure for Italy (1988) from *Jane's Defence Weekly* (28 April 1990).

[f] Estimate for South Korea from Office of Technology Assessment, 18.

*Sources:* Column 1 derived from SIPRI, *Yearbook 1987*, 154–6. Starred figures are derived from Ulrich Albrecht, 'The aborted UN study on the military use of research and development: an editorial essay', *Bulletin of Peace Proposals*, 19:3–4 (1988), 253–4. He gives percentages of defence spending directed towards R&D, which I then multiplied by military spending figures for 1984 from ACDA, *WMEAT 1988*. These are probably too low because they exclude certain indirect state support for military R&D. When direct comparisons could be made, Albrecht's figures were roughly half of the SIPRI figures (with the exception of China, which was double the SIPRI figure). Bracketed figures are very rough estimates.

Column 2 derived from Albrecht, 253–4.

R&D, reflecting the greater effort needed to keep up with the first-tier states. Behind them, R&D spending drops dramatically, to generally less than 5 per cent of military spending. Although these amounts can be significant if concentrated in specific firms or weapons systems, they are indicative of an acceptance that the motors of technological innovation rest securely in the United States and Soviet Union.

The one remaining elusive statistic that would complete this picture is an estimate of the distribution and value of global arms production. There are at least two ways of constructing a ballpark estimate, either from military spending or total transfers. The first estimate assumes that 25–30 per cent of global military spending goes towards military procurement; with world military spending passing the one trillion dollar mark in 1987, this would result in global arms production of approximately $250,000–300,000 million.[14] The second estimate assumes that between one-fifth and one-sixth of total arms production is transferred between states; the roughly $50,000 million in annual arms transfers would therefore suggest total production is also about $250,000–300,000 million.[15] Although these figures do not shed any light on the production and procurement shares of different producers, they do provide a benchmark against which more specific statistics can be evaluated.

Table 10 presents a detailed breakdown by producer for global arms production based on the best available data and drawn from many sources. The resulting high and low totals indicate that global arms production is worth between $260,000 and $290,000 million a year, which corresponds to the above benchmarks. Figures that situate arms production against defence spending and arms exports, and that give the approximate shares of world arms production of different producers, are also presented. Before discussing the data, however, several cautionary notes should be sounded. First, the estimates are gross indices only, as the measure of what qualifies as 'arms production' varies from state to state (and among analysts). As a result the relative ranking of producers may not be exactly accurate, although the orders of magnitude and rough hierarchy certainly are. Second, the estimates for Eastern European and Soviet arms production are especially subject to error, as conversions between market and command economy pricing systems are highly variable. Details on sources and methods are given in the notes. Third, the status of nuclear weapons production in these figures is not consistent: that portion of it that is counted in the defence department budgets has been included in the American, British and French figures, but it appears to have been excluded from the figures for Brazil, India,

91

Israel, Pakistan and Argentina. It is unclear whether or not nuclear weapons production has been included in the Soviet estimates. Fourth, the percentage of production that is exported cannot (usually) be calculated from the figures for production and exports, as it appears that the export percentages are based on a narrower definition of arms production than are the production estimates themselves. Finally, the data are a static snapshot of the mid 1980s and do not take account of subsequent shifts in arms production. The 1980s were a boom period for the military in most parts of the world, and it is clear that domestic procurement budgets and export markets have tightened considerably since then. In the early 1990s there is a large overcapacity in the global arms industry, which appears to be distributed rather evenly across different producers.

But despite the many possible sources of inaccuracy in these figures, several outstanding features of the data are still worth noting. The hierarchical nature of global arms production is clearly manifest, with the United States and the Soviet Union accounting for almost two-thirds of global arms production. Other industrial producers account for approximately 25 per cent of the total, leaving less than 10 per cent for developing states. Several producers in the developing world (China, India, Israel, Brazil) also appear to be as important (in volume terms) as the smaller industrial producers such as Switzerland or Belgium. This at least suggests that the conventional classification of arms producers and exporters into superpower (first-tier), industrialised (second-tier) and developing (third-tier) states may need to be reconsidered. What the figures do not convey, however, is the tremendous disparity in technological capabilities that are present in the global arms production system, and the different motivations for arms exports that these generate. This theme (and the static nature of this snapshot) will be taken up in great detail in succeeding chapters, which discuss the technological basis for the three-tier classification.

Production shares compare relatively well with the export market shares of table 8 above, except that both the United States and the Soviet Union export a lower percentage of their arms production than all other suppliers, whose shares of world arms exports tend to be higher than their shares of global arms production. What this means concretely is that the overall hierarchy of production shares (especially at the top) is relatively unaffected by major shifts in the international arms export market. A decline in American arms exports of 50 per cent, for example, would reduce the American share of global arms production by less than 2 per cent. The reordering of rankings among either industrial or developing world suppliers may be common, but

92

Table 10. *Estimated military production and arms exports (mid 1980s)*

| | Defence spending (000 million US dollars) | Arms exports | % of arms production exported | Estimated arms production (000 million US dollars) | % share of global production |
|---|---|---|---|---|---|
| United States | 261,300 | 10,300 | 11 | 86,000–94,000 | 31.3–34.2 |
| Soviet Union | 276,200 | 18,600 | 16[a] | 92,000–106,000 | 33.4–38.5 |
| France | 31,600 | 4,300 | 40 | 19,400 | 7.1 |
| Britain | 30,100 | 1,400 | 30[a] | 13,900 | 5.1 |
| West Germany | 32,300 | 1,430 | 20[a] | 7,400 | 2.7 |
| Japan | 20,800 | 170 | 3 | 4,900 | 1.8 |
| Poland | 16,900 | 1,230 | 40 | 3,000 | 1.1 |
| Italy | 15,300 | 830 | 60 | 3,000 | 1.1 |
| Canada | 7,800 | 170 | 60 | 3,000 | 1.1 |
| Czechoslovakia | 9,100 | 1,230 | 70 | 1,700 | 0.6 |
| Netherlands | 6,000 | 90 | 30 | 1,500 | 0.5 |
| Spain | 5,900 | 550 | 50 | 1,300 | 0.5 |
| Sweden | 4,200 | 220 | 50 | 1,300 | 0.5 |
| Switzerland | 3,900 | 240 | 40 | 900 | 0.3 |
| Belgium | 3,900 | 280 | 60 | 600 | 0.2 |
| Other industrial | 34,300 | 1,150 | — | 3,500 | 1.3 |
| China | 19,700 | 1,000–1,500 | 15 | 5,000–10,000 | 1.8–3.6 |
| India | 8,000 | 50 | 2 | 2,750 | 1.0 |
| Israel | 6,500 | 750–1,000 | 33[a] | 2,000 | 0.7 |
| Yugoslavia | 2,100 | 400 | 33 | 1,000–1,200 | 0.4 |
| South Africa | 2,800 | 40 | 4 | 1,000 | 0.4 |
| Brazil | 2,700 | 500–1,000 | 75 | 600–1,200 | 0.2–0.4 |
| South Korea | 4,800 | 250 | 40 | 600 | 0.2 |
| Argentina | 2,100 | 200–400 | 30 | 500–1,000 | 0.2–0.4 |
| Taiwan | 5,500 | — | — | 400–800 | 0.2 |
| Turkey | 2,500 | 60 | 10 | 500 | 0.2 |
| Egypt | 6,700 | 500 | n/a | 400–500 | 0.2 |
| Pakistan | 1,800 | 30–40 | 13 | 400 | 0.1 |
| North Korea | 5,400 | 500 | n/a | 200–400 | 0.1 |
| Singapore | 1,000 | 100–25 | 30 | 200–400 | 0.1 |
| Greece | 3,000 | 50 | 70 | 100 | — |
| Other developing[b] | 112,900 | 100–600 | | 1,000 | 0.4 |
| Developing total | 187,500 | 5,000–6,500 | | 16,700–23,900 | 6.4–8.2 |
| Industrial total | 759,600 | 42,000 | | 245,000–267,000 | 94.2–92.1 |
| World total | 947,100 | 47,000–48,500 | 16–19 | 260,000–290,000 | 100 |

*Notes:* [a] Figures from Michael Brzoska, 'Third World arms control: problems of verification', *Bulletin of Peace Proposals*, 14:2 (1983), 166.
[b] Estimate based on the 10 per cent of total employment in arms production (excluding China) estimated for 'others' by Michael Brzoska and Thomas Ohlson (eds.), *Arms Production in the Third World* (London: Taylor and Francis, 1986), 22.
*Sources:* Figures for columns 1 and 2 are averages for the 1984–6 period and are derived from ACDA, *WMEAT, 1988*, except where otherwise noted. I have averaged a longer period wherever the 1984–6 period appeared misleading. Export figures for developing states tend to come from other sources, and therefore the figures in column 2 do not add to the total. Except where noted, the export figures are *not* used with the percentages in column 3 to derive total production figures (or vice versa). In some cases the ACDA export figures are lower than

Table 10 (*cont.*)

those given by independent sources; in others the arms production figures offered appear to use a more inclusive or broad definition of arms production. More specific ranges for arms exports and production for states in the developing world are offered in chapter 7. Exchange rates taken from International Institute of Strategic Studies, *Military Balance, 1985–1986* (London: IISS, 1985).

*United States:* Procurement in the 1985–6 period was 28.8 per cent of the military budget, compared with a 21.7 per cent average for the 1976–80 period. Alex Mintz, '"Guns vs. Butter": a disaggregated analysis', paper presented at the 1989 international studies association meeting, 28 March 1989, 11. Thus the lower production figure is derived from this percentage (plus arms exports, minus imports); the higher figure is based on the export percentage.

*Soviet Union:* Julian Cooper, 'Soviet arms exports and the conversion of the defence industry', paper presented to the United Nations, Department for Disarmament Affairs, Conference on Transparency in International Arms Transfers, Florence, 25–8 April 1990, 4–5, gives figures of 5,300 million rubles (domestic prices) for exports, 34,500 million rubles for procurement, and 3,000 million rubles for imports, giving total production of 36,800 million rubles in domestic prices (he also suggests that 15 per cent of production is exported). SIPRI, *Yearbook 1990*, 165, offers a purchasing power parity conversion rate of $2.5 = 1 ruble, which gives the following figures from Cooper's data:

| (a) | arms exports (domestic prices) | $13,250 million |
|-----|-------------------------------|-----------------|
| (b) | procurement | $86,250 million |
| (c) | arms imports | $ 7,500 million |
| | arms production (a+b−c) | $92,000 million |

The official Soviet figure (cited in SIPRI, *Yearbook 1990*, 163, from *Pravda* (8 June 1989)) for procurement spending is 32,600 million rubles ($81,500 million), which gives total production of approximately $87,000 million.

SIPRI's own estimates (*Yearbook 1990*, 166) are as follows:

| | |
|---|---|
| defence spending: 90–100,000 million rubles | = $225–250,000 million |
| procurement: 40 per cent (Soviet and NATO estimate) | = $ 90–100,000 million |
| assuming exports exceed imports as above | = $ 96–106,000 million |

I have selected the Cooper and SIPRI figures as the low and high ranges for the estimate above. For a discussion of the many difficulties with (and inaccuracies in) estimates of Soviet military expenditures in general see Franklyn Holzman, 'Politics and guesswork: CIA and DIA estimates of Soviet military spending', *International Security*, 14:2 (Fall 1989), 101–31.

*France:* Production figure from Edward Kolodziej, *Making and Marketing Arms: The French Experience and its Implications for the International System* (Princeton: Princeton University Press, 1987), 201. His figure of $15,240 million for 1980 has been corrected for inflation of 5 per cent a year to 1985. Export percentage given in Pierre Dussauge, 'La Baisse des exportations française d'armement et ses répercussions industrielles', *Défense nationale* (January 1988), 79, citing Ministry of Defence figures.

*Britain:* Production total of £11,111 million from Trevor Taylor and Keith Hayward, *The UK Defence Industrial Base: Development and Future Policy Options* (London: Brassey's, 1989), 35.

*West Germany:* Production figure of 23,000 million DM from *Defence* (May 1989).

*Japan:* 1983 production figure of 1,168,589 million yen from Reinhard Drifte, *Arms Production in Japan* (Boulder: Westview Press, 1986), 24. He uses an exchange rate for 1983 of 237 yen to one US dollar. A similar figure (1,200,000 million yen) is given for 1986 in *Jane's Defence Weekly* (9 May 1987).

*Poland:* SIPRI, *Yearbook 1990*, 365, estimates Polish arms production at 3 per cent of industrial production, which gives a production total for 1985 of $3,000 million (at the adjusted 1985 exchange rate of 42 zlotys = $1). Industrial output figures from United Nations, *National Accounts Statistics: Main Aggregates and Detailed Tables, 1985* (New York: United Nations, 1987), 1070.

*Italy:* Production figure based on the average of two estimates, one of $2,500 million and another (for 1983) of $3,650 million. See *Defence Today*, nos. 91–2; Sergio Rossi, 'The Italian defence industry with respect to international competition', *Defence Today*, nos. 77–8 (1984). Percentage of production exported from *Interavia* (October 1985), which also estimated 1984 exports at $1,260, which is in line with the ACDA figure for that year. Rossi confirms the 60 per cent export figure.

*Canada:* Production figures for Canada from John Treddenick, 'The economic significance of the Canadian defence industrial base', in David Haglund (ed.), *Canada's Defence Industrial Base: The Political Economy of Preparedness and Procurement* (Kingston: Ronald Frye, 1988), 30. Production figures in the mid 1980s were exceptionally high because of major offset deals with the United States. More than three-quarters of total production is destined for the United States under a defence 'free trade agreement' (the Defence Production Sharing Agreement), although this does not appear to have been included in the export figures in column 2.

*Czechoslovakia:* Official production figures for 1987 are $966 million, which seems low given that the most recent ACDA export figures for that year are $1,200 million. See *Arms Control Reporter* (1991), section 407.E.1, 35. An export percentage of 70 per cent is given in Jiří Matousek, 'Complex attitude [sic] to conventional arms trade control – reduction of forces/ arms, conversion and deep reduction of weapons sales: the example of Czechoslovakia', paper presented to the United Nations, Department for Disarmament Affairs, Conference on Transparency in International Arms Transfers, Florence, 25–8 April 1990, 4–5. Using this export percentage and the ACDA figure, total production would be around $1,714 million. I have used this figure, as it is lower than Matousek's estimate that military production is 2–3 per cent of GNP but higher than the official figure, and it corresponds well in relative terms with the Polish figure.

*Netherlands:* Export percentage and production figure calculated from Michael Brzoska and Thomas Ohlson, *Arms Transfers to the Third World, 1971–1985* (Oxford: Oxford University Press, 1987), 98.

*Spain:* Export percentage and production figures (222,000 million pesetas) from Assembly of Western European Union, *Defense Industry in Spain and Portugal* (Paris: WEU, 1988), 5, 8. *International Defense Review* (September 1988) also estimates Spanish exports at about 85,000 million pesetas a year (about $500 million) in the mid 1980s.

*Sweden:* Two production estimates are available. The first, derived from the percentage of GNP accounted for by arms production (1.1 per cent) provided in Björn Hagelin, *Neutrality and Foreign Military Sales* (Boulder: Westview Press, 1990), 41, gives a value of about $1,500 million. The second is from Michael Hawes, 'The Swedish defence industrial base: implications for the economy', in David Haglund (ed.), *The Defence Industrial Base and the West* (London: Routledge, 1989), 174. He gives a 1987 procurement figure of about 7,900 million Swedish kroner ($878 million), which, when one subtracts arms imports and adds arms exports, gives a production figure of about $1,000. I have averaged these two figures.

*Switzerland:* Export percentage from *Damoclès*, no. 40 (September/October 1989), which also offers an export total of 578 million Swiss francs ($220 million); production total calculated from Peter Hug, 'Rüstungsproduktion der Schweiz', n.d. (2,409 million Swiss francs); *Damoclès* offers a production figure of $552 million.

*Belgium:* Figure of 35,000 million Belgian francs from Group de Recherches et d'Information sur la Paix, *Dossier*, no. 127 (November 1988). Overall arms production (with a broader definition that includes ancillary material) is estimated by them to be 0.75 per cent of GNP ($945 million).

*Other industrial:* Significant smaller industrial producers include Austria, Finland, Norway, Bulgaria, Romania and Australia. Austrian arms production is about $300 million; Finnish about $150 million (Hagelin, 41). An estimate for Norwegian production can be derived from its employment in arms production, which is probably about half that of Sweden (Brzoska and Ohlson, *Arms Transfers*, 99); this gives a figure of about $600 million. Bulgaria and Romania are estimated to employ between 20,000 and 50,000 workers in arms production (Brzoska and Ohlson, *Arms Transfers*, 103). Using the ratio between employment and output that applies to Poland gives production of between $600 and $1,500 million for each of them. I have estimated

95

Table 10 (*cont.*)

$1,000 for each of them, which accords well with their export figures. Other producers such as Australia probably account for no more than $500 million in total production.

*China:* Chinese figures are particularly imprecise. The 10 per cent export share, employment and industrial output figures are from Brzoska and Ohlson, *Arms Transfers*, 85–8. The upper production figure is calculated from the export percentage, although it appears high given that it would represent about 50 per cent of defence spending. The lower figure is calculated from Sidney Jammes, 'China', in Nicole Ball and Milton Leitenberg (eds.), *The Structure of the Defense Industry* (London: Croom Helm, 1983), 260, 276n.

*India:* Production and exports for 1988 from *International Defense Review* (October 1990). *Defence* (April 1989) offers a 1988 export figure of $45 million.

*Israel:* Export estimates from Aaron Klieman, *Israel's Global Reach* (London: Pergamon-Brassey's, 1985), 65; production figures from Joe Stork, 'Arms industries of the Middle East', *Middle East Report*, 17:1 (January–February 1987). He offers a total production figure for the Middle East (including Turkey and Pakistan) of $4,000 million.

*Yugoslavia:* Production and export figures calculated from Brzoska and Ohlson, *Arms Transfers*, 111 and ACDA, *WMEAT 1988*.

*South Africa:* Production figure from Brzoska and Ohlson, *Arms Production*, 196.

*Brazil:* Export percentage from Brzoska and Ohlson, *Arms Transfers*, 115. Export volume estimate from Alexandre de S. C. Barros, 'Brazil', in James Katz (ed.), *Arms Production in Developing Countries* (Lexington, Mass.: D. C. Heath, 1984), 77. Peter Lock, 'Brazil', in Brzoska and Ohlson, *Arms Production*, 97, offers an estimate of between $800 and $2,000 million, which seems rather high. The production figure is estimated from the detailed figures for the production of the three largest Brazilian arms producing firms presented in Renato Dagnino, 'A indústria de armamentos brasileira: uma tentativa de avaliação', unpublished doctoral thesis, University de Campinas, 1989, 368. He estimates average annual production for the three at about $600 million in the mid 1980s; they probably account for no less than one-half of total production. Patrice Franko-Jones, 'The Brazilian defense industry in crisis', paper presented to the annual conference of the International Studies Association, Washington, 13 April 1990, 1, estimates defence industry sales at $1,000 million in 1986 but only $500 million in 1987.

*South Korea:* Export figure from Janne Nolan, 'South Korea: an ambitious client of the United States', in Brzoska and Ohlson, *Arms Production*, 225; percentage exported from ibid., 32. Total production is calculated from these two figures.

*Argentina:* Production is estimated as 80 per cent of the Brazilian total from the comparative employment figures. V. Millán, 'Argentina: schemes for glory', in Brzoska and Ohlson, *Arms Production*, 37, 49, offers the estimate of $2,200 million, which appears too high (although he notes that some non-defence production is included).

*Taiwan:* Production estimate is based on figures in Brzoska and Ohlson, *Arms Production*, appendix 1. Their estimates for production of major weapons systems are usually between one-quarter and one-eighth of total production figures supplied by other sources, which has been used to calculate this estimate.

*Turkey:* Export figures in Brzoska and Ohlson, *Arms Transfers*, 101. Total production is estimated based on the employment figure given in Brzoska and Ohlson, *Arms Production*, 23, and assumes a similar output per employee as Pakistan.

*Egypt:* Production figure from Jim Paul, 'The Egyptian arms industry', *Merip Reports*, 13:2 (February 1983); export figure from Raimo Väyrynen and Thomas Ohlson, 'Egypt: arms production in the transnational context', in Brzoska and Ohlson, *Arms Production*, 121. The export figure is higher than the production figure because much of Egypt's exports are retransfers of weapons.

*Pakistan:* Brzoska and Ohlson, *Arms Production*, 266, 268, give 30–40 million in exports, 400 million in production and the 10 per cent export figure.

*North Korea:* Production estimate is based on figures in Brzoska and Ohlson, *Arms Production,* appendix 1. Their estimates for production of major weapons systems are usually between one-quarter and one-eighth of total production figures supplied by other sources, which has been used to calculate this estimate. Export figure from ibid., 264.

*Singapore:* Export percentage from Jacquelyn Porth, 'Singapore: a little dragon in arms production', in James Katz (ed.), *Implications of Third World Military Industrialization* (Lexington, Mass.: D. C. Heath, 1986), 236; export and production volume figures calculated from Brzoska and Ohlson, *Arms Production,* 68, 72.

*Greece:* Production and export estimated from Brzoska and Ohlson, *Arms Transfers,* 98 and ACDA, *WMEAT 1988.*

this is unlikely to alter the overall stratification of the system itself. This makes it clear that one cannot treat shifts in the interstate trade in weapons as synonymous with structural changes in the global arms market, and that export policies and participation must be understood against this larger canvas.

## Motive forces in the arms transfer system

Explanations of the motivations driving participants in the arms transfer and production system usually follow a conventional tripartite division into economic, political and military motives. Such a division is analogous to the motive forces introduced in chapter 1: the pursuit of wealth, the pursuit of power and the pursuit of victory in war. This work, however, attempts to explain the evolution of the system itself in terms of the interaction between the constellation of forces that drive different tiers of participants and the momentum of technological change and diffusion. None the less, it is still useful to compile a list of the motives driving (or benefits derived by) individual participants in the global arms transfer system, as a sort of 'checklist' against which the different tiers can subsequently be evaluated. The motives can be classified as follows:

*Pursuit of wealth*

(1) provide foreign exchange and positively affect the balance of payments.
(2) reduce the cost of domestic weapons procurement through economies of scale in production.
(3) maintain employment and infrastructure in defence-related industries.
(4) recoup research and development expenditures.
(5) use military production as an engine of growth for economic development.

*Pursuit of victory in war*

(6)    guarantee independence of arms supply to ensure military security.

(7)    act as a quid pro quo for military base/landing rights (or intelligence-gathering facilities).

(8)    assist friends and allies to maintain an effective (and/or common) defensive posture against external threats.

(9)    substitute for direct military involvement.

(10)  provide testing for new weapons systems.

*Pursuit of power*

(11)  provide access to and influence over leaders and elites in recipient states in pursuit of foreign policy objectives.

(12)  symbolise commitment to the recipient's security or stability against internal or external threats.

(13)  create or maintain a regional balance of power.

(14)  create or maintain a regional presence.

(15)  provide access to scarce, expensive or strategic resources.[16]

According to the analysis in chapter 1, the combination of motives pursued should vary from tier to tier, which provides one method by which the position of specific suppliers in the system can be determined. In the most simple terms, first-tier states, being relatively insensitive to the economic factors under the rubric of the pursuit of wealth, and relatively insulated from the pursuit of victory in war by their technological dominance and size, will concentrate on the pursuit of power in their arms exports. Second-tier states, driven to follow the technological lead, will be driven by the pursuit of wealth. Third-tier states, being both technologically inferior and vulnerable, will be driven by the pursuit of victory in war (or, to phrase it more benignly, the pursuit of security). Although this simplified picture will be elaborated upon in following chapters, the central thesis to keep in mind is that interaction of these different motivations after a period of revolutionary technological innovation directs the evolution of the global arms transfer and production system and helps explain the rapid diffusion of new military technologies, as states attempt to assert their status and independence in the international political hierarchy. Armed with this statistical sketch and this checklist, one can now examine the way in which these motives play themselves out in the contemporary arms transfer and production system.

# 5 THE DOMINANCE OF FIRST-TIER PRODUCERS AND SUPPLIERS

Chapter 4's profile of the international arms transfer system sets the stage for a closer examination of the practices, policies and motivations of the three tiers of suppliers. Each of the following three chapters will examine the scope and evolution of arms transfers, the structure of policy and decision making and the economic dimensions of arms exports and arms production, and conclude by discussing the motive forces that govern the participation of different producers in the arms transfer and production system. Since the contemporary first-tier producers, the United States and the Soviet Union, have complex and vastly different production and decision-making structures, they will be treated separately in the following discussion.

## The evolution of American arms transfers

American arms transfers have not remained relatively constant since 1945, in their volume, destination or composition.[1] Figure 3 presents military deliveries from 1950 to 1988 (by programme), and it indicates a sharp decline in American deliveries after the Korean War and initial European rearmament, with the same high totals (in real terms) not being reached again until the early 1970s. Despite somewhat dramatic ebbs and flows since 1973, total transfers have fluctuated around an annual average of about $16,000 million. The programmes under which the transfers were made also changed radically, and different programmes each had a distinct clientele. Military Assistance Program (MAP) funding was a grant programme directed to NATO members under the European recovery programme and Asian allies during and after the Korean War, and its major recipients between 1950 and 1989 (in million constant 1989 dollars) were: France ($24,029), South Korea ($15,337), Turkey ($14,841), Taiwan ($13,059), Italy ($12,710), Greece ($7,942) and Belgium ($7,100).[2] MAP declined as these states rebuilt their domestic arms industries and assumed responsibility for meeting their military

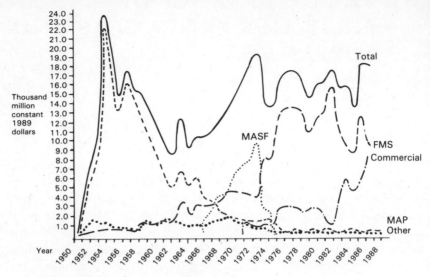

Note:  MAP is Military Assistance Program funding.

FMS is Foreign Military Sales and Foreign Military Construction Sales.

MASF is Military Assistance Service Fund.

Commercial includes all non-government-to-government transfers.

Other includes the International Military Education and Training Program and miscellaneous transfers.

These figures are not directly comparable with Arms Control and Disarmament Agency figures.

Figure 3  United States military deliveries by programme, 1950–88

needs. The Military Assistance Service Fund (MASF) was a grant programme for the Vietnam War; Vietnam, Laos, Thailand, Korea and the Philippines were the major recipients, and it ended when American involvement did. The Foreign Military Sales (FMS) programme, under which most sales are now made, took over the leading role in 1968 (excluding MASF), and the emphasis on arms transfers has shifted with American foreign policy interests. In the 1963–73 period major recipient regions were Europe and East Asia; in the early 1970s the Middle East and Persian Gulf assumed greater prominence, especially as deliveries to Asia declined after the Vietnam War; in the 1984–8 period East Asia and Europe reassumed greater prominence, receiving 22 per cent and 32 per cent of American transfers respectively, while the Middle East share dropped to 27 per cent.[3]

The other key point to note from figure 3 is that American arms transfers shifted in the 1960s from being aid- or grant-based to relying almost entirely on sales, thus marking a return to a more traditional pattern of interstate arms transfers. Three factors contributed to the emergence of export sales as a major foreign policy instrument:

> The first was a search for an inexpensive economic and military assistance instrument. The second . . . centered around efforts to deal effectively with the United States' adverse balance of payments . . . the third . . . was prompted by the concern about problems in logistical cooperation and weapons standardization within the Atlantic Alliance.[4]

Through the 1960s the American balance of payments remained in deficit while Congress reduced military grant assistance and sought less costly alternatives. Congress also placed progressively greater restrictions on MAP decisions, cutting off countries that made unnecessary military purchases, could support their own defence, or traded with Cuba. Congressional pressure on MAP was crucial in the shift from military grant assistance to sales. Finally, the McNamara doctrine of Flexible Response required an increased emphasis on conventional forces for which Americans were not prepared to pay. The result was that arms sales became the preferred tool of military statecraft, doubling in real terms between 1963 and 1968.[5]

The evident tension between the commercial export of arms (and the reaping of economic benefits) and their use as a tool of foreign policy will be discussed below, but it should be noted that in spite of the shift from aid to sales, political considerations (the pursuit of power) remained paramount in American policy. Two other consequences also followed this shift from aid to sales. First, it facilitated the entry of other suppliers into the international market, as they were no longer undercut by American assistance. Previously, other producers were able to sell only to clients to whom the Americans would not provide aid (or to whom they would only sell arms). In pure *sales* competition, these suppliers took advantage of the uncompetitive American pricing policy because prior to 1960 the United States overpriced its arms by valuing surplus equipment at the cost of replacing it with current models.[6] After 1960, however, American products were marketed competitively. Second, since grants were used to acquire finished weapons, the shift to sales meant major recipients such as Italy and Japan began to acquire arms production technology from the United States (and later other suppliers) as grant aid declined.[7]

Transfers steadily increased in the late 1960s under the Nixon

Doctrine's central policy of looking 'to the nation directly threatened to assume the primary responsibility of providing the manpower for its defense'.[8] This required an explicit willingness to give or sell allies the arms required for this role, and the Nixon Doctrine was intended to include a large grant-based security assistance programme. But the Nixon Doctrine ran up against Congressional (and public) pressures to reduce security assistance and the economic constraints posed by the Vietnam War burden, President Johnson's domestic programmes, the 1971 trade deficit and the 1973 oil shock. Under these pressures, the Doctrine translated itself into increased sales, which by 1976 represented 76 per cent of total transfers of $11,346 million (constant 1988 dollars).[9]

Under the tutelage of Secretary of State Henry Kissinger, major arms relationships were opened up with clients such as Iran and Saudi Arabia, who were expected to fulfil the role of regional policemen for American interests. The virtual blank cheque given to these customers, however, produced a fear in some quarters that open-ended arms transfers could endanger American interests, either by entangling the United States (or its allies) in a regional conflict, by reducing its technological lead, or simply by losing political control over the arms transfer process. As one State Department official said: 'Henry used to hand out weapons like hostess gifts. We would think we had sales to country X sealed off and then Kissinger would come back from some trip and tell us he had just agreed to supply another billion or so in arms.'[10]

The Carter Administration adopted a restraint policy (see below) in part as a reaction against these perceived excesses, but although deliveries declined by 25 per cent between 1977 and 1980, they climbed to new heights in the early 1980s, as the Reagan Administration dismantled much of the restraint structure and encouraged exports.[11] The peak year to date for American transfers was 1987, when more than $12,000 million (current 1987 dollars) in arms was delivered. But despite this increase in American transfers, adverse global economic conditions (the debt crisis and recession of the early 1980s) meant global transfers declined from the peak years of 1982–4. In 1984–8 (the most recent years for which data are available), the United States made arms transfers worth $59,500 million to eighty-four states. Three-quarters of these clients, receiving 60 per cent of arms, were in the developing world, although a number of the largest clients were industrial states. America's top clients (in descending order) were: Israel, Saudi Arabia, Japan, Australia, Britain, Taiwan, Egypt, South Korea, West Germany and the Netherlands.[12]

One important shift under the Reagan Administration was a return to the use of aid or concessionary credit sales under the FMS programme (not shown in figure 3) as a major foreign policy instrument. For 1984 and 1985, President Reagan requested $5,636 million and $5,100 million respectively of the FMS programme to be covered by loans or forgiven credits, meaning that approximately half of American arms exports were covered by concessionary agreements.[13] MAP funding also enjoyed a brief resurgence in the mid 1980s, with 1984 and 1985 totals of $747 million and $924 million (this subsequently declined to $467 million for the 1989 fiscal year). The bulk of the money went to clients such as El Salvador, Somalia, the Sudan, Honduras and Morocco, with the only prominent NATO clients (responsible for about 40 per cent of the total) being Turkey and Portugal.[14]

Two more recent changes in the composition of American arms sales that are not reflected in the transfer statistics have been of increasing concern to American policy makers. First, as transfers to allies in Europe and elsewhere have resulted in the emergence of second- and third-tier producers who directly compete with American producers for sales (either in their home state or on the world maket), the technological transfer dimension of American arms sales has become increasingly worrisome. By 1977, the United States was involved in 30 major co-production projects and up to 400 licensed production arrangements, with the number expected to increase in subsequent years.[15] Second, offset arrangements in foreign sales contracts (which can include co-production, local subcontracting, or counter trade) have become increasingly prominent. Both of these factors have economic implications for the benefits that accrue to the United States and the maintenance of its competitive lead in the international arms market, and will be discussed more fully below.

## American policy and decision making for arms transfers

Throughout this period, the decision-making structure for American arms transfers has reflected a strong emphasis on the pursuit of power considerations involved in transfer decisions. The complex edifice of promotion and control began taking shape with the first active government promotion of arms exports when the Office of International Logistics Negotiation (ILN) was established in 1961 as a coordinating office for arms sales. The ILN's primary mandate was to encourage companies to pursue foreign markets, but sales outside NATO were never promoted as vigorously as they were, for example, by British and French sales organisations.[16] Although the Nixon Doctrine encouraged sales, these were closely linked (at least in the minds of policy makers) to security concerns. President Carter's policy reinforced this linkage but with an emphasis on restraint; for example, it required embassies to refrain from offering arms salesmen the same assistance other American firms abroad received. It also required State Department approval for corporate sales promotions, so that in cases where the public refusal to supply a requested weapon would embarrass the client, 'U.S. foreign policy makers ... would be able to evaluate the potential ramifications ... of a given sale before being confronted with a formal request ... resulting from premature promotional actions by U.S. arms sellers.'[17] Although many aspects of the Carter policy were rescinded by the Reagan Administration, the new government's emphasis on increasing arms sales to close allies and on financial credits and concessions effectively kept security and political considerations at the forefront of decision making.[18]

A parallel structure of control evolved alongside the promotion mechanisms. The 1954 Mutual Security Act and 1961 Foreign Assistance Act initiated the legislative constraints and controlled commercial arms sales and military assistance grants. The 1968 Foreign Military Sales Act (proposed by President Johnson to forestall more drastic legislation) formalised this control, as Congress responded to the shift from aid to sales that undermined its influence over arms transfers and hence foreign policy. The Act placed a ceiling on credit sales, barred loans from the Export–Import Bank, limited sales to Africa and Latin America and gave the Secretary of State overall policy control of arms sales to ensure their integration with other American foreign policy goals. Amended over time, by 1976 the renamed Arms Export Control Act included a Congressional veto power (by joint resolution) over proposed sales of more than $50 million.[19] This power was exercised in the 1986 sale of Stinger missiles to Saudi Arabia. In other cases (such as the proposed 1985 sale of air defence equipment to Jordan) the President avoided certain defeat by withdrawing the proposal.[20]

On the executive side, until the early 1970s the Department of Defense controlled the formulation and execution of policy, but as sales increased other bureaucratic actors clamoured for a voice in decision making. Approval of a sale now involves up to twenty steps, can take from a few weeks to several years to complete and involves formal reporting procedures and legislative oversight.[21] In addition to legislative and bureaucratic procedures both the Carter and Reagan Administrations formulated explicit policies concerning arms transfers. The Carter restraint policy viewed arms transfers as an 'excep-

104

tional foreign policy implement, to be used only in instances where it can be clearly demonstrated that the transfer contributes to [our] national security interests'.[22] The policy established an Arms Export Control Board, with members from the Defense, Treasury and State Departments, the Joint Chiefs of Staff, the National Security Council and the CIA, to review potentially controversial sales. A significant number of decisions were reviewed by the President.[23] Although the Reagan Administration changed the policy to view arms transfers as 'an indispensable instrument of American policy', it kept in place much of the control structure, only reducing the administrative level at which decisions were made and accelerating the approval process.[24]

Until the late 1980s, control of American arms transfers was best understood as 'regulation' for political and security ends rather than 'restraint'. The changes in the international environment and in the arms market meant, however, that increased attention began to be paid to the longer-term negative consequences of the diffusion of more advanced military technologies. One sign of this was the 1987 decision to participate in the Western suppliers' Missile Technology Control Regime, which is intended to restrict the diffusion of technologies that can be used for nuclear capable ballistic missile systems.[25] Another, perhaps more clear, example was the 1989 imbroglio over cooperative development with Japan of the FSX fighter, which will see technology transferred to Japan to co-produce an advanced version of the F-16 fighter aircraft.[26] This latter case illustrates the way in which technological considerations and the pursuit of power are increasingly inseparable in the policy-making process.[27]

## The pursuit of wealth in American arms exports

The size and character of the American defence industry, and the small role played by exports in maintaining its well-being and productive base, are important factors in explaining both the American technological lead in military systems and the relative dominance of the pursuit of power as a motive behind arms transfer decision making. Several factors are important here, including the scale and evolution of domestic procurement, the degree of dependence of producers on exports and the overall influence of military production and arms exports on the economy. It is important to note that these represent 'economic' factors (or the pursuit of wealth) in the broadest (or structural) sense, the role played by strict profit–loss considerations being relatively minor.

The decline in arms production that followed the First World War was not duplicated in the post-1945 period, as the Korean conflict, the American–Soviet arms race and the effort to rebuild the military strength of the NATO allies kept American military spending and defence production at levels unprecedented in peacetime. Defense Department budgets averaged $270,000 million a year (in 1991 dollars) between 1950 and 1990, with lows of $210,000 million being reached only after the Korean and Vietnam Wars and a high of $350,000 million reached in 1985. This spending was accompanied by a level of domestic procurement that fluctuated between 20 and 30 per cent of the defence budget.[28] Although defence procurement dropped in 1946–9, the average between 1950 and 1980 remained at about half the Second World War level (in constant dollars). This domestic demand for arms resulted in the creation of a large permanent peacetime defence industrial base and exerted a decisive influence on the role played by the United States in the international arms transfer system.

Perhaps not surprisingly, the high level of domestic demand for arms has meant that few if any individual American defence firms depend upon exports for their financial well-being. Table 11 below details the export dependence of the top ten FMS contractors in the 1982–5 period. Together they accounted for more than one-third of American FMS, and on average they depended upon exports for about 4.5 per cent of their total sales and 11 per cent of their sales of defence equipment.[29] Only three of them depended upon exports for more than 4 per cent of their total sales, and four of them upon exports for more than 10 per cent of their defence production.[30] In case it should be thought that this sample is skewed, it should be noted that 8 of the top 10 defence contractors in the United States are on this list: only Grumman and Rockwell are missing, and exports are 5.3 and 6.0 per cent of their total sales respectively. This pattern of relatively low reliance on exports replicates itself for the top 25 contractors. On the other hand, many of the largest firms tend to be relatively specialised in defence production (with General Electric and Westinghouse as the major exceptions), which means that individual firms are vulnerable to dramatic changes in the level of domestic or foreign arms orders.

It should be noted, however, that these low percentages occur at a time of high domestic procurement. During the mid 1970s, by contrast, when the American defence budget reached its post-Vietnam lows and when the OPEC oil price increases and 1973 Middle East War dramatically increased weapons demand, American firms were much more dependent upon export sales. In the 1970–6 period, 13 of the top 25 defence producers exported more than 15 per cent of their production; 8 of them more than 25 per cent. The overall percentage of

Table 11. *Arms export dependence of the top ten US foreign military exporters, 1982–5*

| Contractor | Total sales (million US dollars) | FMS[a] | FMS/TS (%) | DoD sales | DoD/TS (%) | FMS/DS (%) |
|---|---|---|---|---|---|---|
| McDonnell Douglas | 36,553 | 4,141 | 11.3 | 28,314 | 77.5 | 14.6 |
| General Dynamics | 28,696 | 3,409 | 11.9 | 26,100 | 90.0 | 13.1 |
| Boeing | 44,154 | 3,046 | 0.1 | 17,711 | 40.0 | 17.2 |
| Northrop | 14,479 | 1,533 | 10.6[b] | 4,522 | 31.2 | 33.9 |
| United Technologies | 55,655 | 1,460 | 2.6 | 15,187 | 27.3 | 9.6 |
| Lockheed | 29,751 | 1,039 | 3.5 | 17,554 | 59.0 | 6.0 |
| General Electric | 109,529 | 989 | 0.9 | 18,577 | 17.0 | 5.3 |
| Raytheon | 23,235 | 889 | 3.8 | 11,082 | 47.7 | 8.0 |
| Hughes Aircraft | 20,194 | 746 | 3.7 | 13,163 | 65.2 | 5.7 |
| Westinghouse | 40,243 | 664 | 1.6 | 7,154 | 17.8 | 9.3 |
| Total | 402,489 | 17,916 | 4.5 | 159,364 | 39.6 | 11.2 |

*Notes:* [a] These figures are based on orders, not deliveries, and hence probably overestimate slightly total sales, as cancelled orders are not always deleted.
[b] Northrop's arms exports as a percentage of its total sales for the 1983–6 period dropped to 4.2, and its defence sales as a percentage of total sales dropped to 20.8.
*Source:* Paul Ferrari, Jeffrey Knopf and Raul Madrid, *U.S. Arms Exports: Policies and Contractors* (Washington, D.C.: Investor Responsibility Research Center, 1987). Hughes is a subsidiary of General Motors.

American arms production that was exported rose to approximately 28 per cent.[31] This highlights the degree to which dependence on exports can shift with changing economic and political circumstances.

The other main possible direct economic benefits of arms transfers, the recouping of research and development costs and realisation of economies of scale, are probably not significant for the United States. Chapter 4 noted the large lead the United States possesses in military R&D spending (and its significance for innovation), but the sheer scale of this spending means relatively little attention is paid to recouping R&D costs via exports. One government study suggested that package deals and price cuts offered in contracts reduced the possible savings so that a $10,000 million sales programme will generate an average of only $700 million in savings.[32] In addition, 'the U.S. arms sales mix of weapons, construction and services has shifted somewhat from a mix where savings are high – such as aircraft and missiles – to a mix where savings are negligible or non-existent – such as ships, ammunition, construction and services'.[33]

On the other hand, it is worth noting the effect that the increasing unit cost of weapons has had upon domestic procurement and the significance of exports. In the case of military aircraft, the United

States purchased about 3,000 planes a year in the 1950s, 1,000 a year in the 1960s and 300 a year in the 1970s.[34] This reduces the overall length of production runs, and as initial domestic orders shrink and advanced weapons are sold more quickly, the significance of even small exports for unit cost savings increases, because the drop in average costs is greatest at the early stages of production runs. For example, the sale of 80 F-14s to Iran when the plane had been in production for less than five years meant a recouping of R&D costs of about $161 million; savings would have amounted to only about $70 million if the plane had been in production more than five years.[35]

This trend towards declining numbers of weapons produced is reflected also in the export of American equipment, figures for which are presented in table 12. These figures only present deliveries to the developing world, but as trend indicators they are significant. Since the number of weapons delivered has declined in most categories at the same time as the dollar value of transfers has either risen or stabilised, the potential significance of exports in recouping R&D or unit costs has increased. This effect should be even more important for second- and third-tier suppliers, who are even less able to absorb the burden of high levels of R&D spending either in long production runs or in domestic procurement. One other development that should also be noted is the proportion of American contracts that are for construction and support services, items for which unit cost and R&D savings are zero. Between 1974 and 1978, about $2,391 million a year went on such items, or roughly a quarter of total transfers. Although this has declined to about 7 per cent of total transfers in the 1984–9 period (an annual average of $685 million), this is still a higher level than for other suppliers.[36]

At first glance, it would appear that however low the dependence of the defence industry upon exports, or however mixed the other economic gains, the economy as a whole would benefit from the wealth and employment creation and balance of payments effects of arms transfers. But the evidence on the size of these possible macro-economic benefits suggests that such pursuit of wealth considerations cannot loom large. One government study concluded that the impact of a 10 per cent annual reduction in orders over four years would be a drop in Gross National Product of less than one-tenth of 1 per cent and a concomitant increase of 0.1 per cent in unemployment.[37] The effect of a *total* ban on sales would be an increase in unemployment of roughly 0.3 per cent and a reduction in GNP of less than 1 per cent.[38] The employment effects of transfer reductions would also be limited: the total number of jobs that depend on arms exports (assuming

Table 12. *American weapons delivered to the developing world, major categories, 1976–89*

| Weapons | 1976–9 | 1980–3 | 1986–9 |
|---|---|---|---|
| Tanks and self-propelled guns | 3,121 | 2,759 | 596 |
| Artillery | 2,179 | 2,180 | 760 |
| Naval vessels | 61 | 49 | 4 |
| Submarines | 3 | 0 | 0 |
| Supersonic aircraft | 713 | 398 | 179 |
| Subsonic aircraft | 309 | 193 | 20 |
| Other aircraft | 736 | 139 | 170 |
| Helicopters | 271 | 130 | 112 |
| SAMs | 4,959 | 3,676 | 956 |
| APCs and armoured cars | 6,893 | 5,636 | 642 |

*Note:* The first column covers 1 July 1975–30 September 1979; the others, the periods 1 October–30 September of the given years.
*Sources:* Column 1: Richard Grimmett, *Trends in Conventional Arms Transfers to the Third World by Major Supplier, 1976–1983* (Washington: Congressional Research Service, 1984), 28.
Column 2: Richard Grimmett, *Trends in Conventional Arms Transfers to the Third World by Major Supplier, 1980–87* (Washington: Congressional Research Service, 1988), 65.
Column 3: Richard Grimmett, *Trends in Conventional Arms Transfers to the Third World by Major Supplier, 1982–89* (Washington: Congressional Research Service, 1990), 66.

$10,000 million in annual sales) is estimated at between 380,000 and 600,000, somewhere in the range of 0.5 per cent of total employment and 2–3 per cent of manufacturing employment.[39] Even these calculations for GNP and employment overestimate the impact of arms exports, for they assume that the resources devoted to arms production would not be reallocated if a decline in transfers occurred.

Balance of payments benefits are also suspect. On the surface, arms exports have averaged about 4.5 per cent of total exports over the past two decades, a higher figure than for most other producers (see table 18). But these benefits are only realised if they are not counterbalanced by concessionary arrangements that reduce the domestic benefits of arms exports. These concessions include export contract offset arrangements that guarantee a certain amount of value added at the destination (such as component or sub-assembly); countertrade arrangements that involve the purchase and import of goods from the arms recipient (this can also include barter deals); low interest loans or forgiven credits; and outright military grant aid.[40] The estimated net cost (in lost domestic production) of offset arrangements alone is up to $6,000 million annually, and the sum of all these concessions reduces the effective balance of payments benefits from arms exports by at least half (and perhaps erases them entirely!).[41]

The evidence thus suggests that although the overall influence of military production on the economy may be significant (in terms of percentage of exports), the macro-economic considerations of production for export are relatively minor, and are certainly subordinate to pursuit of power considerations. If maintaining employment and using arms sales to improve the balance of trade were of truly great concern, one would expect the American government to oppose more strenuously the very arrangements it has often helped put in place. Successive Administrations have also denied that economic considerations govern sales decisions, and, as one observer pointed out, if major domestic military procurement decisions can be made on purely political or military grounds, there is no reason to assume that foreign sales decisions (which tend to be much smaller) cannot be also.[42]

## Other motives in American transfer decisions

Military motivations (the pursuit of victory in war) for inaugurating or maintaining an arms transfer relationship are a relatively new phenomenon, as previously strategic access was obtained through colonial possessions. These motivations have also declined in importance in recent years, as the geo-strategic confrontation between the superpowers has waned and as the United States has 'been forced to assume considerable and increasing economic and political costs in order to cling to its still very extensive and dispersed positions'.[43] Although major early deals with the Philippines, Turkey and (to some extent) Iran, Ethiopia and Saudi Arabia resulted in significant military benefits, in recent years such deals have not been consummated with major clients (or have become more strict economic exchanges). Although existing relationships with states such as Oman, Kenya and Morocco do have a military component and are used to maintain strategic access, these states are not major arms clients. Further, existing arrangements (such as with the Philippines) have been subjected to pressures to increase the volume or sophistication of the arms or military aid supplied, thus deterring their expansion or maintenance. Such deals also presuppose a relationship that already has a high degree of shared mutual interests. Finally, the need for bases, landing and overflight rights and intelligence-gathering facilities has declined somewhat in recent years, as a result of improvements in satellite technology and the endurance of aircraft and naval vessels. (One exception to this is the development of rapid deployment forces, which require pre-positioning of supplies and base-use agreements to be effective.)

110

This leaves the pursuit of power as the primary set of motives governing American arms transfer policy decisions. These fundamentally political calculations can operate either as a brake on considerations of military or economic benefits when political costs are incurred by a transfer or as a spur to sales when benefits can be gained. With respect to the former, American policy is more sensitive to political considerations than the policies of second- or third-tier suppliers (West Germany, Japan, Sweden and some others excepted), primarily because of America's different global role. Sales by Britain, France or Brazil to states that are non-aligned, international pariahs, communist-orientated or otherwise unpalatable to American policy makers (such as Libya, Chile and Iraq) support this claim.

With respect to the potential positive political motives, three arguments suggest that these benefits motivate American arms transfer policy. First, all recent American administrations have explicitly acknowledged their pursuit of political gains: the Carter Administration offered ten widely accepted goals served by arms transfers, eight of which were political in the sense used in chapter 4; the Reagan Administration's list contained six broader objectives, five of which were political.[44] Previous and subsequent administrations have also recognised the political benefits of arms transfers: the Nixon/Ford policy stated that one of the factors affecting decisions was 'the position of influence that sales might help support'; the Bush Administration has argued that foreign military sales are vital tools of foreign policy.[45] Although the testimony of officials with vested interests does not prove these are the goals of American policy, this at least accords well with other evidence for the primary role of political motives.

Second, one can infer from the pattern of arms recipients that political justifications entered into American calculations, as shifts have tracked shifts in American foreign policy attention. Beginning with an interest in Europe and the Northern Tier under Truman and Eisenhower, military assistance was provided to help bring countries under Western security arrangements. Most aid had conditions attached; that these were not mere window dressing was proved by the difficulties various states encountered with them. Aid to Burma was suspended when conditions were not met, Iran in the 1950s had difficulty agreeing to them, an Indonesian government fell over the issue, and Mexico and Brazil quarrelled over some stipulations.[46] Among the conditions, recipients were expected to contribute (including a possible troop commitment) to the 'defensive strength of the free world' and to help 'eliminate causes of international tension'. The shift to intense involvement in East Asia was itself followed by one to the

111

Middle East after 1967. Only the last shift could possibly be convincingly explained by economic or purely military motives (leaving aside political economy analyses of the European recovery programme and the Vietnam War).

Finally, the justifications offered before Congress for decisions have frequently relied upon political motives. Recent examples include selling arms to Morocco to facilitate a settlement of the Western Sahara War, demonstrating reliability to the Venezuelans by selling them F-16s, reassuring the Saudis of American support by selling arms to the Yemen Arab Republic, and allowing F-16s and F-18s to be sold to South Asian states.[47] The decision to make future sales to Jordan conditional on direct peace negotiations between Jordan and Israel and the expressed desire in some quarters to put sales to the Saudis on the same footing are also examples of this.[48] Thus although a complex mix of economic, political and military motives is at play in American arms transfers decisions, it is the political motivations that are paramount.

## The evolution of Soviet arms transfers

The motives governing the Soviet Union's arms transfers are similar to those of the United States, but the near-total absence of economic assistance to, and political, social and cultural ties with, client states means the Soviet Union relies even more heavily on arms transfer relationships to achieve its aims.[49] The policy and practice of the Soviet Union in the realm of arms transfers and arms production is, however, more inscrutable than that of virtually any other supplier, for two reasons. First, the Soviets are (even in the era of *glasnost*) reticent to publicise either the scope of activities or the justifications behind specific transfers. Second, available information is often politicised, as writers attempt to prove the Soviet Union is the dominant arms supplier to the developing world or the source of all destabilising transfers. This temptation to adopt what has been called the 'master plan view' of Soviet arms transfers conceals the fact that the practice and motivation of Soviet arms transfers is in many ways similar to the American experience. A longer historical perspective also tempers the 'master plan' thesis by placing the Soviet rise to first-tier status in the context of the traditional behaviour of first-tier suppliers.

In the absence of all but the most general official statistics, the best approach to grasping the dimensions of Soviet transfers is to present a number of estimates to establish a general picture. In the five-year period from 1986 to 1990, official Soviet arms exports were valued at

112

Table 13. *Indices of Soviet arms transfers, 1975–89*

|  | 1975 | 1976 | 1977 | 1978 | 1979 | 1980 | 1981 | 1982 | 1983 | 1984 | 1985 | 1986 | 1987 | 1988 | 1989 |
|---|---|---|---|---|---|---|---|---|---|---|---|---|---|---|---|
| I | 10,491 | 13,906 | 19,900 | 6,522 | 18,740 | 23,344 | 18,094 | 26,153 | 8,118 | 24,868 | 18,705 | 17,997 | 23,187 | 14,654 | 11,230 |
| II | 5,440 | 7,314 | 10,049 | 13,044 | 19,014 | 20,506 | 18,924 | 19,352 | 19,747 | 18,906 | 15,177 | 18,119 | 20,206 | 19,625 | 17,370 |
| III | — | — | — | — | — | 12,359 | 12,787 | 11,041 | 10,961 | 10,585 | 12,796 | 14,579 | 14,718 | 12,464 | 11,652 |
| IV | 3,680 | 4,509 | 7,589 | 10,010 | 11,126 | 9,277 | 8,370 | 7,565 | 7,578 | 7,537 | 8,563 | 10,327 | 10,759 | 8,238 | 8,515 |
| V | 8,163 | 10,192 | 15,495 | 17,953 | 25,617 | 24,045 | 23,097 | 23,152 | 22,547 | 21,734 | 18,689 | 22,388 | 23,037 | 21,400 | — |

*Note:* Figures from SIPRI for the period before 1980 were presented in constant 1975 dollars, and are not directly comparable.

I   Agreement with the Third World, constant 1989 US dollars. Grimmett, *Trends in Conventional Arms Transfers*, various years.
II   Deliveries to the Third World, constant 1989 US dollars. Grimmett, *Trends in Conventional Arms Transfers*, various years.
III   Deliveries worldwide, constant 1985 US dollars, major weapons only. Stockholm International Peace Research Institute, *Yearbook 1990*, 221. Figures for 1980–3 from SIPRI database.
IV   Deliveries to the Third World, constant 1985 US dollars, major weapons only. SIPRI, *Yearbook 1990*, 252.
V   Deliveries worldwide, constant 1988 US dollars. ACDA, *WMEAT*, various years.

113

Table 14. *Weapons delivered to the developing world, major categories, 1982–9*

| Weapon | US | USSR | Western Europe |
|---|---|---|---|
| Tanks and self-propelled guns | 2,849 | 7,265 | 690 |
| Artillery | 2,265 | 13,730 | 4,875 |
| APCs and armoured cars | 4,866 | 13,060 | 2,040 |
| Major naval combatants | 7 | 41 | 51 |
| Minor naval combatants | 31 | 150 | 219 |
| Submarines | 0 | 17 | 15 |
| Supersonic aircraft | 500 | 1,955 | 385 |
| Subsonic aircraft | 190 | 205 | 150 |
| Other aircraft | 305 | 570 | 485 |
| Helicopters | 280 | 1,490 | 550 |
| Guided missile boats | 0 | 21 | 12 |
| SAMs | 3,820 | 26,380 | 3,695 |

*Note:* Western Europe includes France, West Germany, Britain and Italy.
*Source*: Grimmett, *Trends in Conventional Arm Transfers, 1982–89*, 66.

56,700 million rubles, with a 1990 figure of 9,700 million rubles.[50] Table 7 has already provided an overview of Soviet (and others') transfers; table 13 presents five different descriptions of Soviet activity over the past two decades. The measures shown differ in several ways: some count agreements, others deliveries; some count major weapons only, others all weapons; some count only deliveries to the developing world (in practice, virtually all deliveries outside of the Warsaw Pact); all employ different definitions of what is considered as a 'defence item'.[51] It should be noted that the methodologies used to determine the dollar value (export prices) of Soviet arms exports by all the sources in table 13 may seriously underestimate arms transfers, but the available data are insufficient to allow better evaluations. The general trend in Soviet transfers is, however, clearly manifest by all indices (including official figures), with both agreements and deliveries appearing to level off or even decline somewhat from the high levels reached in the early 1980s.[52]

Because of these (and other) problems in comparing American and Soviet transfers in dollar terms, another method of grasping their relative dimensions is to count the number of weapons delivered by type, which table 14 does (including for comparison American and European suppliers). Although the Soviets lead in ten of the twelve categories, a simple comparison of numbers exaggerates the Soviet Union's arms effort, since until recently the arms exported by the Soviet Union have been less sophisticated than equivalent American or European weapons. The Soviet Union's list of clients is also not as long as the United States': until 1960, only about 12 states had received Soviet arms, by 1970 there were 26 recipients, and between 1984 and 1988 50 states received Soviet weapons. Four-fifths of the clients in the last period, receiving 83 per cent of the weapons transferred, were developing world states. The top ten customers in this period were (in descending order): Iraq, India, Vietnam, Cuba, Syria, Afghanistan, Angola, Poland, Ethiopia and Czechoslovakia.[53] This list demonstrates a much greater concentration on key clients in the developing world than for the United States.

Until 1955, the Soviet Union's only arms clients were its Eastern European satellites, North Korea, China and North Vietnam. They received surplus Second World War weapons, and did not receive major quantities of arms, as their political reliability could not yet be guaranteed. Stalin's 'two camp' thesis, which argued that nationalists and anti-colonialists in the developing world were 'acting in bloc with the reactionary bourgeoisie', inhibited the transfer of weapons outside the communist camp, but as the United States shifted its attention in the 1950s away from the Cold War confrontation in Europe, so too did the Soviet Union, its first deals with non-communist states being designed to surmount the encircling system of treaties, pacts and arms deals created by the United States.[54] In 1955 a major deal was signed with Egypt; it was, according to one analyst, 'a demonstrative move intended to serve a specific political aim pursued by both the donor and the recipient'.[55] Whether or not the Soviet Union was acting purposefully, or merely taking advantage of Western blunders in Egypt, is largely irrelevant; what is clear is that the Soviet Union had becomed sufficiently secure in Europe to pursue a more active global policy. The Egyptian deal was rapidly followed by a series of Middle Eastern and Asian agreements with Syria (1955), Yemen (1957), Iraq (1958), Afghanistan (1956) and Indonesia (1958).[56]

This triggered a reaction in American policy under President Kennedy, which recognised that the competition between the Soviet Union and the United States for influence, allies and geo-strategic position was shifting towards the developing world. Through the 1960s both the United States and the Soviet Union simultaneously expanded their list of clients and sought to reduce the costs of their military assistance programmes by shifting from aid to sales or (in the Soviet case) by demanding payment in hard currency. Between 1963 and 1973, the main areas of attention were the Warsaw Pact states, the Middle East and East Asia. Before 1973 Soviet arms were usually provided on credit at a 2.5 to 3.0 per cent interest rate, with a grace

115

period of several years and a 10–12-year (or longer) amortisation period. Repayments were also often made in local currency or with barter arrangments.[57] In the late 1960s and early 1970s, however, three categories of clients became clearly demarcated. Most favoured clients (such as Egypt after 1967) received 20-year credits and up to 50 per cent discounts on list prices; less favoured clients (Iraq and Egypt before 1967) received one-third discounts and shorter credit terms; commercial clients (such as Libya, Algeria and Nigeria) paid list prices and in hard currency.[58]

The growth in Soviet transfers in the 1960s was abetted by two factors. The Sino-Soviet competition meant that the Soviets needed to respond to the Chinese challenge to their leadership of the world communist movement; the direct manifestation of this was competition to support independence and revolutionary movements in Africa and Asia. Second, the Soviets needed to increase the facilities available to their navy to accompany its expanded global role; thus deals for access to facilities were negotiated with clients such as Guinea, Egypt, Somalia, Vietnam, South Yemen and Syria. By the 1970s, the Soviet Union had successfully established a global arms transfer presence that, with short-term fluctuations, was of the same order of magnitude as the United States. The Soviets were still, however, reluctant to supply their clients with top-line weapons, and their attractiveness as a supplier rested more on their willingness to supply rapidly large quantities of weapons at low cost.

The ebb and flow of Soviet arms transfers in the 1970s and 1980s (as indicated in tables 7 and 13) followed a similar pattern as for other suppliers, and tracked changing Soviet foreign policy concerns. The Middle East continued to be the dominant recipient region, although major clients such as Angola, Nicaragua, Afghanistan and Vietnam received large quantities of weapons in connection with continuing conflicts. Deliveries to these clients declined at the end of the 1980s. Iraq was also a major recipient of weapons during the Iran–Iraq War, although there are some signs that military relations with Iran resumed after the 1988 ceasefire.[59] What is of greater interest, though, are two parallel developments: the shift towards supplying the most sophisticated Soviet arms to clients in the developing world (mentioned in chapter 4) and new concern with controlling either the flow of weapons to the developing world, or the diffusion of specific technologies (such as ballistic missiles). Official and unofficial statements have gone far beyond the traditional propagandistic condemnation of imperialist arms merchants, and have included direct criticism of Soviet policies and specific proposals for restraint.[60] Although these concerns have not yet assumed a high priority on the political agenda (and are somewhat contradicted in practice), they do mirror increasing American concerns with the consequences of technological diffusion. More importantly, they are an indicator of the evolution of the global arms transfer and production system to its more mature phases. Such joint interest in restraint was manifest by the agreement by both states (and others) to suspend arms shipments to Iraq in the wake of its invasion of Kuwait.[61]

## The structure of Soviet arms transfer policy and decision making

The structure of Soviet arms transfer decision making is in flux, but like all aspects of policy making it has been highly centralised. Although many departments plan and monitor relations with clients, one does not find a pattern of bureaucratic and legislative division and competition similar to that which complicates American policy making. The three main bodies involved in exports have been the Ministry of Foreign Economic Relations, the Ministry of Defence and the Foreign Ministry.[62] The highest administrative body in this process was the State Committee for Foreign Economic Relations, which reported directly to the Politburo Defence Committee and which was chaired by the General Secretary. The State Committee, which included military experts and had ties with the KGB and economic planners, was divided into a General Engineering Department for arms sales, and a Technical Department for construction and related sales. What is difficult to ascertain is the role of the Foreign Ministry, but it was generally subordinate to party and military concerns. The role of the military was prominent, and in general, 'decision-making [was] carried out at the highest level by top Soviet state and party leaders ... The preparatory work, negotiations and execution of agreements are carried out by various ministries ... However, these ministries only execute[d] directives issued from above.'[63]

While slow to have an impact in this area, the policy of *glasnost* has resulted in some calls for greater openness in decision making. Both *Pravda* and *Izvestia* have urged that the secrecy surrounding the volume and destination of exports be lifted, one author has advocated that control of arms exports be placed under the Supreme Soviet (Committee on Defence and State Security), and officials have acknowledged the need for legislation governing exports.[64] But a loosening of secrecy and regulation is not without its dangers: in 1990 the Soviets experienced their first public arms export scandal, as

117

top-line T-72 tanks were intercepted on their way to the West, having been purchased by a state–private cooperative engaged in hard currency trade.[65]

## The economics of Soviet arms production

The early experience of civil war, the relative technological backwardness of its semi-industrialised economy and the perceived threats from capitalist Europe meant that almost from the outset military production has had a special place in Soviet planning. As David Holloway has noted, 'the requirements of defense [had] an important influence on the whole pattern of industrialization', with defence production receiving the highest priority allocation of scarce and skilled resources, especially under Stalin's 'Red militarism'.[66] This has meant that the Soviet Union has been able to achieve levels of technological development in its arms industries far ahead of the economy as a whole, making its weapons broadly competitive with the West. Much of this progress has been achieved with imports of Western technology, however; in the 1920s and 1930s through purchases, under Lend–Lease during the Second World War, and via illicit transfers since 1945. There are considerable doubts about the indigenous innovative capacity of the Soviet economy in the absence of foreign inputs, and 'the obstacles to indigenous innovation are likely also to hamper the assimilation and diffusion of foreign technology'.[67]

The structure and scale of the Soviet defence industry is ill understood, and all the statistics presented below must be treated with great caution. Aside from the uncertainties of information, production levels and pricing in a command economy are discretionary; this at least in principle liberated decision makers (whether they be policy makers or industrial managers) from worrying about the macro- or micro-economic consequences of decisions and subordinated the entire process to political considerations. It also appears that the domestic prices of weapons produced (that is, the prices used for domestic procurement accounting) were far below the probable real costs of the inputs.[68] But whatever the anomalies, real economic costs and benefits do not vanish: employment is maintained, hard currency is earned, and alternative uses of resources can be contemplated.

The best figures for the scale of domestic arms procurement, arms production and R&D spending are only rough estimates, but they suggest that Soviet arms procurement is about 40 per cent of defence spending and total production worth about $100,000 million.[69] R&D

118

spending is equal to between 20 and 28 per cent of total military spending, or between $55,000 and $75,000 million.[70] Both the procurement and R&D figures are high (in percentage terms) relative to the United States and can only partly be explained by the relatively low amount spent on personnel in a conscript military. On the other hand, the total production figure is in the same range as for the United States.

A high level of both domestic procurement and military spending should make exports less significant in maintaining military production capacity, which appears to be the case. Estimates of the percentage of total defence production that was exported range around 15 per cent, and the best available figures on the export proportion of specific weapons types are presented in table 15.[71] Unfortunately, the figures are too uncertain to allow general conclusions to be drawn. The American government intelligence figures on which most calculations are based change from year to year, and do not make clear whether exports are always included in production figures. Another reason for the variability is that the Soviet armed forces hold large weapons stockpiles, meaning that exports do not always come from current production, and can hence be a high proportion of the total output of a given item over short periods. Thus the figures covering longer periods are probably the most reliable. They suggest that the proportion of exports for most items is higher than in the United States, and that although the overall percentage of arms production that was exported may be relatively low, a high dependence appears in specific areas. But the highest totals appear for items such as artillery and naval vessels, which have comparatively low R&D savings.[72]

Several of the micro- and macro-economic effects of arms exports on the economy are impossible to analyse. With respect to spreading R&D or unit costs, one can only speculate that these factors play a small role (if any) in decision making, because there does not appear to be a point at which they are brought into price determination or export decisions. In addition, exports that are not of top-line equipment are often the equivalent of salvage: as a T-55 tank is taken out of service and exported at low prices, it is replaced by a newer model. Although this reaps hard currency, it does not realise any other benefits.[73] A high proportion of exports also does not translate into a high dependence of specific firms ('design bureaus') or factories on export production for their well-being, since the proceeds of export sales are not returned directly to them. Arms are acquired by the foreign trade agency for domestic prices and sold abroad at foreign trade prices

Table 15. *Percentage of Soviet weapons production exported, various periods*

| Weapons | 1 | 2 | 3 | 4 | 5 | 6 |
|---|---|---|---|---|---|---|
| Tanks and assault guns | 33 | 42 | 21 | 41 | 35 | 23 |
| Field artillery | 71 | — | 30 | 57 | 34 | 45 |
| Armoured cars and APCs | 25 | 34 | 30 | 31 | 25 | 37 |
| Major naval combatants | 53* | 58 | 16 | 63 | 30 | 64 |
| Minor naval combatants | 46* | 70 | 27 | 41 | 36 | — |
| Submarines | 11* | 10 | — | 14 | 13 | 20 |
| Combat aircraft | 32 | 39 | 34 | 34 | 34 | 36 |
| Helicopters | 9 | 24 | 19 | 25 | 16 | 34 |
| SAMs | 7 | — | — | 3* | 7 | — |

*Notes*: Most of these figures are based on various annual statements to Congress by officials of the US Defense Intelligence Agency. Deliveries to Warsaw Pact States are excluded from the calculations in columns 4 and 5.

1 David Holloway, in Ball and Leitenberg, 70–1. Covers the period from 1967 to 1980. Starred figures from David Holloway, *The Soviet Union and the Arms Race*, 2nd edn (London: Yale University Press, 1984), 124, covering the period from 1976 to mid 1981.

2 Ulrich Albrecht, 'Soviet arms exports', in SIPRI, *Yearbook 1983*, 363, covering the period from 1977 to 1981.

3 Calculated from figures in SIPRI, *Yearbook 1985*, 352, covering the period from 1972 to 1983. Figure for field artillery is an approximation.

4 Calculated from SIPRI, *Yearbook 1986*, 218 and Grimmett, *Trends in Conventional Arms Transfers, 1976–83*, 28, covering the period from 1980 to 1983. Starred figure from SIPRI, *Yearbook 1985*, 253 and Grimmett, *Trends in Conventional Arms Transfers, 1976–83*, 28.

5 Calculated from SIPRI, *Yearbook 1985*, 253 and ACDA, *WMEAT, 1969–78* and *1985* for the period from 1974 to 1983.

6 Calculated from SIPRI *Yearbook 1990*, 349, and ACDA, *WMEAT 1988*, 125, covering the period from 1983 to 1987.

(which are higher, and often in hard currency), and the difference (or hard currency) goes directly to the state budget.[74] Exports are probably quite significant in maintaining production lines and employment in certain cases though, as some weapons have continued to be produced after domestic procurement has stopped.[75] In addition, the employment (and other) benefits of military production are receiving greater attention as cuts of up to 20 per cent in military production take effect, and the link between arms exports and maintaining an advanced R&D and defence industrial base is beginning to be discussed openly partly as a defensive reaction to the policy of *konversiya* (conversion to production of civilian goods). Representatives of some design bureaus are also openly advocating that exports be expanded (also via joint production with Western firms) and that the hard currency receipts accrue to the bureaus.[76] This creates certain difficulties for Soviet policy makers, as end producers who are allowed to reap hard currency 'profits' from exports are in reality taking advantage of market distortions all the way down the production line (in labour costs, raw materials, capital costs and so on).[77] Such a change cannot be easily accommodated without general price system reforms.

Overall, military production and arms exports appear to play a larger role in the economy than for most other producers (especially in the high-technology sectors), and arms production may amount to 10 per cent of industrial output. Employment is as a consequence high, with probably roughly 5 million workers directly involved in arms production.[78] Arms transfers also made up (in 1987) about 19 per cent of total exports, and although this is a higher proportion than for other major suppliers, this could simply be a reflection of the low role of trade in the Soviet economy. But when one compares Soviet arms exports as a percentage of GNP with other major producers, the same high dependence on arms emerges: throughout the 1980s, arms exports were about 0.91 per cent of GNP for the Soviet Union, compared to 0.34 per cent for the United States, 0.52 per cent for France and 0.35 per cent for Britain.[79]

The major anomaly in the Soviet system of arms exports is the role of hard currency earnings from arms sales. Although there is a strong consensus that the Soviet drive to acquire influence and weaken the position of the West in the non-aligned developing areas relied almost exclusively on military assistance as the most effective instrument of policy, in recent years the argument that economic forces (the pursuit of wealth) are more evident than the pursuit of power has gained considerable support. This argument is based on the observation that 'the arms now tend to be sold rather than given as bilateral aid, economic prices are often charged, credit terms have become more stringent, interest rates on loans are higher, and deposits of cash payments in hard currency are usual'.[80] Figures suggest that the proportion of arms that were transferred for hard currency rose from below 40 per cent before 1973 to more than 70 per cent by 1980. The estimated value of such exports was between $400 million and $2,600 million a year, and the average percentage of hard currency earnings accounted for by arms was about 18 per cent in the 1970–85 period (with a range from 14–27 per cent).[81] In an economy desperate for hard currency, this cannot help but figure in policy calculations: evidence from specific clients confirms this. Egypt, after its break with the Soviets, was able to purchase arms for hard currency, and hard-pressed clients such as Ethiopia and Zambia have been dunned for payment.[82] Potentially destabilising transfers, such as the sale of Su-24 strike

121

aircraft to Libya in 1989, have been candidly justified on the grounds that 'Libya is virtually the only Soviet client state left that will pay in hard currency, cash on the nail, for modern weapons – [it's] as simple as that.'[83]

The argument explains the shift towards the pursuit of economic benefits as follows. First, without the hard currency income from arms sales the Soviet trade balance with the West would be more negative.[84] Second, the Soviet economy has shifted from a situation in which high growth comes from large-scale investment and better resource utilisation (labour and raw materials) to one in which growth requires the application of greater amounts of technological and capital inputs that must be imported from the West. Third, the supply bottlenecks and excess demand in the Soviet economy create few incentives to export other goods. Fourth, 'the military industries are the only ones in which such supply constraints do not seem to operate. Indeed ... excess capacity is deliberately maintained ... [and] the resources devoted to military R&D are enormous.'[85] The conclusion is that military production is the only sector in which Soviets can compete with the West to offset the costs of imports; thus arms sales must have been consciously pursued for their economic benefits. The implication of this argument, if true, would seriously undermine the argument that all first-tier suppliers are motivated less by economic than political/strategic considerations.

There are, however, counters to this that sustain the argument that economic considerations have not pushed pursuit of power considerations to the background in Soviet arms transfer policy. First, although arms transfers are a relatively high proportion of hard currency earnings, peak earning years were reached in 1973 and 1978; this implies that hard currency earnings were primarily fuelled by transfers to Arab clients during and after the 1973 war and global petroleum price increases. The saturation of these markets, competition from West European suppliers and relative declines in the price of oil also suggest that the usefulness of arms exports as a means for acquiring hard currency may have (at least temporarily) peaked. Second, between 1980 and 1985 (the most recent year for which figures are available) more than 70 per cent of the arms contracted for in hard currency terms were bought on credit; most of these arms will probably never be paid for, making the hard currency benefits illusory.[86] Finally, analysts should not be surprised that the Soviet Union took advantage of the increasing ability (and possibly willingness) of several major clients (Libya, Algeria, Kuwait) to pay for their arms purchases, as did the United States and other producers. The increase in hard currency earnings may ultimately have been a by-product of the same factors that fuelled the American shift from aid to sales: it was desirable to reduce the costs of military assistance programmes, especially as the benefits from them proved to be more limited than previously believed.

## Other motives in Soviet transfer decisions

At various times and with different clients military factors have played a role in Soviet arms transfer decisions. But the argument that 'the Soviet Union . . . has accelerated the use of arms transfers for acquiring strategic access, expanding a once-limited basing network to near global dimensions during an era which is witnessing the withering of previous ideological bars to many arms-transfer client relationships' needs to be greatly moderated.[87] The use of the term 'base' is especially misleading, as most of the access obtained is in the form of limited use of naval and airfield facilities, or as low-level as port calls and refuelling rights. Bases, in the sense normally understood, are only part of Soviet military relations with Cuba and Vietnam, and these arrangements only developed after extensive political ties, not as a result of an arms transfer relationship. The Soviet Union does not have, other than in these states, arrangements similar to the United States in Diego Garcia or the Philippines. Full rights have not been granted by such major clients as Libya, Ethiopia, Angola, Algeria, Iraq, Somalia and Syria, and indeed there have been periodic conflicts over the access demanded by the Soviet Union in return for arms.[88] The quest for base rights must also be seen as an accompaniment to the Soviet navy's expansion into a global naval presence, which suggests that the association of arms transfers with military benefits will probably level off. It is thus hardly correct that the Soviet Union's 'vast expansion of basing assets has been achieved at relatively low cost'.[89]

Other military benefits, such as the testing of weapons or substitution for troops, have played only a minor role in Soviet calculations. Although some evidence for the testing motive exists (the supply of certain weapons to Iraq to quell Kurdish resistance[90]), the repeated failure or poor performance against American weapons hardly suggests that the Soviets would encourage their battlefield use. Accelerated weapons supplies to Middle Eastern clients such as Syria could reflect a desire to forestall a troop commitment, but since it is doubtful that such a commitment was ever envisaged, this cannot be considered a substitute. When a personnel commitment has been required, the Soviets have not (until the Afghanistan experience) been

123

reluctant to act, directly in Egypt (1968–72) or Afghanistan (1980–8), or through Cuban proxies (Angola), or with the supply of East European or Soviet 'volunteers' (Libya or South Yemen).

The division between the pursuit of wealth and pursuit of power motivations also does not accurately describe the Soviet Union's policy-making process. The centralisation of arms transfer decision making means that economic and military costs and benefits were aggregated into an essentially political process, and it is unlikely in such a system that factors such as spreading unit and R&D costs, or maintaining full employment or production lines, have played a large part. Instead, Soviet leaders have taken advantage of, but not led or created, a situation in which economic benefits could be realised.

In addition to these considerations one should note that arms deals were usually the result of high-level contacts between Soviet leaders and their counterparts in the developing states; that the Soviet Union concentrated its exports and efforts on key states (usually those with which it had signed Friendship and Cooperation treaties), and that in the quest for influence and access, Moscow relied on arms transfers because it lacked viable alternatives such as foreign aid, economic investment or technology. From the opening breach of the Northern Tier to initiatives in Asia and Africa, Soviet arms transfer policy has reflected shifting foreign policy concerns and priorities. Finally, the high percentage of concessionary aid and credits supplied to favoured clients (such as India) and the inability of many major clients (such as Syria and Ethiopia) to pay for arms already delivered suggest that in the end, the political calculations of the benefits have been the overriding factors governing the Soviet Union's arms transfers.[91]

## Conclusion: first-tier suppliers, participation in the arms transfer and production system

Although several divergent elements govern American and Soviet participation in the global arms transfer and production system, their policies and practices are by and large what one expects from dominant first-tier producers. The Soviet Union and the United States maintain the largest military production bases, the highest levels of domestic procurement and the most intensive R&D efforts. In the immediate post-1945 period, when their dominance of the global military system was unquestioned, the political benefits derived from arms transfers were paramount in decision making, and the potential economic costs and benefits of arms transfers were ignored. Slowly, however, economic factors entered into arms transfer decisions, with the United States shifting from aid to sales and the Soviet Union charging market prices and demanding hard currency from customers who could afford to pay. The economic benefits accruing to individual producers and the creation of domestic constituencies with an interest in maintaining exports also arguably began to constrain decision makers' ability to exercise the options created by the arms transfer relationship. But the conflict between seeking influence through arms transfers and maintaining one's dominant status in the global military hierarchy was muted.

As the system evolved further, with the progressive diffusion of new technologies and the narrowing of the gap between the weapons possessed by first-tier states and others, the emphasis in American and Soviet thinking shifted from the garnering of influence and allies to a new concern with the protection of one's technological lead. The conflict between the pursuit of these contradictory goals that is suppressed during the early period of unquestioned technological dominance became clear, as the longer-term economic forces involved came into play. Although the Soviet Union had until recently been relatively successful at insulating itself from these pressures, the command economy failed to eliminate the pressures of either global competition or economic logic, especially when competing claims on defence allocations were articulated in the Soviet Union. The advantages that both first-tier producers possessed, such as rapid delivery lower prices or easy terms, were also increasingly challenged, and these challenges reduced the ability of first-tier suppliers to win political advantages as a quid pro quo for arms.

Changes in the international arms market and in the outlook for American and Soviet defence industries provide clear evidence that this cycle of the global arms transfer system is evolving to its more mature stages. International developments in the early 1990s, in particular the end of the Cold War in Europe and a dramatic reduction in the East–West confrontation in the developing world, signal possibly dramatic transformations in American and Soviet arms transfer policy. Again, however, there are contradictory pressures: on the one hand, both the United States and the Soviet Union face declining domestic arms procurement budgets (which increases the desirability of exports) and increased competition from allies for markets. On the other hand, they are pressured to reduce military assistance to clients and wish to exercise greater control over the transfer of destabilising or sensitive technologies and weapons. The above analysis does not

125

predict the direction in which policy will turn, but it suggests that the United States and the Soviet Union, because of their overwhelmingly dominant positions in the global military order, will be better able to balance such competing goals than other participants in the system. But these suggestive indications must be confirmed via an examination of the policies and practices of second- and third-tier suppliers.

# 6 SECOND-TIER PRODUCERS AND SUPPLIERS: THE STRUGGLE TO KEEP PACE

## The evolution of second-tier arms production and transfers

Matters become more complex as one surveys the policy and practice of second-tier arms producers and suppliers. The first difficulty is specifying which states are in the second tier. If membership is determined by production endowments and technological capabilities, tables 9 and 10 confirm that there is a qualitative gap between the production levels and research and development capabilities of the first-tier states and those of the next largest producers or exporters. At the lower end, however, another qualitative break is somewhat harder to distinguish. One task of this chapter will be to delineate with more precision how production capabilities help determine which states are second-tier producers. A second will be to distinguish the different policy stances adopted by these producers towards arms exports. Although the export and production practice of the leading second-tier states (France and Britain) is relatively straightforward, other states in this tier occupy somewhat ambiguous positions vis-à-vis the central dilemma posed by their status in the global arms transfer and production system: how to produce weapons at a sufficiently high level of sophistication to ensure national independence and global status without placing too great an economic burden on the state.

The French experience is the starting point for analysis, primarily because French policy and practice establish the paradigm case to which other second-tier producers conform to a lesser degree. Until the criteria for determining second-tier status are discussed more carefully somewhat later, this chapter will provisionally deal with the export and production activities of the main arms-producing states of the industrialised world: France, Britain, Germany, Spain, Italy, Czechoslovakia, Poland, Japan, Canada and Sweden. (The only significant industrialised producers omitted from this list are Belgium, the Netherlands and Switzerland.) As we shall see, the way in which the system has evolved suggests that not all of them ought automatically to be accorded second-tier status.

## The re-establishment of the European arms industries

Although the degree of destruction of the European industrial infrastructure in the Second World War is often overstated, it none the less took more than two decades for the continental arms industries to re-establish themselves. Until then, the dominance of American and Soviet military technology was nearly complete (with the important exception of Britain), especially in the first postwar generation of technologies. Much of the reconstruction was accomplished (especially in France, Italy, Germany, Poland and Czechoslovakia) with direct and indirect American and Soviet assistance, in the form of technology transfers, markets or military aid. In all but the French and British cases, an immediate trade-off between production of sophisticated weapons and independent arms production was evident, and most producers opted for sophisticated local production, relying on other suppliers for licences to produce key components such as jet engines or advanced electronics.

France was explicit in its use of American aid to rebuild its arms industries: between 1945 and 1955 France received twice as much American military aid as any other NATO member; this aid accounted for about 50 per cent of total French military equipment expenditures.[1] Indirect assistance to its arms industry also came from American purchases of French weapons for NATO forces. This policy coincided with the French goal of rebuilding an independent arms production capability in all weapons systems and gave a particular boost to France's aircraft industry, which built its indigenous design capabilities around the Dassault complex. Today France possesses indigenous design and production capabilities in sophisticated aircraft, tanks, missiles, ships and military electronics.

The British arms industry emerged from the Second World War intact (and with huge capacities), and after the war Britain attempted to resume its traditional great power role, one hallmark of which was the ability to produce the entire range of modern weapons systems, including nuclear weapons. The resources devoted to maintaining its imperial holdings and to European defence meant that for a time, Britain was able to forestall its decline to second-tier status. In certain fields (jet engines) it was perhaps technologically even more advanced than the United States.[2] Although this lead has vanished, Britain has, like France, maintained an across-the-board arms production capability in advanced weapons.

West Germany was a special case, as the Allied prohibition on West German arms production was maintained until 1951. By 1955, when the reconstituted Bundeswehr placed its first orders, production was still modest, and primarily based on American designs.[3] The German arms industry is still more limited in its indigenous design and production capabilities than either France or Britain (the Leopard tank series being the main exception), and Germany eschewed a genuine across-the-board arms production capability, fundamentally for political reasons. Co-production and licensed production arrangements (such as for the HOT and Roland missiles, the Tornado aircraft and the proposed Eurofighter) have been seen as means of enhancing German defence industrial capabilities (especially in aerospace) without reaping the political fallout from a completely independent policy.[4] These limitations have not, however, prevented Germany from becoming a major arms exporter.

Japan is also somewhat of an exceptional case, as until the early 1980s its arms production base was not extensive. A postwar ban on arms production was severely bent during the Korean War, when ammunition, supplies and repair facilities were provided to American forces, and in 1952 the ban was formally lifted, although production remained at low levels through the 1950s.[5] But as American military assistance declined in the late 1950s and early 1960s, licensed production of major weapons systems (all American) of increasing sophistication was expanded. It remained the dominant form of production until the early 1980s. Despite its relatively small defence effort (in relation to its GNP), Japan's large defence budget (in dollar terms), its policy of self-reliance and its increasing presence in high-technology sectors meant, however, that arms production became more prominent, to the point where more than 80 per cent of defence equipment is domestically procured.[6] The Japanese procurement system has also resulted in large contracts to a few firms: the top 6 firms obtain 60 per cent of defence contracts, and as a consequence these 6 are among the 100 largest arms-producing companies (excluding non-market economies). Comparable figures for other second-tier producers are: Britain, 14; France, 9; Germany, 7; Sweden, 4; Italy, 3; Switzerland, 3 (the United States has 47 of the top 100).[7] This large production base is not coupled with a high profile in the export market, however, which perhaps explains the relative lack of attention Japanese defence industries have received.[8]

Other smaller European producers were also later entrants in the

129

arms production and transfer system. Italy relied (as did France) primarily on American assistance and technology to rebuild its arms industry, although licensed production accelerated only in the 1960s as American military aid was ending.[9] Real growth occurred in the 1970s with a ten-fold increase in production. Spain emerged as a significant arms producer even later, with the greatest growth occurring after it joined NATO in 1982. Domestic defence procurement was closely linked with licensed production, and dependence on imported technologies remains high.[10] Neither Spain nor Italy attempted to develop an across-the-board arms production capability, and they specialised in such items as light fighters, helicopters and missiles (Italy) or transport aircraft and small naval vessels (Spain).

The East European arms industries occupied a subordinate position in second-tier arms production, their status being solely a product of integration into the Soviet Union's arms production structure. With the exception of Czechoslovakia, little indigenous production existed in these states prior to 1945. The Polish and Czech industries (the two most significant) were rebuilt in the 1950s under the guidance of the Soviet Union, and their role has been to produce large quantities of less sophisticated weapons under licence from the Soviets.[11] With few exceptions (none highly sophisticated), 'major weapons were not only produced but also modernized according to plans developed in the Soviet Union ... none of the smaller partners alone could carry out production of finished goods from the first stages of design'. It is doubtful that even this level of production will be maintained in these states through the 1990s.[12] But even at low levels of sophistication the momentum of the dynamic of technology and the pursuit of wealth was evident: throughout the 1970s and the early 1980s, non-Soviet Warsaw Pact states increasingly pushed to acquire greater influence in defence industrial decisions, to produce more sophisticated weapons and to increase hard currency exports, with some limited success.[13]

Canada, Sweden and Switzerland all emerged from the Second World War with their defence production bases intact. The Swedish and Swiss defence industrial commitment has been based on the perceived link between independent national arms production and neutrality, although the actual degree of technological independence the two countries now enjoy is limited. Sweden has remained at the forefront of modern fighter production, but important components (such as the engine) are based on licensed technologies.[14] The means of securing at least quasi-independent production is the so-called 'Swedish model', by which a mature foreign-made engine is adapted to Swedish requirements, along with a full transfer of technology.

130

Switzerland concentrates on indigenous production of anti-aircraft guns, ammunition and armoured vehicles. Licensed production of less sophisticated aircraft also occurs.[15] Canada, after flirting in the 1950s with an independent production policy, opted in 1959 (via the Defence Production Sharing Agreement) for near-total integration into the American defence market and for a conscious policy of procuring major weapons systems from foreign sources.[16] As a consequence Canada does not produce a single major weapons system indigenously, but does produce sophisticated components of selected systems (such as gas turbine engines, avionics and flight simulators). These three states (among others), however, also adopted relatively restrained arms export policies that (despite numerous breaches) effectively reduced their ability to maintain a sophisticated defence industrial base.

A fully fledged second tier did not really emerge until the 1970s, as France, Japan and Germany began to satisfy a relatively high proportion of their defence needs and when lesser producers such as Sweden, Czechoslovakia, Spain and Italy had acquired at least limited capabilities to produce modern weapons. Most of these industries developed in the 1960s and 1970s with infusions of military technologies from first-tier states, which is a hallmark of the third phase of evolution in a cycle of the arms transfer system. One major consequence was that the relative demand for arms imports from these states declined, thus forcing exporters to look to new markets in the developing world. Another consequence was that these states began to pursue their own exports vigorously, thus creating by the late 1980s an extremely competitive arms market. The precise position of individual states in the second tier fluctuated according to idiosyncratic national policies and their overall level of industrialisation, but as a group they exhibited a certain cohesiveness. The level of sophistication of their most advanced production was uniformly high, although in many cases it was limited to a few major systems. The reliance on technology from first-tier states was also high, either via direct licensed or co-production, or via a demonstration effect that directed national efforts to reproduce the most advanced weapons developed by the United States or Soviet Union. But most important for our purposes, these states also shared a common dilemma that determined their position in the arms transfer system.

## The scope and direction of second-tier arms transfers

Arms exports tracked the re-establishment of modern arms production for most of these states. Until the early 1960s, the only active exporters were Britain and France, with Britain being most prominent. In the early 1950s, Britain delivered significant amounts of weapons to its colonies and ex-colonies (most prominently to India, Pakistan, Egypt, Jordan and South Africa) and to Western European states.[17] French arms exports remained secondary to rebuilding French forces and fighting colonial wars in the 1950s, and it was not until the early 1960s that France became a major exporter. Early customers for French arms included West Germany, Belgium, Sweden, Israel, India and Pakistan. Two persistent features of second-tier arms exports emerged relatively early, though. First, in both the French and British cases the percentage of major weapons production that was exported was relatively high, as the figures in table 16 illustrate. Since more than 70 per cent of French transfers in this period were aircraft, these figures are representative of the overall export dependence of the industry.[18] Second, even in this early period exports of arms production technology appeared: French trainer aircraft, for example, were produced under licence in West Germany, Finland and Israel.[19]

The 1960s and early 1970s saw several changes in the export shares among the ranks of second-tier arms producers. These shifts are presented in table 17, which charts the relative positions of second-tier suppliers in the international arms market from 1963 to 1988. French arms transfers increased roughly 20 per cent a year between 1960 and 1970, doubling in real terms between 1972 and 1982, and stabilising at this level throughout most of the 1980s (a sharp downturn is apparent in the late 1980s).[20] The French share of the global market climbed in this period from less than 4 per cent to more than 8 per cent. The direction of its sales also shifted to developing world customers: before 1970, two-thirds of deliveries were to other industrialised countries, but by the late 1970s the developing countries accounted for more than four-fifths of arms purchases.[21] By the late 1980s, the Middle East and North Africa alone accounted for almost 80 per cent of French arms exports, with Europe and North America accounting for only about 4 per cent. The most important French clients were Iraq, Egypt, Saudi Arabia and India: they accounted for almost three-quarters of the total.

British arms exports, by contrast, fell sharply in the late 1950s and early 1960s both because other suppliers (notably France and the Soviet Union) re-entered the market aggressively and captured tradi-

Table 16. *Export share of major weapons systems, 1950s*

|  | Share of production exported (%) | Year in service |
|---|---|---|
| *Britain* | | |
| Vampire fighter | 47 | 1946 |
| Hunter fighter | 46 | 1954 |
| *France* | | |
| Ouragan fighter | 47 | 1949 |
| Mystère fighter | 76 | 1952 |
| Djinn helicopter | 50 | 1953 |
| Alouette II helicopter | 40 | 1955 |

*Sources:* British figures from Stockholm International Peace Research Institute (SIPRI), *The Arms Trade with the Third World* (Stockholm: Almqvist and Wiksell, 1971), 378; French figures from Kolodziej, *Making and Marketing*, 47.

Table 17. *Second-tier arms deliveries, 1963–88, four-year averages (million constant 1988 US dollars)*

| Country | 1963–6 | 1967–70 | 1971–4 | 1975–8 | 1979–82 | 1983–6 | 1987–8[a] |
|---|---|---|---|---|---|---|---|
| France | 481 | 507 | 1,450 | 2,512 | 4,202 | 4,833 | 2,340 |
| Great Britain | 557 | 402 | 1,071 | 1,613 | 2,707 | 1,705 | 1,447 |
| West Germany | 360 | 329 | 475 | 1,373 | 1,730 | 1,838 | 1,125 |
| Poland | 412 | 445 | 443 | 856 | 1,125 | 1,304 | 957 |
| Czechoslovakia | 449 | 379 | 531 | 1,164 | 1,167 | 1,250 | 1,045 |
| Italy | 74 | 76 | 295 | 817 | 1,284 | 1,067 | 381 |
| Spain | 7 | 21 | 37 | 118 | 251 | 563 | 297 |
| Bulgaria | 3 | 19 | 19 | 54 | 226 | 541 | 500 |
| Switzerland | 25 | 8 | 95 | 607 | 659 | 383 | 241 |
| Romania | 0 | 1 | 77 | 72 | 456 | 401 | 178 |
| East Germany | 19 | 26 | 87 | 128 | 188 | 401 | 370 |
| Sweden | 47 | 12 | 109 | 144 | 222 | 177 | 219 |
| Belgium | 59 | 22 | 120 | 245 | 197 | 324 | 25 |
| Japan | 32 | 25 | 29 | 80 | 167 | 253 | 92 |
| Canada | 194 | 416 | 402 | 194 | 209 | 195 | 173 |
| Netherlands | 14 | 37 | 118 | 140 | 308 | 118 | 585 |
| Other industrial | 67 | 23 | 157 | 447 | 482 | 815 | 323 |
| Total | 2,799 | 2,748 | 5,514 | 10,564 | 15,580 | 16,169 | 10,299 |
| Share of world exports (%) | 22.2 | 16.7 | 21.5 | 29.1 | 29.2 | 30.0 | 19.7 |

*Note:* [a] Figures for this column are averages for the 1987–8 period only.
*Source:* ACDA, *WMEAT*, various years.

tional British customers and because British arms were uncompetitive, with aircraft especially proving too expensive for most clients.[22] These developments precipitated crises in the arms industry, the cancellation of many projects and a decision to concentrate production in a more narrow range of conventional weapons that had strong export potential. Britain began vigorously exporting first-line weapons that were occasionally superior to those deployed with its own forces, and as a consequence British arms transfers recovered in the late 1960s and early 1970s.[23] They doubled between 1972 and 1983 and stabilised at this level throughout the 1980s, again with a downturn in the late 1970s. As was the case with France, the direction of British exports shifted, with the developing world accounting for 74 per cent of deliveries in the 1983–7 period compared to 60 per cent a decade earlier. The volume of British transfers has, however, been much smaller than France's, and its main clients more diverse: the most recent top five customers for British arms have been Saudi Arabia, the United States, Oman, Switzerland and Turkey; together they accounted for 60 per cent of British transfers.

Although small amounts of arms were delivered earlier, West German transfers began in earnest in the early 1960s when surplus or outdated equipment (tanks, aircraft, small arms) was delivered (often as military aid) to developing states, including Israel, Tanzania and Nigeria.[24] These transfers were driven by political motives: to meet Germany's special responsibilities towards Israel and to enhance West Germany's claim as the only legitimate German state. However, bad experiences in Tanzania and Nigeria, the rupture of relations with Arab states when transfers to Israel became public, and shady end-use transfers (weapons for Italy and Iran appeared in India and Pakistan) 'suggested that this form of aid generated little direct political payoff'.[25] Although a relatively restrictive legal structure had been established as early as 1961 (and is enshrined in the constitution), these experiences contributed to the adoption in 1971 of a policy prohibiting sales to 'areas of tension' that strongly discouraged arms transfers to non-NATO states.[26]

This restrained policy did not forestall Germany's inexorable return to a secure position as a second-tier supplier, and (as will be seen below) economic imperatives have led to a significant erosion of German restraint. Total transfers increased three-fold (in real terms) from the early 1970s to the early 1980s, but have fluctuated considerably since. According to the figures in table 17, West Germany held between 2.2 and 3.4 per cent of the world arms market in the 1980s, but the high proportion of German production that is conducted jointly with other European partners (such as France, Britain and Spain) means that the statistics probably understate German participation in the export market. The locus of German sales also shifted to the developing world, in spite of the regulations: between 1983 and 1987, 73 per cent of transfers went to the developing world, compared to 30 per cent in the 1964–73 period. Major recent customers for German arms have been Argentina, Turkey, Switzerland, Iraq and Colombia.

The next important exporters are Italy and Spain, both relative latecomers to the market. Italian arms exports were negligible until the late 1960s and they increased ten-fold between 1969 and 1979; Spain's exports were almost non-existent until the mid 1970s, and they increased ten-fold between 1977 and 1982. Both enjoyed their highest exports in the early 1980s (with Italy averaging more than $1,000 million and Spain $500 million a year between 1982 and 1986), but these virtually collapsed in the late 1980s as the global market tightened.[27] Both their range of products and their base of clients were relatively narrow, and rested heavily upon transfers to clients such as Libya, Saudi Arabia or Nigeria, all of whom experienced great difficulties with the decline in oil prices of the early 1980s.

It is more difficult to trace the evolution of transfers of the smaller second-tier producers. More than three-quarters of transfers from Poland and Czechoslovakia went to fellow Warsaw Pact members until the early 1980s, at which point Czech exports turned to the developing world. Main Czech clients in the late 1980s (accounting for almost half of total transfers) were Libya, Iraq and Syria. States such as Romania, East Germany and Bulgaria also transferred significant quantities of weapons throughout the 1980s to these same clients (plus an unspecified amount to Iran), which suggests that exports were closely tied to the Iran–Iraq War. Most of these transfers were not major weapons systems, and were adjuncts to Soviet arms transfer decisions or retransfers of Soviet weapons.[28] The group of smaller suppliers that includes Canada, Sweden and Switzerland have seen their relative importance decline since 1963, to the point where in the late 1980s they accounted for just over 1 per cent of global arms transfers (from a high of 2.6 per cent in the mid 1960s). Much of this is a function of their restrictive arms transfer policies, and their clients have consequently seldom been in the developing world or in areas of conflict. Canada, for example, has sold about three-quarters of its arms to the United States and another 15 per cent to Europe, while more than 60 per cent of Swedish exports have been to Europe or North America.[29]

The most important non-participant in the arms export market is

135

Japan, which labours under a virtually complete formal ban on arms exports. Until the mid 1970s, Japanese arms exports averaged less than $15 million (current dollars) annually, and its main clients were other Asian states. Japanese exports appear to have quadrupled in real terms since then, although it is extremely difficult to verify any figures because exports often take the form of semi-finished goods, components, or dual-use items such as helicopters and trucks that have found ready clients in various regions.[30] Japan's position is thus special, although it has not been immune (as will be noted below) to the same pressures faced by other second-tier states to increase exports.

These shifts are clearly documented in the figures in table 17, which mark the emergence of a mature second tier of producers from under the post-1945 shadow of American and Soviet technological dominance. The stabilisation (or slight decline) in exports from second-tier suppliers in the late 1980s reflects the greater competitiveness of the market and the advantages of scale that remain with the first-tier producers. Second-tier participation in the arms export market also correlates highly with their arms production endowments (with the important exception of Japan). Although fluctuations in the shares of specific suppliers have been conditioned by such things as wars (the Middle Eastern and Iran–Iraq conflicts being most important), the ebb and flow of relations with individual clients, and particular policy decisions, these suppliers are all ultimately driven to export by economic pressures that constrain their policy options.

## The economic dimensions of second-tier arms exports

A glance at the macro-economic profile of second-tier arms production and exports would suggest that, with the possible exception of France and the East European producers, the balance of payments or employment benefits of arms exports are not large. Table 18 summarises the available information on the role of arms exports in the economies of major second-tier producers. It measures balance of payments and employment effects via the proportion of arms exports in total exports and the proportion of manufacturing employment accounted for by export production. It also notes the proportion of overall industrial output that is accounted for by arms production. Only Poland and Czechoslovakia have a higher proportion of exports accounted for by arms than the United States (whose average is 4.5 per cent over the past two decades), and this is a function of low participation in international trade and a distorted industrial structure. In addition, the employment effects of arms exports appear (with the probable exceptions of France, Sweden, Spain and Belgium) lower than for the United States. This minimal macro-economic impact is confirmed if one applies the formula used to calculate cost savings to the American defence budget from sales, in which every $1,000 million in exports represents a saving in R&D and unit costs of only $70 million.[31] For Britain, this would represent a saving of less than $100 million a year!

The actual impact of arms exports can only be assessed with input–output economic models (and then only imperfectly) and by accounting for alternative uses of resources, and the evidence on all these factors, as studies of the conversion of military to civilian production suggest, is mixed.[32] But it is almost certain that the macro-economic impact of arms exports is even lower than the figures in table 18 suggest. Lest this static picture be taken too optimistically, however, it should be noted that the proportion of industrial output accounted for by arms production is more than 5 per cent for half of the states listed. Dependence upon arms production appears to have an almost normal distribution around this median. For those states in the upper half (especially France, Britain, Sweden and the Netherlands), this suggests that the macro-economic importance of exports may increase if domestic arms procurement budgets are reduced.

But perhaps the most significant figures in table 18 are those on the percentage of arms production that is exported, as they indicate a much greater role for arms exports than in first-tier states. This suggests that one must look to the micro-economic level, at the structure and scale of second-tier defence industries and their high level of dependence upon exports, to find the fundamental motive forces behind second-tier states' aggressive participation in the global arms transfer system. The most important factor is their relatively small domestic procurement base, which results in higher unit costs for weapons and lower levels of R&D spending. This eventually forces a choice between dependence on imported technologies, special-isation in weapons systems of particular national importance, or abandonment of the quest to remain at the technological frontier. Britain's House of Commons Defence Committee captured the essence of the dilemma when it observed that 'to try to stay at the forefront of weapons technology may make the cost of independence unacceptably high, but there is little point in seeking to remain independent if it means relying on outdated equipment which will not be effective in countering the threat posed by an increasingly sophisti-cated enemy'.[33]

Table 18. *The economics of arms exports for second-tier producers, mid 1980s*

| Country | Arms production | Arms exports | % of production exported | % of exports | Employment from arms exports | Exports as % of manufacturing employment | Production as % of industrial output |
|---|---|---|---|---|---|---|---|
| | (million US dollars) | | | | | | |
| France | 19,400 | 4,300 | 40 | 4.0 | 130,000 | 2.7 | 15.6 |
| Britain | 13,900 | 1,400 | 30 | 1.4 | 120,000 | 2.2 | 14.1 |
| West Germany | 7,400 | 1,430 | 20 | 0.7 | 50,000–60,000 | 0.7 | 3.9 |
| Japan | 4,900 | 170 | 3 | 0.1 | Negligible | Negligible | 1.3 |
| Poland | 3,000 | 1,230 | 40 | 6.5 | 40,000 | 1.1 | 3.0 |
| Italy | 3,000 | 830 | 60 | 1.1 | 70,000 | 1.7 | 3.3 |
| Canada | 3,000 | 170 | 60 | 0.2 | 20,000 | 1.0 | 5.9 |
| Czechoslovakia | 1,700 | 1,230 | 70 | 6.5 | 35,000–70,000 | 1.4–2.9 | 2.7 |
| Netherlands | 1,500 | 90 | 30 | 0.1 | 10,000 | 1.0 | 6.9 |
| Spain | 1,300 | 550 | 50 | 2.2 | 50,000–85,000 | 2.3–4.0 | 2.9 |
| Sweden | 1,300 | 220 | 50 | 0.7 | 20,000 | 3.8 | 6.5 |
| Switzerland | 900 | 240 | 40 | 0.8 | 12,000 | 1.7 | n.a. |
| Belgium | 600 | 280 | 60 | 0.5 | 20,000 | 2.6 | 3.5 |

*Note: Japan:* Arms production as a percentage of total industrial production is estimated as 0.5 per cent by *Far Eastern Economic Review* (22 February 1990).

*France:* Employment figures from Edward Kolodziej, *Economic Determinants of the Transfer of Arms and Military Technology under the French Fifth Republic* (Illinois: University of Illinois, Office of Arms Control, Disarmament and International Security, 1983), 23; Dussauge, 79.

*Italy:* Employment figures from *Défense & armement Héraclès* (February 1990).

*Sources:* Sources for figures, except where noted, are the same as for table 10. Figures for arms production and percentage of production cannot be used to calculate column 3. Figures in columns 5 and 6, unless otherwise noted, are calculated from Brzoska and Ohlson, *Arms Transfers*, 72–110, and from the International Labour Office, *Year Book of Labour Statistics* (Geneva: ILO, 1986), 414–25. Column 7 is calculated from United Nations, *National Accounts Statistics*.

The aggressive pursuit of arms exports is often seen as a way out of this difficult choice to abandon in one way or another the quest for independence in arms production. When short weapons-production runs are the norm, arms exports generate relatively greater economies of scale by spreading R&D costs and moving down the learning curve at its steepest point. That this path was chosen by many second-tier states is reflected in the median (and perhaps average) figure for arms exports as a proportion of total arms production in table 18, which is about 50 per cent (excluding the exceptional case of Japan). It should be noted that the percentages in column 3 are not derived from columns 1 and 2, and are based on more accurate country case studies that avoid what appears to be the systematic under-counting of arms exports in the United States Arms Control and Disarmament Agency figures.[34] This suggests immediately that however limited the macro-economic benefits, arms exports are crucial to the economic well-being of second-tier defence industries.

This high reliance on exports is confirmed when one examines specific firms or weapons systems, which the data in table 19 summarise. All of the major second-tier producers are represented, and almost all of the firms are among the top 100 world arms producers, so they constitute a representative sample. The median reliance upon exports (as a percentage of total arms production) is about 50 per cent, which corresponds well to the figures in table 18.[35] Unfortunately, no export dependence figures are available for West German firms, although their reliance upon exports is probably lower than for other suppliers. What is most significant is that the greatest reliance upon exports appears in the high-technology production sectors such as aircraft, aircraft engines, electronics, helicopters or missiles. Lower figures appear for items such as vehicles and ships, which, although incorporating state-of-the-art technology, are based upon less sophis-ticated technologies. Second-tier exports are as a result skewed towards such items: in France aerospace products have since 1965 always averaged more than 60 per cent of total arms exports, and in Britain three-quarters of British arms exports in the 1970s were aerospace equipment.[36] These high-technology sectors are also the most critical for maintaining highly skilled employment: French government figures, for example, estimate that 50 and 37 per cent respectively of the jobs in aerospace and defence electronics industries are created by exports.[37]

This concentration on sophisticated items, where the unit and R&D savings are greatest, runs somewhat counter to the trend in first-tier suppliers and reflects the great pressures to reduce unit costs and

139

Table 19. *Dependence upon exports of major second-tier arms-producing firms, mid 1980s*

| Firm | Country and rank | | Products | Arms production % of production | Arms exports % of arms production | World rank |
|---|---|---|---|---|---|---|
| Thomson | Fr | 1 | Electronics | 36 | 60 | 12 |
| Aérospatiale | Fr | 2 | Helicopters/missiles | 49 | 50 | 22 |
| DTN | Fr | 3 | Ships | 100 | 5 | 24 |
| Dassault | Fr | 4 | Aircraft | 70 | 70 | 28 |
| GIAT | Fr | 5 | Tanks | 100 | 40 | 45 |
| SNECMA | Fr | 6 | Engines | 45 | 53[a] | 59 |
| Matra | Fr | 8 | Missiles | 14 | 75 | 81 |
| British Aerospace | Br | 1 | Aircraft | 54 | 55 | 7 |
| GEC | Br | 2 | Electronics | 35 | 45[b] | 14 |
| Rolls-Royce | Br | 3 | Engines | 40 | 42[b] | 39 |
| Thorn EMI | Br | 4 | Electronics | 20 | 35[b] | 41 |
| Ferranti | Br | 5 | Electronics | 80 | 40 | 44 |
| VSEL | Br | 6 | Ships | 100 | 30 | 55 |
| Aeritalia | It | 1 | Aircraft | 64 | 65 | 53 |
| Fiat Aviazone | It | 2 | Engines | 81 | 60[c] | 63 |
| Oto Melara | It | 3 | Vehicles | 98 | 55 | 74 |
| Agusta | It | 4 | Helicopters | 72 | 80 | 75 |
| MBB | Ge | 1 | Aircraft | 49 | n/a | 29 |
| AEG | Ge | 2 | Electronics | 18 | n/a | 41 |
| MTU | Ge | 3 | Engines | 52 | n/a | 50 |
| Siemens | Ge | 4 | Electronics | 2 | n/a | 57 |
| Rheinmetall | Ge | 5 | Artillery | 35 | n/a | 62 |
| Krauss-Maffei | Ge | 10 | Vehicles | 53 | (33)[d] | 91 |
| Casa | Sp | 1 | Aircraft | 65 | (70)[e] | 49 |
| ENASA | Sp | 2 | Vehicles | 55 | (45)[f] | — |
| Bofors | Sw | 1 | Artillery | 50 | 50[g] | — |
| Nobel | Sw | 2 | Artillery/missiles | 23 | n/a | — |

*Notes:* [a] *Jane's Defence Weekly* (4 October 1986).
[b] Taylor and Hayward, 49.
[c] *Flight International* (5 July 1986).
[d] Krauss-Maffei's status dropped in the late 1980s as a result of the end of the Leopard tank production series (it had been in the German top five until then). Its export figure is calculated from the deliveries of Leopard tanks in the 1970s. From Bernd Huebner, 'The importance of arms exports and armament cooperation for the West German defence industrial base', in Haglund, 139, 142.
[e] Derived from Vicenç, Fisas, *Las armas de la democracia* (Barcelona: Editorial Critica, 1989), 34 and SIPRI, *Yearbook 1990*, 327.
[f] Derived from Fisas, 61 and *Technologia militar* (1 January 1984).
[g] Data from 1982 from *Financial Times* (4 November 1982).
*Sources:* Unless otherwise indicated, figures are from Brzoska and Ohlson, *Arms Transfers*, passim and SIPRI, *Yearbook 1990*, 326–8. Bracketed figures are rough estimates.

spread R&D expenditures. It cannot be emphasised too strongly how important such savings are: according to one estimate, the final unit cost of the Leopard I tank was reduced by 57 per cent through exports.[38] All estimates for unit cost savings depend on the precise slope of the learning curve, but one estimate for aircraft argues that a doubling of production from 400 to 800 units lowers costs by 15 per cent, with an increase to 1,200 units lowering costs by a further 13 per cent.[39] This suggests that the savings from exports of high technology items could be considerably higher than the $70 million per $1,000 in sales cited above. (If the above calculations are correct, an aircraft valued at $15 million for 400 domestically procured units would decrease in cost to $12.75 million if 400 units were exported, a saving of $900 million (or a saving of $176 million per $1,000 million sales, assuming no sales costs or discounts).) It should also be noted that the prices charged for export items are often higher than for domestic procurement: Dassault's Mirage III was sold abroad for 13.05 million francs, while the French price was only 4.66 million![40]

In the most extreme cases exports are essential to keep a full production line open: Dassault estimates that it must produce 40 planes annually in order to maintain production teams; with French government orders of only 28 and 33 respectively in 1988 and 1989, a minimum of approximately 25 per cent of production must be exported.[41] Sweden has projected that a minimum proportion of one-third of its production of the Gripen fighter must be exported in order for the plane to be affordable; France's Rafale cost estimates assume that one-half of production will be exported.[42] These floors are well above the average figures for export dependence of first-tier states. During several years of interrupted domestic orders, French AMX tank production was also maintained only through exports. As one official from the French firm Thomson succinctly summarised it, 'the day we stop exporting . . . that's it. We close up shop.'[43] Anticipated (or past) declines in levels of military procurement and stretched-out procurement programmes only exacerbate this problem. In France, for example, arms exports as a percentage of defence procurement and exports together increased from 14.8 per cent in 1970 to 38.1 per cent in 1980 and 42.5 per cent in 1982.[44] One consequence has been that the defence industry in many second-tier states has become so export-orientated that force readiness is often sacrificed to meet export demands and weapons are designed for the export market rather than to meet domestic military needs.[45] Overall, therefore, the promotion of arms exports to lower unit costs for domestic forces, maintain a healthy defence industry, and stay at the forefront of military technology is much stronger for second-tier than for first-tier producers, and is perhaps a decisive consideration shaping arms transfer policies.[46]

## Policy and decision making for arms transfers

The decision-making structure of the dominant second-tier producers and the actual policies they pursue reflect these relatively strong economic imperatives and the concomitant weak influence of other (political or military) considerations. This results in essentially two responses towards arms exports, which Michael Brzoska has dubbed the 'Japanese' and 'French' models.[47] France's government-backed export policy aggressively seeks markets without strong political restraints and promotes exports in order to maintain a strong, autonomous, defence industrial base at the technological frontier. Similar policies are followed by Britain, Italy and Spain. Japan does not allow (in principle) the export of goods 'used by military forces and directly employed in combat', and its policy is based upon 'a desire to eradicate the image of Japan as a militaristic nation making profit from wars'.[48] Similar policies (although without the taint of the Second World War) are followed by Canada, Sweden and Switzerland. West Germany is somewhat of an anomaly: its declared policy appears 'Japanese'; its volume of exports and actual policies appear more 'French'. Poland and Czechoslovakia throughout the 1970s and 1980s pursued 'French' policies within the limits established by the Warsaw Pact, although in early 1990 the new Czech government announced that it was immediately ending arms exports.[49]

In France, both arms production and arms exports are conducted with the integral participation of state agencies. The Délégation générale pour l'armement (DGA) was created in 1961 as the umbrella organisation under which all production is monitored. One branch, the Délégué aux relations internationales (DRI), works closely with corporations to promote the varied products. It 'plays a key role in discovering prospective clients, facilitating their contact with French arms manufacturers ... cueing French arms makers to the possibilities of foreign sales, organizing the contractual, financial and credit terms for arms sales, and providing administrative support'.[50] A special government committee, the Comité interministériel pour l'études des exportations de matériels de guerre (CIEEMG), which includes representatives from the Defence, Economic and Foreign Affairs Ministries, makes final sales decisions, reports directly to the Prime Minister and is the forum for any debate. However, this committee is effectively subordinated to the DRI and only reviews requests from firms to export weapons; it does not initiate sales as a matter of policy. Thus although the government is involved in a complex web of public–private sector relations covering all aspects of arms exports, sales are initiated primarily on a bureaucratic or commercial level, not a political one.

British policy towards arms sales is similar, although it is more secretive about the dimensions of its trade and does not disclose the details of its deals with individual clients. An annual official figure for defence sales has been published since 1968, but:

> no attempt is made to claim that the figures are accurate and no indication of their significance is ventured ... it is not clarified if [these figures] include receipts, orders, deliveries or progress payments; nor is it stated what categories of defence equipment are included or excluded ... nor is it known whether the figures for one year are calculated on the same basis as the next.[51]

Sales promotion is conducted by the Defence Exports Sales Organisation (DESO), established in 1966, but unlike France, Britain's arms industry has clearer lines of demarcation between the private and public sector (bidding for contracts, for example, is done on a more competitive basis). Policy is decided by an Arms Working Party, an interdepartmental committee chaired by the Foreign Office that makes most routine sales decisions. Difficult decisions are referred to a Cabinet Committee, which again suggests that the political implications of sales enter the process after commercial decisions.[52] In practice, the Ministry of Defence is the dominant actor in arms sales decisions. Although elected officials do enter the decision-making process, their role is more to lend credence and weight to the pursuit of deals, as was the case with India and Saudi Arabia.[53]

The political and military considerations governing current British and French policy are thus weak, and act only as brakes on possible excesses rather than as positive justifications for exports. This is a clear change since the 1950s, during which time both states attempted to use arms transfers and military aid as positive tools of influence with small but active programmes of military aid based on a residual perception of their first-tier status.[54] Britain's perception of its first-tier status was reflected in its stated policy on arms exports: in 1955 a government White Paper that noted that 'the general policy of H.M. government on the sale of arms is primarily governed by political and strategic considerations: only when these have been satisfied are economic considerations – i.e., the contribution of arms sales to export earnings – taken into account'.[55] In France, arms exports were also until the 1960s 'primarily influenced by strategic and foreign policy considerations', connected with the Gaullist vision.[56]

But this primacy of political motivations did not last beyond the 1960s in either Britain or France. By 1970 official French policy deliberately eschewed the seeking of political benefits vis-à-vis client states, and 'arms were treated like any other good or service that could ... enhance public welfare'.[57] As Defence Minister Michel Debré stated, France 'does not set any political conditions, as certain powers do, in selling its arms'.[58] Further, despite frequent assertions that French arms sales were carefully controlled and governed by political and military considerations (such as helping clients to ensure their self-defence and guarantee autonomy from the superpowers), the breaching of embargoes, non-suspension of contracts when conflicts have erupted and violation of end-use clauses allow one to question what, if any, restrictions had been applied in practice.[59] An example of where the locus of power rested was France's desire to maintain good commercial relations with Argentina after the Falklands/Malvinas War. Although an embargo was instituted when the conflict began, transfers of aircraft and Exocet missiles resumed in November 1982 and there were allegations that the embargo had been broken.[60] Other examples would include France's reluctance to join the United Nations embargo on arms sales to South Africa (finally adhered to in 1977), its embargo on arms sales to Israel in 1969 (after pressure from Middle Eastern oil suppliers), and the promotion of sales to oil suppliers.[61] What one ought to conclude from this is *not* that successive French governments have ignored entirely the political implications of arms transfers (as in some cases they have clearly played a role), but rather only that political benefits to France are accorded a low priority in decision making on arms transfers.

The British appear to have tempered their sales policy with political considerations only slightly more frequently than the French: embargoes (formal or informal) were placed on exports to Chile (temporarily after 1973), India and Pakistan (during the 1965 war), Uganda (under Amin), South Africa and Taiwan.[62] Britain also does not justify its transfers for the military benefits they may produce; the last such debate was over continuing arms sales to South Africa as a means of defending the Cape shipping lanes.[63] Thus in general Britain follows a policy of 'commercial pragmatism': weapons sales have no strings attached, an end-use requirement is not a normal part of contracts and 'sales are rarely portrayed now as instruments of an active foreign policy'.[64]

Spain and Italy have until recently been equally aggressive participants in the arms transfer system, placing few prima facie restrictions on their exports. Italian exports have been dominated by commercial considerations, although Italy attempted to implement new regulations following several questionable sales to Iran and Iraq in the early 1980s.[65] The ensuing political struggle pitched those opposed to all exports against those wishing to adopt policies and a promotional apparatus on the French model; the struggle culminated in a 1990 legislative proposal that was decidedly liberal, and that accelerated the export approval process.[66] Spain likewise has an open export policy that bans deliveries to a few specific countries and 'zones of conflict'; deliveries to Iran and Iraq during their war illustrate the laxity of such policies.[67]

The legal apparatus for controlling arms exports is often a poor guide to the actual intent of policy. French arms exports, for example, are controlled by restrictions that include a prohibition on the supply of arms to belligerents in open conflict, a refusal to sell weapons that can be used for repression to countries engaged in it, and caution over the transfer of high-technology weapons.[68] British exports are prohibited to states that post a direct threat to British security and are under a UN embargo (or other such special circumstance); they are also intended not to upset regional stability, be used for internal repression, threaten British dependencies or undermine Britain's multilateral arms control policies.[69] Neither Italy nor Spain has a clear policy framework for arms exports, although there is an expressed intention to follow NATO restrictions on technology transfers and Western embargoes. In all cases actual transfers often belie these policies.

Many of the smaller second-tier suppliers have followed the Japanese approach and adopted formally 'restrictive' arms export policies, the characteristic feature of which is 'that arms are not supplied to countries where this may, directly or indirectly, involve the supplier in a local or international conflict'.[70] In Sweden and Switzerland, restrictions are the logical concomitant of a neutral stance that shuns involvement in areas of conflict and interprets 'conflict' fairly rigorously (although pressure has increased in Sweden for an easing of export restrictions).[71] Canada's close integration with the American defence market has allowed it to maintain a restrictive policy on transfers without necessarily sacrificing arms production.[72] Since again legal strictures do not always reflect actual practice, the best test of restrictive policies is a counterfactual: could these states sell their defence products more widely if a more liberal policy were adopted? In the Japanese case the answer is clearly 'yes': one Japanese study concluded in 1982 that were Japan to participate fully in the arms trade, it would corner 40 per cent of the defence electronics, 60 per cent of the ship-building and 25–30 per cent of the aerospace markets.[73] The answer is more ambiguous for the other restrictive suppliers, in part because the small size of their production base may make their arms uncompetitive. The relatively low share of exports from these states that has been destined for the developing world (or for regions such as the Middle East) suggests, however, that they at least deliberately forwent these markets.

The West German situation acutely illustrates the dilemmas facing all second-tier producers and highlights the economic and techno-logical forces at work. Legal strictures and sensitivity to the taint of arms exports resulted in a restrictive policy and the establishment of an extensive 'munitions list' that required licensing of all potential military exports.[74] The policy was designed to prevent transfers to 'areas of tension' and to avoid politically sensitive transfers. These concerns also prevented the establishment of a government-sanctioned sales promotion agency equivalent to that of Britain or France and meant that neither political leverage and influence nor potential military benefits have been (since the 1960s) a factor in German arms export decisions. In practice, however, the policy has operated on a case-by-case approach, which has resulted in various pressures being placed on what began as a strict restraint policy.

These pressures progressively eroded the underlying desire to exercise restraint from about the mid 1970s, as defence producers began to argue the case for the economic benefits derived from arms exports and as irregular procurement cycles threatened the develop-ment of an advanced defence industrial base.[75] As a consequence the policy was weakened in degrees: veto power over exports of co-produced weapons was relinquished, the concept of 'areas of tension' was deleted from the restraint policy (in 1982), and Asian states were permitted to buy German weapons. The long-standing pressure from unions and industry groups to sell the Leopard II tank to Saudi Arabia, which sparked a major debate before being finally refused in 1986, indicated how far restraint had been eroded. Recent scandals involv-ing military technology sales to Libya and Iraq have, however, resulted in a tightening of export regulations since 1989.[76] Probably the greatest breach in the restraint policy, however, was in co-production and licensed production (which represent a large part of the German industry), as government guidelines concluded that participation in these projects was more important than export control. For example, in 1983 the German government waived the right to veto sales of Tornado aircraft to Saudi Arabia, even though

German firms hold a 42 per cent interest in the plane and the previous government had refused the sale.[77] Other major co-production projects include surface-to-air missiles (with France), helicopters (assembled in Spain), and tanks (licensed to Argentina, but with a German engine). The missiles have appeared in Syria and the helicopters in Iraq, although neither of these transfers would be likely to pass German export guidelines.[78] Thus, although Germany's special political position has acted as a brake on arms exports, the economic imperatives that face all second-tier producers have progressively made their presence felt.

The majority of analysts have argued that the restrictive suppliers are also experiencing a similar evolution in policy, which would lead one to project an inevitable 'commercialisation' of the arms market. In Japan, for example, industry groups have long pressed for a relaxation of restraints, and the legal regime contains many loopholes.[79] But the fact that similar economic imperatives have been linked to different political responses indicates that economic considerations do not deterministically shape the choices of decision makers. Likewise, it is a mistake to search for a particular balance struck between political and economic incentives, as if the two were somehow equivalent. It is more productive to regard the economic imperatives to export arms as *structural* constraints that limit the 'agency' that policy makers can possess, irrespective of their intentions (or the political pressures they face). Political considerations are the product of a complex concatenation of historical and social factors, and Herbert Wulf's conclusion on the German case, that the economic imperatives behind 'the global military system inevitably but almost inadvertently produce[s] an export-oriented arms manufacturing system', is not necessarily generalisable to all second-tier producers (although its underlying point is correct).[80]

## The restructuring of European defence production

A high level of arms exports is not the only means by which to resolve the dilemma created by rising unit costs and shorter production runs that second-tier arms producers face. Three other possible solutions have received increased attention since the mid 1980s, at least among the European NATO members: collaborative development and production of advanced weapons, coordinated procurement policies and rationalised and restructured defence industrial sectors. Although *ad hoc* efforts under all these headings have been undertaken since the 1960s, 'the accumulation of economic pressures and the evolution of a new political climate in Western Europe are . . . beginning to create the conditions in which a more comprehensive system of European cooperation may be developing'.[81] The literature on the nature and evolution of this cooperation is vast, and a full examination of this topic is not germane to this study.[82] What is important to note, however, is how this cooperation reflects the operation of the same underlying forces that created and reinforced the need for high levels of arms exports from second-tier states.

The initial impetus behind coordinated procurement was NATO's desire to match the much more integrated Warsaw Pact forces by imposing greater standardisation and interoperability on its array of incompatible weapons systems.[83] But decision makers realised that strict adherence to military requirements and the acquisition of lowest-cost weapons (i.e. some form of free market competition in procurement) would almost inevitably result either in American domination of NATO procurement or in the emergence (through industrial restructuring) of monopolistic pan-European producers. The latter solution would require a geographically restricted free market and essentially create a quasi-autarkic European defence industrial base on the scale of a first-tier producer (or at least one of about half the size). Both solutions acknowledge the inability of second-tier producers to maintain autonomous national production at the technological frontier without adopting the scale of production required to compete internationally.[84]

But growing recognition of the economic imperatives surrounding modern arms production does not mean that a continentalist solution will be adopted. The same considerations that generated autonomous national production and arms exports have intervened to link coordinated procurement to cooperative weapons development according to the principle of *juste retour*, which shares development and production tasks among participating states according to their proportion of investment and procurement.[85] The hallmark projects in this regard are the Tornado multi-role combat aircraft and the Eurofighter (the former a German, British and Italian effort, with Spain joining these three for the latter), although projects for the collaborative development of missiles, helicopters, frigates, radars and other aircraft have all been undertaken.

This tension between pan-European market integration and national protection is reflected in what is perhaps the most important official statements on this issue, the study report prepared in 1986 for NATO's Independent European Programme Group (IEPG) and subsequent action plan adopted in 1988. The report simultaneously advocated removing 'obstacles which restrict free trade' while agreeing that the 'maintenance and development of the industrial base and national technologies will remain a national priority'.[86] These contradictory impulses, plus the fact that the political oversight, management and sponsorship of these activities is being conducted under several (and often competing) auspices, strongly suggests that some combination of national and continental policies is most likely to evolve in Europe.[87] In all cases, attention will be paid to the threat of American domination.

Two observations are most significant for the arms transfer system, however. First, collaborative arms development and coordinated procurement among European producers is merely an extension of arms export strategies. The leap from arms transfers that already include technology transfers or production offsets to fully shared production is small: technology, production and R&D costs are simply divided on a more formal and explicit basis (between relative equals), in return for which a larger and more stable market for the final product is guaranteed. Thus only the emergence of a genuinely integrated pan-European arms production and procurement market would undermine the need for continued high levels of second-tier exports, either among second-tier states or outside.

Second, all outcomes are still 'second-best' choices to the preferred strategy of subsidised autonomous national production and exports, for they involve serious compromises in national decision-making autonomy that are still anathema to most producers. Confirmation of this comes from several angles. First, cooperation appears necessary only after declines in exports to the developing world in the 1980s, increased competition from other suppliers and continuing increases in the cost of weapons have essentially exhausted the gains to be achieved from high levels of exports. Second, the benefits of collaboration are often less substantial than they first appear, as economies of scale are not fully realised because of inevitable duplication and excess bureaucracy.[88] Third, military requirements must also often be compromised in cooperative procurement. The withdrawal of states from high-profile projects also belies the rhetoric of cooperation and underlines the continued strength of national imperatives.[89] Finally, industrial restructuring has proceeded initially on a national level, with little genuinely transnational integration of production appearing until after single national prime contractors for major weapons systems (such as British Aerospace, Saab-Scania, Thomson-CSF and MBB-Daimler Benz) have emerged. Restructuring is also driven by the industrial over-capacities that arise from the pursuit of autarkic defence production.[90] Whatever the outcome, these choices all demonstrate that the advance of technology and the evolution of the arms production and transfer system have meant that leading second-tier suppliers can no longer maintain independent, across-the-board, production of sophisticated weapons.

## Conclusion

It is clear from the above discussion that economic considerations are the primary motive forces that shape second-tier states' participation in the global arms transfer system. That this receives explicit confirmation in the policy statements of leading second-tier producers should come as no surprise. In France, the aggressive pursuit of exports rests on a consensus on maintaining an independent and self-reliant foreign policy that 'guarantee[s] the material base of an autonomous defence and . . . extend[s] the influence of France in Europe and the world'.[91] The 1972 White Paper on Defence spelled this out:

> Our military industrial policy should . . . guarantee the realization, today and tomorrow, of the arms programs which the [nation's] defense needs . . . it is necessary . . . to maintain and modernize an industrial potential which assures us in the area of armament a sufficient independence in order that the effectiveness of our defense is not tributary to foreign industrial constraints which would compromise our liberty of decision.[92]

British policy also emphasises the economic benefits of arms sales, and of these, 'the most important area . . . does not lie in employment or even in the balance of payments situation, but in maintaining the technology [that we have] in this country'.[93]

These economic forces affect policy making in a special way. They do not enter directly as macro-economic considerations such as easing the balance of payments or recovering costs, as these benefits have proved uncertain.[94] Rather competition in technological and industrial development (the pursuit of wealth as defined in chapter 1) rears its head as the motive driving second-tier suppliers, as it did in the earlier waves of the arms transfer system. This competition forces a choice between independence and technological achievement that does not exist for first-tier producers, which in turn acts as a structural constraint on second-tier decision making. It does not dictate the precise contours of policy, but restricts the range of possible responses, as the ultimate choice made by a state depends on a host of other factors. The policies of the restrictive suppliers demonstrate that states are free to sacrifice the quest for independence in the pursuit of other motives. In a paradoxical way, the impossibility of achieving meaningful independent arms production for states such as Canada or Switzerland has increased their margin of manoeuvre in policy making, while condemning them to fall from second-tier status.

It now ought to be possible to draw the line between second-tier and other producers more distinctly and to explain more clearly how this analysis fits with the model sketched in chapter 1. By the most rigid criterion, the ability to produce indigenously a full range of weapons at or near the existing technological frontier, only three states would qualify as second-tier: France, Britain and (possibly) Germany. This would be unduly restrictive, however, for two reasons. First, even these states depend to some degree on key inputs from other producers: in the 1980s about one-third of the value added in French arms production was imported, and between 10 and 30 per cent of the Tornado fighter is imported from the United States (depending on the model).[95] Second, one of the main identifying features of second-tier status is the ability to *reproduce* technologies, which does not require complete self-reliance.

Thus, for example, Sweden's inability to design a jet engine for its newest fighter ought not automatically to disqualify it from the second tier, as Sweden does possess the ability to produce an engine under licence and to adapt it to its own needs, demonstrating a significant (although not total) degree of autonomy. Admitting producers such as Sweden to the second tier requires that one invoke another threshold criterion: the ability to manufacture (independently or with imported components in an independent design) a wide range of modern weapons. Producers such as Sweden and Italy meet this standard, but below the Swedish or Italian threshold, however, the claims to second-tier status of producers such as Belgium, Switzerland or Canada are increasingly suspect, as they possess only a specialised and limited production capability, have no meaningful design independence in major systems, and play a declining role in the arms transfer system.[96] Producers such as Czechoslovakia or Poland have also probably lost (or are losing) their temporarily prominent niche in the global arms transfer system.[97]

Although a certain degree of unavoidable ambiguity remains because the evolution of the system and the continuing diffusion of technology mean that producers such as Spain and Italy have probably not reached their final position in the hierarchy, the outline of the evolutionary path of second-tier production is clear. From the early 1950s until the 1960s, the leading second-tier producers could make a credible, but inevitably short-lived, claim to first-tier status as long as competition was low and high levels of exports compensated for declining domestic procurement. This was followed by a period in which autonomous national production of advanced systems was sustained by the export of increasingly sophisticated systems, and lesser second-tier producers emerged. But this period too was ephemeral, and these producers were forced to export their arms-making technology (which will be documented in chapter 7) and then abandon the quest for independent national production of the most advanced systems.

The economic pressures that manifest themselves as the system matured and technology evolved now dictate that a new balance be struck between production on the scale of first-tier states and preservation of national independence, especially as leading second-tier producers are forced to initiate a new round of catch-up as the technologies listed in table 6 come into production. Thus the future portends a strategic alliance between leading second-tier producers willing to accept some dilution of national autonomy as long as they remain dominant partners (France, Britain, Germany and Japan) and lesser producers (Italy, Spain, possibly Sweden) who are willing to sacrifice independence in pursuit of the technological grail. The remaining producers will either opt out (through increasing specialisation) or be forced out of the second tier.

All of this presages a continued large role for arms exports. If second-tier suppliers attempted to control the supply pipeline to major recipients, they would have to reduce and specialise their defence industries, accept higher weapons procurement costs, and abandon competition in advanced technology with the superpowers. These unpalatable choices make restraint unlikely. The results of the most recent French attempts to exercise some restraint illustrate the outcome. In the early years of François Mitterrand's presidency, he promised to reduce exports to colonial, fascist or racist states and ordered offensive weapons to be removed from the Paris Air Show. But when opening the next Air Show in 1983 (complete with offensive weapons), Mitterrand admitted that 'since 1981, I have dealt with the French nation in its true reality. Our striving for national independence is supported by the army and the defence [establishment] who need the means to [carry out their missions]. And to have the means, we need access to foreign markets.'[98]

# 7 DEPENDENT PRODUCTION AND EXPORTS IN THE THIRD TIER

## The rise of third-tier arms producers

Third-tier states are fundamentally motivated to produce arms by a desire to escape or ameliorate their subordinate position in the global arms transfer and production system. Although they are not completely powerless, the scale of the effort they can mount and their status as late entrants in the market condemns most of them to be frustrated in this quest. An examination of the evolution of third-tier arms production and exports through the contemporary period confirms both the imperfections in the process of technological diffusion and the evolutionary pattern of the global arms transfer and production system that was sketched in chapter 1. Third-tier producers can be identified by one of three criteria:

(a) they can only produce weapons at a level of sophistication far below the existing technological frontier.
(b) the sophisticated weapons that they can produce are restricted to only one or two weapons systems.
(c) they remain dependent upon imports of critical sophisticated subsystems, and little or no transfer of the knowledge required to go beyond the simple reproduction or copying of weapons occurs.

Although for the moment all arms-producing states in the developing world will be treated as members of the third tier, these criteria will allow a more subtle and dynamic picture to be drawn eventually that would allow for some (albeit rare) movement between tiers and that could elevate the potential status of some producers in the developing world.

Arms production on a limited scale spread beyond the industrialised states relatively early in the post-1945 period. The output of the

153

only serious early producers (Argentina, Egypt, India, China and North Korea) was limited to ship-building and small arms.[1] In Argentina, the industry expanded upon a production base that had existed since the 1930s. In Egypt, China and India, considerable help was obtained (especially in the nascent aircraft industry) from German engineers and specialists; China also began manufacturing Soviet-licensed weapons systems during this period. These early efforts were devoted to meeting domestic demands for arms, not to the export market, as large surpluses of Second World War weapons were then on offer. Most efforts were based entirely on imported Second World War technologies and did not thrive or even survive in the same form beyond the 1950s, with the major exception of China.

Between the late 1950s and the early 1970s important new efforts to produce modern arms were undertaken in Israel, South Africa, India and Brazil. The first three states were motivated by the pursuit of victory in war (perhaps better understood in these cases as the more defensive 'pursuit of security') in the face of uncertain arms supplies and continuing conflicts, while Brazil was driven by the pursuit of regional power and hegemony. None of these efforts were expressly designed to provide a large export capacity, and they concentrated at the outset on only a few types of weapons: simple aircraft, naval vessels, artillery and vehicles. Chinese arms production also began its involuntary drive for self-sufficiency after the Sino-Soviet split isolated China from its most important source of technology. Reverse engineering of weapons was consequently a major source of innovation and advance in Chinese arms production.[2]

Arms production in Israel began seriously in 1956, when licences were purchased from France for aircraft components, electronics and ammunition.[3] This progressed to include naval construction, expanded missile and tank production (and modification), and development of the indigenously designed Kfir fighter based on French blueprints and an American engine. After the 1967 war and France's subsequent decision to stop supplying weapons and technology, Israel shifted to arms production based on American designs and components and intensified its efforts to guarantee continued supplies of weapons. In the South African case, anticipation of the 1963 and 1964 United Nations' resolutions prohibiting exports of weapons and arms-manufacturing technology to South Africa triggered an intense effort in the early 1960s to secure military technologies. In 1961 alone, 127 licences for arms production were secured, and although there was little arms production in South Africa before the embargo, between 1963 and 1977 South Africa was able to purchase designs and licences to produce virtually all types of weapons systems.[4] Most of the technology was obtained from France, Italy and other European producers. As a result, by 1972 the Ministry of Defence could claim that South Africa was 'absolutely self-sufficient with regard to internal needs'.[5] In spite of numerous evasions of the embargo, it has, however, limited South Africa's capability to produce more sophisticated weapons.

India was motivated to expand its arms production base in the 1960s by its rivalries and wars with China and Pakistan, its bid for regional hegemony and political independence, and its desire for technological advancement.[6] Arms technology for licensed production was obtained from Britain (for tank, aircraft and ship construction), West Germany and the Soviet Union (for aircraft). In the late 1960s and early 1970s Brazilian arms production also accelerated, driven also by the quest for regional hegemony and technological progress. The drive for self-reliant arms production was boosted in 1968 and 1977, when the United States first cut military aid and then criticised Brazil's human rights record, resulting in Brazil's abrogation of its military assistance agreement. As Brazil's former Air Force Minister noted in 1977, 'the time has come to free ourselves from the United States and the countries of Europe. It is a condition of security that each nation manufacture its own armaments.'[7] This defence-industrialisation drive, when coupled with a strong export orientation and an emphasis on the technological factor in economic development, ensured Brazil's rapid rise in the ranks of both producers and exporters. Technology was obtained from a variety of mostly West European sources. But despite the rhetoric of self-reliance in both states, progress towards indigenous production was slow, and many setbacks or failures were experienced.[8]

In the 1970s a great expansion of third-tier arms production efforts occurred, as more states began producing arms and a greater variety of weapons systems were tackled. Prominent new (or rising) producers included North and South Korea, Taiwan and Egypt. Tanks, various missile systems, major naval vessels, helicopters and a variety of aircraft projects were launched (see table 21 below). Most of these were based upon first-generation post-1945 technologies, and none were at the forefront of existing weaponry. The technology to support these efforts was obtained from many sources, but what united all efforts was a desire to use the technology transfer process to create increasingly independent arms production. This was usually formalised in contracts that specified the way in which (and pace at which) technology was to be transferred. The 1961 agreement to produce the

Indian Vijayanta tank from the original British Vickers Mk1 was proto-typical: the first forty tanks were British-made, but the tank was then to be assembled and later manufactured in India. By 1980 India claimed that the tank was 95 per cent indigenously produced (although, as will be seen below, this did not reflect the same degree of independence).[9] Although even the most advanced third-tier producers have not achieved self-sufficiency, their ability to resist supplier pressure or cope with supply restrictions has been increased by a capacity to produce at least some weapons and components.[10]

South Korean and Taiwanese efforts relied almost exclusively on American technology, and their expansion of production in the 1970s was a direct result of a perceived weakening of the American security umbrella.[11] The most sophisticated projects that were undertaken (the American F-5 aircraft and assorted armoured vehicles) incorporated essentially 1960s technology and little genuine technology transfer. In the late 1980s more ambitious efforts were undertaken (especially in South Korea) as the advancing industrial sector was able to support more sophisticated production of such items as armoured vehicles and rocket launchers.[12] North Korean arms production was driven by the industrialisation and quest for self-sufficiency that followed the Korean War, and all necessary technology was obtained from the Soviet Union. Its production base does not appear to have progressed significantly from the levels reached in the early 1970s.

Egyptian efforts to build a modern arms industry date from 1948, when the war with Israel highlighted the urgency of expanding arms production.[13] By the early 1960s, minimal capabilities in ammunition, armoured vehicles and missile production had been created, but production depended upon imports of crucial components and technology.[14] In the early 1970s these efforts took on new momentum with the establishment of the Arab Organisation for Industrialisation (AOI), which pooled Saudi Arabian and Gulf capital and Egyptian labour and plant to secure joint ventures and co-production agreements with Western (primarily European) firms to produce jet fighters, missiles and vehicles.[15] Egypt pursued its efforts after the dissolution of the AOI in 1979 (as a consequence of the Egyptian–Israeli peace), and licences to assemble Mirage fighters, surface-to-air missiles and the American M-1 tank were obtained.[16] The shortage of capital for new projects, however, has meant that Egypt's efforts have had only limited success, and production is mainly limited to assembly, component production or low-technology items. Egypt's future progress in all likelihood depends upon the recreation of the AOI under some other guise.

156

All statistics concerning third-tier arms production ought to be treated with the greatest caution, although some order of magnitude figures can be offered. The data in table 20 estimate that production (under licence or indigenous) of major weapons systems in the developing world (excluding China) rose from $3 million in 1950 to $1,147 million (constant 1975 dollars) by 1984. These figures are trend indicators and do not reflect total production as they include only major weapons systems (fighter aircraft, helicopters, missiles, battle tanks and major fighting ships), which few developing states could produce until recently. Other estimates of total military production in the developing world are higher. One has it increasing from roughly $2,500 million in 1970 to $6,170 million in 1980, with a projection for 1990 of $11,000 million.[17] This confirms the roughly four-fold increase in the value of third-tier arms production between 1970 and 1990. The snapshot estimate of total production offered in chapter 4 (also presented in more detail in table 24) is even higher: it places third-tier arms production at between $16,000 and $23,000 million a year in the mid 1980s. (The gap between the figures in table 20 and the other estimates is not as large as it first appears. If production of other developing world states (especially China) is included and figures are converted to current dollars, then 1984 production of major weapons would be at least $5,000 million. Much of the remaining difference could be accounted for by production of non-major weapons.)

This expansion of production has been accompanied by an increase in the number of states producing major weapons systems from 3 in 1965 to 11 in 1984.[18] Table 21 provides an overview of the expansion of third-tier arms production of major weapons systems, although without providing details on the sophistication of the systems produced. It suggests a relatively even distribution across weapons systems, although when one includes non-major systems a clear hierarchy of production appears, with 24 states able to build ships (major and minor vessels), 13, aircraft, 8, missiles and 7, tanks and armoured vehicles.[19]

The precise ranking for third-tier arms producers is difficult to determine exactly, but an approximate descending order of the top 10 would be: China, Israel, India, Yugoslavia, Brazil, South Africa, South Korea, Taiwan, Argentina and Turkey (see table 24 below).[20] These top 10 states account for probably about 85 per cent of third-tier arms production, although about 20 other states produce some weapons, usually either small arms and ammunition or simple licensed or co-produced systems. Among these 10, one finds great variability in the sophistication of the weapons they produce and breadth of

Table 20. *Value of production of major weapons systems in the developing world (constant million 1975 US dollars)*

| Year | Indigenous production | Licensed production | Total |
|---|---|---|---|
| 1950 | 2 | 1 | 3 |
| 1955 | 6 | — | 6 |
| 1960 | 11 | — | 11 |
| 1965 | 33 | 34 | 67 |
| 1970 | 92 | 182 | 274 |
| 1975 | 349 | 298 | 647 |
| 1980 | 470 | 510 | 980 |
| 1984 | 635 | 512 | 1,147 |

*Note:* The People's Republic of China, Yugoslavia and Turkey are not included in these statistics. The People's Republic of China's annual arms production alone would double or triple the total figures.
*Source:* Brzoska and Ohlson, *Arms Production*, 8. Production is defined as indigenous when the 'essential stage of development of a certain weapon or weapons system has been carried out in the country'.

Table 21. *Number of third-tier states producing major weapons, various years*

| Weapons system | 1965–9 | 1970–4 | 1975–9 | 1980–4 |
|---|---|---|---|---|
| Fighters | 2 | 5 | 6 | 8 |
| Helicopters | 2 | 4 | 6 | 6 |
| Missiles | 2 | 4 | 7 | 7 |
| Battle tanks | 1 | 1 | 3 | 6 |
| Major naval craft | 1 | 4 | 5 | 6 |

*Source:* Brzoska and Ohlson, *Arms Production*, 23.

production they have striven for, and the way in which they participate in the arms transfer system. Rather than presenting detailed examinations of specific cases, however, this chapter will concentrate on two issues that unite them and that confirm the overall role of third-tier production in the global transfer and production system: their continued dependence on technology from first- and second-tier suppliers, and their inability to move beyond a relatively low level of sophistication in production.

## Patterns of third-tier arms exports

This increase in production has been paralleled by a similar, albeit less dramatic, increase in exports from third-tier suppliers, with the two most significant periods of expansion occurring in the early 1970s and mid 1980s. Many new producers, observing the failed efforts of the previous two decades, concluded that an arms production base could only be maintained with an export-based industry. None of the early production efforts in North Korea, Argentina, South Africa and Egypt bore long-term fruit, and although there were many reasons for this, the absence of exports (and concomitant inability to make production lines economically viable) doubtless played some role. States such as Brazil and Israel, by contrast, in the early 1970s coupled their drive towards domestic production with the realisation that 'production itself could only be economically viable if there were weapons markets other than the Brazilian armed forces'.[21] In the 1980s exports were given another boost by the expansion of arsenals that followed the 1978 oil price increases and by the demand for arms for the Iran–Iraq War. Unlike the first period of expansion, these factors were much more ephemeral.

According to the United States Arms Control and Disarmament Agency figures presented in table 22, third-tier states' exports increased from $365 million in 1963 to $1,316 million in 1975 and a high of $6,779 million in 1984 (constant 1988 dollars). The most recent data (which are probably not complete) suggest that third-tier arms exports declined to $5,525 million in 1988. These recent totals are roughly consistent with the figures in table 24 below, which estimate developing world arms exports at between $4,700 and $6,000 million annually in the mid 1980s. In addition, the number of third-tier states that export arms has increased from 14 in 1963–6 to 25 in 1987–8, which means that almost all new suppliers are in the third tier (it should be noted, however, that many of these states are only retransferring weapons). The third-tier proportion of total transfers has also increased, although not quite in a linear fashion. But the relatively consistent increase in these figures creates at least a prima facie suspicion that this represents not an ephemeral conjunction of circumstances, but a durable shift (as in many other production sectors) of arms-manufacturing and industrial capability to the developing world.

Several characteristics of exports from these states that are not conveyed by these statistics should be noted. First, a large proportion of the increase in third-tier exports is accounted for by the increased

159

Table 22. *Developing world arms exports (constant million 1988 US dollars)*

| Year | Value | % of world total |
|------|-------|------------------|
| 1963 | 365   | 3.2  |
| 1966 | 647   | 4.2  |
| 1969 | 468   | 2.7  |
| 1972 | 2,361 | 9.0  |
| 1975 | 1,316 | 4.9  |
| 1978 | 2,131 | 4.8  |
| 1981 | 3,748 | 6.6  |
| 1984 | 6,779 | 11.5 |
| 1987 | 5,036 | 9.0  |
| 1988 | 5,525 | 11.4 |

*Note:* Includes major and minor weapons systems. The figures for 1972 are unusually high because of large Chinese arms sales that year.
*Source:* ACDA, *WMEAT*, various years.

activities of one or two producers. The number of third-tier producers of any importance remains small, and some (such as India, Taiwan and South Africa) have almost no exports. The most important third-tier exporters are China, Brazil, Israel, Egypt, North Korea and Yugoslavia, and probably between 50 and 60 per cent of third-tier transfers are accounted for by the first three states. Although other states that are not major exporters have attempted (or are attempting) to increase their exports (including Argentina, South Korea and India), many of these projects can be described as rather unrealistic 'schemes for glory', few of which will succeed in an increasingly competitive market.[22] Second, the vast bulk of the arms transferred are relatively unsophisticated or uncomplicated weapons such as small arms, ammunition, armoured vehicles, light fighters or naval craft, areas in which first- and second-tier sellers do not necessarily have a comparative advantage. Third, most of the customers for these arms are also less wealthy states in the developing world or states that otherwise have difficulty obtaining weapons from first- and second-tier suppliers (such as Iran and Iraq during their war). Finally, these data (the best available) unfortunately cover the mid 1980s, a period when the global arms market was artificially stimulated by the Iran–Iraq War. This conflict provided an unanticipated boost to third-tier industries because of the partial embargoes under which both combatants laboured. Subsequent figures indicate a near-collapse in arms exports for some major suppliers such as Brazil (and even for producers such as France).[23]

The picture of export and production capabilities presented by the

Table 23. *A comparison of arms transfer data for selected third-tier suppliers, mid 1980s*

|  | Independent sources | ACDA figures |
|---|---|---|
| China | 1,000–1,500 | 1,292 |
| Israel | 750–1,000 | 478[a] |
| South Africa | 40 | 27 |
| Brazil | 500–1,000 | 400 |
| South Korea | 250 | 222 |
| Argentina | 200– 400 | 62 |
| Egypt | 500 | 103 |
| Pakistan | 30– 40 | 110[b] |
| North Korea | 500 | 333 |
| Singapore | 100– 25 | 23 |

*Notes:* [a] Perhaps the most extreme example is the contrast between Israel's officially reported figure of $1,470 million in exports in 1988, of which $400 went to the United States (*Jane's Defence Weekly* (24 June 1989)). ACDA (*WMEAT 1989*) reported exports of $140 million for that year.
[b] Pakistan's exports are inflated by a reported volume of $300 million in 1984.
*Sources:* Sources for column 1 are given in table 24 below. Column 2 from ACDA, *WMEAT 1988*, average figure for the 1984–6 period.

above statistics may also be inaccurate or unreliable because of poor data, weapons retransfers and value-added double counting. The first problem is confirmed by the contrasting estimates of exports from major third-tier suppliers provided in table 23, which compares official American figures to those provided by other sources. They suggest, unless other sources are always exaggerated, that the most widely used figures (those of the United States Arms Control and Disarmament Agency) may understate third-tier exports by as much as 100 per cent. The other two problems, although they are difficult to quantify, result in the opposite error, overstatements of third-tier production capabilities. In 1981, for example, Egypt earned $200 million as a commission on European arms transferred through it to Iraq, yet this was counted as 'arms sales' in the data; North Korean transfers of Chinese weapons to Iran appear to have been similarly conducted.[24] Sanctioned or unsanctioned transfers from existing stocks of weapons (such as Egyptian or North Korean transfers of Soviet arms) also occur. The third problem, overestimation of the actual domestic value-added in third-tier arms production because of the high level of imported components, is probably even more severe and more difficult to quantify, except in rare cases. Brazil's aircraft producer Embraer, perhaps the only major third-tier firm for which detailed information is available, acknowledged that the average import content of its aircraft production between 1985 and 1988 was 61 per cent, making its actual value-added production (and the consequent contribution to export earnings) much lower.[25]

## Motivations for third-tier arms production

What motivates a third-tier state to develop or maintain an independent arms production capability? If arms were traded as purely commercial goods and the pursuit of wealth were the only governing motivation, the pattern of production would correspond to the distribution of international comparative advantage, with perhaps different tiers of suppliers meeting the demands of different market segments. But the evidence suggests that other incentives are also at work. Among the possible motives that have been identified one finds the following:

(1) guarantee continued arms supplies to counter threats to security.
(2) provide a symbol or index of effective regional or international power.
(3) catalyse economic modernisation efforts.
(4) develop local skills and technologies.
(5) substitute for imports to save hard currency and improve the balance of payments.

One point upon which there is little disagreement is that the primary motivation behind the *initiation* of arms production is to reduce or eliminate dependence on uncertain and unreliable external sources of supply when faced with identifiable threats to security.[26] Evidence for this is the near-perfect relationship between a state's having been involved in a conflict and/or subjected to embargoes and its initiation of weapons production. All of the current major developing world arms producers (India, China, Brazil, Egypt, Israel, South Korea, South Africa, Chile, Argentina, Taiwan, Pakistan) have had significant restrictions placed on their ability to acquire weapons at various points in the past two decades.[27] The motivation of the pariah states and those producers who face direct military threats (Egypt, Israel, South Africa, Taiwan and South Korea in particular) is also clear.

This motivation falls under the rubric of the 'pursuit of victory in war', and can be understood as the natural response of states in potentially conflictive relationships, operating under the security dilemma in a self-help international system. Arms production is not initiated from the 'pursuit of wealth', for many of these states have demonstrated a preference for purchasing their security at less expense on the international market. Neither is it generally catalysed by the much broader 'pursuit of power', although (as will be seen) this factor is important in explaining both the outer limits of arms production capabilities and the motivations of some producers. But once the decision to initiate arms production is taken and entrenched as a canon of national policy, economic factors such as achieving viable production runs become important determinants of production and export policy. The scenario is on the surface similar to that of second-tier states, but the dilemmas are even more acute. Second-tier states wish to retain an autonomous high-technology and research and development capability, and possess the level of wealth, economic infrastructure and defence spending to make this possible. Third-tier states usually possess none of these, and most often simply want to keep their factories operating.

The critical evidence for determining if 'pursuit of wealth' considerations are important is whether arms production contributes positively or negatively to economic performance. Although this question has been legitimately posed to first- and second-tier producers (but not dealt with in this work), it has loomed larger in discussions on arms production in the developing world as a debate between those who argue that investment in arms production wastes scarce resources and those who argue that arms production can help catalyse economic development. A resolution to this debate could shed light on the motives driving arms production: if arms production is ultimately a net economic burden, pursuit of victory in war and pursuit of power considerations triumph over the pursuit of wealth.

Before we engage in this debate, an overview of the best estimates for the macro-economic impact of arms production in the developing world must be given. Table 24 presents the best available figures, although in many cases these figures are no better than rough (albeit educated) guesses and should be treated accordingly. On the one hand, figures for producers such as Argentina, India, Pakistan, Brazil and Israel almost certainly exclude resources devoted to nuclear weapons development programmes, which should technically be included as arms production. On the other, considerations of national prestige and domestic competition for scarce resources often result in the inflation of export and production figures. Brazil provides perhaps the most egregious example of this: a 1979 'study' estimated that production in more than 350 defence firms was worth

Table 24. *The economics of arms production for third-tier producers, mid 1980s*

| Country | Arms production (million US dollars) | Arms exports | % of production exported | % of total exports | Employment from arms production (thousands) | Employment from arms exports as % of manufacturing employment | Production as % of industrial output |
|---|---|---|---|---|---|---|---|
| China | 5,000–10,000 | 1,000–1,500 | 10–20 | 6–7 | 2,000–6,000 | 3.6–10.8 | 5.0–10.0 |
| India | 2,750 | 50 | 2 | Negligible | 280 | 4.5 | 6.3 |
| Israel | 2,000 | 750–1,000 | 30–35 | 15 | 90 | 30.0 | 49.7 |
| Yugoslavia | 1,000– 1,200 | 400 | 33 | 5 | 60 | 2.5 | 7.2 |
| South Africa | 1,000 | 40 | 4 | Negligible | 100 | 7.2 | 8.2 |
| Brazil | 600– 1,200 | 500–1,000 | 70–80 | 4 | 75 | 1.0 | 1.0– 2.0 |
| South Korea | 600 | 250 | 40 | 1 | 30 | 1.0 | 2.5 |
| Argentina | 500– 1,000 | 200– 400 | 20–40 | 2–4 | 60 | n/a | 1.0– 2.0 |
| Taiwan | 400– 800 | Negligible | Negligible | Negligible | 50 | n/a | n/a |
| Turkey | 500 | 60 | 10 | 4 | 50 | 6.0 | 3.8 |
| Egypt | 400– 500 | 500 | n/a | 16 | 75 | 4.4 | 11.8 |
| Pakistan | 400 | 30– 40 | 10–15 | 1 | 40 | 7.2 | 7.7 |
| North Korea | 200– 400 | 500 | n/a | 30 | 55 | 4.0 | n/a |
| Singapore | 200– 400 | 100– 125 | 30 | Negligible | 11 | 3.9 | 4.7– 9.4 |
| Greece | 100 | 50 | 70 | 1 | 20 | 12.7 | 1.8 |
| Other developing | 1,000 | 100– 600 | n/a | n/a | 80 | — | — |
| Total | 16,700–23,900 | 4,700–6,000 | — | — | 3,000–7,000 | — | — |

*Sources:* Sources for figures, except where otherwise noted, are the same as for table 10. Figures for arms production and arms exported cannot be used to calculate column 3. Employment estimates (except where noted) are from Brzoska and Ohlson, *Arms Production*, 22 and from the International Labour Office, *Year Book of Labour Statistics* (Geneva: ILO, 1986), 414–25. Exchange rates (where required) from International Institute of Strategic Studies, *Military Balance, 1985–1986* (London: IISS, 1985).

*Israel:* Figures from Brzoska, 'Third World arms control', 166.

*Turkey:* Employment figures from Brzoska and Ohlson, *Arms Transfers*, 101. Total production is estimated based on the employment figure and assuming a similar output per employee as Pakistan. Ömer Karasapan, 'Turkey's armaments industries', *Middle East Report*, 17:1 (January–February 1987), 27 reports 1985 arms exports of $400 million (much of which is small arms and ammunition), and more than 40,000 employees. No overall production figure is given, but a total of between $500 and $800 million would be reasonable.

*North Korea:* Percentage of manufacturing employment from Brzoska and Ohlson, *Arms Production*, 262.

*Singapore:* Employment figures in Bilveer Singh, 'ASEAN's arms industries: potential and limits', *Comparative Strategy*, 8:2 (1989), 255.

164

approximately $4,800 million, a figure that does not appear justified when the output of major firms is aggregated.[28]

There does not appear to be any consistent pattern in the macro-economic impact of third-tier arms production. The volume of production varies by a factor of ten, the percentage of production that is exported ranges from virtually zero to around 70 per cent, the position of arms exports in total exports is likewise variable, and the role of arms production in domestic manufacturing ranges between 1 and 50 per cent. No consistent correlation between total production and other factors is evident. This confirms one argument of this book: that the concept of third-tier production (or any classification system) must be justified in terms that do not depend on these sorts of indicators, and that the most important factors are technological (sophistication and depth of production capabilities). It also makes it extremely difficult to untangle the possible motives behind arms production.

Perhaps the most crucial figures that shed light on the macro-economic impact of arms production (and its relationship to economic development) are those of the last column. Unlike the second tier, there is no even distribution of arms production as a percentage of industrial production, but rather three distinct groups: the top 5 producers, for whom arms production is greater than about 6 per cent of industrial production; a middle group of 3 or 4 states (Brazil, Argentina, South Korea and probably Taiwan), for which arms production is less than 2.5 per cent of industrial output, and a bottom group of 3 states (Egypt, Pakistan and Singapore), for which arms production is again a significant industrial activity. It is not surprising that the largest producers have the highest proportion of industrial activity devoted to arms production, and the economic benefits for (and linkages to) the economy are probably strong enough to ensure that arms production is a stable activity. Arms production in the middle group, however, appears to be an enclave industrial activity of minor overall economic significance, which suggests that macro-economic benefits such as catalysing economic development are unlikely to be either important or realisable. The last group demonstrates a somewhat skewed industrial structure since its overall level of industrialisation is low and arms production is of great importance. These producers will have the greatest difficulties in advancing technologically, as the backward and forward linkages in the economy that are necessary to support increasingly sophisticated arms production are likely to be weak. The real measure of the importance of arms production for these states will only be measured via less tangible benefits such as technological progress or skill development, benefits that are unlikely to be realised by all third-tier producers when competition for markets is stiff.

The 1973 publication of Emile Benoit's study of the relationship between defence expenditures and economic growth started a continuing debate on the role of military production in the local economy.[29] The investment effort required to build an arms industry and the demands for procurement it creates can be regarded as allocative choices that exclude the achievement of other economic development goals. Although Benoit suggested there was no negative relationship between defence expenditures and economic growth, he also predicted that if states began to produce weapons, their economies would be adversely affected. As Nicole Ball notes, if 'military-related investment ... occur[s] at the expense of more productive civil-sector investment, or encourage[s] an overly heavy emphasis on capital-intensive techniques of production', it might 'ultimately reduce the growth potential of the economy'.[30]

Three possible motives for production, all falling under the pursuit of wealth, are under scrutiny here: saving foreign exchange, catalysing economic modernisation and developing local skills and technologies. In practice, however, indigenous production of arms above the most basic level of sophistication in third-tier states has turned out to be more expensive than imports of the same item. If much of this money were spent in the local economy, a higher price would not be problematic, but the evidence suggests that the import of components and subsystems for indigenous production may drain more scarce foreign exchange than the import of completed weapons![31] Such efforts also usually require heavy direct government subsidies. Finally, the capital-intensive nature of arms production is economically inefficient in an economy with a labour surplus, and if the defence sector employs a significant proportion of scarce investment capital or technical talent, it may impede capital investment and formation.[32]

This simple economic analysis of costs and benefits may be somewhat misleading, however. As the examples in chapters 2 and 3 suggest, if backward and forward linkages to the economy can be established from an advanced industrial sector such as arms production, significant spin-off and multiplier benefits for the development of relevant civil industries may occur.[33] The military sector can also be used to induce R&D spending and accelerate skill formation. For some states (most notably Brazil), the development of an arms industry appears to have been treated as a form of export-led industrial development, rather than dominated by concerns for import-substitution. But these spin-offs have proved difficult to find: Saadet Deger's study of the Indian case 'fails to reveal any significant evidence of spin-off'.[34] Robert Looney's broader study is less pessimistic, and points out that the macro-economic effects of military industrialisation should not be considered separate from overall patterns of military spending. His statistical study concludes that 'the macro-linkages from the arms industry to the economy enable third-world arms producers to minimize most of the adverse impacts on the economy often associated with increased military burdens'.[35] Arms production may thus not provide major spin-off benefits, but may at least ameliorate the negative impact of military spending.

One cannot resolve this debate here, but a historical perspective suggests that broader pursuit of wealth considerations also play a major role in motivating arms production. The focus on macro-economic benefits or security considerations and a concentration on individual cases have tended to highlight idiosyncratic factors and conceal underlying capacities. But when one examines which states have become arms producers and exporters, there appear to be common socio-economic sources of (and limits to) military-industrial development. Several analysts have attempted to correlate indicators of social and economic development (such as manufacturing as a proportion of GNP, numbers of scientists and engineers, level of development of the iron and steel industries, and size of the military) with the distribution of arms production capabilities in the Third World to discover if the ranks of actual producers correspond to expected producers, and some suggestive evidence has emerged.[36]

Stephanie Neuman found significant correlations between the size of the military and GNP with arms production, especially in Latin America and Asia, where 'the existence of a large military to provide an adequate market, combined with a generous national income and a sizable population to support the necessary industrial infrastructure, significantly affect a state's long-term ability to produce major weapons systems'.[37] Leaders were India, China, Brazil and Argentina; anomalies (with smaller than expected arms industries) were Mexico and Pakistan. In the Middle East and Africa, however, security motives rather than underlying endowments appear to determine arms production capacity. Israel is by far the largest producer, and nowhere near the largest in size or military manpower; Iran, Egypt and Nigeria have industries smaller than would be expected based on factor endowments (although this suggests that their potential for future growth may be greatest). Saadet Deger's composite index ranking the arms production *potential* of Third World states also found a highly ordered system among the 6 major producers, but a less orderly relationship for the remaining 11 states studied.[38]

These correlations all suffer somewhat from being mere static snapshots. Given the relatively short history of third-tier arms production, the favourable market conditions of the past two decades and the inevitable early experiments in production, some disorder in the lower ranks is to be expected. In addition, one could argue (with a version of Gershenkron's 'late industrialisers' thesis) that states such as Pakistan or Chile will have great difficulty in reaching their niche in the hierarchy.[39] The fact that their potential market niche is already occupied by other producers creates high barriers to entry that are difficult to overcome, and that would require government support and intervention on a scale much greater than that required in early defence industrialisers. Such an effort is probably beyond the reach of most of these states.

How can this be integrated into a coherent explanation of the motives governing third-tier arms production? With few exceptions (such as Mexico), the attractiveness of an arms industry as a symbol of national power is such that few states with the capacity to maintain one will forgo it. As one analyst notes: 'industrial capabilities are necessary – and almost sufficient – to explain arms production'.[40] The implication of these analyses is that although third-tier arms production may be catalysed by the pursuit of victory in war, it appears more to be determined by the achievement of a specific level of development. This suggests that it is initially driven by pursuit of power or victory in war considerations (and by possible economic benefits), but that it does not evolve autonomously from the overall limits set by economic endowments (which fall under the pursuit of wealth). Despite the fact that ephemeral factors such as arms embargoes have played a role in determining the ranks of current third-tier arms producers, states such as Pakistan, Chile and Iraq will never become solidly entrenched third-tier members alongside Brazil, India, China and Israel, and may even lose their existing weapons production capability.

## Motive forces driving arms exports and mechanisms of control

The logical concomitant of the narrow production base and limited local demand for arms would be high levels of exports (as a proportion of production, not total volume) from third-tier producers. Yet the data of table 24 present a conflicting picture, and the dependence upon exports of the third-tier industries varies from almost no exports by producers such as India and Taiwan to extremely high levels of dependence in Brazil. Leaving aside these outliers for a moment, the range of export dependence is generally about 20–30 per cent. This is consistently *lower* than for the second tier, but higher than for the first tier. It suggests either that third-tier states are not strongly motivated to export arms, or that this drive is frustrated by other factors.

Since almost all third-tier states manifest a desire to pursue exports aggressively, it is most likely that other factors intervene to make high levels of exports impossible in most cases. Information on arms transfer decision making is sparse, but policies controlling or restricting arms exports appear to be almost non-existent. In Brazil, for example, exports are almost purely *laissez-faire* decisions by manufacturers, and despite giving support to the marketing efforts of the arms industry, the government 'is careful to emphasize the private, commercial nature of the transactions'.[41] As one official noted, 'we're looking to the Third World and we'll sell to the right, the left and the center'. The only major exceptions to this policy to date appear to have been restraint in supplying Libya and South Africa, although indications in 1990 were that exports would be given 'a more political and less commercial orientation'.[42] When given the opportunity, Brazil has exported up to 70 per cent of its production. In Israel, there are 'few controls, even fewer inhibitions' on arms transfer decisions, and the policy presumption has been that 'unless presented with solid political or diplomatic reasons to the contrary, requests for arms ought to be answered affirmatively'.[43] In Yugoslavia, a 1979 law made promotion of arms exports an official policy goal.[44] Producers such as China and Chile also demonstrated how few political restraints they laboured under by supplying both sides in the Iran–Iraq War, and (as noted above) many lesser exporters have voiced ambitious plans to increase their arms exports.[45] In virtually all these cases, the bureaucratic structures to deal with arms transfer decision making are primitive or non-existent, and no strong anti-sale lobbies exist. Great pride is usually taken in the ability to produce and export arms, which is seen as recognition and confirmation of one's independent status in the international system. In extreme cases (such as Brazil in the mid 1980s) arms export levels rose so high that production decisions cease to be related in any meaningful way to national defence needs.[46]

This drive to export is indirectly confirmed by the economic importance of arms exports in foreign trade. For the major third-tier exporters arms transfers generally represent a higher percentage of total exports than in other tiers, with three states (Israel, Egypt and North Korea) counting arms exports for more than 15 per cent of total exports. These three are somewhat exceptional; Israel because of the militarisation of its industrial infrastructure; Egypt and North Korea because of high levels of arms retransfers. More normal figures, between 4 and 7 per cent, appear for China, Brazil, Yugoslavia and Turkey. Nevertheless, these totals are higher than for all non-East European producers except the United States, and they make it clear that the balance of payments and hard currency benefits of arms exports may be important. What is also noteworthy is how clearly these export percentages correlate with high absolute dollar values of arms exports: this suggests that most third-tier producers will be extremely sensitive to fluctuations in the arms market. Given the deteriorating terms of trade facing the developing world, these producers can hardly afford to neglect export opportunities that present themselves.

This strong export orientation makes competition at the lower end of the market fierce, and one can then distinguish three general categories of third-tier exporters: the 'aggressive opportunists', the 'non-participants' and the 'involuntary restricters'. In the first category are producers such as Brazil, South Korea or Argentina. In the second category fall India and China, whose industries do not depend on exports for their well-being because of a large domestic procurement base, although both manifested a willingness to increase exports to high real levels in the late 1980s, perhaps in recognition of the foreign exchange benefits that accrue. China is also most unusual because it has had a small but vigorous military aid policy, a feature more commonly associated with first-tier states.[47] In the third category fall international pariahs such as Taiwan and South Africa, who find their customer lists severely restricted in spite of the relatively high quality of their production.

Other idiosyncratic factors also render the market unpredictable for most third-tier suppliers, whatever their general orientation. The usual geographical concentration of third-tier sales (with Israel and Argentina enjoying success in Latin America and Egypt and Brazil in the Middle East, for example) means that fortunes are tied more directly to particular conflicts or spending patterns. The equally great concentration (with some exceptions) on one or two weapons systems suitable for export (such as artillery or vehicles) also precipitates wide fluctuations in export sales as demand for a particular system in which one producer enjoys a market advantage ebbs and flows. As a consequence of all these factors, the production base in all but the largest producers (China, India, Israel, Yugoslavia) is unstable, as domestic procurement or state subsidies are unable to compensate fully for these fluctuations.

## The third-tier ladder of production

One prominent line of analysis has attempted to explain the evolution and growth of third-tier arms production as an internally driven dynamic process that leads from arms importer to fully indigenous and autonomous arms producer. Such an evolution would certainly be consistent with the desire for autonomy expressed by third-tier decision makers. This process is usually described as a 'ladder of production', and although the number of stages varies, these heuristic constructs all present some variation on the following stages:

(1) capability of performing simple maintenance.
(2) overhaul, refurbishment and rudimentary modification capabilities.
(3) assembly of imported components, simple licensed production.
(4) local production of components or raw materials.
(5) final assembly of less sophisticated weapons; some local component production.
(6) co-production or complete licensed production of less sophisticated weapons.
(7) limited R&D improvements to local licence-produced arms.
(8) limited independent production of less sophisticated weapons; limited production of more advanced weapons.
(9) independent R&D and production of less sophisticated weapons.
(10) independent R&D and production of advanced arms with foreign components.
(11) completely independent R&D and production.[48]

This composite picture captures the sophistication of the weapons produced as well as the independence of production; most typologies fail to capture the former element, thus seriously limiting their descriptive utility.[49] Although such models may be intended as purely descriptive devices, most explicitly assume that linear progress through the stages occurs as a consequence of military industrialisation. Andrew Pierre notes that 'trying to bypass any of these steps may be risky'; James Katz argues that 'there is a "natural history" in the actualization of a weapons-system production program'; and Ron Ayres argues that his typology captures the 'normal pattern of

171

development of arms industries'.[50] Neuman concludes that 'the Iranian experience suggests that an escalator of development leading to some form of indigenous production is the end product of the arms transfer process', and Herbert Wulf argues that 'the domestic production of arms in Third World countries often follows a fairly uniform step-by-step pattern. Know-how gained serves as a basis for subsequent phases.'[51] Progress through the stages will admittedly be erratic, but the assumption is that at least some developing world arms industries (the Indian, Chinese or Brazilian, for example) will reach the level of complete indigenous design and production. Further, as other states reach an appropriate level of industrial development, they too may attempt to create indigenous arms industries, leading to an ever-increasing number of developing world arms producers at the bottom rungs.

But this conception of the evolution of third-tier arms production is incorrect. The most important developing world arms producers (Israel, India and Brazil) have been unable to ascend to higher levels of production and have not progressed beyond stage eight. Lesser producers (such as Egypt or South Korea) have had great difficulty progressing beyond stages six or seven. Although the most advanced producers have developed an across-the-board capability of producing major air, land and sea weapons, they have reached a plateau near the point where limited local R&D and limited independent production of advanced weapons occur.[52] Progression along the stages of production is also never uniform, and the development of indigenous arms industries often skips over several stages or regresses to lower rungs on the ladder.[53] And (as will be shown below) third-tier producers have neither successfully freed themselves from dependence upon imported components nor captured the process of technological innovation.

Several examples of failed progress beyond limited production of advanced weapons in even the most ambitious and serious projects can be given. Brazil's most advanced aircraft programme was undertaken in 1980 with its decision to participate (with a 30 per cent stake in development and production) in the Italian AMX fighter project. All subsequent aircraft projects have been at or below this level of independence and sophistication, and all have involved high levels of foreign technical assistance, confirming that Brazil's aircraft industry is far from attaining an advanced indigenous R&D capability.[54] Israel's advanced Lavi fighter was initiated in 1980 as a low-cost second-level aircraft; by the time it was cancelled in 1987 at the prototype stage, it had been redesigned to compete with the F-16 and more than $1,800 million had been spent on it (most of which was American military assistance). Even in this case, 55 per cent of the final product was to have been imported, with the engines and much of the avionics being American-made. The possibility of manufacturing the engine in Israel was dropped when estimates of development costs were revealed to be higher than $2,000 million![55] India's Arjun tank project, which was conceived in 1974 and intended to be wholly Indian-designed, had still not entered into service by 1989. It had been downgraded to 55 per cent local content, with crucial components (the diesel engine, transmission, communications and fire-control systems) having to be imported (and with major cost overruns).[56] A similar tale can be told for other sectors of the Brazilian, Israeli and Indian defence industries, all of which have discovered that 'the gap between initiation of design work and actual production is painfully long, and the resultant systems are obsolete even before they are deployed'.[57]

For the secondary developing world producers (such as Egypt or South Korea), a similar plateau was reached at a lower rung on the ladder. Egypt's most advanced aircraft programme, a 1978 deal for assembly and production of the French Alpha Jet, had reached the stage of co-production of a less advanced system (stage six) by 1983, with roughly 48 per cent of the components being produced in Egypt (none, however, of the highly sophisticated ones). All attempts to move beyond this to co-production of the Mirage 2000 or the F-16 were unsuccessful, and in 1988 General Dynamics was still conducting the maintenance on the F-16.[58] The highest level reached by Egyptian armoured vehicle production was limited independent R&D and production of more advanced weapons (stage eight).[59] The South Korean arms industries, which did not begin serious production until the mid 1970s, manifest a different pattern, with production beginning at relatively high levels, but uneven progress. In aircraft, for example, the first indigenous programmes (the local assembly of American helicopters and F-5E fighters) were at stage five.[60] These were followed by ambitious plans (launched in 1987) for a Korean Fighter Project that would be a multi-stage operation involving initially local assembly, progressing to co-production with a 60 per cent Korean share. If successful, this programme would be at stage eight, but it is difficult to see how the Korean industry could advance beyond this level in the foreseeable future.

The major break that limits third-tier production appears to fall between stages eight and nine on the ladder, with progress beyond limited R&D being rare. The expectation that this plateau is not simply temporary is based on four observations. First, the motor of techno-

173

logical innovation (and R&D spending) remains firmly anchored in the first tier, with three-quarters of world military R&D being conducted in the United States and the Soviet Union and the third tier accounting for less than 5 per cent.[61] Developing world arms industries are unlikely to progress to the point where they can produce indigenously key highly sophisticated components of the most advanced weapons (such as jet engines, propulsion systems for armoured vehicles, advanced avionics and fire control systems, or advanced armour). Second, the advancing technological frontier means that the *relative* level of sophistication of third-tier arms industries is not increasing. Egypt's aircraft and armoured vehicle industries, for example, were at the same relative level of production in the early 1960s as in 1988![62] This will not be overcome until and unless technological innovation in armaments slows.

Third, progress up the ladder of production for all (or even many) third-tier producers implies a linear expansion of global arms production; such an expansion is not possible unless one assumes a constantly expanding global arms market (or the suspension of market forces). The relatively great dependence of many of these producers (notably Brazil, Yugoslavia, South Korea and Israel) on exports suggests that increased competition and market saturation will make it extremely difficult for third-tier producers with smaller domestic procurement bases to enter the market and compete effectively, except in narrow product niches. Many existing enclave industries may even perish, especially where government support has been crucial to their survival to date. Finally, the historical evidence demonstrates that the process of technological diffusion is neither smooth nor unproblematic, and that the progressive development of arms production capabilities is rare. The entire argument of this book implies rather that one should expect significant qualitative breaks in production capabilities and different stopping points for producers with different factor endowments. When the evolution of third-tier production is analysed in a fashion that takes account of the broader structural forces at work in the global arms transfer and production system, the relatively stable structure of the system is confirmed.

## Technology transfer and the continued dependence of third-tier arms production

The continued dependence of third-tier producers on first- and second-tier suppliers for arms production technology is another indicator of their subordinate status in the arms transfer system. It is

Table 25. *Degree of independence of third-tier production by weapons projects, late 1980s*

| | | | | Degree of Independence | | | | | |
|---|---|---|---|---|---|---|---|---|---|
| Weapons system | Local effort | Near-local effort | Reverse engineered | One imported component | Two plus imported components | Local frame only | Local assembly only | Unknown | Total |
| Aircraft | — | 1 | — | 3 | 25 | 17 | 7 | 6 | 59 |
| Naval vessels | 1 | — | — | 10 | 27 | 15 | 7 | 13 | 73 |
| Missiles | 5 | 1 | 2 | 2 | 1 | 1 | — | 13 | 25 |
| Armoured vehicles | 8 | — | 3 | 7 | 25 | 16 | 6 | 15 | 80 |
| Soft-skin vehicles | 12 | — | 2 | 6 | 4 | 1 | — | 4 | 28 |
| Artillery | 5 | 1 | 13 | 3 | 1 | 1 | — | 3 | 27 |
| Various | — | — | — | 1 | — | 1 | — | — | 2 |
| Totals | 31 | 3 | 20 | 32 | 83 | 51 | 20 | 54 | 294 |

*Source*: author's data base. The number of producers examined is twenty-five. I am grateful to Tom Quiggan for having compiled this table. See also Tom Quiggan, 'Production, dependence and appropriate technologies: arms production in the lesser developed countries', unpublished Master's thesis, York University, Toronto, 1990, 20.

175

demonstrated by the data of table 25, which covers the level of independent production achieved by third-tier producers in all weapons systems except small arms. Of the almost 300 projects identified, only about 10 per cent qualified as independent or nearly independent production. The majority of these projects were relatively uncomplicated systems such as armoured and unarmoured vehicles or artillery; half of the 34 projects are multiple rocket launchers or towed artillery systems that fire unguided rockets, are not linked to central fire control systems and are optically aimed.

The pattern of dependence is clear in the more sophisticated systems such as aircraft, missiles and naval vessels. About half of the projects undertaken are attempts to build these systems, which is not surprising given the association of military prowess with high-profile weapons such as aircraft and missiles. But in 80 per cent of the cases where information is available, third-tier producers depend upon advanced producers for two or more critical weapons subsystems for aircraft, missile or naval production. These usually include the engines or power plants (including transmissions) and the electronics packages (guidance or radar). The mere incorporation of these into a locally built platform cannot be considered as an independent production capability, although the prominence and prestige value of such projects ensure that great effort is made to give such items a 'made at home' label. Estimates of the domestic content of production (such as were offered above) are usually based on the dollar value of local value-added content, which does not accurately reflect the degree of technological dependence involved. High-profile sophisticated projects such as Argentina's TAM tank or Condor missile, Israel's Lavi fighter or Merkava tank or India's Arjun tank may receive the most attention, but they neither represent the bulk of production nor reflect independent capabilities in critical weapons subsystems.

When one breaks down these projects by producer, the expected concentration of production appears, with the top 3 producers (by number of projects), China, Israel and Brazil, accounting for almost 30 per cent of all the projects, and the top 6 (adding South Korea, Yugoslavia and Taiwan) accounting for half of the projects. Virtually all of the more sophisticated weapons production occurs in these states.[63] Even this overstates capabilities somewhat, for only Israel, China and Brazil have attempted (with limited success) to make the transition from licensed to indigenous production of aircraft, and only one main battle tank (the Israeli Merkava) can be considered as indigenously designed. Only 7 producers (Argentina, Brazil, China, India, Israel, South Africa and Taiwan) possess what could loosely be considered an across-the-board production capability, and the production of at least 2 of these states, Argentina and South Africa, is not at a high level of sophistication.[64]

But this evidence triggers two different conclusions. The first, which is consistent with the ladder of production model sketched above, argues that a considerable decrease in dependence is an eventual consequence of domestic arms production: as Ilan Peleg concludes, 'self-production of weapons gives a nation more freedom of action in its foreign affairs and makes it less dependent upon other actors'.[65] Attempting to be more analytically precise, Andrew Ross concludes that *technological* dependence differs fundamentally from *import* dependence, and that 'in the long run, technological dependence in the defense sector . . . can be superseded, and the developing world's defense industries will come to rival those of the advanced industrial world'.[66] Against this one finds the argument that whatever success may be enjoyed in creating autonomous arms production, 'toute indépendance des pays du Tiers-Monde reste illusoire devant le quasi-monopole de la recherche-développement des pays développés'.[67] Some analysts go so far as to argue that sophisticated arms production actually *increases* third-tier states' dependence on industrialised states.[68]

There appears, however, to be a confusion here between reliance and dependence. Continued heavy *reliance* upon imported components or technology is not sufficient by itself to measure *dependence*, because it does not assess if the relationship is 'costly to break' (i.e. if the recipient state is vulnerable to changes in supply).[69] The most clear example of high reliance but low dependence would be trade in a commodity for which substitutes were readily available at only a slightly higher cost. There are three reasons for thinking that although developing world arms producers will continue to rely on inputs from developed arms industries, they have reduced (and will continue to reduce) their vulnerability to supplier controls in many cases.

First, the majority of co-production and licensed production agreements for third-tier production are with second-tier producers. Table 26 details the pattern of agreements since 1950, and presents two estimates of overall licensed production activity. The top four second-tier licensers (France, Britain, West Germany and Italy) are responsible for about 50 per cent of all licensed production and co-production deals, or almost double that accounted for by first-tier producers. The position of first-tier supplies has also been eroded since 1976, as second-tier suppliers have become most active in the export market. First-tier suppliers, who are most likely to implement supply

Table 26. Licensing agreements with developing world producers

| Licenser | SIPRI data | | | | | IFSH data |
| --- | --- | --- | --- | --- | --- | --- |
| | 1950–8 | 1959–67 | 1968–76 | 1977–84 | Total | Total |
| United States | — | 3 | 17 | 11 | 31 | 43 |
| Britain | 2 | 5 | 7 | 7 | 21 | 22 |
| France | 1 | 3 | 5 | 12 | 21 | 25 |
| West Germany | — | 1 | 6 | 10 | 17 | 44 |
| Soviet Union | 1 | 4 | 5 | 5 | 15 | 11 |
| Italy | — | 1 | 4 | 1 | 6 | 16 |
| Belgium | n/a | | | | | 7 |
| Spain | — | 1 | 2 | 1 | 4 | — |
| Israel | — | — | 1 | 2 | 3 | — |
| Switzerland | — | — | 1 | 1 | 2 | — |
| Netherlands | 1 | — | — | — | 1 | 5 |
| Sweden | — | — | 1 | — | 1 | — |
| Austria | — | — | — | 1 | 1 | — |
| Bulgaria | — | — | — | 1 | 1 | — |
| Brazil | — | — | — | 1 | 1 | — |
| South Korea | — | — | — | 1 | 1 | — |
| Other | n/a | | | | | 19 |
| Total | 5 | 18 | 49 | 54 | 126 | 192 |

*Sources*: SIPRI data are from Brzoska and Ohlson, *Arms Production*, 306–49. The data from the Institut für Friedensforschung und Sicherheitspolitik (University of Hamburg) data base are for 1980, and are from Herbert Wulf, 'Arms production in Third World countries: effects on industrialization', unpublished paper, 9. They include small arms, and count Greece, Yugoslavia, Turkey and Portugal as developing countries, which means that they have broader coverage than the SIPRI data. China is excluded from both sets, which artificially reduces the pre-1968 figures (and the totals) for the Soviet Union.

restrictions, also concentrate their agreements with a few clients: the United States had the largest number of contracts but only 9 clients; the Soviet Union only 2. More than half of the American agreements since 1977 have been with only 4 clients, Israel, South Korea, Chile and Taiwan. France, Britain and Germany all had as many as or more clients than the United States; Italy and Spain both had 4 clients; Israel had 2; and Switzerland 1.[70]

This is not the pattern one would expect given the level of sophistication and overall market presence of first-tier suppliers, but it is consistent with the argument that first- and second-tier states face different motivations for participating in the global arms transfer and production system. Second-tier producers are much more prone to sacrifice or dilute their technological lead in order to maintain their productive base, and are much more reliant upon export opportunities. They are therefore less likely to demand end-use restrictions, and hence reliance may not translate into dependence. First-tier producers are much more sensitive both to the political significance of arms transfers and the importance of their technological lead, and hence are less attractive as a source of technology.

Second, the political salience and visibility of the supply of weapons subsystems tend to be lower than for the weapons themselves. Jet fighter engines or dual-use electronics are (ceteris paribus) less controversial than the fighters themselves, and are less likely to be subject to the embargo pressures that can be placed on high-profile items (although this may change). It is also more difficult to control the traffic in items that are dual-use, or not complete systems (through, for example, end-use restrictions).[71] In the arms market, if the political salience of the products exported declines (or their ease of black market transfer increases), then dependence will also decrease.[72]

Third, the number of alternative suppliers for any given subsystem is also relatively high (compared to completed systems), which increases substitutability. Although the most important components are unsubstitutable in the strict sense (an engine is needed to drive an armoured vehicle), the learning that is the by-product of the creation of an arms production capability at least increases the ability of states to adapt existing and available hardware to new uses.[73] Substitutions can be made between different suppliers of engines, armaments, electronics and so forth. Significant modifications can also occur: Iraq, for example, was able to strap boosters on to Scud missiles and reduce the payload to give them a range sufficient to strike Teheran during the Iran–Iraq War.[74] Even on the lowest rungs of the evolutionary ladder (local repair and servicing), important independence is

179

gained.[75] Thus although the reliance of third-tier producers on imported technology continues, it can qualitatively change in such a way that it may not produce a great deal of influence for the supplier states. It is thus mistaken to conclude that dependence is remaining stable or perhaps even increasing.[76]

## Conclusion

By the criteria introduced at the outset of this chapter, all the states in the developing world are limited to third-tier production, however large the volume of arms they produce or export. None currently possess either the breadth or sophistication of production to cross the threshold to second-tier production, and only two or three of the largest could conceivably do so in the future. These would include China, India, and perhaps Brazil or Israel. Prospects for promotion of the last two are extremely uncertain; Brazil because it is so export-dependent that it has been unable to maintain its production base intact during a market decline; Israel because it has probably neared the outer limit of production (with the Lavi fighter) that can be attained by a state with fewer than five million people. All four have at least managed to grasp the technological skills needed to adapt weapons systems to their military or market needs, thus manifesting one critical attribute of the advanced technological development characteristic of second-tier production. The remaining third-tier producers, however, have not moved beyond the simple reproduction of existing technologies, and are unlikely to be able to move with an advancing technological frontier without continued infusions of technology from first- and second-tier states.

Again, the pace of technological innovation emerges as a crucial factor shaping global patterns of arms production and transfers, especially in the early phases of a technological wave or cycle. Although some movement up the so-called ladder of production is evident, and although dependence may not be increasing, as defence technologies advance in sophistication third-tier arms industries find it increasingly difficult to maintain their relative position in the global arms transfer and production system. The crises experienced by the Brazilian, South Korean and Taiwanese arms industries in the late 1980s hint at the sombre future that may face most third-tier producers. As Patrice Franko-Jones notes for Brazil,

> while Brazilian defense production was closely tied to the automotive sector, scale economies could be derived from like processes and bulk purchases ... [but] as systems became more sophisticated, costs,

180

including those for research and development, increased markedly
and domestic sourcing became less common.[77]

Arms production may for a time proceed ahead of the overall level of
economic and technological development of the economy, but it can
do so only as an enclave industry vulnerable to the vicissitudes of the
global market. As arms production experience is gained and technologies are acquired, however, arms industries can plant deeper roots in
an advancing economy and perhaps act as an engine of growth. But
these circumstances will be rare.

The motivations governing third-tier states' participation in the
arms transfer system can be summarised as follows: the initial decision
to produce weapons systems is driven by the narrow pursuit of victory
in war (security) or the pursuit of power (regional hegemony or global
status). Sustained success then depends on possession of the requisite
economic infrastructure capabilities. The heavy burden of production
pushes most states to pursue exports, and when exports can be
achieved, other possible military or political benefits from arms
transfers are subordinated to the goal of industrial growth or survival.
Thus both pursuit of power and pursuit of wealth motivations play a
role (at different stages) in explaining third-tier arms production and
exports, which moves us beyond the simple dichotomous debate over
which of the two motives dominates.[78]

This chapter confirms the hierarchical and stratified structure of
global arms production and implies that the future is likely to witness
neither a large increase in the number of third-tier producers of major
weapons, nor an expansion of the third-tier share of the world arms
export market much beyond its current limits.[79] An increase in the
number of third-tier suppliers is also unlikely, as virtually the entire
growth in the volume of third-tier exports has been the result of
intense efforts by states such as Brazil and Israel that are willing and
able to take advantage of any market opportunities. The seemingly
durable shift in the 1980s from a sellers' to a buyers' market means that
the arms trade will be governed more by the intentions of recipients
than those of suppliers. Although it may be true that 'strong military,
political and economic stimuli exist for further expansion of domestic
arms production', these stimuli in themselves are not sufficient to
overcome the structural and technological impediments that stand in
the way of such an expansion.[80] If a virtuous conclusion can be drawn,
it is that at least in the realm of arms production the world is not likely
to witness an ever-increasing militarisation of relations between and
within states.[81]

# 8 THE SUBORDINATE ROLE OF ARMS RECIPIENTS

## A statistical overview

The global arms transfer and production system involves more than just the producers of arms: it enmeshes all major and most minor states as patrons or clients in a complex web of military relationships that includes not only weapons, but arms production technology, spare parts and supplies for weapons, and military training assistance. Chapters 2 and 3 noted how the subordinate status of recipient states in the arms transfer system was confirmed by their dependence upon external arms supplies and, occasionally, by their inability even to adopt the military and political organisation required to operate modern weapons; this chapter will examine contemporary arms recipients in the same light. Although almost all states, including the largest producers, are also arms recipients, the discussion will concentrate on those recipients who either do not produce arms or straddle the line between recipient and third-tier status.

A full discussion of the role of arms recipients in the contemporary arms transfer system would require a separate book. The issues it would raise include the relationship between arms acquisitions and the quest for security (both interstate and internal), the link between spending on weapons and economic development, and the use of arms transfer and military aid relationships as a tool of influence by arms producers.[1] What this chapter presents, however, is an overview of the main patterns of arms acquisitions, a brief discussion of the motives driving arms recipients and an explanation of how they have responded to their subordinate position in the global military hierarchy.

Between 1945 and 1950, the most important arms recipients were Eastern and Western European countries and China (both the nationalists and the communists), lesser recipients being Greece, Iran, Turkey, North and South Korea and the Philippines. During the 1950s, military assistance by the Soviet Union and United States delivered to their European allies dwarfed that provided to all other regions: 70–80 per cent of the more than $17,000 million (in current dollars) of transfers by the United States between 1950 and 1957 went to Europe.[2] As European rearmament reached its completion in the early 1960s the locus of the arms trade shifted south, fuelled also by the decolonisation movement and continued conflict in South-East Asia. Table 27 details this shift by giving the regional shares of global arms imports between 1963 and 1987. The shift in the locus of arms transfers is confirmed as Europe, which accounted for 43 per cent of transfers in 1963–7, accounted for fewer than 20 per cent in the 1980s. The major recipient regions after 1970 were the Middle East and Africa, both of which more than trebled their share of arms acquisitions between 1963 and 1987 (Algeria and Libya are included as African states, accounting for most of the increase in the African category). In the 1980s, imports to South Asia assumed greater prominence, consistent with the rising wealth of the region. Regions other than the Middle East and Africa show little or no increase, or even (in East and South Asia) a decrease in their share of acquisitions. Given the increase in real terms of transfers over this period, this does not mean that these regions purchased fewer arms, only that the increase in global transfers was concentrated in a few states.

Table 28, which lists the top 10 customers at different dates within this period, confirms the disappearance of European purchasers from the upper echelons and their replacement primarily by Middle Eastern recipients. Five of the 10 largest recipients in 1963 were European; 3 were European in 1972, but none were European in the 1980s. In 1982, 8 of the top 10 were in the Middle East (including Algeria and Libya in this definition), and although this declined slightly to 5 by 1988, the Middle East still contains most of the large recipients. The identity of the top recipients in table 28 and the regional focus of attention have shifted, but the top 10 states have always accounted for about 50 per cent of global arms acquisitions (although recent statistics suggest that this percentage may be declining slightly). Such market concentration is more striking when one considers that this is less than one-tenth of the total number of arms recipients. Characterising the shift in arms transfers from the developed to the developing world over the past three decades as a global phenomenon is thus misleading, and one should be wary of generalisations about dramatic overall increases in arms acquisitions in the developing world.[3] In fact, only a small number of suppliers and recipients are active participants and account for the bulk of transfers. There appears to be only a slow erosion of this concentration of customers at the top of the market, and at the bottom,

Table 27. *Regional distribution of arms imports, 1963–87 (percentage shares)*

| Years | 1963–7 | 1968–72 | 1973–7 | 1978–82 | 1983–7 | (% population 1982) |
|---|---|---|---|---|---|---|
| Africa | 4.2 | 3.6 | 11.3 | 18.7 | 12.3 | (9.8) |
| East Asia | 28.7 | 34.6 | 15.6 | 10.7 | 11.5 | (35.1) |
| Latin America | 3.1 | 3.6 | 4.8 | 6.8 | 7.4 | (8.1) |
| Middle East | 9.2 | 16.6 | 33.6 | 37.5 | 37.8 | (3.1) |
| North America | 3.0 | 3.5 | 2.0 | 1.7 | 1.5 | (5.6) |
| Oceania | 2.0 | 1.4 | 0.9 | 1.0 | 1.5 | (0.5) |
| South Asia | 6.8 | 4.3 | 4.0 | 3.9 | 7.3 | (20.4) |
| NATO Europe | 20.3 | 18.3 | 10.2 | 8.7 | 7.4 | (7.1) |
| Warsaw Pact | 19.1 | 11.2 | 14.7 | 8.3 | 10.4 | (8.2) |
| Other Europe | 3.6 | 2.7 | 2.8 | 2.7 | 2.4 | (2.0) |
| Developed | 41.7 | 28.9 | 25.7 | 19.5 | 20.9 | (23.1) |
| Developing | 58.3 | 71.1 | 74.3 | 80.5 | 79.1 | (76.3) |

*Note:* Regions are classified as follows:
*Africa*: does not include Egypt.
*East Asia*: Mongolia, both Koreas, both Chinas, Japan and from Burma to Indonesia.
*Latin America*: Mexico south, all Caribbean states.
*Middle East*: Egypt to the Persian Gulf, Iran and Cyprus.
*North America*: Canada and the US.
*Oceania*: Australia, New Zealand, Fiji, Papua New Guinea.
*South Asia*: Afghanistan, India, Pakistan, Nepal, Bangladesh, Sri Lanka.
*Other Europe*: Albania, Austria, Finland, Ireland, Malta, Spain, Sweden, Switzerland, Yugoslavia.
*Developed*: all of NATO, except Greece and Turkey; all of the Warsaw Pact except Bulgaria; Japan, Australia, New Zealand, Finland, Austria, Ireland, Sweden and Switzerland.
*Developing*: all others.
*Source:* ACDA, *WMEAT*, various years.

more states purchase arms than ever before (albeit in small quantities): 89 in 1963, 91 in 1972 and 112 in 1988.[4]

The changing identity of the top clients during the periods presented is not surprising, given that states that are (or have been) at war have the highest requirements for arms, and that most clients make major arms purchases in a cyclical pattern of military modernisation. No state appears on all four lists in table 28, and roughly half of the states seem to disappear from the top 10 over each decade (the 1988 data see only 3 states dropped from 1982). The fact that a state does not appear consistently in the top 10 does not, however, mean that it disappears from the upper ranks of arms purchasers, and most recipients remain major clients for parts, repairs and other services throughout the life of the equipment. One should also not conclude that arms acquisitions by states that are not in the top 10 or 20 are unimportant: many smaller states (measured by population or Gross

Table 28. *Top ten arms recipients, selected years*
*(million constant 1988 US dollars)*

| | 1963 | | | 1972 | |
|---|---|---|---|---|---|
| | dollar value | % of world total | | dollar value | % of world total |
| West Germany | 1,660 | 14.6 | South Vietnam | 4,040 | 15.4 |
| Indonesia | 840 | 7.4 | North Vietnam | 3.030 | 11.6 |
| Italy | 770 | 6.8 | West Germany | 1,700 | 6.5 |
| India | 660 | 5.8 | Egypt | 1,390 | 5.3 |
| Egypt | 530 | 4.7 | Iran | 1,330 | 5.1 |
| East Germany | 470 | 4.1 | South Korea | 880 | 3.4 |
| Iraq | 380 | 3.3 | East Germany | 860 | 3.3 |
| Poland | 370 | 3.2 | Israel | 760 | 2.9 |
| Soviet Union | 330 | 2.9 | Syria | 710 | 2.7 |
| South Vietnam | 320 | 2.8 | Poland | 660 | 2.5 |
| Total | 6,330 | 55.6 | Total | 15,360 | 58.6 |

| | 1982 | | | 1988 | |
|---|---|---|---|---|---|
| | dollar value | % of world total | | dollar value | % of world total |
| Iraq | 8,600 | 14.8 | Iraq | 4,600 | 9.5 |
| Saudi Arabia | 3,880 | 6.7 | India | 3,200 | 6.6 |
| Libya | 3,880 | 6.7 | Saudi Arabia | 3,000 | 6.2 |
| Syria | 3,150 | 5.4 | Afghanistan | 2,600 | 5.3 |
| Egypt | 2,300 | 4.0 | Iran | 2,000 | 4.1 |
| India | 2,060 | 3.5 | Israel | 1,900 | 3.9 |
| Cuba | 2,060 | 3.5 | Cuba | 1,700 | 3.5 |
| Iran | 1,940 | 3.3 | Angola | 1,600 | 3.3 |
| Algeria | 1,460 | 2.5 | Vietnam | 1,500 | 3.1 |
| Israel | 1,140 | 2.0 | Syria | 1,300 | 2.7 |
| Total | 30,470 | 52.4 | Total | 23,400 | 48.1 |

*Source:* ACDA, *WMEAT*, various years.
*Note:* Numbers have been rounded to avoid the impression of greater accuracy.

National Product) have rapidly expanded their military establishments and expenditures on sophisticated modern arms, particularly in Southern Africa and Central America. What may be an unexceptional acquisition in one region may be a large and qualitatively significant acquisition in another, and thus one must examine arms acquisitions in the context of specific local conflicts or competitions.

Suppliers and recipients are brought together in more detail in table 29, which gives the major suppliers' market shares by region over

Table 29. *Percentage market share of major suppliers by region, various years*

| Supplier | US | Soviet Union | Britain | France | West Germany | Italy | China | Warsaw Pact | Other |
|---|---|---|---|---|---|---|---|---|---|
| *Region* | | | | | 1964–73 | | | | |
| Africa | 17 | 28 | 11 | 26 | 3 | — | 4 | 2 | 9 |
| East Asia | 74 | 16 | 1 | — | — | — | 6 | — | 3 |
| Latin America | 42 | 13 | 8 | 16 | 4 | — | — | — | 17 |
| Middle East | 34 | 50 | 5 | 3 | — | — | — | 3 | 5 |
| South Asia | 9 | 55 | 4 | 9 | 1 | — | 11 | 5 | 6 |
| Oceania | 80 | — | 13 | 5 | — | — | — | — | 2 |
| NATO Europe | 83 | — | 1 | 5 | 7 | — | — | — | 4 |
| Warsaw Pact | — | 70 | — | — | — | — | — | 29 | 1 |
| Other Europe | 47 | 31 | 3 | 7 | 2 | — | 4 | — | 6 |
| | | | | | 1976–80 | | | | |
| Africa | 4 | 53 | 2 | 11 | 7 | 6 | 1 | 3 | 13 |
| East Asia | 50 | 26 | 5 | 2 | 1 | 1 | 3 | — | 11 |
| Latin America | 10 | 29 | 11 | 17 | 6 | 6 | — | — | 20 |
| Middle East | 37 | 32 | 7 | 9 | 4 | 2 | — | 2 | 8 |
| South Asia | 6 | 64 | 5 | 10 | 1 | 1 | 7 | 3 | 3 |
| Oceania | 58 | — | 19 | — | 13 | — | — | — | 10 |
| NATO Europe | 69 | — | 4 | 4 | 10 | 3 | — | — | 10 |
| Warsaw Pact | — | 59 | — | 1 | — | — | — | 37 | 3 |
| Other Europe | 39 | 21 | 7 | 6 | 3 | 2 | — | — | 23 |
| | | | | | 1984–8 | | | | |
| Africa | 5 | 66 | 2 | 5 | — | 4 | 1 | 6 | 12 |
| East Asia | 42 | 41 | 2 | 1 | 1 | 1 | 1 | — | 11 |
| Latin America | 12 | 55 | 1 | 5 | 8 | 2 | — | 5 | 12 |
| Middle East | 18 | 30 | 4 | 14 | 2 | 1 | 9 | 5 | 18 |
| South Asia | 6 | 73 | 1 | 9 | 2 | 1 | 2 | 1 | 4 |
| Oceania | 88 | — | 4 | 1 | 2 | — | — | — | 5 |
| NATO Europe | 80 | — | 3 | 4 | 7 | 1 | — | — | 4 |
| Warsaw Pact | — | 67 | — | — | — | — | — | 28 | 6 |
| Other Europe | 51 | 12 | 9 | 2 | 12 | 3 | — | — | 12 |

*Source:* ACDA, *WMEAT*, various years.

time. No single supplier exclusively dominates any region (although some come close), and both first-tier suppliers have a significant presence in virtually all regions. The distribution of shares also reflects traditional lines of influence, the presence of major clients and the waxing and waning impact of specific policies. For example, the American absence from the Latin American market in the 1980s is the direct consequence of restraint policies implemented in the 1960s and 1970s. Soviet dominance in Africa and South Asia in the 1970s and 1980s results from a major presence in Libya, Algeria, Ethiopia and India. France's initially large market share in Africa was a consequence of the close military ties it maintained with its former African colonies;

Britain did not maintain such ties and saw its market share in Africa decline precipitously from 1960. Whatever the idiosyncratic reasons behind particular market share distributions, second- and third-tier suppliers appear to present a genuine alternative to clients in all regions.

## The diffusion of sophisticated weapons and the growth of arsenals

This somewhat abstract picture of the distribution of weapons throughout the arms transfer system can be made more concrete with some figures on the actual size of arsenals in various regions. Table 30 documents the growth in weapons arsenals in various regions, and although it does not take into account the sophistication of the equipment, it does give some indication of the especially important increases in the military potential of states in the developing world. Given that the bulk of arms traded between states flow from north to south, these data appear at first glance to manifest clearly what Edward Kolodziej has called the progressive 'militarization of international relations' as a consequence of a dramatic increase in military capabilities in the developing world.[5] But a closer examination of the data in table 30 highlights the extremely uneven distribution of armaments around the world and the different regional rates of build-up. It also makes clear that military capabilities in the developing world still do not compare with the vast weapons arsenals held by NATO and Warsaw Pact states at the end of the 1980s (although these are shrinking dramatically).

The Middle East and North Africa account for about half the tanks and armoured fighting vehicles in the developing world (excluding China). Egypt alone has more tanks than there are in all of Latin America or Sub-Saharan Africa! East Asia and China possess the next largest arsenals, while Sub-Saharan Africa and Latin America remain relatively less well armed. The most rapid growth of arsenals has occurred in Sub-Saharan Africa, although this is in part a result of the small size of the military establishments that existed in the early post-independence period. Within each region, the two or three states with the largest arsenals always account for a high percentage of the total regional arsenal. In South Asia, India possesses about 50 per cent of the tanks, 40 per cent of the armoured fighting vehicles and 30 per cent of the combat aircraft. In Sub-Saharan Africa, Ethiopia possesses 35 per cent of the tanks, South Africa has 50 per cent of the armoured fighting vehicles, and South Africa, Angola and Mozambique together have one-third of the aircraft. In Latin America, Cuba possesses more than 50 per cent of the tanks, and Brazil and Argentina one-third of the armoured fighting vehicles. In East Asia, North and South Korea possess more than 50 per cent of the tanks and roughly one-third of the combat aircraft. In the Middle East, Egypt, Israel and Syria have 45 per cent of the tanks and 28 per cent of the aircraft.

Table 31 supplements this by documenting the increase in the number of states possessing advanced weapons. What it does not document is that as the weapons transferred to recipients have become more sophisticated, the gap between the technologies possessed by first-tier states and their clients has shrunk. Although it is difficult to demonstrate precisely how narrow this gap has become, it has reached the point where weapons are delivered to the best customers simultaneously with their introduction into national forces. The production lines for the American F-14 and F-16 were shared with foreign recipients, the Soviet Union supplied its best clients with arms such as the MiG-27 and MiG-29 fighters or SA-9 surface-to-air missiles as they entered Soviet service, and France allowed Egypt to acquire the Mirage 2000 as its own forces did.[6] This is a far cry from the late 1960s, when the United States attempted (ultimately unsuccessfully) to slow the pace of introduction of supersonic aircraft into Latin America.[7]

The diffusion of modern weapons is thus much more 'lumpy' or uneven than is suggested by a simple picture of progressive (and perhaps accelerating) global militarisation. What appears to be at work is a combination of two factors: the dynamics of military build-ups within the context of a specific conflict (such as the Arab–Israeli confrontation), and the pursuit of hegemony and status within a particular regional 'security complex' (such as the Indian sub-continent).[8] Both factors are also either amplified or turned down by the influence of internal domestic political struggles and decisions. In any event, it is difficult to make sense of this evidence without a more subtle account of the motive forces driving arms acquisition processes.

When one focuses on a particular high-profile or sophisticated weapons system, a similar (albeit more frightening) picture of the struggle for pre-eminence in a global or regional military hierarchy emerges. Ballistic missiles and combat aircraft capable of delivering conventional, chemical or nuclear warheads have proliferated rapidly in the developing world over the past decade, with even states that have little or no arms production capability attempting to acquire such items. Approximately 20–5 states in the developing world now possess some type of ballistic missile; 13–16 states possess weapons

Table 30. *Number of weapons by region and weapons system, selected years*

| | North Atlantic Treaty Organization | | |
| | 1975–6 | 1982–3 | 1988–9 |
| --- | --- | --- | --- |
| Main battle tanks | 20,144 | 27,789 | 32,458 |
| Other AFVs | 35,584 | 58,864 | 71,127 |
| Combat aircraft | 11,256 | 10,662 | 11,576 |
| Helicopters | 11,169 | 13,617 | 14,699 |
| Naval vessels | 2,090 | 2,973 | 2,991 |

| | Warsaw Pact | | |
| | 1975–6 | 1982–3 | 1988–9 |
| --- | --- | --- | --- |
| Main battle tanks | 54,350 | 64,500 | 71,640 |
| Other AFVs | 40,705 | 84,330 | 88,835 |
| Combat aircraft | 9,724 | 9,407 | 10,585 |
| Helicopters | 2,758 | 4,452 | 6,273 |
| Naval vessels | 2,180 | 2,624 | 2,872 |

| | Middle East and North Africa | | |
| | 1975–6 | 1982–3 | 1988–9 |
| --- | --- | --- | --- |
| Main battle tanks | 11,070 | 19,762 | 23,181 |
| Other AFVs | 14,311 | 24,342 | 28,818 |
| Combat aircraft | 2,594 | 3,621 | 3,921 |
| Helicopters | 884 | 2,307 | 2,209 |
| Naval vessels | 432 | 605 | 711 |

| | Sub-Saharan Africa | | |
| | 1975–6 | 1982–3 | 1988–9 |
| --- | --- | --- | --- |
| Main battle tanks | 500 | 1,962 | 2,186 |
| Other AFVs | 2,457 | 7,079 | 9,182 |
| Combat aircraft | 461 | 780 | 1,088 |
| Helicopters | 221 | 543 | 802 |
| Naval vessels | 164 | 263 | 253 |

| | South Asia | | |
| | 1975–6 | 1982–3 | 1988–9 |
| --- | --- | --- | --- |
| Main battle tanks | 2,996 | 4,293 | 5,250 |
| Other AFVs | 1,538 | 2,364 | 3,165 |
| Combat aircraft | 1,240 | 1,040 | 1,293 |
| Helicopters | 338 | 500 | 516 |
| Naval vessels | 145 | 155 | 241 |

| | East Asia | | |
| | 1975–6 | 1982–3 | 1988–9 |
| --- | --- | --- | --- |
| Main battle tanks | 5,250 | 6,870 | 8,829 |
| Other AFVs | 4,249 | 11,129 | 15,516 |
| Combat aircraft | 2,315 | 3,083 | 3,106 |
| Helicopters | 939 | 1,858 | 2,337 |
| Naval vessels | 982 | 1,253 | 1,938 |

Table 30 (*cont.*)

| | People's Republic of China | | |
| | 1975–6 | 1982–3 | 1988–9 |
| --- | --- | --- | --- |
| Main battle tanks | 8,500 | 10,500 | 9,000 |
| Other AFVs | 3,600 | 4,600 | 4,800 |
| Combat aircraft | 4,340 | 5,980 | 6,730 |
| Helicopters | 350 | 403 | 463 |
| Naval vessels | 1,035 | 1,177 | 1,472 |
| | Latin America and Caribbean | | |
| | 1975–6 | 1982–3 | 1988–9 |
| Main battle tanks | 805 | 1,673 | 2,213 |
| Other AFVs | 2,245 | 4,615 | 6,996 |
| Combat aircraft | 940 | 1,118 | 1,279 |
| Helicopters | 601 | 941 | 1,025 |
| Naval vessels | 500 | 588 | 574 |

*Notes:* IISS data are subject to great variation from year to year; these figures are meant as trend indicators only. 'Main battle tanks' includes heavy and medium tanks; 'Other AFVs' includes light tanks, reconnaissance vehicles, armoured personnel carriers and infantry fighting vehicles; 'Combat aircraft' includes fighter, strike, reconnaissance, counter-insurgency and ASW aircraft; 'Naval vessels' includes all surface and submarine vessels of greater than 100 tons displacement (excluding hovercraft).
*Source:* International Institute of Strategic Studies, *The Military Balance* (London: IISS, various years).

Table 31. *Number of developing countries with advanced military systems, 1950–85*

| | 1950 | 1960 | 1970 | 1980 | 1985 |
| --- | --- | --- | --- | --- | --- |
| Supersonic aircraft | — | 1 | 28 | 55 | 55 |
| Missiles | — | 6 | 25 | 68 | 71 |
| Armoured vehicles | 1 | 38 | 72 | 99 | 107 |
| Main battle tanks | — | 32 | 39 | — | 62 |
| Modern warships | 4 | 26 | 56 | 79 | 81 |

*Source:* Edward Kolodziej, *Making and Marketing*, 183. Figures for main battle tanks estimated from Brzoska and Ohlson, *Arms Transfers*, 12.

with a range greater than 200 kilometres.[9] Around 5 states in the developing world may acquire the capability to produce missiles by the year 2000.[10] Although most of these missiles are relatively primitive and not capable of delivering large warheads with a great deal of accuracy, their presence changes the complexion of conflicts by their possible effect on crisis stability, deterrence and escalation. The most widely distributed of all ballistic missiles is the Soviet Scud-B: it has a range of 280 kilometres (with a payload of 1,000 kilograms), is based upon 1960s technology (albeit with subsequent modifications), and has been acquired by at least eight states.

Not surprisingly, the most prominent possessors (and potential producers) of ballistic missiles are India, China, Brazil, Iraq, Israel, Iran, Egypt, North Korea, South Korea and South Africa, almost all of whom rank highly among third-tier arms producers. The acquisition of such weapons has been driven by regional rivalries (Iran–Iraq, South Korea–North Korea, China–India–Pakistan, Israel–Egypt–Iraq) and the quest for international status and recognition (Brazil, Argentina, South Africa), as much as by any military considerations. As one Indian analyst described India's Agni missile, '[its] role as a weapon is the least of its roles. It is a confidence builder and a symbol of India's assertion of self-reliance not merely in defence but in the broader international political arena as well.'[11] Because ballistic missile proliferation signals the diffusion of some of the most advanced technologies hitherto monopolised by first- and second-tier states, it has also been the focus of control efforts by these suppliers. These have centered on the Missile Technology Control Regime (MTCR), formally acceded to by seven Western states in 1987.[12] The success of this regime is mixed: although it appears to have slowed or even halted several specific missile development programmes (in Egypt, Argentina, India and Iraq), it enjoys only limited membership (and does not include the Soviet Union), has limited enforcement, and does not cover all systems that could contribute to a ballistic missile capability.[13]

Ballistic missiles are only the most prominent sophisticated weapons that have been diffused to a narrow range of states in the developing world. Other advanced weapons such as combat aircraft and modern tanks have also been distributed to a relatively small number of prominent recipients. About 40 states possess modern fighter/interceptor aircraft, although only 8 states in the developing world (India, Israel, Saudi Arabia, Cuba, Iran, Iraq, North Korea and Syria) possess the most advanced models (the F-15 and MiG-29). Sophisticated strike aircraft such as the F-16, Su-24, Tornado and Mirage 2000 also are in limited distribution, with only 16 states possessing such planes.[14] Advanced main battle tanks are possessed by only 13 developing world states.

The chemical and nuclear weapons that could be delivered by such systems have been the subject of long-standing efforts at control. Efforts to restrict the proliferation of nuclear weapons have centered around the Nuclear Non-Proliferation Treaty and the London nuclear suppliers group; efforts to control the diffusion of chemical weapons have focused on the chemical and biological weapons convention negotiations and the informal twenty-one nation 'Australia group' of states that export chemical feedstocks that could be used to produce weapons.[15] These efforts need not be discussed in detail; what is worth noting is that however successful efforts have been, they have not entirely stopped the diffusion of nuclear and chemical weapons technologies. At least four states in the developing world are on or across the nuclear weapons threshold (Israel, India, Pakistan, South Africa), with several others (among them Brazil, Argentina, Iraq, Iran and South Korea) having at one point pursued a nuclear weapons programme.[16] Chemical weapons can in principle be produced by almost any state that possesses an advanced chemical industrial plant (to produce fertilisers or pharmaceuticals, for example), and the number of states that possess chemical weapons has been estimated at between 10 and 25.[17]

The attractiveness of nuclear and chemical weapons and ballistic missiles is paradoxically enhanced by efforts to control their diffusion. Relatively common sophisticated weapons (such as tanks, armoured vehicles or supersonic aircraft) are unlikely to be monopolised by one or two states in a region, and hence a decisive advantage (military or psychological) is difficult to achieve. If achieved, it can often be quickly countered with arms acquisitions. But ballistic missiles and chemical or nuclear weapons, on the other hand, might create an advantage that is less likely to be easily offset by arms transfers to possible opponents. In addition, such weapons provide the sting of modern warfare by enhancing countervalue (or deterrent) capabilities, capabilities that could prove to be even more significant than a battlefield advantage. Acquisition or production of such weapons is thus worth the much greater relative effort it entails.

This again confirms the uneven diffusion of modern weapons and the hierarchical nature of the global military system, as the same few states (either prominent third-tier arms producers or states in zones of conflict such as the Middle East or Southern Africa) reappear on all these lists. Loosely comparable hierarchical rankings appear in absolute terms whether one compares the distribution of particular weapons, the size of arsenals, arms acquisitions or military spending. This at least implies that the evolution of the arms transfer system since 1945 has been driven more by states' quest to place themselves in the hierarchy than by internal factors. To assess this more systematically, however, requires that one examine more closely the motive forces that govern arms acquisitions.

## Motives governing arms acquisitions

As the above discussion suggests, it will be difficult to gen-eralise about global patterns of arms acquisitions, since these are usually governed by a constellation of political or security consider-ations unique to a region or state. As Robert Rothstein points out in a broader context, 'there is no such thing as "the" security problem in the Third World: differentiation within the Third World itself is growing . . . and there are unique factors in each case that make grand generalizations inherently suspect'.[18] One can at least identify, however, three sets of motives states have for acquiring arms: internal (including securing the regime against internal threats or using mili-tary development as a vehicle for social and economic modernisation), regional (including guaranteeing security, fighting wars and acquiring regional influence or hegemony), and systemic (including the pursuit of status, power and prestige).[19] These motives have usually been discussed in the broader context of military expenditures and the quest for security in both the developed and the developing world, with the acquisition of modern weapons merely being part of this quest. To complicate the analysis further, there is little reason to expect that one motive or set of motives will predominate or emerge as a norm. Attempts to determine the relative weight of internal, regional or systemic motivations have tended to show, however, that systemic or regional security motivations are more important, a finding that accords well with the emphasis in this book on factors inherent in the self-help nature of international politics.[20]

The internally driven motivations for acquiring arms (as a concomi-tant to the creation of a modern military establishment) have been highlighted by three groups of authors: those who argue that the military can act as a force for modernisation, those who concentrate on the contested nature of security for most states in the developing world, and those who argue that arms acquisitions and military spending contribute to underdevelopment. The first group of authors (writing mainly in the 1950s and 1960s) argued that the military played a prominent role because in many developing countries it was the only modern social and political institution that could affirm (or create) national identity against a historical backdrop of inter-ethnic, inter-religious, or inter-tribal rivalry. In addition, it provided a focus for economic, social and political modernisation by educating and train-ing individuals in technical skills that could be used outside the military, and it allegedly socialised its members to a modern world view with hierarchical and ordered relationships based on efficiency and merit, not background and family ties.[21] Such arguments co-incided well with the thrust of American arms transfer and military aid policies of the time, which were justified on the grounds that if the military was to govern the state along the path to modernisation (or at least play a major role), it ought to acquire modern weapons and training.[22]

The second group of authors focused on the weak legitimacy of specific regimes or of the state itself, and the fact that power resides frequently with a small elite (often the military) that possessed weak ties of identification and loyalty with the majority of the population. The resulting weak legitimacy can trigger violent and frequent challenges to the regime or state.[23] Thus an important motive for acquiring arms is to maintain the security of a regime and integrity of state borders in the face of internal threats to its survival: threats that can arise from an ethnic or religious minority agitating for secession, from political insurgencies of the right or left, or from political discontent with authoritarian and repressive rulers. The Sikhs in India, the Karens in Burma and the Tamils in Sri Lanka are examples of the first kind of threat. The contras in Nicaragua, the UNITA movement in Angola and the 'Sendero Luminoso' (Shining Path) in Peru are examples of the second. Resistance to Idi Amin's rule in Uganda, General Augusto Pinochet's regime in Chile and the Shah's dynasty in Iran are examples of the last type of internal threat. Civilian politicians who govern under the shadow of the military can also be forced to purchase the loyalty of the military with arms imports, in an attempt to guarantee their security against their own armed forces.

In a more negative light, a third group of authors argued that the acquisition of modern weapons is driven by a more dysfunctional internal process of militarisation that has resulted in a dispropor-tionate role for the military within a state, increased its claim on national resources and distorted economic, social and developmental priorities.[24] Military spending and arms acquisitions can also have political and cultural/ideological consequences by increasing the pres-tige of 'military values' in politics.[25] The literature on the impact of military expenditures on economic growth and development does not often directly address the issue of arms acquisitions, although as Nicole Ball points out, 'in the public mind, security expenditure in the Third World is firmly linked with the arms trade. It is commonly assumed that a large portion of all developing countries' security outlays are used to purchase weapons and related services from abroad.'[26] This is misleading, for the bulk of military spending in the developing world goes to operating and personnel costs, not on arms procurement. In India, for example, the proportion of the military budget devoted to personnel, operations and maintenance over the period from 1951 to 1979 was always greater than 80 per cent (although it slowly declined over this period). In states as diverse as Ghana, Malaysia, the Philippines, Morocco, Argentina, Brazil and Chile, operating costs were more than two-thirds of military spending throughout the 1970s (the last period for which reliable data are available).[27] This suggests that whatever factors influence the degree of militarisation and military spending, it is not likely to be linked causally to levels of arms acquisitions.

The 'regional' motivations for arms acquisitions encompass the classic national security justification for arms acquisitions – the need to protect and defend a state's citizens and their way of life from possible aggression by other states; this has been the most common justification offered.[28] The increase in arms transfers since 1960 can therefore be partly explained by the demand created by the process of decolonisation and the unleashing of regional or local conflicts that had hitherto been suppressed. As the newly independent states in Africa and Asia assumed responsibility for their own defence, former colonial constabularies or police forces were transformed into national armed forces. Military spending, arms transfers and even arms production (where possible) were thus elements of the larger struggle of new states to assert their sovereignty. This process had, not surprisingly, the inadvertent result of triggering many arms races, as the difficulty in distinguishing between offensive and defensive military preparations started an action–reaction cycle of arms purchases in the absence of any necessary intention on either side to start a war. An example of this would be the Latin American race to acquire supersonic jet fighters in the 1960s. Peru was the first state to acquire such planes; by 1975 Argentina, Brazil, Chile and Venezuela had all followed suit. No war broke out, none was intended, and all states were forced to spend more than they would have wanted on national defence.

In many cases, especially in Africa and the Middle East, the weapons acquired far exceeded the absorption capacity of the state. In Iran (perhaps the most egregious example), the Shah acquired in the 1970s such a quantity of sophisticated weapons that an American government report acknowledged that 'Iran will not be able to absorb and operate within the next five to ten years a large proportion of the sophisticated military systems it has purchased.'[29] Several American studies 'concluded that the military threats to Iran's northern and western borders could best be addressed by the steady, systematic development and training of its military forces, rather than the rapid introduction of massive quantities of complex high-technology equipment'.[30] The pattern has been repeated throughout North and Sub-Saharan Africa, where the weapons acquired have been 'usually inappropriate for the environment and absorptive capacity of recipient nations'.[31] One result has been an influx of foreign technicians and advisors to maintain and operate the weapons, a result that does not increase the independence of recipient states but rather confirms their subordinate status in the arms transfer system.

Arms can also be acquired to fight a war, and the pattern of arms acquisitions in the Arab–Israeli context since 1955 suggests that arms races triggered by this motive are probably the most costly and dramatic. States anticipating a war often argue (correctly or not) that small differences in the quality and quantity of weapons available at the outset can make a great deal of difference in the outcome or duration of the fighting. Because most of the wars since 1945 have been fought by states with no domestic arms industry, and because suppliers are frequently reluctant to make massive deliveries during a war, most recipients driven by this motive attempt to build large weapons stockpiles to avoid a potentially crippling dependence on uncertain resupply during a conflict.[32] The main practitioners of stockpiling have been those Middle Eastern states that have experienced such pressures. For example, Syria has about 1,100 older tanks and some aircraft in storage, while Israel has about 100 planes in reserve, and its domestic industry to draw upon. Libya had throughout the 1980s up to 450 MiG-23 and MiG-25 aircraft (and up to 1,200 tanks) stored still in their crates, and Saudi Arabia in 1984 acquired 1,600 air-to-ground missiles, explicitly to provide a sixty-day war-fighting reserve.[33] When one compares the forces available in the Middle East at different periods in the 1970s and 1980s (as presented in table 30 above), this progressive escalation in the quantity of weapons is clear, and a similar arms build-up (albeit from a much lower base) has appeared in Africa, another zone of endemic conflict.[34] It should be noted, though, that such stockpiling can also be a manifestation of a regional arms race triggered by interstate insecurities and not an attempt to secure greater independence from suppliers. The interaction of these two motives can in fact help trigger or escalate regional arms races.

The pursuit of regional influence and hegemony often accompanies these other motives. States that wish to assume a higher regional or global profile often assume that military prowess is the means of advancement, irrespective of whether or not the weapons are acquired to meet a definable threat in a militarily appropriate fashion. If one can fly a squadron of advanced fighter planes over the capital on independence day, this is (much like a national airline and national palace) a sign of power that commands respect. Thus states such as Libya and Venezuela acquired sophisticated arsenals that either could not be maintained or operated or could not be justified by clear threats to security. In Libya, although huge quantities of tanks and aircraft were acquired during the 1970s and 1980s, the relatively poor performance of the Libyan army against Chad suggests that its more sophisticated equipment was not effectively used.[35] The 1982 acquisition by Venezuela of F-16 fighters, defended on the grounds of a putative threat from Cuba, appears less credible after one notes that Cuba does not possess an aircraft with a range capable of attacking Venezuela and returning to base.[36] Weapons acquisitions by other states such as India, Iran or Iraq that often appear to be explained by specific conflicts or wars can also be seen as part and parcel of a claim to regional political or military hegemony. Arms acquisitions by these states can also be seen (correctly or not) as a means of excluding external powers or reducing the dependence that arises from their relative position in the international hierarchy of power.[37]

Both the internal and the regional sets of motivations explain the acquisition of modern weapons as fundamentally driven by factors operating at the level of the state (or groups of states). Yet there remains the possibility that arms acquisitions (especially in the developing world) are driven by 'systemic' forces: either by the direct influence and interests of arms suppliers operating within the market, or by the widespread acceptance of a particularly narrow understanding of how states (and peoples) can achieve security. The former argument is present in explanations that link changes in patterns of arms acquisitions to such factors as the rising cost of oil imports for industrial states, and there is at least *ad hoc* evidence that the dramatic increase in weapons sales to Iran and other oil-rich Gulf states after 1973 was in part driven by arms suppliers eager to recycle petrodollars and reap quick profits.[38] The latter, more subtle, explanation is advanced by those who argue that 'the threat system established by the arms race and violence in international relations serves to promote the interests of the military and to encourage militaristic tendencies'.[39] Whether or not this 'threat system' is established or reinforced by the dominant states in the global arms transfer and production system or simply a product of the self-help nature of international politics is debatable. What cannot be ignored, however, is the fact that this construction of international politics (with its emphasis on the

197

sovereign state) is neither neutral nor necessarily appropriate for many recipient states. As two authors adopting this perspective argue, 'the principle of sovereignty is a mechanism of structural coercion that creates and legitimates material inequality that disempowers Third World state actors and which thereby forces those interested in capital-intensive militarization to do so on a dependent basis'.[40] On this account, it is not surprising that the same forces that drive other states to produce arms will push those states that cannot produce modern weapons at least to acquire them, even if this process actually confirms their subordinate position in the global hierarchy by reinforcing the anarchic structure of international politics.

It is ultimately impossible to disentangle these motives for arms acquisitions completely; and more importantly, the state-level and system-level processes may operate in tandem. One state may purchase weapons for reasons of prestige or to suppress internal dissent, yet the operation of the security dilemma may drive its neighbours inevitably to interpret this as a possible threat. An expensive and unnecessary arms race may be triggered, and the result might even be an armed conflict. The simple equation that many arms recipients make between a military establishment and security, between possession of more advanced arms and greater security, and between independence of arms supply with autonomy of action coincides well with the interest of first-tier suppliers in using arms transfers as a tool of influence, or of second- and third-tier suppliers in increasing arms exports.

## The recipients' responses

The dynamic of technological change and diffusion outlined in chapter 1, and the inability of most recipient states to achieve autonomous arms production or even to make effective use of modern weapons, suggests that their subordinate position in the global arms transfer and production system is unchanging. It would be an error, however, to conclude that recipients are utterly unable to ameliorate their subordinate position in the face of the monopoly of military technology possessed by suppliers, and the influence this bestows upon suppliers (especially upon first-tier states).[41] While the dependence of recipients may make arms transfers an effective instrument of influence for supplier states over the medium term, over the long run they increase the drive to greater military self-reliance by recipients. Greater self-reliance can be won by recipients in two ways:

(1) by increasing also the dependence of their weapons suppliers on them – providing these suppliers with their strategic resources – the desired outcome in this case is a more *symmetrical interdependence*; and

(2) by reducing their dependence on any single foreign supplier of arms ... the desired outcome [being] *lower dependence*.[42]

The first of these depends on idiosyncratic factors in particular patron–client relationships (such as military bases and strategic access), and will not be dealt with. Within the second set of responses, however, one can distinguish several means by which recipients can lower their dependence on particular suppliers, including diversifying sources of supply or changing primary suppliers, stockpiling weapons, retransferring weapons and making alternative arrangements for financing arms acquisitions.

The most significant evidence for attempts to alter the relationship between suppliers and recipients is the increased tendency of arms recipients to diversify their sources of supply. On the surface, the diversification of supply sources is a militarily inefficient and expensive policy, as complex modern weapons require an integrated approach from initial training to final usage. Prosaic examples would be the different ammunition needed by different weapons or the need for consistent and coherent training procedures that can be incorporated into established or primitive military structures. The integration of more sophisticated weapons with other systems (such as the links required between surveillance aircraft, ground stations and interceptors) almost dictates that equipment from multiple suppliers will be difficult to operate efficiently. When such integration can develop, it often requires the duplication of essential support services; the problems NATO planners experienced with equipment integration attest to this. Thus one cannot expect less advanced military forces, with already enormous difficulties in absorbing modern weapons, to embark on a policy of supplier diversification for purely military or economic reasons.

But most recipient states have diversified their sources of supply whenever possible. Table 32 breaks down the dependence of clients upon primary suppliers in different periods since the early 1960s. Between 1964 and 1973, 102 of 122 states depended upon one supplier for more than 60 per cent of their weapons. By the 1984–8 period, only 86 of 132 states (65 per cent) were in this position. This reduction of dependence was most apparent in the Middle East and Latin America, where by 1984–8 about half of arms recipients acquired weapons from multiple suppliers. That these two regions are prominent is not surprising, given that both have experienced supply restrictions over the past three decades: in the Middle East as a consequence of regional wars; in Latin America, as a consequence of American policies.

One can also find numerous examples of states that have switched primary suppliers while perhaps not actually reducing their level of dependence. Examples of such switches would include Egypt (1976), Somalia (1977), Ethiopia (1976), the Sudan (1974), Libya (1971), Nicaragua (1979), and Angola and Mozambique after 1976. All shifts but one (Somalia) occurred directly or indirectly as a result of regime change, which suggests that there is a high degree of rigidity in the policy options entertained by a specific regime and reinforces the importance of the *perception* within the client state's policy-making elite that different options exist. Switching suppliers at least demonstrates some degree of independence from suppliers, and is especially significant given the near-total obsolescence of previously acquired weapons that it creates (as the Egyptian experience suggests).

In addition to diversifying their sources of arms supply or changing suppliers, recipients can stockpile weapons, transfer weapons among themselves, pay for weapons previously obtained as grant aid, or seek alternative sources of military aid.[43] Evidence for the tendency to stockpile weapons as a means of achieving greater independence was offered above. With respect to weapons retransfers, although American (and probably Soviet) arms contracts prohibit arms transfers to third parties without authorisation, the arms supplied by second- and third-tier suppliers often contain no such provisions. As a result, many states, particularly in the Middle East and Africa, have transferred weapons among themselves as a way of avoiding supplier restrictions. In the 1973 Middle East war, Libya lent Egypt two squadrons of Mirage fighters, and Iraq shipped tanks to Syria.[44] After the war, Kuwait and Saudi Arabia paid for 86 Mirages for Egypt, and in 1982, Libya sent 20–30 MiG-21s to Syria to replace its losses against Israel.[45] Although in most cases support was minor, the Iran–Iraq War, which saw American and Soviet equipment transferred to both combatants by many suppliers without the approval of either supplier, suggests that retransfers can take on major proportions.[46] These transfers are not confined to the Middle East, although they are most common there.

Dependence upon a patron for the means of paying for arms is also a potentially great source of influence for the patron, and it is in this light that one must see the shift from military aid towards purely commercial transactions. Although this shift has occurred in part

Table 32. *Degree of dependence of recipients on suppliers, various years (number of states)*

|  |  | 1964–73 | 1976–80 | 1984–8 |
|---|---|---|---|---|
| Africa | Sole | 11 | 4 | 14 |
| | Predominant | 17 | 20 | 10 |
| | Multiple | 6 | 18 | 16 |
| Europe | Sole | 13 | 4 | 9 |
| | Predominant | 12 | 20 | 13 |
| | Multiple | 3 | 3 | 5 |
| East Asia | Sole | 7 | 6 | 6 |
| | Predominant | 4 | 5 | 5 |
| | Multiple | 3 | 4 | 4 |
| Latin America | Sole | 8 | 3 | 6 |
| | Predominant | 9 | 4 | 6 |
| | Multiple | 5 | 13 | 12 |
| Middle East | Sole | 3 | 3 | 3 |
| | Predominant | 10 | 11 | 7 |
| | Multiple | 1 | 2 | 6 |
| North America | Sole | 1 | 0 | 1 |
| | Predominant | 1 | 1 | 0 |
| | Multiple | 0 | 1 | 1 |
| South Asia | Sole | 1 | 1 | 1 |
| | Predominant | 3 | 1 | 3 |
| | Multiple | 2 | 3 | 1 |
| Oceania | Sole | 0 | 0 | 1 |
| | Predominant | 2 | 2 | 1 |
| | Multiple | 0 | 2 | 1 |
| Total | Sole | 44 | 21 | 41 |
| | Predominant | 58 | 64 | 45 |
| | Multiple | 20 | 46 | 46 |
| $n =$ | | 122 | 131 | 132 |

*Note:* A 'sole' supplier provides 90 per cent of a client's arms, a 'predominant' supplier more than 50 per cent of them, and 'multiple' suppliers less than 50 per cent for any one supplier.
*Source:* ACDA, *WMEAT*, various years.

because of first-tier suppliers' desire to reduce foreign military expenditures, it has also been conditioned by recipients' desire to reduce their vulnerability to exercises of influence. Clients who pay for their arms are less likely to have 'unmet demands' that could be manipulated by a patron state in its interest.

Middle Eastern states have again been particularly adept at easing such potential pressures by transferring funds between themselves, often to purchase weapons from second- and third-tier suppliers that have no strings attached. After the 1967 war, for example, the oil-producing Arab states agreed to provide money to front-line states in the Arab–Israeli conflict: $250 million was pledged to Egypt, and $100 million and $14 million to Jordan and Iraq respectively.[47] During the 1973 war, Algeria, Libya and some oil-producing states agreed to pay for the airlifted arms to Egypt which the Soviets were not prepared to supply cheaply. Between 1973 and 1978 Egypt received more than $5,800 million from the Gulf states; this aid played a major role in allowing Egypt to reduce its military dependence on the USSR before it received American military aid.[48] The Saudis also granted Jordan $350 million to purchase American air defence equipment. After 1978, the political nature of this cooperation became clear when Egypt was punished for the Camp David accords by the suspension of Arab military and economic aid. Syria and Jordan became the primary recipients, with respective pledges of $1,850 and $1,250 million annually being made at the 1978 Baghdad summit. Neither party, however, received the total amount pledged, and aid to Syria was cut as disenchantment with its regional policies set in.[49] Such aid is also not confined to the Arab–Israel conflict: Oman was granted $1,800 million for the 1984–94 period by the Gulf Cooperation Council to help fight its insurgents.[50]

Israel has adopted a different strategy to insulate itself from American pressure by placing its military assistance and arms transfer relationship on a long-term footing. That this is a direct reaction against pressure exerted upon it is clear: Israel first tried to gain such concessions as part of its agreement to the Golan Accords, and the Americans informally promised to determine arms supplies to Israel on a long-term instead of an annual basis.[51] In 1975 this informal agreement was codified when the Memorandum of Agreement appended to the Sinai II agreements pledged the United States 'to make every effort to be responsive ... on an ongoing and long-term basis to Israel's military equipment and other defense requirements'.[52] The overall result has been that since 1973 American–Israeli arms negotiations have seldom focused on individual transactions but rather on long-term military modernisation and technology transfer programmes. The cumulative effect of such moves (as American attempts to exercise influence over Israel in various policy areas in the 1980s suggest) has been a clear reduction in the influence the United States can muster.

Although inter-Arab financial ties and the American–Israeli relationship are unique, and although it is unlikely that another region could develop this level of cooperation to thwart the influence of external powers, these developments do illustrate what recipient states will do to ameliorate their subordinate position in the arms transfer system if they have the means.[53] The various recipients' responses, which are usually triggered by exercises of influence against them, are part of a process that can result in great reductions in the influence which supplier states can extract from arms transfer relationships. The upshot of all these strategies is that the ability of suppliers to manipulate bilateral arms transfer relationships for political ends appears to have been greatly weakened by these changes in the structure of the arms transfer system. In so far as following any of these strategies also provides a precedent, or creates a perception that other alternatives exist, the real decline in dependence upon suppliers may actually be greater than the figures of table 32 suggest.

## Conclusion

The importance of examining the changing structure of the recipient market, the different motives behind states' arms acquisitions and the different patterns of acquisitions that have developed over the past few decades does not lie in the answer to the simple question of who gets what. Rather such data are important indicators of patterns of hierarchy and hegemony in the global arms transfer and production system. The attempt by recipient states to acquire arms in order simultaneously to guarantee their security (as states or regimes) and to ameliorate their regional or global position is merely part of the same larger pattern that is manifest throughout the different tiers of the system. Although recipient states are subordinate, they are not utterly powerless. A learning curve of sorts appears to be at work, in which continued contact with patron states allows the client to uncover means by which the relationships can be manipulated to its benefit, and over time strengthens its belief that its environment is (or should be) controllable.

But there are limits to this learning process, and although this struggle can reduce dependence on arms suppliers in particular bilateral relationships of influence, it seldom fundamentally alters the structurally subordinate position of recipient states. The global military system remains extremely hierarchical, and the underlying dynamic of the global arms transfer and production system in the post-1945 period remains the quest of states to reach the highest possible point in the league tables of international or regional military capabilities. Idiosyncratic factors such as the policies pursued by different leaders or the impact of specific wars can push a state beyond a position in the international (or regional) ranking of power that is warranted by its underlying economic base or factor endowments, but such deviations do not undermine the structure of the system itself.

However successful recipient states are at acquiring and learning to use advanced weapons, their structurally subordinate position is at the core the product of an inability to grasp the art of producing and operating advanced weapons in an appropriate socio-cultural, economic and political context. Recipient states are unable to move beyond the most simple level, that of 'technology I' (the ability to operate and maintain the weapons), to acquire the skills needed to reproduce or copy modern technological artifacts (not just military ones). Such states remain prey to the vicissitudes of the arms market and the machinations of regionally more powerful states (such as India, Brazil, China or Egypt) that have managed to ascend at least to third-tier status. It is important to realise, however, that their inability to produce weapons is not in itself the reason for the subordination of recipient states; it is rather a reflection of other more profound economic, political and socio-cultural inequalities in the international system.

# CONCLUSION

As Stephanie Neuman and Robert Harkavy point out, 'for the most part the arms transfer literature has confined itself to asking and answering descriptive questions about who is buying what from whom for how much and how this affects the U.S.–USSR balance. Only recently has the world's attention been drawn to the . . . complex interrelationships between arms transfers and developments within and among nations.'[1] This book has focused on the latter set of complex relationships at the general or systemic level in order to provide a better understanding of arms transfers as a phenomenon of international relations and to reduce the conceptual chaos that is often found in the literature. The intent was not to develop a rigorous 'theory' or 'model' of the global arms transfer and production system, but rather to provide a framework within which diverse phenomena can be better explained. Thus instead of embarking on a detailed and purely descriptive study of a particular aspect of the arms transfer system, the book cast its net more widely to answer such questions as: 'What are the constituent elements of an arms transfer "system"?' 'What motives govern states' participation in arms transfers?' and 'What are the implications of these factors for the emergence and evolution of the system?'

Existing analyses of the arms trade, although often well documented and informative, also generally lack the historical perspective required for this task. They most often fail to acknowledge that the current arms transfer system has historical antecedents with which it may or may not share common features, and do not concern themselves with the broader historical forces that shape the order within which states operate.[2] This ahistorical and anti-systemic bias overstates the freedom of states to shape the military and security environment within which they operate and obscures the real and profound structural constraints on their choices. To paraphrase Marx, leaders of states may make their own history, but not in the time and place of their choosing.

Although one should not accord the global arms transfer and production system the status of an independent exogenous force for change that explains the rise and fall of particular states or the transformations of the state system, it performs three functions within the international system: it distributes the means for fighting wars and winning conflicts, it helps establish a state's location in the international and regional military hierarchy (and is the means for enforcing regional hegemony), and it is the mechanism for the diffusion of the technology of arms production. It is also a focal point at which a number of the broader forces that drive the evolution of the international system (which I have called the pursuit of power, wealth and victory in war) come together. It thus provides a useful intellectual vantage point from which to begin exploring the interaction of these forces.

The forces motivating states' action within the international system and the dynamic of technological innovation drive the arms transfer system to evolve along the 'life cycle' that was sketched in chapter 1. This life cycle is catalysed by 'revolutionary' technological innovation, and its first manifestation is the emergence of centres of advanced arms production that monopolise new techniques based on their underlying factor endowments and their 'pursuit of power'. The advantages that weapons based on new technologies can bring drive other states to acquire them, and thus they are diffused throughout the system. States that are not among the initial first tier soon attempt to eliminate the near-monopoly of the means of producing advanced weapons that first-tier states possess by acquiring the technologies to produce the weapons themselves. But the uneven distribution of economic and socio-cultural endowments results in the imperfect diffusion of new technologies (and the ability to reproduce them) throughout the system and gives rise to a second and third tier of producers. The diffusion of military technology and techniques is not smooth or linear, and the system remains highly stratified. Although the rate of incremental innovation in first-tier states slows in the later stages of each cycle, the barriers to movement between tiers remain relatively high as the intense competition between a slowly growing number of suppliers increases the importance of underlying economic endowments as the prime determinant of a state's location in the global military hierarchy. At the bottom of the hierarchy, weak states attempt to acquire the means of producing military technology, either to fortify their position vis-à-vis strong states, or to exercise their own form of local dominance, but such attempts nearly always have limited success.

The historical material presented in chapters 2 and 3 confirms this picture of a hierarchically organised and stratified system. In the first epoch, catalysed by the cannon and gunpowder revolution, Britain, Sweden and the Low Countries emerged as the first-tier innovative foci of arms production and trade. In the second (associated with the technological innovations of the Industrial Revolution), Britain, France and Germany assumed this role. As technology was diffused throughout the system, other states, often driven by deliberate government policies, struggled to maintain or assume an equal role on the world stage. Many states gained a secure foothold as second-tier suppliers, but few mastered the new technologies of military production sufficiently to elevate their status to the first tier. In the sixteenth century, Italy enjoyed a brief tenure as a first-tier producer, while Germany (in the seventeenth) failed to consolidate its first-tier position. Spain and Russia, both in the seventeenth and nineteenth centuries, failed to climb beyond the second tier. Below these producers the diffusion of new weapons to less-developed regions spawned imitative third-tier arms production in states as diverse as the Ottoman Empire, Portugal, Japan, China and India, and the mastery of 'advanced' technology that these states acquired was sufficient to allow them to play a powerful regional role. Even further down the hierarchical ladder one finds simple consumers of arms, the weakest of whom were unable to adapt their military and social structures to the exigencies of the new weapons and thus eventually faded away.

How well does the pattern of change in the contemporary global arms transfer system correspond to this evolutionary model?[3] At the outset, it is clear that the brief period from 1950 to 1970, which formed the basis for most assessments of the structure and evolution of the arms transfer system, was a poor starting point for analysis. The roots of the contemporary system can be traced to the interwar period, when the expected quiescent phase that could have followed (given the slowed pace of innovations still based on technologies of the Industrial Revolution) was superseded by a new technological 'revolution', the rise of the superpowers and the break with the previous arms transfer system these developments precipitated. The primacy of the United States and the Soviet Union was confirmed during the Second World War, and the rapid pace of technological change within the twentieth-century 'revolution in mobility' foreshadowed the massive investments in research and development that would be required of states wishing to stay at the forefront of military technology after 1945.[4] After 1945, the United States and the Soviet Union eclipsed other potential or former first-tier suppliers (with Britain maintaining its first-tier position until the late 1950s), and the evolutionary dynamic of the arms transfer system began to take shape. The initial focus was on the trade in weapons themselves (technology I), and the first-tier states' near-monopoly of modern military technologies granted them a temporary capability both to concentrate on the political significance of arms transfers and to manipulate arms transfers as effective tools of foreign policy. The size of the American and Soviet domestic arms markets also permitted a much lower reliance on exports to maintain a healthy industry, which facilitated the use of arms transfers as tools of political influence. Prior first-tier states had only pursued such a policy with much difficulty. The fate of the English arms industry in the seventeenth century under a restrictive government policy and the French experience of the late nineteenth century (when government policy was forced to pursue exports to harness the indigenous capacity for innovation) testify to this.

But the dynamic process of technology diffusion commenced in the 1950s with transfers of arms production technologies via licensed and co-production arrangements to the alliance partners of both superpowers. Such transfers ensured that producers such as France, Czechoslovakia, Italy and Japan (among others) could either rise to or maintain second-tier status, as their domestic arms industries acquired the skills to adapt weapons to specific requirements and to innovate incrementally (technology III). British, French and German efforts to stay abreast of current technological developments, and Italian and Spanish efforts to join the second tier, highlight how difficult the struggle to maintain such status is. These difficulties mean that the motivation of second-tier producers for participating in the arms transfer system is distinct from that of first-tier suppliers: low levels of domestic procurement and relatively small research and development establishments force a greater reliance on exports and a forswearing of the potential political benefits that can be derived from arms transfer relationships. The shift in British and French policy in the 1960s to a more commercial orientation (and the rapid rise in their exports in the 1970s) and West Germany's emergence as a major exporter in the face of serious domestic political inhibitions confirm this phenomenon. Although second-tier states seldom contribute to the advancement of military technology, as the locus of technological innovation is firmly rooted in the first tier, the emergence of alternative second-tier suppliers reduces the ability of first-tier states to dominate the system and to manipulate transfers for political ends.

Throughout the 1970s and 1980s, sophisticated weapons were

further diffused throughout the system. On the demand side several states in the developing world (including India, China, Israel, Brazil and Egypt) sought also to acquire not only the weapons themselves but the means to reproduce them (technology II), in order to establish a strong regional political or military presence. Second-tier producers were the greatest suppliers of technology to these states as first-tier states tentatively attempted to control the haemorrhage of their monopoly of advanced technologies. But weak economic, industrial and technological infrastructures hindered the progressive advance of third-tier industries, and in an environment in which military technology continued to advance rapidly these states were unable to narrow significantly the technological gap (in weapons production) between themselves and first-tier producers. Several recent efforts at third-tier production will almost certainly fail to flourish, as the pursuit of power and victory in war is ultimately overwhelmed by critical economic or technological weaknesses.

Third-tier arms production will remain a marginal activity in the system as these producers are (almost always) restricted to producing a narrow range of weapons systems and continue to depend on technological inputs from the first and second tier. The fact that third-tier producers relentlessly pursue arms exports in order to maintain their fragile defence industrial bases, and their limited success at this effort, underscores their vulnerability to the vicissitudes of the market. Although the limited independence of supply and increased margin of manoeuvre against weaker (pure recipient) states that they gain does improve their position somewhat and further diminishes the dominance exercised by first-tier states throughout the system, the subordinate status of third-tier producers in the system will not be ameliorated until and unless the pace of technological innovation in armaments slows.

It may indeed be the case that the current wave of the arms transfer and production system is entering a stage in which the rate of technological innovation in the core slows, as the cost, for example, of 'Stealth' bombers reaches $500 million a plane and the engineering design capabilities of aircraft exceed the physical human capacity to fly them. The increasingly 'baroque' nature of military technology itself, with innovations less and less related to military demands, points to the exhaustion of the process of innovation within the particular set of technologies associated with the 'revolution in mobility'.[5] One consequence of this is that the gap between the sophistication of the weapons possessed by different tiers of suppliers and recipients is narrowing, although the gap in production capabilities may remain

209

extremely wide for an indefinite time. Another implication is that the stratified structure of the system will be reinforced, with entry into a higher tier becoming increasingly difficult as the system is driven by what are fundamentally economic or market considerations. Finally, the influence derived from arms transfers will increasingly become an idiosyncratic product of involvement in evanescent and unpredictable conflicts, rather than a systemic characteristic of first-tier status.

The analysis presented in this book of the structure of the global arms transfer and production system does not support a rigidly deterministic account of the future position of particular states within the system. Structural constraints do not dominate or dictate the choices of agents, although they do establish the outlines or broad borders that shape and limit these choices. It was noted above that ascent to a higher tier is extremely difficult, but descent is of course less difficult. Second-tier producers such as Canada, the Netherlands or Belgium are finding it increasingly difficult to maintain an autonomous advanced defence production base, and in an environment in which the global confrontation between East and West has vanished, these states may choose to abandon the struggle. A similar decline (from first- to second-tier status) may even be imposed on the Soviet Union, as state power is fragmented or radically decentralised. Current third-tier producers such as Argentina, Chile or North Korea could conceivably abandon their efforts, while India and China could (in the distant future) possibly ascend to second-tier status, albeit only after a great deal of industrial development takes place. Japan or united Germany, on the other hand, could also certainly support greater defence industrial infrastructures, and may even be capable of sustaining a first-tier military research and development and procurement establishment, although this is certainly not indicated by current political developments.

In addition, the model's successive epochs based on revolutions in military technology should not lead one to conclude that the international arms transfer system endlessly replicates itself in timeless monotony. Its history is instead evolutionary: successive epochs, while following a similar pattern, differ from each other in important respects and are at the same time influenced by traces of prior history and other broader forces. For example, the underlying shift in economic thought from mercantilism to capitalism led to a changed perception of the role of arms exports; from an initial unwillingness to export arms and military technology, first-tier producers accepted that exports allowed them to maintain their innovative capabilities and productive base. In addition, the changing mechanisms (and ideologies) of state intervention in the economy gave rise to different mechanisms of control and regulation: from tight mercantilism, to nineteenth-century *laissez-faire*, to the complex state–producer–recipient relations that characterise the late twentieth-century edifice of promotion and control.

Perhaps the most important progressive development is the changed relationship between technology and the state, which has witnessed the state increasingly harnessing the process of techno-logical innovation to its ends. The Italian city-states' attempts to develop siege defences against the new weapons of the sixteenth century were defensive reactions to exogenously introduced military innovations, but by the eighteenth century 'planned invention, organized and supported by public authority, becomes an unmistak-able reality'.[6] For the first time, weapons were developed whose use could be anticipated, rather than the previous process of reluctant adaptation to exogenous technological change. This process acceler-ated throughout the Industrial Revolution and culminated in the Manhattan Project, which 'forged the last link in the chain between pure theory and practical policy'.[7] But this new realm of competition was only open to states that could mobilise increasingly large amounts of resources. Just as the Italian city-states faded into insignificance in the sixteenth and seventeenth centuries as a result of technological changes that required the mobilisation of resources on a scale beyond their means, the military technologies of the twentieth century demanded an effort that could only be met by 'superpowers'.[8]

Although the 'wave' model describes only imperfectly what is doubtless a more complex reality, it does suggest that attempts to understand specific changes in the current arms transfer system need to be carefully rooted in an understanding of its history, structure and dynamic. When this is done, one can distinguish between durable and ephemeral trends and significantly amend the conclusions drawn by many current analyses of the arms transfer system. For example, one contemporary analysis of global arms transfers concluded that 'the political factors that dominated the arms trade in the recent past are yielding to market forces . . . the arms trade is returning to its patterns prior to World War II, when the trade in military equipment was not dramatically different from the trade in many other industrial pro-ducts'.[9] When these developments are placed in a historical context, it becomes clear that arms have only rarely and briefly been traded as freely as any other commodity, with all or most participants imposing few restrictions. Even during the height of the *laissez-faire* era, arms transfers were manipulated in one way or another by states. The global distribution of arms production capabilities, however, is significantly determined by 'market forces', if by this one means the underlying economic infrastructure and capabilities of states. Finally, the evolutionary dynamic marks not a return to pre-1945 patterns, but part of a larger process of the diffusion and reproduction of military technology.

The most important feature of the arms transfer system identified in this book is its three-tiered structure, which ultimately determines membership in a tier by such criteria as the arms production base, military research and development capabilities, the technological sophistication of production, and domestic procurement and export dependence. (By contrast, most previous efforts to classify arms producers into tiers have usually been based on relative shares of the export market, with authors distinguishing either two or three tiers.[10]) First-tier states innovate at the technological frontier and possess an across-the-board production capability for sophisticated weapons. They possess the largest domestic markets and research and development establishments, and although they are the dominant exporters, they do not depend on exports for the survival of their industries. Second-tier states produce weapons at or near the technological frontier and adapt them to their needs, but possess much smaller R&D, domestic procurement and production bases. Their industries hence depend heavily on exports or subsidies and are limited by the length of their production runs from producing arms as cheaply as first-tier states. Third-tier producers reproduce existing technologies but are unable to innovate. Their industries are often enclaves in a less industrialised economy, and major political and economic investments are needed to override these disadvantages. Third-tier suppliers' share of global production and exports is limited, and their comparative export advantage lies in specialised niches for unsophisticated weapons.

This classification is not a mere terminological quibble, for it has concrete analytical consequences. If one classifies arms suppliers by their share of the export market, for example, it appears reasonable to argue that the relatively linear decline in first-tier suppliers' market shares will continue. An analysis rooted in underlying endowments and production bases, on the other hand, leads one to conclude that market shares will stabilise at or near present levels.[11] The rise of French sales in the 1970s and early 1980s, for instance, was argued by some to signal an impending rise to first-tier status.[12] A better understanding of the motivations governing the French pursuit of arms exports and its underlying defence industrial endowment makes clear that such a rise was the result of a short-term constellation of forces. The retrenchment of the French arms industry and the increasing competition provided by Britain and West Germany suggest that this development was a function of such factors as the oil price rise; the lack of second-tier competition in the late 1960s and early 1970s and the desire of certain clients to diversify their supply sources. Similarly, the argument that 'the structure of the international arms market is changing ... Slowly, but perceptibly, the market is becoming less concentrated and more diffuse' must acknowledge that this diffusion has almost reached its limits, and that it marks not a dramatic change in the structure, but an evolution along an easily understood life cycle.[13]

Several future characteristics of the global arms transfer and production system can be projected from this analysis of the evolutionary dynamic of the system. First, the system will be characterised by excess capacities in arms production in more and more states, as a result both of declining demand and the expanded efforts of second-tier states such as Spain and Italy and third-tier states such as Brazil. Already, European arms producers are experiencing a tremendous contraction of demand and production, which will only be further reinforced by conventional arms control treaties.[14] In the United States and the Soviet Union, the apparently inevitable downward pressures that will be exerted on military spending (at least in the medium term) will put tremendous economic pressures on arms producers. In such an increasingly competitive environment, 'ascendent' producers such as Japan and South Korea (or a more integrated European arms industry) may find their efforts overwhelmed by the advantages possessed by existing producers. All producers may find that greater state intervention is required in order to sustain industries that are otherwise not economically viable.

In this increasingly competitive environment the arms market will remain concentrated rather than becoming more diffuse: only states that can support either high levels of subsidisation or cooperative efforts will be able to sustain advanced weapons production, and other producers will maintain their foothold in the system only with difficulty. But this possibility reminds us that the global arms transfer and production system cannot be analysed in strict economic terms, and that the 'pursuit of power' by states is an important element required to explain the evolution of the system. If arms were produced, bought and sold as simple commodities, one would anticipate over time the emergence of an international division of labour based on the diffusion of technology, economies of scale and comparative

213

advantage. To the extent that these principles accurately describe economic behaviour, one would expect a highly concentrated arms transfer system that persisted or even grew more rigid over time.[15] That this is not entirely the case is a function of the *interaction* between political and economic factors, which strikes a balance between the economic imperatives that push towards a concentrated system and the political imperatives that motivate every state to produce arms if it can.

As the current system moves into its mature stages, in which the technologies of arms production are widely (if imperfectly) diffused throughout the system and the pace of technological innovation in the first-tier states slows, greater emphasis will be placed on the processes of technology transfer by suppliers and recipients. Already co-production, offsets and licensed production arrangements dominate major weapons deals; what the future may hold is genuine inter-nationalisation of production. As Trevor Taylor points out, this can take the form of 'international collaborative development and pro-duction; sub-contracting from overseas; and multinational corporate defence structures'.[16] Examples would include the ill-starred Egyptian–Argentinian–Iraqi Condor II missile, the Brazilian–Italian AMX fighter consortium, or the contracting activities of Northrop in South Korea and Taiwan or General Dynamics in Turkey.[17] These efforts are directly analogous to the early twentieth-century activities of the large British, French and German arms-producing firms, and are a hallmark of a mature system in which participants are driven to relinquish their technological monopolies by the imperative of survival.

The future possibilities for exercising control and restraint over the arms trade must be understood against this backdrop. As the gap between the weapons possessed by first-tier states and strong recipients narrows, one would expect increased efforts to control the diffusion of advanced weapons in order to maintain the remaining narrow margin of advantage. But the diffusion of technologies makes this goal more difficult to achieve as it becomes more difficult for states, individually or in concert, to exercise even tacit restraint over transfers. This is especially true as the emphasis in trade shifts to the technologies of arms production rather than the weapons themselves. It is the persistent efforts of third-tier states to produce arms and recipient states to obtain them that drives the system to evolve, as participation in the arms transfer system teaches the weak that they are not eternally powerless. An understanding of the logic of such a dynamic process is too often absent from the arms transfer literature.

Whatever the future outlines of the system, it is clear that we must link the study of arms transfers to an understanding of the underlying motivations and prospects for arms production. Further, the global arms transfer and production system is itself a product and a reflection of broader forces at work in international politics: arms are sought (and produced) as part of the enduring quest for security, independence and well-being that we have associated with the sovereign state. In so far as individuals and states (especially in a post-Cold War world) strive to transcend the self-help nature of international politics to create other means of achieving security, the forces that give rise to arms production and transfers can perhaps be muted or even overcome. If this occurs, much of the underlying motivation that drives states to procure and produce weapons might also be overcome, and a genuine 'demilitarisation' of global politics could occur. But in so far as states remain locked into what they perceive to be a permanent struggle to survive, or to improve their position in a global hierarchy of power and influence, arms transfers and arms production will be persistent accompanying features of the landscape. In any case, arms transfers and production cannot be understood outside of their historical context or the structure of world politics, and must be seen as part of the greater web of economic, diplomatic and socio-cultural interactions between weak and strong states.

# APPENDIX
# ARMS TRANSFER DATA
# SOURCES AND PROBLEMS

Any publication using arms transfer data ought to acknowledge the severe, and possibly crippling, shortcomings of such data. Several specific and general problems can be highlighted which make conclusions based on statistical manipulation of the data extremely tentative. This appendix merely sketches the problems; readers are encouraged to consult the more detailed studies noted throughout.

There are four main sources of arms transfer information: The United States Arms Control and Disarmament Agency (ACDA) annual publication *World Military Expenditures and Arms Transfers*; the Stockholm International Peace Research Institute *Yearbook of World Armaments and Disarmament* (and related publications using the same data base); the International Institute of Strategic Studies (IISS) annual *The Military Balance*; and other (usually country-specific) studies. The ACDA data have been relied upon most in this book, because they possess three advantages other sources do not: they include all suppliers and recipients, they attempt to capture all transfers (not just major weapons systems), and they present at least roughly comparable dollar figures for arms deliveries.[1] SIPRI data, on the other hand, include only deliveries of major weapons systems (aircraft, armour and artillery, guidance and radar systems, missiles and warships), and they also detail major identified arms agreements in their comprehensive data base of arms transfers since 1950. *The Military Balance* does not provide aggregate arms transfers data (although it does include a listing of major arms agreements of the preceding year), but it does present information on states' equipment inventories, which can be used to gain a sense of what arms have been transferred over time. This is especially useful in discussing the possible military utility of the arms transferred, which is not possible with ACDA data.

Although ACDA and SIPRI data can be correlated, there are occasionally major differences between the two sources (in part based on the fact that SIPRI uses only public sources, while ACDA relies on information generated from within the American intelligence community).[2] The two correlate highly on arms deliveries (for example, shares of arms imported by different regions), but much more poorly on the distribution of market shares to producers, with considerable differences in the shares assigned to the United States and the Soviet Union.[3] Thus information from the two sources should not be mixed. In addition, although the two sources do correlate, ACDA figures are generally 1.8–2.0 times higher than SIPRI data, as a result of the latter's restriction to major weapons transfers.[4] On the other hand, when compared to studies of arms transfers by specific states, ACDA data appear (as indicated in table 23) sometimes to underestimate their volume seriously.

Since the ACDA data are presented in an annual publication that covers the preceding ten years, and since all figures are subject to annual revision, the figures presented in this book are based upon a composite data base derived from several different volumes of ACDA statistics. For any given year, the most up-to-date statistics available were used. In addition, a common deflator was constructed to convert current dollars from 1963 to 1987 into constant 1988 dollars. There are several potential sources of error in this process, and small errors in recent data are magnified as one moves further back. Given these sources of error, the gross dollar value statistics should be used as trend indicators only.

Four specific problems with the ACDA (and other) data are worth mentioning, if only to alert the reader to the massive pitfalls facing macro-statistical manipulations of it. First, the valuation of Soviet weapons transfers is extremely problematic, even assuming that all transfers are sooner or later made public (usually by the recipient). Soviet weapons prices are not made public, and in its command economy they would in any case bear little relationship to actual production costs (as noted in chapter 5). The model used by ACDA to value the weapons estimates the costs of producing Soviet equipment in the United States.[5] Among the problems with this method, it ignores the possibly large unit-cost savings accruing from long Soviet production runs and standardised production and the large differences in capital and labour costs (which means that an economically efficient production process in the Soviet Union that has a high labour component will be more costly in the United States). Both these effects probably result in overestimation of Soviet arms transfers.[6] In addition, in the mid 1980s ACDA revised upwards its estimates of Soviet arms exports since 1977 by approximately 40 per cent. This was based *not* upon any new discoveries of transfers, but simply upon a revision

217

of the pricing system used to value Soviet weapons. Since the data and methodology upon which the ACDA figures are based are not public, it is impossible to assess whether or not this revision was justified.[7] The result is that any attempt to place either the United States or the Soviet Union in 'first place' according to the dollar volume of arms transfers is probably specious. It also suggests that it is wrong to assume that 'transfer values can be compared on a cross-national basis'.[8]

Second, ACDA (and to a lesser extent SIPRI) data appear consistently to underestimate the exports of producers other than the United States and the Soviet Union. Edward Kolodziej's study of French arms transfers found a discrepancy of, on average, *2.59 times* over the period 1963–75![9] ACDA data, using what appears to be the same, or even a better, definition of what constitutes an arms transfer, arrive at a figure much lower than official French statistics. Similar dramatic findings appear for Britain and for third-tier states, with ACDA estimates ranging from one-fifth to one-third of what specific country studies have found.[10] SIPRI data do not appear to be much better.

Third, annual fluctuations and short-term variations in the arms trade render any short-term detection of trends extremely dubious. One or two large deals, which may involve deliveries stretching over many years, can easily skew the figures for a particular year, especially since the decision concerning which year in which to count any given deal is somewhat arbitrary. Large French and British contracts with Middle Eastern states often created this distortion. In this respect, SIPRI's use of five-year moving averages to isolate trends from fluctuations is more appropriate than ACDA's presentation, but also less informative. Currency fluctuations and conversion problems also make it difficult to determine the 'real volume' of transfers and production. Dramatic fluctuations in exchange rates can distort the statistics, which are always presented in American dollars, as can the choice of exchange rate to use for comparison. The use of an American price deflator based on the Gross National Product to obtain constant dollar values is also problematic since inflation in the military production sector varies widely.[11] It is virtually impossible, however, to correct these sources of error.

Finally, changes in the arms trade itself have created serious problems for data collection.[12] The rise of offsets, licensed production and co-production arrangements make it difficult to untangle the import or domestic content of weapons. The increase in transfers of components or subsystems (especially of such sophisticated items as electronics packages) for weapons production or retrofits of existing weapons platforms is also not captured by data that count only completed weapons systems. The data needed to assess the true dimensions of the arms trade to take these factors into account would have to be impossibly precise and detailed, even if the relevant information were publicly available. Lost among these details is the question: 'To what end are these data sought?', for ultimately, the answer to the question 'What is an arms transfer?' depends on what issue is being studied.

These methodological problems, coupled with the extreme unreliability of much of the information in the first place, make arms transfer data some of the least useful in the world of statistics gathering. None of the available sources present a fully reliable measure of arms transfers and production. The secrecy and uncertainty surrounding arms deals, and the hidden interests of the groups disseminating the information (third-tier producers wishing to exaggerate their performance; second-tier producers wishing to conceal it; the American intelligence community's diverse interests) are well known, but often such sources of error are put aside in the search for statistical valid assertions based on seemingly solid data. Until the arms transfer data sources are much more reliable, any manipulations of this sort are best left unattempted.

# NOTES

## Introduction

1 United States, Arms Control and Disarmament Agency, *World Military Expenditures and Arms Transfers, 1989* (Washington: Arms Control and Disarmament Agency, 1990). Hereafter cited as ACDA, *WMEAT*.

2 For variety I use the term 'arms trade', 'arms transfer' and 'international/global arms transfer (and production) system' interchangeably. The most inclusive is 'global arms transfer and production system', and is borrowed from Edward Kolodziej, *Making and Marketing Arms: The French Experience and its Implications for the International System* (Princeton: Princeton University Press, 1987).

3 John R. Hale, *War and Society in Renaissance Europe, 1450–1620* (London: Fontana Press, 1985), 219–29. The specific concept of a 'Military Revolution' is taken from Michael Roberts and will be detailed in chapter 2.

4 This point is well made by John Vincent in his review article, 'Change and international relations', *Review of International Studies*, 9:1 (January 1983), 63–70.

5 Here I can only offer examples of these approaches: Hedley Bull and Adam Watson (eds.), *The Expansion of International Society* (Oxford: Oxford University Press, 1984); Immanuel Wallerstein, *The Modern World System*, vols. I and II (New York: Academic Press, 1974, 1980); Ernest Gellner, *Nations and Nationalism* (Oxford: Basil Blackwell, 1983); Michael Howard, *War in European History* (Oxford: Oxford University Press, 1976); William McNeill, *The Pursuit of Power* (Oxford: Basil Blackwell, 1983); Robert Gilpin, *War and Change in World Politics* (Cambridge: Cambridge University Press, 1981); Paul Kennedy, *The Rise and Fall of the Great Powers* (New York: Random House, 1987); and William Thompson, *On Global War: Historical–Structural Approaches to World Politics* (Columbia: University of South Carolina Press, 1988).

6 Fernand Braudel, *On History*, trans. Sarah Matthews (London: Weidenfeld & Nicolson, 1980), 35.

7 Aaron Karp, 'The trade in conventional weapons', in Stockholm International Peace Research Institute, *SIPRI Yearbook of World Armaments and Disarmament, 1988* (Oxford: Oxford University Press, 1988), 175.

8 Ibid., 197

9 The contributions to Thomas Ohlson (ed.), *Arms Transfer Limitations and Third World Security* (Oxford: Oxford University Press, 1988) are the most

prominent, but see also, *inter alia*, Michael Brzoska, 'The arms trade – can it be controlled?', *Journal of Peace Research*, 24:4 (December 1987), 327–31; Janne Nolan, 'The conventional arms trade: prospects for control', working paper 42 (Canberra: National University of Australia, 1988); Keith Krause, 'Constructing regional security regimes and the control of arms transfers', *International Journal*, 45:2 (Spring 1990), 386–423; Herbert Wulf, 'Recent trends of arms transfers and possible multilateral action for control', paper presented to the United Nations Conference on Transparency in International Arms Transfers, Florence, 25–8 April 1990.

10  Thomas Ohlson, 'Introduction', in Ohlson (ed.), 11.

11  'Arms and men', *Fortune Magazine*, 9 (March 1934), 52.

12  These were written by respectively, Helmuth Engelbrecht and F. C. Hanighen, George Seldes, Otto Lehmann-Russbüldt and A. Habaru. Full citations for these works may be found in the bibliography.

13  Union of Democratic Control, *Patriotism Ltd.: An Exposure of the War Machine* (London: Union of Democratic Control, 1933), 5.

14  *Fortune*, 120. In Fenner Brockway's *The Bloody Traffic* (London: Victor Gollancz, 1933), 284, one finds the admission that 'the nationalization of the [arms] industry would mean that the Bloody Traffic would be pursued by Governments instead of private corporations ... the wealthiest and most powerful Governments would undoubtedly use their ability to produce armaments as a weapon in their foreign policy'.

15  See John Wiltz, *In Search of Peace: The Senate Munitions Inquiry, 1934–36* (Louisiana: Louisiana State University Press, 1963).

16  John D. Scott, *Vickers: A History* (London: Weidenfeld & Nicolson, 1962), 245.

17  See League of Nations, *Statistical Yearbook of the Trade in Arms and Ammunition* (Geneva: League of Nations, various years).

18  Together with supporting studies, the latter work 'penetrated more deeply into the whole area of arms transfers than any [previous] scholarly research enterprise'. Amelia Leiss et al., *Arms Transfers to Less-Developed Countries* (Cambridge, Mass.: Massachusetts Institute of Technology, Center for International Studies, 1970), iv.

19  See, for example, Geoffrey Kemp, 'The international arms trade: supplier, recipient and arms control perspectives', *Political Quarterly*, 42 (1971), 380–2.

20  Paul Hammond, David Louscher, Michael Salomone and Norman Graham, *The Reluctant Supplier: U.S. Decision Making for Arms Sales* (Cambridge, Mass.: Oelgeschlager, Gunn and Hain, 1983), 266–71; Anne Cahn, Joseph Kruzel, Peter Dawkins and Jacques Huntzinger, *Controlling Future Arms Trade* (New York: McGraw-Hill, 1977). These would be representative writings of each group.

21  See, for example, Andrew Pierre, 'Arms sales: the new diplomacy', *Foreign Affairs*, 60 (Winter 1981–2), 266–304; Kolodziej, *Making and Marketing Arms*; Frederic Pearson and Edward Kolodziej, 'The political economy of making and marketing arms: a test for the systemic imperatives of order and welfare', occasional paper 8904 (St Louis: Center for International Studies, University of Missouri–St Louis, April 1989).

22 As, for example, the argument that 'the import of modern weapons entails a multitude of complex dependencies . . . this in turn offers the suppliers a broad spectrum of influence, if not pressure, on recipients' behaviour in the fields of foreign and defence policy'. Wolfgang Mallmann, 'Arms transfers to the Third World: trends and changing patterns in the 1970s', *Bulletin of Peace Proposals*, 10 (1979), 303.

23 See, for example, Ohlson (ed.), passim; Helena Tuomi and Raimo Väyrynen (eds.), *Militarization and Arms Production* (London: Croom Helm, 1983).

24 Stephanie G. Neuman and Robert E. Harkavy (eds.), *Arms Transfers in the Modern World* (New York: Praeger Publishers, 1980), vii.

25 See, for examples of the lack of consensus on this point: Michael Klare, 'The arms trade: changing patterns in the 1980s', *Third World Quarterly*, 9:4 (October 1987), 1257–81; Michael Brzoska and Thomas Ohlson, 'The future of arms transfers: the changing pattern', *Bulletin of Peace Proposals*, 16 (1985), 129–37; Karp, 'The trade in conventional weapons'; Stephanie Neuman, 'The arms market: who's on top?', *Orbis*, 33:4 (Fall 1989), 509–29; Andrew Ross, 'The international arms market: a structural analysis', unpublished paper presented at the annual meeting of the International Studies Association, Washington, 12 April 1990.

## 1 Motive forces in the evolution of the arms transfer and production system

1 See Robert Looney, *Third-World Military Expenditure and Arms Production* (London: Macmillan Press, 1988), passim.

2 Mary Kaldor, *The Baroque Arsenal* (London: André Deutsch, 1981), 3. For a useful survey of this literature see William Thompson, *On Global War: Historical–Structural Approaches to World Politics* (Columbia: University of South Carolina Press, 1988), chapters 6–8.

3 Clive Trebilcock, 'British armaments and European industrialization, 1980–1914', *Economic History Review*, 2nd series, 26 (1973), 254.

4 See Saadet Deger, *Military Expenditure in Third World Countries: The Economic Effects* (London: Routledge & Kegan Paul, 1986), 171–6; Looney, 208, 212.

5 Thomas Esper, 'Military self-sufficiency and weapons technology in Muscovite Russia', *Slavic Review*, 28 (1969), 186. He cites mercantilist scholars such as Eli Heckscher and Edmond Silberner to this effect.

6 Esper, 185.

7 John Beeler, *Warfare in Feudal Europe* (Ithaca: Cornell University Press, 1971), xv.

8 See Robert Gilpin, *War and Change in World Politics* (Cambridge: Cambridge University Press, 1981), especially 175–85; Paul Kennedy, *The Rise and Fall of the Great Powers* (New York: Random House, 1987); George Modelski, 'The long cycle of global politics and the nation-state', *Comparative Studies in Society and History*, 20:2 (April 1978), 214–35.

9 John Stanley and Maurice Pearton, *The International Trade in Arms* (London:

Chatto & Windus, 1972), 5; Jost Delbrüch, 'International traffic in arms –
legal and political aspects of a long neglected problem of arms control and
disarmament', *German Yearbook of International Law*, 24 (1981), 116. See also
Agnès Courades Allebeck, 'Arms trade regulations', in Stockholm International Peace Research Institute, *SIPRI Yearbook of World Armaments and
Disarmament, 1989* (Oxford: Oxford University Press, 1989), 319, 334.

10 The distinction between the 'pursuit of power' and 'pursuit of victory in
war' is contestable. Although the two are related, the latter is distinct in
two senses. First, over the short and medium term, particular wars can
have contrary effects (on the arms transfer system) to those resulting from
the pursuit of power. Second, unless one reads the historical record
deterministically, the outcome of major wars has not been foreordained by
the initial relative power positions of combatants (except by tautological
definition). In a sense, this analysis posits the relative autonomy of war
(and preparations for it) as a historical force. Not all authors would accept
this assertion, but for an interesting analysis see the contributions by
Martin Shaw and John Hall in Martin Shaw (ed.), *War, State and Society*
(London: Macmillan Press, 1984).

11 Esper, 185. The same point is made for both Petrine and late nineteenth-
century Russia by Alexander Gerschenkron, *Economic Backwardness in
Historical Perspective* (Cambridge, Mass.: Harvard University Press, 1962),
16–21, 131.

12 John Nef, *War and Human Progress* (New York: Russell and Russell, 1950),
65. Nef's book is essentially a polemic against Sombart's thesis. See also
J. M. Winter (ed.), *War and Economic Development* (Cambridge: Cambridge
University Press, 1975); Karen Rasler and William Thompson, *War and State
Making* (Boston: Unwin Hyman, 1989).

13 A. H. John, 'War and the English economy, 1700–1763', *Economic History
Review*, 2nd series, 7 (1954–5), 330.

14 John, 329; Phyllis Deane, 'War and industrialization', in Winter (ed.), 91.

15 Richard Bean, 'War and the birth of the nation state', *Journal of Economic
History*, 33 (1973), 203–21; John Hale, *War and Society in Renaissance Europe,
1450–1620* (London: Fontana Press, 1985), 232–52; Rasler and Thompson,
89–154.

16 Immanuel Wallerstein, 'The future of the world economy', in Terence
Hopkins and Immanuel Wallerstein (eds.), *Processes of the World-System*
(Beverly Hills: Sage Publishing, 1980), 172. See also Christopher Freeman,
'Technological innovation, diffusion, and long cycles of economic develop-
ment', in Tibor Vasko (ed.), *The Long Wave Debate* (London: Springer-
Verlag, 1987), 295–309.

17 Gilpin, 177.

18 Martin van Creveld, *Technology and War* (New York: The Free Press, 1989),
1.

19 Maurice Pearton makes an analogous distinction between technologies II
and III as follows: 'the first is the complexity of the task of producing
advanced weapons (or indeed any advanced technology); the second is the
complexity of the relationships required to initiate and manage such tasks'.

Maurice Pearton, *Diplomacy, War and Technology since 1830* (Lawrence: University Press of Kansas, 1984), 7.

20 William McNeill, *The Pursuit of Power* (Oxford: Basil Blackwell, 1983), 84, 89. Fernand Braudel, *The Structures of Everyday Life*, vol. I of *Civilization and Capitalism*, trans. Siân Reynolds (London: Fontana Paperbacks, 1985), 393–5, also makes this point.

21 Lynn White, *Medieval Technology and Social Change* (Oxford: Oxford University Press, 1962), 1–38; Carlo Cipolla, *Guns, Sails and Empires: Technological Innovation and the Early Phases of European Expansion, 1400–1700* (New York: Minerva Press, 1965), passim; Daniel Headrick, *The Tools of Empire: Technology and European Imperialism in the Nineteenth Century* (Oxford: Oxford University Press, 1981), 83–126.

22 Edward Kolodziej, *Making and Marketing Arms: The French Experience and its Implications for the International System* (Princeton: Princeton University Press, 1987), 319.

23 Cited in T. S. Ashton, *The Industrial Revolution, 1760–1830* (Oxford: Oxford University Press, 1968), 11.

24 Braudel, *Structures*, 386; Wang Ling, 'On the invention and use of gunpowder and firearms in China', *Isis*, 37:109–10 (July 1947), 160–78; Ahmad al-Hassan and Donald Hill, *Islamic Technology* (Cambridge: Cambridge University Press, 1986), 111–20.

25 White, 28.

26 Gilpin, 177, 177–85.

27 Pearton, *Diplomacy*, 7–9; Kaldor, passim.

28 Pearton, *Diplomacy*, 9.

29 See Freeman, 299–300; Joseph Schumpeter, *Business Cycles*, vol. I (New York: McGraw-Hill, 1939), 87–8, 87–102.

30 Advanced electronics and computers could also possibly revolutionise future warfare by providing genuinely stand-off and 'smart' weapons, but applications to date have been more incremental than revolutionary.

31 A. G. Kenwood and A. L. Lougheed, *Technological Diffusion and Industrialization before 1914* (New York: St Martin's Press, 1982), 5.

32 See James Kurth, 'The political consequences of the product cycle: industrial history and political outcomes', *International Organization*, 33:1 (Winter 1979), 2–5.

33 For exceptions see Kaldor, passim; Andrew Ross, 'Security and self-reliance: military dependence and conventional arms production in developing countries', unpublished doctoral thesis, Cornell University, 1984; Stephanie Neuman, 'International stratification and Third World military industries', *International Organization*, 38:1 (Winter 1984), 187–91.

34 Daniel Headrick, *The Tentacles of Progress: Technology Transfer in the Age of Imperialism* (Oxford: Oxford University Press, 1988), 9.

35 Nathan Rosenberg, *Inside the Black Box: Technology and Economics* (Cambridge: Cambridge University Press, 1982), 8. See also Carlo Cipolla, 'The diffusion of innovations in early modern Europe', *Comparative Studies in Society and History*, 14 (1972), 46–52.

36 Melvin Kranzberg, 'The technical elements in international technology transfer: historical perspectives', in John McIntyre and Daniel Papp (eds.),

*The Political Economy of International Technology Transfer* (New York: Quorum Books, 1986), 32.

37 The link between capacity transfer and the ability to adapt technology is explored by Robert Roberge, 'Peripheral industrialization and the technology transfer process', in F. E. Ian Hamilton, *Industrialization in Developing and Peripheral Regions* (London: Croom Helm, 1986), 1–15. He argues that early Canadian industrial development, which depended on technological imports, differed from that of other technology importers of the time precisely because Canada possessed the ability to *adapt* the technologies acquired.

38 Adapted from Kenwood and Lougheed, 12.

39 Political will may also be needed for civilian technological transfers. As Kenwood and Lougheed note: 'the existence of certain political requirements for successful industrial growth reminds us that ... the diffusion process ... is a cultural, social, political and psychological process, as well as an imitation of artifacts' (Kenwood and Lougheed, 13).

40 As Hamilton points out, there is a natural 'tendency to downgrade the somewhat inelegant solutions which local innovators may develop in favour of the more sophisticated solutions from abroad. In the short term these imported solutions may be cheaper and quicker to implement than those which have been developed locally, but in the long term they imply a dependency on the donor country' (Hamilton, 5). This dilemma is extremely acute in the defence sector, where military establishments are most susceptible to this sort of comparison.

41 Romain Yakemtchouk, *Les Transferts internationaux d'armes de guerre* (Paris: Pedone, 1980), 26.

42 Gerald Berg, 'The sacred musket: tactics, technology and power in eighteenth-century Madagascar', *Comparative Studies in Society and History*, 27:2 (April 1985), 262.

43 On the latter, see Berg, and Jack Goody, *Technology, Tradition and State in Africa* (London: Hutchinson, 1980), 39–56.

44 The term 'baroque', as used by Kaldor, refers to 'perpetual improvements to weapons that fall within established traditions ... the hardware becomes more complex and sophisticated [and] results in dramatic increases in the cost of individual weapons. But it does not increase military effectiveness' (Kaldor, 4–5).

## 2 The emergence of a global arms transfer and production system

1 The diffusion in the late Bronze Age does not run from Greece, but rather to it. Anthony Snodgrass, *Early Greek Armour and Weapons* (Edinburgh: Edinburgh University Press, 1964), 204, 210.

2 Barton Hacker, 'Greek catapults and catapult technology', *Technology and Culture*, 9:1 (January 1968), 47.

3 Ibid., 46; E. W. Marsden, *Greek and Roman Artillery* (Oxford: Oxford University Press, 1969), 48–64, 65–85.

4 Thucydides, *The Peloponnesian War*, trans. Rex Warner (Harmondsworth: Penguin Books, 1972), 608–9.

5 Frank Walbank, 'Trade and industry under the Later Roman Empire in the West', in *Cambridge Economic History*, 2nd edn, vol. II (Cambridge: Cambridge University Press, 1987), 116–17; C. R. Whittaker, 'Late Roman trade and traders', in Peter Garnsey et al. (eds.), *Trade in the Ancient Economy* (London: Chatto & Windus, 1983), 165, points out that although arms production was state controlled, the scale and centralisation of production were minimal, and based upon an 'estate-centered' economy.

6 Romain Yakemtchouk, *Les Transferts internationaux d'armes de guerre* (Paris: Pedone, 1980), 24; Walbank, 116–17.

7 John Beeler, *Warfare in Feudal Europe* (Ithaca: Cornell University Press, 1971), 14; Claude Gaier, *Four Centuries of Liège Gunmaking* (London: Sotheby, Parke Bernet, 1977), 17.

8 Information and quotations in this paragraph from Yakemtchouk, 24–6.

9 Claude Gaier, *L'Industrie et le commerce des armes dans les anciennes principautés belges du XIIIe à la fin du XVe siècle* (Paris: Société d'Edition 'Les Belles Lettres', 1973), 158–9.

10 Michael Roberts, 'The military revolution, 1560–1660', reprinted in *Essays in Swedish History* (London: Weidenfeld & Nicolson, 1967), 195, 195–255. See also Geoffrey Parker, *The Military Revolution: Military Innovation and the Rise of the West, 1500–1800* (Cambridge: Cambridge University Press, 1988).

11 William McNeill, *The Pursuit of Power* (Oxford: Basil Blackwell, 1983), 79, 69–79; Roberts, 205. See in general Michael Howard, *War in European History* (Oxford: Oxford University Press, 1976); John Hale, *War and Society in Renaissance Europe, 1450–1620* (London: Fontana Press, 1985).

12 Fernand Braudel, *The Structures of Everyday Life*, vol. I of *Civilization and Capitalism*, trans. Siân Reynolds (London: Fontana Paperbacks, 1985), 393.

13 Gaier, *Four Centuries*, 57.

14 Braudel, *Structures*, 393.

15 Details on technological developments from Braudel, *Structures*, 386, 392; A. R. Hall, 'Military technology', in Charles Singer et al. (eds.), *A History of Technology*, vol. III (London: Oxford University Press, 1957), 347–76; James R. Partington, *A History of Greek Fire and Gunpowder* (Cambridge: W. Heffer & Sons, 1960), 101–29. The first pictorial representation of a cannon dates from 1326, and is preserved in Christ Church, Oxford (McNeill, 84). Cast bronze and iron cannon also appear to have been developed in China earlier, the first evidence dating from 1288. They may even have been initially diffused to Europe, rather than the other way around. See note 76 below.

16 For discussions of these evolutionary changes, see McNeill, 83–8; Braudel, *Structures*, 388, 392, 395; Hall, 'Military technology', passim; Philippe Contamine, 'Les Industries de guerre dans la France de la Renaissance: l'exemple de l'artillerie', *Revue historique*, 271 (1984), 272.

17 Claude Gaier, 'Le Commerce des armes en Europe au XVe siècle', in *Armi e Cultura Nel Bresciano 1420–1870* (Brescia: Ateneo di Brescia, 1981), passim; Robert Lopez, 'The trade of Medieval Europe: the South', in *Cambridge Economic History*, 2nd edn, vol. II (Cambridge: Cambridge University Press, 1987), 393–7.

18 Gaier, 'Le Commerce', 156; McNeill, 67, 80.

19 Gaier, 'Le Commerce', 157.

20 See Frederic Lane, *Navires et constructeurs à Venise pendant la Renaissance* (Paris: SEVPEN, 1965), 125–39.

21 See Djurdjica Petrović, 'Fire-arms in the Balkans on the eve of and after the Ottoman conquests of the fourteenth and fifteenth centuries', in Vernon Parry and M. E. Rapp (eds.), *War, Technology and Society in the Middle East* (London: Oxford University Press, 1975), 172–9.

22 Richard Rapp, *Industry and Economic Decline in Seventeenth-Century Venice* (Cambridge, Mass.: Harvard University Press, 1976), 11.

23 McNeill, 80, 84.

24 Rapp, 8; Carlo Cipolla, *Before the Industrial Revolution*, 2nd edn (New York: Norton, 1980), 187.

25 McNeill, 89. Venice kept a peacetime arsenal of gunpowder worth more than the annual receipts of the city. Braudel, *Structures*, 395. See also Parker, 12, for details on the high costs of new fortifications and arsenals.

26 Fernand Braudel, *The Mediterranean*, trans. Siân Reynolds (London: Collins, 1973), vol. I, 201. Export figures from Hale, 221.

27 Gaier, *L'Industrie*, 169; Gaier, 'Le Commerce', 162.

28 Gaier, *L'Industrie*, 171; Helmuth Engelbrecht and F. C. Hanighen, *Merchants of Death: A Study of the International Armament Industry* (New York: Dodd, Mead and Company, 1934), 14.

29 Gaier, *Four Centuries*, 31.

30 McNeill, 113; Yakemtchouk, 27. Details on the later development of the Liège industry in Gaier, *Four Centuries*, 57, 93.

31 John Nef, 'Mining and metallurgy in Medieval civilisation', in *Cambridge Economic History*, 2nd edn, vol. II (Cambridge: Cambridge University Press, 1987), 729–30; H. R. Schubert, 'The superiority of English cast-iron cannon at the close of the sixteenth century', *Journal of the Iron and Steel Institute*, 161 (February 1949), 85–6.

32 Charles Ffoulkes, *The Gun Founders of England* (London: Arms and Armour Press, 1969), 11, 106; O. F. G. Hogg, *English Artillery, 1326–1716* (London: Royal Artillery Institution, 1963), 13, 16.

33 Ffoulkes, 87; T. F. Tout, *Firearms in England in the Fourteenth Century* (London: Arms and Armour Press, 1968), reprinted from *English Historical Review*, 26 (1911), 20, 31, 39, disagrees, concluding that 'the evidence of our records is that all persons having anything to do with the making of cannon or arms were Londoners, not foreigners ... there is no evidence of any imported gunpowder in England in the fourteenth century'.

34 Ffoulkes, 4–5, 30; Hogg, 18–20. As Tout, 31, notes, Henry VIII 'was forced to employ the great Flemish craftsman Hans Poppenruyter, who provided him with at least 140 guns ... owing to the backward condition of the industry in England'.

35 H. Schubert, 'The first cast-iron cannon made in England', *Journal of the Iron and Steel Institute*, 146 (1942), 131–40, argues that the development of iron-casting techniques was impeded by Henry VIII's initial importation of foreigners to cast in bronze.

36 Carlo Cipolla, *Guns, Sails and Empires: Technological Innovation and the Early*

*Phases of European Expansion, 1400–1700* (New York: Minerva Press, 1965), 41; Ffoulkes, 23, 74.

37 A. Rupert Hall, 'Early modern technology, to 1600', in Melvin Kranzberg and Carroll Pursell, Jr. (eds.), *Technology in Western Civilization*, vol. I (Oxford: Oxford University Press, 1967), 86; Brian Awty, 'The continental origins of the Wealden ironworkers, 1451–1544', *Economic History Review*, 34 (1981), 524–39.

38 Figures for England from Cipolla, *Before the Industrial Revolution*, 287; for France from Contamine, 253.

39 Ffoulkes, 74, quoting *State Papers Domestic Elizabeth* 1574, xcv 15, 16 and xcv 61, 70 and 22. This interdiction was reinforced by bills in 1610 and 1614, although some exports continued. Cipolla, *Guns, Sails*, 63; Schubert, 'Superiority', 86.

40 Ffoulkes, 75; Schubert, 'Superiority', 86; Richard Lewinsohn, *The Profits of War through the Ages* (London: G. Routledge and Sons, 1936), 27.

41 John Nef, *War and Human Progress* (New York: Russell and Russell, 1950), 80.

42 Quoted in Elton Atwater, 'British control over the export of war materials', *American Journal of International Law*, 33 (April 1939), 292.

43 Ffoulkes, 82; Cipolla, *Guns, Sails*, 67–8. By the 1630s a fuel crisis had also bitten deeply into founding and metal-working in general.

44 McNeill, 122; Hale, 225.

45 Nef, *War and Human Progress*, 79.

46 Ibid., 80; McNeill, 86n.

47 Nef, *War and Human Progress*, 69; Gaier, 'Le Commerce', 159.

48 Braudel, *Structures*, 395.

49 As Carlo Cipolla points out, 'through the ages, the main channel for the diffusion of innovations has been the migration of people'. Carlo Cipolla, 'The diffusion of innovations in early modern Europe', *Comparative Studies in Society and History*, 14 (1972), 48.

50 Gaier, 'Le Commerce', 162, estimates that in 1412 French production could meet only a hundredth of demand!

51 Hale, 226.

52 Ibid., 223, 226.

53 Gaier, *Four Centuries*, 62; Cipolla, 'Diffusion', 49–50; Hale, 220.

54 Contamine, 278.

55 Cipolla, *Guns, Sails*, 67–8; McNeill, 86, 181–2.

56 Richard Hellie, *Enserfment and Military Change in Muscovy* (Chicago: University of Chicago Press, 1971), 152, 154; Thomas Esper, 'Military self-sufficiency and weapons technology in Muscovite Russia', *Slavic Review*, 28 (1969), 189, 195. Iron shot also was in use by 1510, twenty or thirty years after its development. Arcadius Kahan, *The Plow, the Hammer and the Knout* (Chicago: University of Chicago Press, 1985), 156.

57 Esper, 196, 201. He notes as adaptation the use of iron rather than clay moulds for cannon. Richard Hellie also notes the constant improvement of weapons coming out of the Tula factory and the innovation of the horse pack mortar. Richard Hellie, 'The Petrine army: continuity, change, and impact', *Canadian–American Slavic Studies*, 8:2 (Summer 1974), 242.

58 Esper, 200. Although most of these cannon went to Holland, it is doubtful that this was their final destination.

59 McNeill, 176n. This was also roughly the number of Russian artillery in service until the 1760s. Peter increased cast-iron production from twelve plants with an annual output of 2,000 tons to fifty-two plants turning out 20,000 tons by 1725. Esper, 206–7.

60 Figures on imports and output from Esper, 203–7; Kahan, 98; Hellie, *Enserfment*, 183; Hellie, 'The Petrine army', 240. Firearms output averaged 21,000 a year between 1714 and 1778.

61 Esper, 208.

62 I. A. A. Thompson, *War and Government in Habsburg Spain, 1560–1620* (London: Athlone Press, 1976), 235–7. Bronze cannon were cast, however, in the 1560s.

63 Hale, 223, 229; Braudel, *Mediterranean*, 839. A typical agreement required a high percentage of employees to be Spanish and to be trained in gun-founding techniques, but as Thompson points out: 'again and again foreigners were brought over in the vain hope that they would train a school of Spaniards able to take over after them. They never did.' I. A. A. Thompson, 244, 253. See I. A. A. Thompson, 237–9, 245–6, for details of the administrative reforms and state finances.

64 McNeill, 113; I. A. A. Thompson, 241.

65 Cipolla, *Guns, Sails*, 35n; I. A. A. Thompson, 238. These export restrictions only expanded regulations adopted in 1488 that 'forbade the export ... not only of artillery ... but of "handguns, crossbows and bolts, lances, cuirasses and shields, casques, helmets and beavers, and other forms of weapons and equipment"'. Hale, 226.

66 Quoted in Hale, 223.

67 Cipolla, *Guns, Sails*, 31–2. See also R. A. Kea, 'Firearms and warfare on the Gold and Slave Coasts from the 16th to the 19th centuries', *Journal of African History*, 12:2 (1971), 186. He points out that 'officially the Portuguese were forbidden to sell firearms to non-Christians, ostensibly on politico-religious grounds, but more credibly because, during the fifteenth, sixteenth and seventeenth centuries Portugal was largely dependent on Flemish and German gunsmiths'.

68 David Caldwell, 'The Royal Scottish Gun Foundry in the sixteenth century', in Anne O'Connor and D. V. Clarke (eds.), *From the Stone Age to the 'Forty-Five* (Edinburgh: John Donald Publishers, 1983), 427–9. Caldwell, 430, 436, notes that there is no record of successful casting after 1558.

69 Parker, 38, 167n; Tadeusz Nowak, 'Wpłw Rozwoju Nauki i Techniki na Wojskowść Polską XVI–XVII w', *Kwartalnik Historii Nauki i Techniki*, 26 (1981), 39–56.

70 Information on Hungary from Gusztáv Heckenast, 'Equipment and supply of Ferenc II Rákóczi's army', in János Bak and Béla Király (eds.), *From Hunyadi to Rákóczi: War and Society in Late Medieval and Early Modern Hungary* (New York: Brooklyn College Press, 1982), 421–31.

71 Petrovic 170–89, notes that fewer than eighty bombards were produced before the end of the fourteenth century, but that by 1410 bronze cannon

were being founded there. Hand firearms followed the same pattern of diffusion.

72 Details on Turkey from McNeill, 61; Braudel, *Mediterranean*, 802; A. Z. Hertz, 'Armament and supply inventory of Ottoman Ada Kale, 1753', *Archivum Ottomanicum*, 4 (1972), 98–100; Halil Inalcik, 'The socio-political effects of the diffusion of fire-arms in the Middle East', in Parry and Rapp, 202–10.

73 Cipolla, *Guns, Sails*, 111n, 110.

74 Ahsan Jan Qaisar, *The Indian Response to European Culture and Technology (A.D. 1496–1707)* (Delhi: Oxford University Press, 1982), 47; Braudel, *Mediterranean*, 201. On the debate over whether firearms were introduced by the Muslims or the Portuguese, see Iqtidar Alam Khan, 'Early use of cannon and musket in India, A.D. 1442–1526', *Journal of the Economic and Social History of the Orient*, 24:2 (May 1981), 146–64; Syed Abu Zafar Nadvi, 'The use of cannon in Muslim India', *Islamic Culture*, 12:4 (October 1938), 405–18.

75 Delmer Brown, 'The impact of firearms on Japanese warfare, 1543–98', *Far Eastern Quarterly*, 7 (1948), 236, 241; Parker, 140.

76 Joseph Needham christened these weapons eruptors to distinguish them from true guns, in which the projectile closely fits the barrel. Joseph Needham, 'The guns of Khaifêng-fu', *Times Literary Supplement* (11 January 1980), 39–42. Robert Temple, *The Genius of China* (New York: Simon and Schuster, 1986), 243–6, dates the first true gun cast in China from 1288 (about fifty years earlier than it can be dated in Europe) and the first cast-iron gun from the fourteenth century, again before the Europeans. See also L. C. Goodrich, 'Early cannon in China', *Isis*, 55:2 (August 1964), 193–5.

77 Information in this paragraph from Qaisar, 18–19, 47, 50–1; Cipolla, *Guns, Sails*, 111–28; Parker, 144; Brown, passim. Nadvi, 409, 412, however, dates Indian cannon-casting with Turkish founders from the 1560s.

78 Parker, 136.

79 Braudel, *Mediterranean*, 801; Braudel, *Structures*, 392.

80 Parker, 127; Cipolla, 'Diffusion', 51.

81 Qaisar, 50, 44; Parker, 128–30.

82 Cipolla, *Guns, Sails*, 129.

83 Inalcik, 211.

84 David Ayalon, *Gunpowder and Firearms in the Mamluk Kingdom* (London: Vallentine, Mitchell and Company, 1956) 4, 46.

85 Parker, 205n; Roger Savory, *Iran under the Safavids* (Cambridge: Cambridge University Press, 1980), 43–4. Inalcik, 207–9, notes that the Safavids recovered some of their losses by the seventeenth century, when their military techniques changed.

86 A. C. Hess, 'Firearms and the decline of Ibn Khaldun's military elite', *Archivum Ottomanicum*, 4 (1972), 181–7.

### 3 From the Military Revolution to the Industrial Revolution

1 Basil Collier, *Arms and the Men: The Arms Trade and Governments* (London: Hamish Hamilton, 1980), 118.

2 David Dougan, *The Great Gun Maker: The Story of Lord Armstrong* (Newcastle upon Tyne: Frank Graham, undated), 56; Robert O'Connell, *Of Arms and Men* (Oxford: Oxford University Press, 1989), 165. William McNeill, *The Pursuit of Power* (Oxford: Basil Blackwell, 1983), 88, 142, places the end of revolutionary innovation as early as 1477. The technology of founding bronze and cast-iron guns also changed little from the sixteenth to the eighteenth centuries. David Caldwell, 'The Royal Scottish Gun Foundry in the sixteenth century', in Anne O'Connor and D. V. Clarke (eds.), *From the Stone Age to the 'Forty-Five* (Edinburgh: John Donald Publishers, 1983), 432.

3 McNeill, 141n, 167–8; O'Connell, 157–8, 179.

4 McNeill, 141, 172–5. O'Connell, 159, cites the example of the Marquis de la Frezelière's new chamber designs for French guns that greatly reduced the weight of cannon. The military melted down all his pieces after his death.

5 O'Connell, 189, 148–60, 189–93.

6 Transfers in this paragraph noted in: Gunther Rothenberg, *The Art of Warfare in the Age of Napoleon* (London: Batsford, 1977), 120–1; Claude Gaier, *Four Centuries of Liège Gunmaking* (London: Sotheby, Parke Bernet, 1977), 60; Romain Yakemtchouk, *Les Transferts internationaux d'armes de guerre* (Paris: Pedone, 1980), 31; W. O. Henderson, 'The rise of the metal and armament industries in Berlin and Brandenburg 1712–1795', *Business History*, 3:1 (December 1960), 66.

7 McNeill, 202–3, 210. Geoffrey Best, *War and Society in Revolutionary Europe, 1770–1870* (Leicester: Leicester University Press, 1982), 94, 144. O'Connell, 175, notes that Revolutionary France rapidly transformed itself into a major small-arms producer, turning out 750 muskets a day compared to the European production total of 1,000.

8 Charles Ffoulkes, *The Gun Founders of England* (London: Arms and Armour Press, 1969), 113.

9 Ffoulkes, 87; McNeill, 167.

10 See Barton Hacker, 'The weapons of the West: military technology and modernization in 19th-century China and Japan', *Technology and Culture*, 8:1 (January 1977), 43–55; Thomas Kennedy, *The Arms of Kiangnan: Modernization in the Chinese Ordnance Industry, 1860–1895* (Boulder: Westview Press, 1978), 13.

11 Figures from J. E. Inikori, 'The import of firearms into West Africa 1750–1807', *Journal of African History*, 18:2 (1977), 339–68. The thesis that arms imports had a decisive state-building impact (although not always as dramatic an impact on the outcome of wars) is advanced by W. A. Richards, 'The import of firearms into West Africa in the eighteenth century', *Journal of African History*, 21:1 (1980), 43–59. See also Gerald Berg, 'The sacred musket: tactics, technology and power in eighteenth-century Madagascar', *Comparative Studies in Society and History*, 27:2 (April 1985), 261–76; R. A. Kea, 'Firearms and warfare on the Gold and Slave Coasts from the 16th to the 19th centuries', *Journal of African History*, 12:2 (1971); Joseph Smaldone, *Warfare in the Sokoto Caliphate* (Cambridge: Cambridge University Press, 1977), 94–124.

12 Humphrey Fisher and Virginia Rowland, 'Firearms in the Central Sudan', *Journal of African History*, 12:2 (1971), 222.
13 Fisher and Rowland, 201.
14 O'Connell, 191–2.
15 Maurice Pearton, *The Knowledgeable State* (London: Burnett Books, 1982), 20–1.
16 Karen Rasler and William Thompson, *War and State Making* (Boston: Unwin Hyman, 1989), 66, 95, 102. For a general discussion of the social, political and economic changes that underlay this military transformation see Best, passim.
17 Clive Trebilcock. '"Spin-off" in British economic history: armaments and industry, 1760–1914', *Economic History Review*, 22:3 (1969), 477.
18 Alfred Cochrane, *The Early History of Elswick* (Newcastle upon Tyne: Mawson, Swann and Morgan, 1909), passim; John Dick Scott, *Vickers: A History* (London: Weidenfeld & Nicolson, 1962), 25.
19 Collier, 47; Scott, 32.
20 Scott, 20–43; Clive Trebilcock, *The Vickers Brothers: Armaments and Enterprise 1854–1914* (London: Europa Publications, 1977), 22, 30–42.
21 Dougan, 91; Trebilcock, '"Spin-off"', 480.
22 Scott, 33; Dougan, 104; Collier, 47.
23 Trebilcock, *Vickers*, 21.
24 William Manchester, *The Arms of Krupp* (Toronto: Little, Brown and Company, 1964), 27. Details of eighteenth-century efforts are given in Henderson, 63–74.
25 Pearton, *Knowledgeable State*, 79–80; Manchester, 78–92.
26 Customers detailed in Dougan, 103; Collier, 47. The relocation offer was later made to Armstrong. Pearton, 48; Manchester, 91.
27 Manchester, 89, quoting Alfred Krupp. He also pressed the Prussian navy to buy local products when they considered purchasing Armstrong weapons. Manchester, 91.
28 Manchester, 101; Pearton, *Knowledgeable State*, 115, 144; Fenner Brockway, *The Bloody Traffic* (London: Victor Gollancz, 1933), 58; 'Arms and men', *Fortune Magazine*, 9 (March 1934).
29 James Dredge, *The Work of Messrs. Schneider and Company* (London: Bedford Press, 1900), 7.
30 François Crouzet, 'Recherches sur la production d'armements en France (1815–1913)', *Revue historique*, 98:251 (January–March 1974), 50, 64; François Crouzet, 'Remarques sur l'industrie des armements en France (du milieu du XIXe siècle à 1914)', *Revue historique*, 98:251 (April–June 1974), 409.
31 Crouzet, 'Remarques', 412; Joseph Roy, *Histoire de la famille Schneider et du Creusot* (Paris: Marcel Rivière et Cie, 1962), 35–6.
32 Dredge, 7, 250; Roy, 75.
33 Roy, 77.
34 Roy, 89; Crouzet, 'Remarques', 418. It should be noted that military production was only 61 per cent of its total production. Crouzet, 'Recherches', 65, gives no figures for Schneider, but argues that 'les fournitures de cette société à la France étaient très supérieures à ses exportations'.
35 Based on calculations from Crouzet, 'Recherches', 50, 65–6.

36 Dredge, 249–50. For an overview of the period see Lother Hilbert, 'Der zunehmende waffenexport seit den 1890er Jahren', in Fritz Klein and Karl Otmar von Aretin (eds.), *Europa um 1900* (Berlin: Akademie Verlag, 1989), 59–72.

37 John Stanley and Maurice Pearton, *The International Trade in Arms* (London: Chatto & Windus, 1972), 5.

38 Roy, 77. Crouzet, 'Remarques', 415 n2, suggests that the freeing of exports was justified 'par la nécessité de combattre le chômage, de ne plus abandonner le marché des armes aux Anglais et aux Allemands et de créer dans le privé une réserve de capacité utilisable en temps de guerre' and by 'l'achèvement de la réfection du matériel de l'Armée vers 1885 et ... l'insuffisance des commandes de la Marine'.

39 Trebilcock, *Vickers*, 19.

40 Brian Bond, *War and Society in Europe, 1870–1970* (London: Fontana, 1984), 44. Most technical advances in French arms were also produced or adopted first in private firms. Crouzet, 'Remarques', 410.

41 Pearton, *Knowledgeable State*, 47.

42 Ibid., 47. Manchester, 100–3. Quotation cited in Manchester, 94.

43 Pearton, *Knowledgeable State*, 102.

44 McNeill, 302.

45 John Rawlinson, *China's Struggle for Naval Development, 1839–1895* (Cambridge, Mass.: Harvard University Press, 1967), 76; Elton Atwater, 'British control over the export of war materials', *American Journal of International Law*, 33 (April 1939), 293–4.

46 Pearton, *Knowledgeable State*, 143, 145.

47 Ibid., 97.

48 Helmuth Engelbrecht and F. C. Hanighen, *Merchants of Death: A Study of the International Armament Industry* (New York: Dodd, Mead and Company, 1934), 124; Bond, 70. A good discussion of various market-sharing arrangements can be found in Collier, 64–80.

49 Alan Milward and S. B. Saul, *The Economic Development of Continental Europe, 1780–1870* (London: George Allen & Unwin, 1973), 183. They note that by 1896 the Nobel explosives empire had factories in eleven European states.

50 Clive Trebilcock, *The Industrialization of the Continental Powers, 1780–1914* (London: Longman Group, 1981), 282.

51 Ibid., 344; Trebilcock, '"Spin-off"', passim; Clive Trebilcock, 'British armaments and European industrialization, 1890–1914', *Economic History Review*, 2nd series, 26 (1973), 254–72. One reason for possible high spin-offs was the relatively high proportion of R&D spending, which was in the range of 6–12 per cent of net profits. Trebilcock, *Vickers*, 4.

52 Eighty-four such ships were sold before 1914. Other examples cited in Dougan, 138; McNeill, 263n; Trebilcock, *Vickers*, 22; Scott, 53–4; Pearton, *Knowledgeable State*, 83.

53 Dougan, 151; Pearton, *Knowledgeable State*, 115; Scott, 84.

54 Trebilcock, *Industrialization*, 346–7; his italics. This is also substantially the argument of R. A. Webster, *Industrial Imperialism in Italy 1906–1914* (Berkeley: University of California Press, 1975).

55 For details see Trebilcock, 'British armaments', 260–2, quoting the Vickers archives. See also R. J. Harrison, 'British armaments and European industrialization, 1890–1914: the Spanish case re-examined', *Economic History Review*, 2nd series, 27:4 (1974), 620–4.

56 See Jacob Kipp, 'The Russian Navy and private enterprise', in Benjamin Cooling (ed.), *War, Business and World Military-Industrial Complexes* (Port Washington, New York: Kennikat Press, 1981), 84–105.

57 Clive Trebilcock, 'British armaments', 265, 262–8; Trebilcock, *Industrialization*, 283.

58 McNeill, 156–7.

59 Joseph Borus, 'The military industry in the War of Independence', in Béla Király (ed.), *East Central European Society and War in the Era of Revolutions, 1775–1856* (New York: Brooklyn College Press, 1984), 519–37.

60 See David F. Good, *The Economic Rise of the Habsburg Empire, 1750–1914* (Berkeley: University of California Press, 1984), 166; Richard Rudolph, *Banking and Industrialization in Austria-Hungary* (Cambridge: Cambridge University Press, 1976), 114–15; Trebilcock, *Industrialization*, 347–8.

61 Roger Owen, *The Middle East in the World Economy 1800–1914* (New York: Methuen, 1981), 71; David Ralston, *Importing the European Army: The Introduction of European Military Techniques and Institutions into the Extra-European World, 1600–1914* (Chicago: University of Chicago Press, 1990), 94; Ervand Abrahamian, *Iran Between Two Revolutions* (Princeton: Princeton University Press, 1982), 52–4.

62 Stanford Shaw and Ezel Shaw, *History of the Ottoman Empire and Modern Turkey*, vol. II (Cambridge: Cambridge University Press, 1977), 86, 122–3, 236, 245; Owen, 62–3; Ralston, 57. In the early 1900s, weapons were also purchased from Britain and the United States. Shaw, 286.

63 Owen, 117, 63. Owen, 110, notes that 'by the mid-1870s, the army contained 84 batteries of field guns and the navy 4 major warships, 8 frigates and 9 corvettes, almost all purchased in Europe' and (p. 199) that by 1904 the army was equipped with German artillery and rifles.

64 For details see Ushisaburo Kobayashi, *Military Industries of Japan* (New York: Oxford University Press, 1922), 3–23, 30–5, 45, 53–5, 183. See also D. Eleanor Westney, 'The military', in Marius Jansen and Gilbert Rozman (eds.), *Japan in Transition: From Tokugawa to Meiji* (Princeton: Princeton University Press, 1986), 169–71, 174; Umetani Noboru, *The Role of Foreign Employees in the Meiji Era in Japan* (Tokyo: Institute of Developing Economies, 1971), 10–11, 23–6. Exports went to Australia and the Philippines.

65 Ralston, 143, 142–72.

66 Kobayashi, 161, 180–97; Trebilcock, *Industrialization*, 383, 151n.

67 Rawlinson, 21; Stanley Spector, *Li Hung-chang and the Huai Army* (Seattle: University of Washington Press, 1964), 152–94; Thomas Kennedy, 18–33. Cannon and firearms were produced in China in limited quantities before 1839, but these were based entirely on technologies that were becoming rapidly obsolete.

68 The key principles of the 'self-strengthening' movement, as codified by Li Hung-chang in 1874, were:

    (1) the training of troops in the use of modern weapons;

(2)   the production of modern weapons;
(3)   the building of modern ships;
(4)   the securing of funds for these purposes;
(5)   the development of a corps of bureaucrats capable of dealing with these . . . problems.

Stanley Spector, 175; Ralston, 117–18.

69 Thomas Kennedy, 129–35; Rawlinson, 67–81, 110. See Rawlinson, 41–52, 88, for a detailed description of the process of technology transfer and production (from French managers) at the Foochow dockyard, which included training abroad for employees.

70 Rawlinson, 104, 144–5; Stanley Spector, 174, 192–3; Thomas Kennedy, 121–47. For an analysis of the different responses in Japan and China see Hacker, 49–55.

71 Thomas Kennedy, 150–1. For a general discussion of the problems of military change and reform in traditional societies, see Ralston, passim.

72 R. W. Beachey, 'The arms trade in East Africa in the late nineteenth century', *Journal of African History*, 3:3 (1962), 453, quoting a British official's memo. See also Sue Miers, 'Notes on the arms trade and government policy in Southern Africa between 1870 and 1890', *Journal of African History*, 12:4 (1971), 574.

73 For a discussion of the military impact of the new weapons, see Smaldone, 110–24; Shula Marks and Anthony Atmore, 'Firearms in Southern Africa: a survey', *Journal of African History*, 12:4 (1971), 517–30; Anthony Atmore, J. M. Chirenje and S. I. Mudenge, 'Firearms in South Central Africa', *Journal of African History*, 12:4 (1971), 545–56; J. J. Guy, 'A note on firearms in the Zulu kingdom with special reference to the Anglo-Zulu War, 1879', *Journal of African History*, 12:4 (1971), 557–70.

74 Scott, 34, 86; Pearton, *Knowledgeable State*, 108.

75 Trebilcock, 'Legends of the British armaments industry: a revision', *Journal of Contemporary History*, 5:4 (1970), 14, his italics. The best discussions of the relationship between government and arms producers in this period are Pearton, *Knowledgeable State*, 95–154 and McNeill, 223–306. McNeill concludes that the command economy for military production is the norm, and that this period was unique; Pearton that this period witnessed the beginnings of the later close relationship between government policy and the process of technological innovation.

76 New entrants were in South America, where Brazil, Chile and Argentina launched limited third-tier arms production projects. Frank McCann, 'The Brazilian Army and the pursuit of arms independence, 1899–1979', in Cooling, 171–86; Michael Brzoska and Thomas Ohlson (eds.), *Arms Production in the Third World* (London: Taylor and Francis, 1986), 35, 79, 251. For an overview of the period see Lother Hilbert, 'Waffenexport. Aspekte des internationalen Waffenhandels nach dem Ersten Weltkreig', in Jürgen Hedeking et al. (eds.), *Wege in die Zeitgeschichte* (Berlin: De Gruyter, 1989), 415–32.

77 Scott, 148–9; Roy, 114. Figures in this paragraph from Robert Harkavy, *The Arms Trade and International Systems* (Cambridge, Mass.: Ballinger, 1975), 61, 69, 74, 79.

78 Details of British policy in Atwater, 'British control', 299–301; Scott, 262.
79 Roy, 125; Jeffrey Clarke, 'Land armament in France', in Cooling, 40.
80 Pearton, *Knowledgeable State*, 198. The annual subsidy reached 400 million gold francs.
81 See the comprehensive discussion in Anthony Chan, *Arming the Chinese: The Western Armaments Trade in Warlord China, 1920–1928* (Vancouver: University of British Columbia Press, 1982). He points out that limited arms production also occurred in China during this time.
82 Pearton, *Knowledgeable State*, 199–200. Export figures from Engelbrecht and Hanighen, 241.
83 Harkavy, 146.
84 Manchester, 320.
85 Ibid., 330. Details of the secret rearmament that follow, unless otherwise noted, come from him.
86 Richard Lewinsohn, *The Profits of War through the Ages* (London: G. Routledge and Sons, 1936), 192; Pearton, *Knowledgeable State*, 193; Manchester, 331–5.
87 Harkavy, 84.
88 Prime Minister Lloyd George, quoted in Anthony Sampson, *The Arms Bazaar* (London: Hodder & Stoughton, 1977), 70.
89 Stockholm International Peace Research Institute, *The Arms Trade with the Third World* (Stockholm: Almqvist and Wiksell, 1971), 92.
90 'Arms and men', *Fortune Magazine*, 120.
91 See John Wiltz, *In Search of Peace: the Senate Munitions Inquiry, 1934–6* (Louisiana: Louisiana State University Press, 1963); Scott, 245–55.
92 Uri Ra'anan, 'Soviet arms transfers and the problem of political leverage', in Uri Ra'anan, Robert Pfaltzgraff and Geoffrey Kemp (eds.), *Arms Transfers to the Third World: The Military Buildup in Less Industrialized Countries* (Boulder: Westview Press, 1978), 131.
93 Details and figures in David Holloway, *The Soviet Union and the Arms Race*, 2nd edn (London: Yale University Press, 1984), 7–8. Some weapons, such as aircraft and artillery, had also been acquired in the 1920s under the Rapallo treaty. Brockway, 93.
94 Engelbrecht and Hanighen, 165. Details on production are from Benedict Crowell and Robert Wilson, *The Armies of Industry*, vol. I (New Haven: Yale University Press, 1921), 26, 41, 48, 195–8. It should be noted, however, that the American Expeditionary Force was primarily equipped with French weapons. McNeill, 322.
95 Brockway, 124, 125. The first figure comes from Thomas Morgan, president of the All-American Aeronautical Chamber of Commerce, testifying before the Nye Committee. Others (Pratt and Whitney and United Aircraft) estimated the total at only 36 per cent (1936). Collier, 175.
96 O'Connell, 192–3. Some argue that the ascendance of the 'American system of manufactures' was clear by 1850: the British Enfield arsenal of 1854 was built almost entirely with American machines. Crouzet, 'Remarques', 421. Trebilcock, 'British armaments', 257, argues, however, that the overall state of the American arms industry at the turn of the century was far behind that of Britain. Interestingly, just as Britain was driven to perfect

cast-iron cannon by economic factors (the high cost of imported copper), American manufacturing was driven by the high cost of labour and market size factors.

97 Elton Atwater, *American Regulation of Arms Exports* (Washington: Carnegie Endowment for International Peace, 1941), 8.

98 Ibid., 177. Intermittent embargoes during specific conflicts were more easily agreed to: among these were the 1905 embargo of the Dominican Republic, the 1912 embargo of Mexico, the 1937 Spanish Civil War embargo and the 1938 embargo of Japan.

99 Harkavy, 56.

## 4 An overview of the post-1945 global arms transfer system

1 Figures for unit costs and employment from Jacques Gansler, *The Defense Industry* (Cambridge, Mass.: MIT Press, 1980), 15–17, 97, 286; Nicole Ball, 'Appendix I: the United Kingdom', in Nicole Ball and Milton Leitenberg (eds.), *The Structure of the Defense Industry* (London: Croom Helm, 1983), 358–9; Edward Kolodziej, *Making and Marketing Arms: The French Experience and its Implications for the International System* (Princeton: Princeton University Press, 1987), 142. Gansler, 83, notes that the average real increase in unit costs has been about 5 per cent a year, which doubles the cost of equipment in thirteen years.

2 Stockholm International Peace Research Institute, *The Arms Trade with the Third World* (Stockholm: Almqvist and Wiksell, 1971), 215. It should be noted, however, that Britain did not begin exporting weapons based on post-1945 designs until the mid 1950s.

3 See, for an example of such an error, Andrew Ross, 'The international arms market: a structural analysis', paper presented at the International Studies Association annual meeting, Washington, 12 April 1990.

4 The figures for 1982 and 1983 were as high as 13.5 and 11.3 per cent respectively.

5 Thomas Snitch, 'Eastern European involvement in the world's arms market', in United States, Arms Control and Disarmament Agency, *World Military Expenditures and Arms Transfers, 1972–82* (Washington: Arms Control and Disarmament Agency, 1982), 117. Hereafter cited as ACDA, *WMEAT*.

6 Romania supplied Iraq with $825 million in arms between 1978 and 1982, Snitch, 97, 117.

7 Michael Brzoska and Thomas Ohlson, *Arms Transfers to the Third World, 1971–1985* (Oxford: Oxford University Press, 1987), 135.

8 Stockholm International Peace Research Institute (SIPRI), *SIPRI Yearbook of World Armaments and Disarmament 1987* (London: Oxford University Press, 1987), 153–62; Ulrich Albrecht, 'The aborted UN study on the military use of research and development: an editorial essay', *Bulletin of Peace Proposals*, 19:3–4 (1988), 252–4. The total is estimated at $85–100,000 million by SIPRI and $100–105,000 million by Albrecht.

9 SIPRI, *Yearbook 1987*, 154.

10 Ibid., 154; Stephanie Neuman, 'International stratification and Third

World military industries', *International Organization*, 38:1 (Winter 1984), 190. Neuman estimates that the United States and Soviet Union together account for 85 per cent of all R&D expenditure, and with Britain and France, 90 per cent.

11 SIPRI, *Yearbook 1987*, 154–6, gives $173 million; Albrecht, 253, calculated for 1984, gives $194 million; the $300 million estimate comes from the Organization of Economic Cooperation and Development, *Science and Technology Indicators: Basic Statistical Series, Recent Results: Selected S&T Indicators 1981–86* (Paris: OECD, 1986).

12 Judith Reppy, 'The United States', in Ball and Leitenberg, 23.

13 Albrecht, 254.

14 Military spending figure from ACDA, *WMEAT 1988*, 1. Twenty-five per cent is the average procurement figure for the United States between 1950 and 1980. Reppy, in Ball and Leitenberg, 24.

15 The estimate of one-fifth to one-sixth of total production transferred comes from Michael Brzoska and Thomas Ohlson (eds.), *Arms Production in the Third World* (London: Taylor and Francis, 1986), 32.

16 Numerous authors have compiled similar lists, including: William Lewis, 'Political influence: the diminished capacity', in Stephanie G. Neuman and Robert Harkavy (eds.), *Arms Transfers in the Modern World* (New York: Praeger Publishers, 1980), 189–90; Geoffrey Kemp and Steven Miller, 'The arms transfer phenomenon', in Andrew Pierre (ed.), *Arms Transfers and American Foreign Policy* (New York: New York University Press, 1979), 45–63; Andrew Pierre, *The Global Politics of Arms Sales* (Princeton: Princeton University Press, 1982), 14–27; Lewis Sorley, *Arms Transfers under Nixon* (Lexington: University Press of Kentucky, 1983), 34–5; Michael Klare, 'Soviet arms transfers to the Third World', *Bulletin of the Atomic Scientists* (May 1984), 28–9; Cyrus Vance, 'Report to Congress on arms transfer policy', 30 June 1977, summarised in Paul Hammond, David Louscher, Michael Salomone and Norman Graham, *The Reluctant Supplier: U.S. Decision Making for Arms Sales* (Cambridge, Mass.: Oelgeschlager, Gunn and Hain, 1983), 32–3.

## 5 The dominance of first-tier producers and suppliers

1 There are a number of good surveys of American policy and practice. See, *inter alia*, Stockholm International Peace Research Institute (SIPRI), *The Arms Trade with the Third World* (Stockholm: Almqvist and Wiksell, 1971), 138–54; Michael Klare, *American Arms Supermarket* (Austin: University of Texas Press, 1984); Andrew Pierre (ed.), *Arms Transfers and American Foreign Policy* (New York: New York University Press, 1979); Paul Hammond, David Louscher, Michael Salomone and Norman Graham, *The Reluctant Supplier: U.S. Decision Making for Arms Sales* (Cambridge, Mass.: Oelgeschlager, Gunn and Hain, 1983).

2 United States Department of Defense, Defense Security Assistance Agency, *Fiscal Year Series* (Washington: Department of Defense, 1990). This programme continued earlier efforts for Greece and Turkey under the Truman Doctrine.

3 Calculated from United States, Arms Control and Disarmament Agency, *World Military Expenditures and Arms Transfers, 1989* (Washington: Arms Control and Disarmament Agency, 1989). Hereafter cited as ACDA, *WMEAT*.

4 David Louscher, 'The rise of military sales as a U.S. foreign policy instrument', *Orbis*, 20 (Winter 1977), 936, 936–51.

5 Hammond et al., 45, 47–8. Transfers increased from $4,204 million in 1963 to $10,234 million in 1969 (constant 1988 dollars).

6 Harold Hovey, *United States Military Assistance* (New York: Frederick A. Praeger, 1966), 183.

7 See David Louscher and Michael Salomone, *Technology Transfer and U.S. Security Assistance: The Impact of Licensed Production* (Boulder: Westview Press, 1987), 39–63; Fabrizio Battistelli, *Armi: nuovo modello di sviluppo?* (Turin: Giulio Einaudi Editore, 1980), 126–42; Office of Technology Assessment, *Arming our Allies: Cooperation and Competition in Defense Technology* (Washington: Office of Technology Assessment, May 1990), 61–72; Reinhard Drifte, *Arms Production in Japan* (Boulder: Westview Press, 1986), 10–13.

8 Richard Nixon, quoted from his 1968 Guam speech in Hammond, 75. For details see Lewis Sorley, *Arms Transfers under Nixon: A Policy Analysis* (Lexington: University Press of Kentucky, 1983). See also Stephen Gibert, 'Implications of the Nixon Doctrine for military aid policy', *Orbis*, 16:3 (Fall 1972), 661–81.

9 See Hammond et al., 125–68, for statistics.

10 Quoted by Jo Husbands in 'How the United States makes foreign military sales', in Stephanie G. Neuman and Robert E. Harkavy (eds.), *Arms Transfers in the Modern World* (New York: Praeger Publishers, 1980), 171. See also Richard Moose and Daniel Spiegel, 'Congress and arms transfers', in Pierre, *Arms Transfers*, 236.

11 ACDA, *WMEAT 1988*, 107. These figures are not directly comparable with those of figure 3. Note that in the late 1980s ACDA stopped including military construction sales in American arms transfer figures, arguing that as they did not constitute actual transfer of military capabilities they artificially inflated American figures. ACDA, *WMEAT 1987*, 144.

12 ACDA, *WMEAT 1989*.

13 US Department of State, *International Security and Development Cooperation Program*, Special Reports 108 (April 1983) and 116 (April 1984), 8. This declined to about $4,000 million for the fiscal 1989 year. Defense Marketing Services, *International Defense Intelligence*, 5 December 1988.

14 *International Security and Development Cooperation Program*, Special reports 108 (April 1983) and 116 (April 1984), 8; *Jane's Defence Weekly* (14 May 1988).

15 Klare, *American Arms Supermarket*, 164, citing figures from the Office of Munitions Control and the Congressional Research Service.

16 Anthony Sampson, *The Arms Bazaar* (London: Hodder & Stoughton, 1977), 116–17.

17 United States, Congressional Research Service, *Changing Perspectives on U.S. Arms Transfer Policy*, a report prepared for the Subcommittee on International Security and Scientific Affairs, Committee on Foreign Affairs,

House of Representatives, 97th Congress, 1st session (Washington: U.S. Government Printing Office, 1981), 29; *Munitions Control Newsletter 47*, 1977; reprinted in *Review of the President's Conventional Arms Transfer Policy*, hearings before the Subcommittee on International Security and Scientific Affairs, Committee on International Relations, House of Representatives, 1–2 February 1978 (Washington: Government Printing Office, 1978), 77–80.

18 The Reagan Administration sought, for example, to increase government-to-government sales by 28 per cent in 1988. *International Herald Tribune* (3 May 1988).

19 For a full discussion of the changes that culminated in the 1976 Act, see S. Scott-Morrison, 'The Arms Export Control Act: an evaluation of the role of Congress in policing arms sales', *Stanford Journal of International Studies*, 14 (Spring 1979), 108–9; Philip Farley, 'The control of United States arms sales', in Alan Platt and Lawrence Weiler, *Congress and Arms Control* (Boulder: Westview Press, 1978), 111–34.

20 A summary of American restraint in sales to the Middle East can be found in William Bajusz and David Louscher, *Arms Sales and the U.S. Economy* (Boulder: Westview Press, 1988), 63–70. A further unsuccessful legislative initiative (the 'Biden–Levine' bill) that would have required exports to receive an affirmative vote in Congress was launched in 1987. *Jane's Defence Weekly* (21 May 1987); *Defence & Foreign Affairs* (May 1987).

21 Husbands, in Neuman and Harkavy, 158; M. T. Smith, 'U.S. Foreign Military Sales: its legal requirements, procedures and problems', in Uri Ra'anan, Robert Pfaltzgraff and Geoffrey Kemp (eds.), *Arms Transfers to the Third World: The Military Buildup in Less Industrialized Countries* (Boulder: Westview Press, 1978), 362, 383–4; Klare, *American Arms Supermarket*, 54–76.

22 From President Carter's statement, reprinted in *Changing Perspectives on U.S. Arms Transfer Policy*, 122. The policy included commitments to do the following:

(a) reduce the dollar volume of transfers.
(b) foreswear development of weapons systems for export.
(c) prohibit co-production agreements for major weapons systems.
(d) tighten regulations on the retransfer of equipment.
(e) refuse to introduce more advanced weapons systems into a region.
(f) abstain from using government personnel abroad to promote American weapons.

It was riddled with exceptions and subject to reinterpretation, curious accounting or outright reversal. See Jo Husbands, 'The arms connection: Jimmy Carter and the politics of military exports', in Cindy Cannizzo (ed.), *The Gun Merchants: Politics and Policies of the Major Arms Suppliers* (New York: Pergamon Press, 1980), 25–45; Comptroller General of the United States, *Arms Sales Ceiling Based on Inconsistent and Erroneous Data* (Washington: Office of the Comptroller General, 12 April 1978); *Changing Perspectives on U.S. Arms Transfer Policy*, 26.

23 Husbands, in Neuman and Harkavy, 160.

24 James Buckley, Under-Secretary of State for Security Assistance, Science and Technology, quoted in *Conventional Arms Sales*, hearing before the

Committee on Foreign Relations, Senate, 28 July 1981 (Washington: Government Printing Office, 1981), 12.

25 Robert Shuey, 'U.S. legislative responses to missile proliferation', paper presented at the International Studies Association annual meeting, Washington, 13 April 1990; Robert Shuey, 'Missile proliferation: a discussion of U.S. objectives and policy options', Congressional Research Service Report for Congress, 90–120 (21 February 1990).

26 Proponents of the sale argued that Japan would otherwise develop its own fighter; opponents worried that the technologies transferred would create competition for American civilian and military aircraft manufacturers. This attention is also reflected in a growing specialist literature on the subject. See Klare, *American Arms Supermarket*, 163–82; Louscher and Salomone, *Technology Transfer*; David Haglund and Marc Busch, '"Techno-nationalism" and the contemporary debate over the American defence industrial base', in David Haglund (ed.), *The Defence Industrial Base and the West* (London: Routledge, 1989), 234–77; and the report by the Office of Technology Assessment, *Arming our Allies*.

27 This was reflected by a 1989 move by the Senate to increase the Commerce Department's role in reviewing arms cooperation agreements. *Aviation Week and Space Technology* (7 August 1989).

28 Defence spending figures from Office of Technology Assessment, *Arming our Allies*, 10–11. Procurement figures from Judith Reppy, 'The United States', in Nicole Ball and Milton Leitenberg (eds.), *The Structure of the Defense Industry* (London: Croom Helm, 1983), 24; Alex Mintz, '"Guns vs. butter": a disaggregated analysis', paper presented at the International Studies Association annual meeting, London, 28 March–1 April 1989, 11; Jacques Gansler, *The Defense Industry* (Cambridge, Mass.: MIT Press, 1980), 12. Peaks in procurement were associated with the Korean War, the Cuban Missile Crisis and the Vietnam War. Procurement in the 1985–6 period was 28.8 per cent of the military budget, compared with a 21.7 per cent average for the 1976–80 period.

29 The 11 per cent figure is an increase from the estimated 5 per cent of total defence production that was exported in the pre-1970 period. SIPRI, *Arms Trade*, 135.

30 The figures were somewhat higher for the top ten FMS contractors (who accounted for 56 per cent of sales) in the 1979–80 period. Only Northrop depended upon arms sales for its well-being, with 41 per cent of its total sales being arms exports! The other nine ranged between 1 and 17 per cent, the norm being less than 10 per cent. Council on Economic Priorities, 'Weapons for the world: 1982 update', *Newsletter* (December/January 1981–2), 3, 6.

31 Gansler, *Defense Industry*, 209; Reppy, in Ball and Leitenberg, 24; ACDA, *WMEAT, 1986*.

32 This is less than 0.5 per cent of the defence budget. From *Budgetary Cost Savings to the Department of Defense Resulting from Foreign Military Sales*, staff working paper of the US Congressional Budget Office (Washington: Congressional Budget Office, 24 May 1976).

33 Anne Cahn, 'Arms sales economics: the sellers' perspectives', *Stanford*

*Journal of International Studies,* 14 (Spring 1979), 138. Savings on specific items can, however, be important: the Air Force recoups $745,000 in R&D for each F-16 exported. Tom Martin and Rachel Schmidt, *A Case Study of the F-20 Tigershark,* Rand report P–7495–RGS (Santa Monica: Rand Corporation, 1987), 23.

34 Gansler, *Defense Industry,* 17, 21.

35 Lewis Snider, 'Do arms exports contribute to savings in defense spending?', in David Louscher and Michael Salomone (eds.), *Marketing Security Assistance* (Lexington, Mass.: D.C. Heath, 1987), 61n. See SIPRI, *Arms Trade,* 379–83, for a discussion of this. These gains appear to be smaller in the ship-building and electronics sectors.

36 The total for the *entire* period 1950–73 was $1,851 million (current) dollars. Department of Defense, *Foreign Military Sales, Foreign Military Construction Sales, and Military Assistance Facts* (Washington: Department of Defense, September 1983 and September 1989). Most of these agreements were with Saudi Arabia.

37 Details of the Treasury Department's study are discussed in United States Congressional Research Service, *Implications of President Carter's Conventional Arms Transfer Policy,* report prepared for the Committee on Foreign Relations, US Senate (Washington: Government Printing Office, 1977), 37–8.

38 United States, Congressional Budget Office, *The Effect of Foreign Military Sales on the U.S. Economy,* staff working paper (Washington: Congressional Budget Office, 23 July 1976).

39 The first figure is from Edward Fried, 'An economic assessment of the arms transfer problem', in Pierre, *Arms Transfers,* 269; the second from Bajusz and Louscher, 53, 57–60. Anne Cahn, 'The economics of arms transfers', in Neuman and Harkavy, 179, cites a Carter Administration study that estimates employment at 520,000; the Congressional Budget Office figure, in *The Effect of Foreign Military Sales,* is 420,000. The percentage of manufacturing employment is calculated from International Labour Office, *Year Book of Labour Statistics* (Geneva: ILO, 1986), 414–25.

40 Details from Erik Pratt, 'Trading guns for butter: net-export earnings from the arms trade', paper presented at the International Studies Association annual meeting, London, 28 March 1989, 10, 14–26. The exact figure depends on the source chosen to measure arms transfers, and ACDA figures tend to be somewhat low on this point. See also Stephanie Neuman, 'Coproduction, barter and countertrade: offsets in the international arms market', *Orbis,* 29:1 (Spring 1985), 183–213; Tracy DeCourcy, 'Countertrade and the arms trade in the 1980s', in Louscher and Salomone (eds.), *Marketing Security Assistance,* 165–84.

41 Pratt, 23–5.

42 Interview with Paul Warnke, former head of the Arms Control and Disarmament Agency (25 September 1984).

43 Robert Harkavy, 'The new geopolitics: arms transfers and the major powers' competition for overseas bases', in Neuman and Harkavy, 143.

44 US Senate, Committee on Foreign Relations, *Arms Transfer Policy* (Washington: Government Printing Office, 1977), 11–12; US House of Repre-

sentatives, Committee on Foreign Affairs, *Changing Perspectives on U.S. Arms Transfer Policy* (Washington: Government Printing Office, 1981).

45 United States Department of State, 'U.S. foreign military affairs', *Current Policy* (July 1975), 3; State Department classified report to Congress, January 1990, reported in *Jane's Defence Weekly* (10 February 1990).

46 Details in SIPRI, *Arms Trade*, 157–8.

47 See *Arms Sales in North Africa and the Conflict in the Western Sahara*, hearing before the Subcommittees on International Security and Scientific Affairs and on Africa, Committee on Foreign Affairs, House of Representatives, 25 March 1981; *Proposed Sale of F-16s to Venezuela*, hearing before the Committee on Foreign Relations, Senate, 5 February 1982; *Proposed Arms Transfers to the Yemen Arab Republic*, hearing before the Subcommittee on Europe and the Middle East, Committee on Foreign Affairs, House of Representatives, 12 March 1979; *International Herald Tribune* (4/5 March 1989).

48 *The Times* (6 June 1985; 7 February 1986); *International Herald Tribune* (28 September 1985).

49 Rajan Menon, *Soviet Power and the Third World* (London: Yale University Press, 1986), 166–237; Mark Kramer, 'Soviet arms transfers to the Third World', *Problems of Communism*, 36:5 (September/October 1987), 52–68; George Hudson, 'The economics of Soviet arms transfers: a policy dilemma', in Louscher and Salomone (eds.), *Marketing Security Assistance*, 65–78.

50 Official figures reported by Deputy Prime Minister Igor Belousov, in *Pravitelstyenny Vestnik*, reprinted in *Foreign Broadcast Information Service* (9 January 1991), FBIS–SOV–91–006, 45. If one uses the SIPRI purchasing power parity conversion rate of $2.5 = 1$ ruble, then total Soviet arms exports between 1986 and 1990 are $141,750 million, which is higher than all the figures in table 13. This may, however, be a conversion artifact, since Belousov also reported that deliveries of specific items declined dramatically in the same period – missiles by 64 per cent, tanks by 25–30 per cent and aircraft by 53 per cent.

51 SIPRI includes only major weapons systems and not service or construction contracts; the Congressional Research Service data include construction services; and the ACDA data include virtually all defence-related items. For a brief discussion of statistical problems see the appendix, and Moshe Efrat and Peter Wiles, *The Economics of Soviet Arms* (London: Suntory-Toyota International Centre for Economics and Related Disciplines, London School of Economics, 1985).

52 The *increase* of the early 1980s, however, may be in part a statistical artifact (which also affects the data of tables 6 and 7), as the United States Arms Control and Disarmament Agency changed its pricing estimates for Soviet weapons and revised upwards the value of Soviet deliveries since 1977 by approximately 40 per cent. It is impossible to assess whether or not this revision is justified. ACDA, *WMEAT 1987*, 6.

53 SIPRI, *Arms Trade*, 184 and ACDA, *WMEAT, 1972–1982*, 95–8.

54 SIPRI, *Arms Trade*, 189n, quoting a 1949 statement by E. Zukov, a Soviet authority on the colonial issue. For details of the Soviet relationship with its East European satellites, see Daniel Papp, 'Soviet military assistance to

243

Eastern Europe', in John Copper and Daniel Papp (eds.), *Communist Nations' Military Assistance* (Boulder: Westview Press, 1983), 13–21.

55 Uri Ra'anan, *The USSR Arms the Third World: Case Studies in Soviet Foreign Policy* (Cambridge, Mass.: MIT Press, 1969), 29.

56 Stockholm International Peace Research Institute, *The Arms Trade Registers* (London: MIT Press, 1975), passim; SIPRI, *Arms Trade*, 196–201.

57 Rajan Menon, 'The Soviet Union, the arms trade and the Third World', *Soviet Studies*, 24 (July 1982), 381–2.

58 Moshe Efrat, 'The economics of Soviet arms transfers to the Third World – a case study: Egypt', *Soviet Studies*, 35 (October 1983), 440; Moshe Efrat, 'Disentangling the economics of Soviet arms trade: are Western assessments really reliable?', *Osteuropa Wirtschaft*, 32:1 (March 1987), 41–2.

59 The Soviet Union reportedly agreed to supply Iran with 100 tanks and to construct an advanced radar network. *Defence and Foreign Affairs Weekly* (10–16 July 1989).

60 I am indebted to William Potter and Adam Stulberg's unpublished paper 'The Soviet Union and ballistic missile proliferation' (April 1990) for this information.

61 *New York Times* (3, 4 August 1990).

62 *Izvestia* (20 February 1990); Roger Pajak, 'West European and Soviet arms transfer policies in the Middle East', in Milton Leitenberg and Gabriel Sheffer (eds.), *Great Power Intervention in the Middle East* (New York: Pergamon Press, 1979), 155; Michael Brzoska and Thomas Ohlson, *Arms Transfers to the Third World, 1971–1985* (Oxford: Oxford University Press, 1987), 41.

63 SIPRI, *Arms Trade*, 180–1; Brzoska and Ohlson, *Arms Transfers*, 41.

64 *Izvestia* (2 February 1990); *The Independent* (19 April 1989). Andrei Kozyrev, head of the international organisations division of the Foreign Ministry, acknowledged in *Izvestia* that 'in general the amounts of arms sold internationally are being registered rather accurately'.

65 *Izvestia* (20 January 1990); *Le Monde* (2 February 1990); *International Herald Tribune* (3 February 1990).

66 David Holloway, *The Soviet Union and the Arms Race*, 2nd edn (London: Yale University Press, 1983), 9, 117–23.

67 David Holloway, 'Western technology and Soviet military power', in Mark Schaffer (ed.), *Technology Transfer and East–West Relations* (New York: St Martin's Press, 1985), 177–8. The United States Defense Department reported in 1982 that the United States led the Soviets in 14 of 20 basic technology areas, was equal in 4 and lagged in 2.

68 Julian Cooper, 'Soviet arms exports and the conversion of the defence industry', unpublished paper prepared for the United Nations, Department for Disarmament Affairs, conference on Transparency in International Arms Transfers, Florence, 25–8 April 1990, 3.

69 Stockholm International Peace Research Institute, *SIPRI Yearbook of World Armaments and Disarmament, 1990* (London: Oxford University Press, 1990), 162–5. Hereafter referred to as SIPRI, *Yearbook 1990*. See also Cooper, 4–5, and table 10 for a detailed explanation of how these figures were arrived at. Michael Checinski, 'An estimate of current Soviet military-industrial

output and of the development of the Soviet arms industry', *Osteuropa Wirtschaft*, 29:2 (June 1984), 138–52, estimates Soviet arms production ('military-industrial end product') at about 68,000 million rubles, giving a total of $170,000 million, far above the other estimates. His methods, however, are based upon calculations of total employment in unions connected with arms production and upon Soviet industrial output figures.

70 SIPRI, *Yearbook 1990*, 164–5. This accords well with the figures in Holloway, *Soviet Union and the Arms Race*, 133 (after correcting for inflation) and with the estimate of 25 per cent given in Ulrich Albrecht, 'The aborted UN study on the military use of research and development: an editorial essay', *Bulletin of Peace Proposals*, 19:3–4 (1988), 253–4.

71 Three estimates for the overall percentage of production that is exported, all of which coincide, are Cooper, 5; Michael Brzoska, 'Third World arms control: problems of verification', *Bulletin of Peace Proposals*, 14:2 (1983), 166; Holloway, *Soviet Union and the Arms Race*, 124.

72 Figures in David Holloway, 'The Soviet Union', in Ball and Leitenberg, 70–1, suggest, however, that the greatest *growth* of exports has occurred in combat aircraft and tanks, where considerable savings could be enjoyed.

73 *Armed Forces Journal International* (December 1989). The T-55 is sold for around $115,000.

74 Cooper, 5.

75 Production of the T-55 tank and MiG-21 and Su-17 aircraft fits this category. Patrick Rollins, 'Soviet arms transfers to the Third World, 1980–84', in David Jones (ed.), *Soviet Armed Forces Review Annual, 1985–86* (Gulf Breeze: Academic International Press, 1987), 203; *Jane's Defence Weekly* (16 September 1989).

76 Cooper, 7–8 discusses the advocacy of exports by the Mikoyan–Gurevich (MiG) bureau. See also SIPRI, *Yearbook 1990*, 355–8; *New York Times* (17 June 1989); *Jane's Defence Weekly* (16 September 1989, 10 February 1990).

77 For the best (if dated) explanation of accounting and pricing of weapons in the Warsaw Pact see Michael Checinski, 'The costs of armament production and the profitability of armament exports in Comecon countries', *Osteuropa Wirtschaft*, 20:2 (1975), 123–6, 131–6.

78 Industrial output figure from Assembly of Western European Union, *Konversiya – Conversion in Soviet Military Industry* (Paris: WEU, 1990), 7. SIPRI, *Yearbook 1990*, 348, cites estimates of up to 20 per cent of industrial production and 8 million workers, but in light of recent information these seem somewhat high.

79 Dervied from ACDA, *WMEAT 1988*.

80 Saadet Deger, 'Soviet arms sales to developing countries: the economic forces', in Robert Cassen (ed.), *Soviet Interests in the Third World* (London: Sage Publications, 1985), 161. For other examples of this view see: Hudson in Louscher and Salomone, 65–78; Wharton Associates, *Soviet Arms Trade with the Non-Communist Third World in the 1970s and 1980s* (Washington: Wharton Economic Forecasting Associates, 1984), 24–7; Gur Ofer, 'Economic aspects of Soviet involvement in the Middle East', in Yaacov

Ro'i (ed.), *The Limits to Power* (London: Croom Helm, 1979), 67–93; Pajak in Leitenberg and Sheffer, 155; Menon, 'The Soviet Union', 383–8; Hammond et al., 264; Rollins, 203.

81 Figures from Wharton, 24; Menon, *Soviet Power*, 210; Robert Cutler, Lauré Després and Aaron Karp, 'The political economy of East–South military transfers', *International Studies Quarterly*, 31:3 (September 1987), 279. Higher figures (28 per cent on average) are given in Hudson in Louscher and Salomone, 71.

82 Karen Dawisha, *Soviet Foreign Policy towards Egypt* (London: Macmillan Press, 1979), 181; Anthony Cordesman, 'U.S. and Soviet competition in arms exports and military assistance', *Armed Forces Journal International*, 118 (August 1981), 67.

83 Soviet representative quoted in *Military Technology* (October 1989).

84 Hudson in Louscher and Salomone, 71, estimates that it would be increased by about 14 per cent.

85 Robin Luckham, 'Soviet arms and African militarization', in Robert Cassen (ed.), *Soviet Interests in the Third World* (London: Sage Publications, 1985), 104; Elizabeth Kridl Valkenier, *The Soviet Union and the Third World: An Economic Bind* (New York: Praeger, 1983), 24–5, gives evidence for this shift in Soviet thinking.

86 Cutler et al., 278. Syria alone owes more than $15,000 million for its arms purchases, *International Herald Tribune* (21 November 1989).

87 Harkavy in Neuman and Harkavy, 132.

88 For example, in the wake of the 1976 Lebanese War, when Soviet arms shipments were curtailed to express displeasure with Syrian policy, Syria retaliated by closing port facilities. Harkavy in Neuman and Harkavy, 149n; Menon, *Soviet Power*, 228–35.

89 Harkavy in Neuman and Harkavy, 141. He suggests that the cost is low because 'many bases certainly have been acquired merely by allowing extensive cash arms sales'. This has not been the case in Ethiopia, Syria, Mozambique, Cuba, Vietnam or India. This leaves only Iraq and Libya, whose base grants have hardly been extensive, and the smaller African states such as Congo, Guinea and Benin, all of which have received concessionary arms aid.

90 Andrew Pierre, *The Global Politics of Arms Sales* (Princeton: Princeton University Press, 1982), 22.

91 India signed in 1980 a $1,700 million arms package with a seventeen-year loan at 2.5 per cent interest. Menon, 'The Soviet Union', 383, 395n. As Soviet discontent with regional policies mounted, the Syrians were pressed for payment and did not receive all the arms they sought. It owes the Soviet Union $15,000 million for arms, and the delivery of sophisticated weapons (Su-24 bombers, MiG-29 fighters and SS-23 missiles) has been repeatedly delayed. *International Herald Tribune* (21 November 1989); *Flight International* (16 September 1989). Ethiopia also has been refused an increase in military aid. *Afrique Défense* (July 1989). See also United States Central Intelligence Agency, *Communist Aid Activities in Non-Communist Less Developed Countries, 1979 and 1954–1979* (Washington: Central Intelligence Agency, 1980), 4.

## 6 Second-tier producers and suppliers: the struggle to keep pace

1 Details on postwar reconstruction and military aid from Edward Kolodziej, *Making and Marketing Arms: The French Experience and its Implications for the International System* (Princeton: Princeton University Press, 1987), 41–8. France received about $10,000 million in military aid up to 1954. See also Pierre Dussauge, *L'Industrie française de l'armement* (Paris: Economica, 1985).

2 Peter Lock, 'Towards a European arms industry?', occasional paper 27 (Hamburg: Centre for the Study of Wars, Armaments and Development, 1989), 1. For details see Trevor Taylor and Keith Hayward, *The UK Defence Industrial Base: Development and Future Policy Options* (London: Brassey's, 1989).

3 Michael Brzoska, 'The Federal Republic of Germany', in Nicole Ball and Milton Leitenberg (eds.), *The Structure of the Defense Industry* (London: Croom Helm, 1983), 111–16.

4 Alistair Edgar, 'The MRCA/Tornado: the politics and economics of collaborative procurement', in David Haglund (ed.), *The Defence Industrial Base and the West* (London: Routledge, 1989), 46–85.

5 Details from Marie Söderberg, *Japan's Military Export Policy* (Stockholm: University of Stockholm, 1986), 51–5; United States, Office of Technology Assessment, *Arming our Allies* (Washington: Office of Technology Assessment, 1990), 61–8.

6 In 1989 Japan had the sixth largest defence budget in the world. Stockholm International Peace Research Institute, *Yearbook 1990* (Oxford: Oxford University Press, 1990), 193. Hereafter cited as SIPRI, *Yearbook*.

7 Figures for defence procurement from Office of Technology Assessment, 104–5; for the top 100 arms firms, from SIPRI, *Yearbook 1991*, 285.

8 The only book-length study is Reinhard Drifte, *Arms Production in Japan* (Boulder: Westview Press, 1986). See also Söderberg, 50–89; Office of Technology Assessment, 61–72, 102–10.

9 Fabrizio Battistelli, *Armi: nuovo modello di sviluppo?* (Turin: Giulio Einaudi Editore, 1980), 126–42, dates Italian production in the following phases: 1949–56, absolute dependence; 1956–68, partial dependence; 1968–today, complementary production. David Louscher and Michael Salomone, *Technology Transfer and U.S. Security Assistance: The Impact of Licensed Production* (Boulder: Westview Press, 1987), 42–9, date the emergence of Italian production after 1963. See also Sergio Rossi, 'Italy', in Ball and Leitenberg, 214–56.

10 See Vicenç Fisas, *Las armas de la democracia* (Barcelona: Editorial Critica, 1989), 43–51; Evamaria Loose-Weintraub, 'Spain's new defence policy: arms production and exports', in SIPRI, *Yearbook 1984*, 137–48; Louscher and Salomone, *Technology Transfer*, 73–8.

11 See Michael Checinski, 'The Warsaw Pact/Comecon and the Polish and Czechoslovak military-industrial complex', *Osteuropa Wirtschaft*, 33:1 (March 1988), 37–56; Stephen Tiedtke, 'Czechoslovakia', in Ball and Leitenberg, *The Structure of the Defense Industry*, 181–213.

12 Katarzyna Zukrowska, 'East European international arms transfers and

prospects for limitation', paper presented to the United Nations conference on Transparency in International Arms Transfers, Florence, 25–8 April 1990, 17. A list of systems produced in the non-Soviet Warsaw Pact states that highlights the unsophisticated nature of East European production can be found in SIPRI, *Yearbook 1990*, 360–2. Since 1989 Czechoslovakia has undertaken to end its arms exports and substantially cut production. Projected production for 1992 is only $133 million. This policy has not been without controversy, as demonstrated by a proposed sale of 300 T-72 tanks to Syria. See *Arms Control Reporter* (1991), section 407.E.1, pp. 33, 35–6; *International Herald Tribune* (25 January 1990, 5 May 1991); *Financial Times* (7 May 1991).

13 Checinski, 'Warsaw Pact/Comecon', 44–6, 56; Michael Checinski, 'Warsaw Pact/CEMA military-economic trends', *Problems of Communism*, 36:2 (1987), 15–28.

14 *Defence* (July 1987); *Aviation Week and Space Technology* (9 January 1989); Michael Hawes, 'The Swedish defence industrial base: implications for the economy', in Haglund, *Defence Industrial Base and the West*, 173–80.

15 See Björn Hagelin, *Neutrality and Foreign Military Sales* (Boulder: Westview, 1990), 36–7.

16 Robert Van Steenburg, 'An analysis of Canadian–American defence economic cooperation: the history and current issues', in David Haglund (ed.), *Canada's Defence Industrial Base: The Political Economy of Preparedness and Procurement* (Kingston: Ronald Frye, 1988), 189–219; Canada, Department of External Affairs, *Task Force on Europe 1992: Report of the Working Group on Defence Products* (Ottawa: External Affairs, 1989), 20–4; *Jane's Defence Weekly* (20 May 1989).

17 Stockholm International Peace Research Institute (SIPRI), *The Arms Trade with the Third World* (Stockholm: Almqvist and Wiksell, 1971), 216–17.

18 Ibid., 250.

19 Kolodziej, *Making and Marketing*, 46–7.

20 Sales for 1989 dropped even further, and declined 40 per cent from 1988. *Le Monde* (4–5 March 1990). A recovery (in orders, at least) to 'normal' levels occurred in 1990. *Jane's Defence Weekly* (23 March 1991). Unless otherwise noted, figures in this section from United States, Arms Control and Disarmament Agency, *World Military Expenditures and Arms Transfers* (Washington: ACDA, various years). Hereafter cited as ACDA, *WMEAT*.

21 Andrew Pierre, *The Global Politics of Arms Sales* (Princeton: Princeton University Press, 1982), 84. ACDA figures for 1979–83 put the developing world total at 97 per cent!

22 Britain's biggest customers, India, Pakistan (who together accounted for half of British arms exports in the 1950s), Egypt, Iraq, Jordan and South Africa, all turned to other suppliers. Britian's Lightning interceptor cost 2 million dollars, compared to the roughly equivalent F-104 at $1.5 million and the even less expensive MiG-21. SIPRI, *Arms Trade*, 217, 229.

23 In the aircraft industry, for example, between 1943 and 1965 seventy-three projects were undertaken, of which twenty-five produced more than 100 planes, five more than 500, and only two more than 1,000. SIPRI, *Arms*

*Trade*, 228–9; Lawrence Freedman, *Arms Production in the United Kingdom: Problems and Prospects* (London: Royal Institute of International Affairs, 1978), 31.

24 For a complete list of West German deliveries, 1951–74, see Hans Rattinger, 'West German arms transfers to the non-industrial world', in Uri Ra'anan, Robert Pfaltzgraff and Geoffrey Kemp (eds.), *Arms Transfers to the Third World: The Military Buildup in Less Industrialized Countries* (Boulder: Westview Press, 1978), 234–7.

25 Mike Dillon, 'Arms transfers and the Federal Republic of Germany', in Cindy Cannizzo (ed.), *The Gun Merchants: Politics and Policies of the Major Arms Suppliers* (New York: Pergamon Press, 1980), 109–10; SIPRI, *Arms Trade*, 308–14.

26 Frederic Pearson, 'Of leopards and cheetahs: West Germany's role as a mid-sized arms supplier', *Orbis*, 29 (Spring 1985), 172–3; Frederic Pearson, '"Necessary evil": perspectives on West German arms transfer policies', *Armed Forces and Society*, 12:4 (Summer 1986), 531–4; SIPRI, *Yearbook 1983*, 275–80.

27 The Italian collapse precipitated a crisis in the industry and debate over the way arms exports were regulated. See *Jane's Defence Weekly* (9 April 1988; 9 July 1988; 20 January 1990).

28 The most important exception was an indigenously produced Czech jet trainer. See Michael Brzoska and Thomas Ohlson, *Arms Transfers to the Third World* (Oxford: Oxford University Press, 1987), passim.

29 Ernie Regehr, *Arms Canada* (Toronto: Lorimer, 1987), 17; Hagelin, 64. Asia accounts for almost all the rest of Swedish sales. Swiss and Finnish arms sales are similarly concentrated, although probably about 20 per cent of Swiss arms have gone to the Middle East. Hagelin, 66–8.

30 Drifte, 74–8. Japanese equipment has appeared in Chad, Burma (Myanmar), Saudi Arabia, Zaire, Sweden and South Korea.

31 From *Budgetary Cost Savings to the Department of Defence Resulting from Foreign Military Sales*, staff working paper of the US Congressional Budget Office (24 May 1976).

32 See Herbert Wulf, 'The West German arms industry and arms exports', *Alternatives*, 13:3 (July 1988), 332–4.

33 From *Implementing the Lessons of the Falklands Campaign* (London: Her Majesty's Stationery Office, 6 May 1987), 88–9, quoted in Taylor and Hayward, xiv.

34 See Edward Kolodziej, 'Measuring French arms transfers', *Journal of Conflict Resolution*, 23:2 (June 1979), 210.

35 For a comprehensive list of the proportion of French weapons production that has been exported by weapons systems, see Kolodziej, *Making and Marketing*, 96–8; Dussauge, *L'industrie*, 81.

36 Edward Kolodziej, *Economic Determinants of the Transfer of Arms and Military Technology under the French Fifth Republic* (Illinois: University of Illinois, Office of Arms Control, Disarmament and International Security, 1983), table 3; Lawrence Franko, 'Restraining arms exports to the Third World: will Europe agree?', *Survival*, 21:1 (1979), 16.

37 Jean Klein, 'France and the arms trade', in Cannizzo, 143, citing *Le Projet de loi de finances pour 1976*, Assemblée nationale.

38 Bernd Huebner, 'The importance of arms exports and armament cooperation for the West German defence industrial base', in Haglund (ed.), *Defence Industrial Base and the West*, 139. This figure appears somewhat high. Jean-Paul Hébert, *Les Ventes d'armes* (Paris: Syros/Alternatives, 1988), 137–42, argues that the French government has not realised these unit cost savings with lower procurement costs.

39 Andrew Latham, 'Conflict and competition over the NATO defence industrial base: the case of the European Fighter Aircraft', in Haglund (ed.), *Defence Industrial Base and the West*, 91–2. The first American F-15 fighter plane required 600,000 person-hours for construction, the hundredth unit required 90,000 hours and the thousandth unit only 40,000. Ulrich Albrecht, 'New strategies of mid-sized weapons exporters?', The Federal Republic of Germany and Italy: *Journal of International Affairs*, 40:1 (Summer 1986), 133.

40 Hébert, 125.

41 *Damoclès*, 41 (November/December 1989), 14; *International Defence Intelligence* (20 February 1989); *Flight International* (10 October 1987).

42 *Aviation Week and Space Technology* (9 January 1989); Andrew Moravcsik, 'The European armaments industry at the crossroads', *Survival*, 32:1 (January/February 1990), 82n. Exports of the Gripen could equal half of production.

43 Klein in Cannizzo, 144; Hébert, 146–7. Thomson official cited in Lewis Snider, 'Do arms exports contribute to savings in defense spending?', in David Louscher and Michael Salomone (eds.), *Marketing Security Assistance* (Lexington, Mass.: D. C. Heath, 1987), 43.

44 SIPRI, *Yearbook 1984*, 186–7.

45 SIPRI *Arms Trade*, 257; Lawrence Freedman, 'Britain and the arms trade', *International Affairs* (London), 54:1 (July 1978), 377–92; Hammond, 224, 243; Hébert, 120.

46 For a similar conclusion based on statistical analysis of defence spending and arms exports see Snider in Louscher and Salomone, 41–63.

47 Brzoska characterises different strands in West German policy in this way. Cited in Wulf, 'West German arms industry', 335n.

48 Drifte, 74; Brzoska and Ohlson, *Arms Transfers*, 102.

49 Statement by Foreign Minister Jiri Dienstbier, *International Herald Tribune* (21 January 1990). Polish policy is unclear, although Polish arms may be uncompetitive in a freer market in any case. Zukrowska, 21–6.

50 Edward Kolodziej, *French Arms Transfers and the Military-Industrial Complex* (Chicago: Chicago Council on Foreign Relations, 1981), 16, 15–20. The DRI is the enhanced and upgraded version of the Direction des Affaires Internationales (DAI). Kolodziej, *Making and Marketing*, 263–5. For a comprehensive description of the French policy-making apparatus, see Kolodziej, *Making and Marketing*, 239–79; Jacques Isnard, 'Marketing weapons systems: an analysis of France's export apparatus', *Defence & Armament*, 20 (June 1983).

51 Martin Edmonds, 'The domestic and international dimensions of British

arms sales', in Cannizzo, 69. See also Frederic Pearson, 'The question of control in British defence sales policy', *International Affairs* (London), 59:2 (Spring 1983), 211–38.

52 Pierre, *Global Politics*, 105; Pearson, 'Question of control', 213–15, 237.

53 *Guardian* (9 November 1985, 8 December 1985, 7 May 1985).

54 Britain gave military aid averaging $68 million a year between 1964 and 1968 to India, Jordan, Kenya, Pakistan and Malaysia. SIPRI, *Arms Trade*, 217–21. France used military aid and cooperation agreements to maintain a strong position in its former African colonies; twelve such agreements were signed in 1960–1, and in 1960 there were more than 100 French garrisons in Black Africa. Such agreements usually granted military aid and training in return for base rights and occasionally preferential access to natural resources. John Chipman, 'French military policy and African security', *Adelphi Paper*, 201 (London: International Institute for Strategic Studies, 1985), 5–7.

55 SIPRI, *Arms Trade*, 215, quoting the 1955 White Paper, 'The export of surplus war material'.

56 Kolodziej, *Making and Marketing*, 135.

57 *Ibid.*, 158. Kolodziej links this shift to an underlying transformation in France's perception of its role in Europe and the world.

58 Quoted in Edward Kolodziej, 'France and the arms trade', *International Affairs* (London), 56 (January 1980), 60. By 1981 France possessed only six garrisons in Black Africa, and only 6 of its 12 defence agreements had been maintained.

59 Klein in Cannizzo, 156. For the 'self-defence and national independence' argument, see Kolodziej, *French Arms Transfers and the Military-Industrial Complex*, 4; Kolodziej, *Economic Determinants*, 14.

60 SIPRI, *Yearbook 1983*, 483–7.

61 Pierre, *Global Politics*, 84. 'Although arms-for-oil is never officially acknowledged as a policy, the assurance of future supplies of oil is clearly an important motivation for French leaders.'

62 Freedman, *Arms Production*, 39; Pearson, 'Question of control', 226. There is strong evidence that the embargo to South Africa may have been breached. SIPRI, *Yearbook 1984*, 190.

63 SIPRI, *Arms Trade*, 242–8. There was a recrudescence of the issue in 1970.

64 SIPRI, *Arms Trade*, 226–7; Freedman, 'Britain and the arms trade', 386. The term 'commercial pragmatism' is Freedman's.

65 Marco De Andreis, 'Italian arms exports to Iran and Iraq', *Note & richerche*, 18 (Rome: Centro studi di politica internazionale, 1988).

66 Albrecht, 'The Federal Republic of Germany', 132; *Defense & Armament Héraclès* (February 1988); *Armed Forces Journal International* (November 1988). The proposal was suspended as of early 1990 because of the implications of change in Eastern Europe for technology transfer regulations. *Defense News* (9 April 1990); Agnès Courades Allebeck, 'Arms trade regulations', in SIPRI, *Yearbook 1989*, 332–4.

67 Loose-Weintraub, 146; Fisas, 84–92.

68 Klein, 154–5. See also Kolodziej, *Making and Marketing*, 294–7 on public

criticism of French policy. For an overview of legislative controls see Allebeck, 319–38.

69 From 'Foreign policy aspects of overseas arms sales', memorandum submitted by the Foreign and Commonwealth Office to the House of Commons, Foreign Affairs Committee (4 March 1981).

70 SIPRI, *Arms Trade,* 17. In 1971 SIPRI placed Sweden, Switzerland, West Germany, Japan, Italy and Canada in this category.

71 On the Swedish debate see *Armed Forces Journal* (June 1990). Finland and Austria have similar policies, although for slightly different reasons. See Hagelin, *Neutrality,* 49–60.

72 John Lamb, 'Canada, arms transfers and arms control', unpublished paper (1987), 12–20.

73 Jacques Gansler, *Affording Defense* (Cambridge, Mass.: MIT Press, 1989), 312. See also Pierre, *Global Politics,* 120. Less optimistic analysts have argued that Japanese exports would suffer from not having been tested in battle. *Far Eastern Economic Review* (22 February 1990).

74 Pearson, 'Leopards and cheetahs', 171; Pearson, '"Necessary evil"', 531–7.

75 Michael Brzoska, 'The erosion of restraint in West German arms transfer policy', *Journal of Peace Research,* 26:2 (1989), 165–77.

76 *Middle East Economic Digest* (2 November 1985); *International Herald Tribune* (30–1 August 1986). *The Times* (London) (29 January 1991). In 1990 Germany again refused to sell tanks and other equipment to Saudi Arabia. *International Herald Tribune* (12 October 1990).

77 SIPRI, *Yearbook 1984,* 193; Brzoska and Ohlson, *Arms Transfers,* 91; Michael Feazal, 'New liberal arms export rules force review of German policy', *Aviation Week and Space Technology* (2 December 1985), 27–8. The first waiver was actually made in 1971.

78 Feazal; Rattinger in Ra'anan et al., passim; Pierre, *Global Politics,* 113.

79 Söderberg's thesis is that 'it is impossible for Japan to say outside the field of military export'. Söderberg, 2. Drifte, 74–9, is more cautious. See also Hagelin, *Neutrality,* 103–11, on the erosion of restraint in Sweden and Switzerland and Lamb, 19–23, for the Canadian experience.

80 Wulf, 'West German arms industry', 319–20.

81 Ian Gambles, 'Prospects for West European security co-operation', *Adelphi Paper,* 244 (London: International Institute for Strategic Studies, 1989), 42.

82 See, inter alia, Moravcsik, 65–85; Michael Brzoska, 'The structure of arms production in Western Europe beyond 1992', occasional paper 26 (Hamburg: Centre for the Study of Wars, Armaments and Development, 1989); Martyn Bittleston, 'Co-operation or competition? Defence procurement options for the 1990s', *Adelphi Paper,* 250 (London: International Institute for Strategic Studies, 1990); Lock, 'Towards a European arms industry?'; Pauline Creasey and Simon May, *The European Armaments Market and Procurement Cooperation* (London: Macmillan Press, 1988); Terrell Covington et al., *A Review of European Arms Collaboration and Prospects for its Expansion under the Independent European Program Group,* Rand report N–2638–ACQ (Santa Monica: Rand Corporation, 1987).

83 On past efforts see Michael Brenner, 'Strategic interdependence and the

politics of inertia', *World Politics*, 23:4 (July 1971), 635–64; Hammond et al., 209–19, 226–35, 244–7.

84 Brzoska, *The Structure of Arms Production*, 16. There is debate over whether an autarkic European solution could be technologically competitive. For a positive view, see Independent European Programme Group, *Towards a Stronger Europe* (2 vols., Brussels: Independent European Programme Group, 1986), vol. II, 22–33.

85 For a good discussion of the tension between the 'free market' and *juste retour* principles of cooperation see Moravcsik, 71–7.

86 See *Towards a Stronger Europe*, vol. I, 3, 5. It also supports *juste retour* and the establishment of a common European military research programme. A good analysis is presented in William Walker and Philip Gummett, 'Britain and the European armaments market', *International Affairs* (London), 65:3 (1989), 419–42.

87 The European Community, the Western European Union and the NATO Council of Armaments Directors have also been active in this area. For a description of possible alternatives see Brzoska, *The Structure of Arms Production*, 16–17; Moravcsik, 77; Walker and Gummett, passim.

88 In the Tornado project, for example, reduced unit costs were offset by the additional costs of collaboration, with significant saving coming only from development costs. *Towards a Stronger Europe*, vol. II, 119. Moravcsik, 75, however, argues that these inefficiencies are often overestimated.

89 On the compromises in military requirements inherent in collaboration, see Edgar in Haglund, 49–50. West Germany withdrew from the ASRAAM air-to-air missile project (leaving Canada, Norway and Britain), and France, Italy and Britain withdrew from the NATO frigate programme (leaving Canada, West Germany, the Netherlands and the United States). Royal United Services Institute, *Newsbrief* (January 1990); SIPRI, *Yearbook 1990*, 343–4. Continued West German participation in the Eurofighter has also been put in doubt. *Globe and Mail* (28 December 1989).

90 Walker and Gummett, 432–5. The recent spate of international take-overs and joint ventures suggests this may be changing. SIPRI, *Yearbook 1990*, 335–8; *Armed Forces Journal International* (January 1989); Bittleston, 27–8; Lock, 'Towards a European arms industry?', 3.

91 Klein in Cannizo, 134.

92 Quoted in Edward Kolodziej, 'Determinants of French arms sales: security implications', in Patrick McGowan and Charles Kegley, *Threats, Weapons and Foreign Policy* (Beverly Hills: Sage Publications, 1980), 154–65.

93 Speech by Sir Ronald Ellis, Head of Defence Sales Organisation, 18 October 1978. Reprinted in Royal United Services Institute, *RUSI*, 124 (June 1979), 4–5.

94 As one British study pointed out, arms transfers did not recoup research and development costs but did help keep production lines open. Cited in Pierre, *Global Politics*, 104.

95 Lock, 'Towards a European arms industry?', 13; Moravcsik, 78.

96 On Italian dependence upon imported technologies see Louscher and Salomone, *Technology Transfer*, 47–9. Official Swedish policy has shifted to recognise this dependence, as its stated goal is now simply to 'hold

together' a domestic manufacture and adaptation capability. Björn Hagelin, 'At arms' length or arm in arm? Sweden and West European military production', paper presented at the International Studies Association annual meeting, Washington (March 1989), 10.

97 Cutler et al., 289 and Tiedtke in Ball and Leitenberg, 206–8, echo this conclusion.

98 President François Mitterrand, *Le Monde* (2–3 October 1983), cited in J. Aben, 'The French Socialists confronted with the problem of arms exports', *Defense Analysis*, 2:4 (December 1986), 310, 316. Translation corrected by author.

## 7 Dependent production and exports in the third tier

1 Michael Brzoska and Thomas Ohlson (eds.), *Arms Production in the Third World* (London: Taylor and Francis, 1986), 9–12, 19, 36; Jacquelyn Porth, 'Argentina', in James Katz (ed.), *Arms Production in Developing Countries* (Lexington, Mass.: D. C. Heath, 1984), 63; John Frankenstein, 'People's Republic of China: defense industry, diplomacy and trade', in Katz, (ed.), *Arms Production*, 89–94.

2 See Frankenstein in Katz (ed.), *Arms Production*, 91–5.

3 Robert Harkavy and Stephanie Neuman, 'Israel', in Katz (ed.), *Arms Production*, 197.

4 Signe Landgren, *Embargo Disimplemented: South Africa's Military Industry* (Oxford: Oxford University Press, 1989), 41. Ewan Anderson, 'South Africa', in Katz (ed.), *Arms Production*, 333; Michael Brzoska, 'South Africa: evading the embargo', in Brzoska and Ohlson (eds.), *Arms Production*, 204–7, lists the systems produced.

5 Anderson in Katz (ed.), *Arms Production*, 333.

6 See Herbert Wulf, 'India: the unfulfilled quest for self-sufficiency', in Brzoska and Ohlson (eds.), *Arms Production*, 126–8; Raju Thomas, 'India: the politics of weapons procurement', in James Katz (ed.), *The Implications of Third World Military Industrialization: Sowing the Serpent's Teeth* (Lexington, Mass.: D. C. Heath, 1986), 158.

7 Quoted in Michael Moodie, *Sovereignty, Security and Arms* (Beverly Hills: Sage Publications, 1979), 23. For a detailed discussion of Brazilian arms production, see Andrew Ross, 'Security and self-reliance: military dependence and conventional arms production in developing countries', unpublished doctoral thesis, Cornell University, 1984, 175–8, 189–95; Alexandre de S. C. Barros, 'Brazil', in Katz (ed.), *Arms Production*, 73–87; Renato Peixoto Dagnino, 'A indústria de armamentos brasileira: uma tentativa de avaliação', unpublished doctoral thesis, University de Campinas, 1989; and Patrice Franko-Jones, *The Brazilian Defense Industry* (Boulder: Westview Press, forthcoming).

8 See Thomas Graham, 'India', in Katz (ed.), *Arms Production*, 170–2 for a list of successes and failures in the Indian aircraft industry; on Brazil's travails see Patrice Franko-Jones, 'The Brazilian defense industry in crisis', paper presented to the annual conference of the International Studies Association, Washington, 13 April 1990.

9 Ross, 'Security and self-reliance', 421; United States Arms Control and Disarmament Agency, *World Military Expenditures and Arms Transfers 1968–77* (Washington: ACDA, 1978), 18. Hereafter cited as ACDA, *WMEAT*.

10 Harkavy and Neuman in Katz, 198–9, 202, claim that in this Israeli case 'what has been mitigated by [the] indigenous defense industry perhaps, is the kind of precarious dependence for resupply of consumables exhibited in the larger and longer 1973 war'.

11 See Kwang-Il Baek and Chung-in Moon, 'Technological dependence, supplier control and strategies for recipient autonomy: the case of South Korea', in Kwang-Il Baek, Ronald McLaurin and Chung-in Moon (eds.), *The Dilemma of Third World Defense Industries* (Inchon: Center for International Studies, Inha University, 1989), 156–61; Janne Nolan, *Military Industry in Taiwan and South Korea* (London: Macmillan Press, 1986), 45–83.

12 Author's data base. South Korea is also producing parts of the F-16 and a battle tank (the K-1) based upon an American design. Baek in Baek and Moon, 161. Taiwan is also attempting to build a medium tank and sea-to-sea missile of modern design, although in both cases with imported components. The tank is built with an imported M-60 hull.

13 Mohammed El-Sayed Selim, 'Egypt', in Katz (ed.), *Arms Production*, 126–7. He quotes President Nasser as later saying: 'I have been waiting for the day in which we can rely upon ourselves in this crucial military sector. When we were fighting in Palestine, our ammunition was limited whilst Israel got all that it needed.'

14 Selim in Katz (ed.), *Arms Production*, 130; Brzoska and Ohlson (eds.), *Arms Production*, 107–9.

15 See Raimo Väyrynen and Thomas Ohlson, 'Egypt: arms production in the transnational context', in Brzoska and Ohlson (eds.), *Arms Production*, 114–20, for a description of the weapons produced.

16 Up to two-thirds of Egypt's exports in the 1980s went to Iraq, other customers being Somalia, the Sudan and Zaire. Väyrynen and Ohlson in Brzoska and Ohlson (eds.), *Arms Production*, 120–1. The United States also granted agreement in principle to the licensing of production of the M-1 tank. *Le Monde* (1 July 1987).

17 Saadet Deger, *Military Expenditure in Third World Countries* (London: Routledge & Kegan Paul, 1986), 151. Her data are calculated from Wassily Leontief and Faye Duchin, *Military Spending: Facts and Figures, Worldwide Implications and Future Outlook* (New York: Oxford University Press, 1983).

18 Derived from Brzoska and Ohlson (eds.), *Arms Production*, 8, 10, 23. The producers of major weapons systems in 1965 were the People's Republic of China, India and North Korea.

19 From Stephanie Neuman, 'International stratification and Third World military industries', *International Organization*, 38:1 (Winter 1984), 175.

20 This is consistent with the list in Brzoska and Ohlson (eds.), *Arms Production*, 10.

21 Barros, in Katz (ed.), *Arms Production*, 80; Gerald Steinberg, 'Israel: high-technology roulette', in Brzoska and Ohlson (eds.), *Arms Production*, 182–8.

22 Wulf in Brzoska and Ohlson (eds.), *Arms Production*, 140; V. Millán 'Argentina', in Brzoska and Ohlson (eds.), *Arms Production*, 48; Janne Nolan, 'South Korea: an ambitious client of the United States', in Brzoska and Ohlson (eds.), *Arms Production*, 225. In Brazil, for example, industry officials were projecting 1986 exports of $5,000 million! Peter Lock, 'Brazil', in Brzoska and Ohlson (eds.), *Arms Production*, 96.

23 A saturation of demand (cyclical or more durable) may also have been reached. Brazilian arms exports in 1988 were recorded at $380 million, on total sales of only $500 million. Franko-Jones, 'The Brazilian defense industry in crisis', 1; ACDA, *WMEAT 1989*.

24 Selim, in Katz (ed.), *Arms Production*, 156n. For details of the routes followed by Chinese weapons to Iran and Iraq see Yitzhak Shichor, 'Unfolded arms: Beijing's recent military sales offensive', *The Pacific Review*, 1:3 (1988), 323–4.

25 Dagnino, 347. See also Ross, 'Security and self-reliance', 261. Neuman, 'International stratification', 197, points out that typically the costs of a jet aircraft 'breaks down into one-third for the airframe, one-third for the engine and one-third for the avionics ... most developing countries are dependent upon major suppliers for the latter two items'.

26 See Michael Brzoska, 'The impact of arms production in the Third World', *Armed Forces and Society*, 15:4 (Summer 1989), 509; Moodie, 26; Steven Miller, 'Arms for the Third World: indigenous weapons production', occasional paper 3 (Geneva: Geneva Programme for Strategic and International Security Studies, 1980).

27 Ilan Peleg, 'Military production in Third World countries: a political study', in Patrick McGowan and Charles Kegley (eds.), *Threats, Weapons and Foreign Policy* (Beverly Hills: Sage Publications, 1980), 216. Neuman, 'International stratification', 186–7. Chile's industry was spurred by the partial embargo instituted by President Carter; Taiwan announced a determination to produce fighter planes after the 1982 Reagan Administration decision not to sell F-5Gs or F-16s; and Pakistan's 'frantic efforts to make [itself] as self-sufficient as possible in arms production ... was a result of the experience in the 1965 Indo-Pakistan War and the American embargo. Smaller producers such as Indonesia and Malaysia have also had their military industrialization efforts spurred by procurement difficulties.' Bilveer Singh, 'ASEAN's arms industries: potential and limits', *Comparative Strategy*, 8:2 (1989), 253.

28 The study is cited in Ross, 'Security and self-reliance', 191. Dagnino, 368, questions the larger figure; Franko-Jones, 'The Brazilian defense industry in crisis', 1, also notes that actual sales in 1987 were *one-quarter* of the estimated $2,000! The difference may be accounted for partly by non-military production in the firms in question.

29 Emile Benoit, *Defense and Economic Growth in Developing Countries* (Lexington, Mass.: D. C. Heath, 1973); Nicole Ball, 'Defense and development: a critique of the Benoit study', in Helena Tuomi and Raimo Väyrynen (eds.), *Militarization and Arms Production* (London: Croom Helm, 1983), 39–56; David Whynes, *The Economics of Third World Military Expenditure* (London: Macmillan Press, 1979), 69–77; Deger, 185–209.

30 Nicole Ball, *Security and Economy in the Third World* (Princeton: Princeton University Press, 1988), 106.

31 Indian domestically produced planes were 150–70 per cent of the cost of equivalent imports, and the foreign exchange component of the domestically produced MiG-21 was 8.3 million rupees, compared to a cost of 6-7.5 million rupees for an imported aircraft. Signe Landgren-Backstrom, 'The transfer of military technology to Third World countries', in Tuomi and Väyrynen, 200, 204; Ian Clark, 'Soviet arms supplies and Indian Ocean diplomacy', in Larry Bowman and Ian Clark (eds.), *The Indian Ocean in Global Politics* (Boulder: Westview Press, 1981), 156; Deger, 158–9. Two other noteworthy cases are Israel's Lavi fighter and Merkava tank. Steinberg in Brzoska and Ohlson, 165. The Lavi was estimated to have an eventual unit cost as high as $24 million, compared to no more than $17 million for a licence-produced F-16. Galen Roger Perras, 'Israel and the Lavi fighter-aircraft: the Lion falls to earth', in David Haglund (ed.), *The Defence Industrial Base and the West* (London: Routledge, 1989), 204–5.

32 Lance Taylor, 'International adjustment to the oil shocks and the arms trade', unpublished paper cited in Ball, *Security and Economy*, 106.

33 Carole Evans, 'Reappraising Third-World arms production', *Survival*, 28:2 (March–April 1986), 101; Whynes, 52–3.

34 Deger, 153, 175, 171–6.

35 Robert Looney, *Third-World Military Expenditure and Arms Production* (London: Macmillan, 1988), 67. He also notes that it appears to worsen income distribution. Ibid., 68.

36 Neuman, 'International stratification'; Herbert Wulf, 'Developing countries', in Nicole Ball and Milton Leitenberg (eds.), *The Structure of the Defense Industry* (London: Croom Helm, 1983), 310–43; Peleg, 209–30; Deger, 164–71; Arthur Alexander et al., *Modelling the Production and International Trade of Arms: An Economic Framework for Analyzing Policy Alternatives*, Rand report N–1555–FF/RC (Santa Monica: Rand Corporation, 1981), 15–19. A study of Latin American producers suggests that in addition to the factors cited 'arms production necessitates a certain economic environment', in which integration into the world economy (via trade and investment) plays a major role. Robert Looney and P. C. Frederiksen, 'Profile of current Latin American arms producers', *International Organization*, 40 (Spring 1986), 746, 752.

37 Neuman, 'International stratification', 183–6.

38 Deger, 170. Her top six producers were ranked as follows, in descending order of actual production, with potential production scores in brackets: Israel (6), India (3), Brazil (2), Yugoslavia (1), South Korea (4), Turkey (5).

39 Alexander Gershenkron's thesis is, loosely, that late nineteenth-century industrialisers such as Germany and Russia required greater levels of state intervention to achieve industrial development because the benefits of technological diffusion (i.e. not having to invest in R&D) were outweighed by the barriers to entry. Alexander Gershenkron, *Economic Backwardness in Historical Perspective* (Cambridge, Mass.: Harvard University Press, 1962), 5–30. See also Andrew Ross, 'Military import substitution in the developing world: the market, industrialization, the state and dependency', paper

presented to the annual conference of the International Studies Association, London, March 1989, 11–13.

40 Alexander et al., 17. Of course, industrial capabilities are not strictly speaking a sufficient condition to explain arms production, because there exists at least one exception (Iran, Mexico). It is probably closer to a necessary condition, as there are no examples of states that do not have the necessary industrial endowments to produce arms, but are doing so. This is almost, however, true by tautology. See Ross, 'Security and self-reliance', 152, for a challenge to this thesis.

41 Patrice Franko-Jones, '"Public private partnerships": lessons from the Brazilian armaments industry', *Journal of Interamerican Studies and World Affairs*, 29:4 (Winter 1987–8), 59–60; Lock, 99.

42 First quotation from Franko-Jones, '"Public private"', 59. See also *Le Monde* (25 March 1986). The 1990 policy statement is from Foreign Minister Francisco Rezek, quoted in *The Globe and Mail* (Toronto) (11 October 1990).

43 Aaron Klieman, *Israel's Global Reach* (London: Pergamon-Brassey's, 1985), 107.

44 Michael Brzoska and Thomas Ohlson, *Arms Transfers to the Third World, 1971–1985* (Oxford: Oxford University Press, 1987), 111–12. This was defended both as part of the official policy of non-alignment and to maintain a healthy arms production base.

45 *Le Monde* (23 December 1986); Shichor, 322–4. States that have voiced this intention include Argentina, South Korea, India and South Africa.

46 Klieman, 116; Moodie, 25. Some estimates have up to 90 per cent of production being exported. Thomas Ohlson, 'Third World arms exporters – a new fact of the global arms race', *Bulletin of Peace Proposals*, 13:3 (1982), 217.

47 Graham in Katz (ed.), *Arms Production*, 178; *International Defense Review* (November 1990); *Defence* (April 1989); Shichor, 320–30; Anne Gilks and Gerard Segal, *China and the Arms Trade* (London: Croom Helm, 1985), 29–83.

48 I am grateful for the research assistance of Ken Boutin for this section. See also Ken Boutin, 'Import substitution or exports?: the determinants of arms production in developing countries', unpublished master's thesis, York University, Toronto, 1990. He lists several 'ladder of production' models, the most significant of which are: International Institute for Strategic Studies, *The Military Balance, 1979–1980* (London: IISS, 1979), 103; Moodie, 46–7; Andrew Ross, *Arms Production in Developing Countries: The Continuing Proliferation of Conventional Weapons*, Rand report N–1615–AF (Santa Monica: Rand Corporation, 1981), 4–6; James Katz, 'Understanding arms production in developing countries', in Katz (ed.), *Arms Production*, 8; David Louscher and Michael Salomone, *Technology Transfer and U.S. Security Assistance: The Impact of Licensed Production* (Boulder: Westview Press, 1987), 4–7; and Stephanie Neuman, 'Arms transfers, indigenous defence production and dependency: the case of Iran', in Hossein Amirsadeghi, *The Security of the Persian Gulf* (London: Croom Helm, 1981), 131–50. None of the models examined has eleven steps.

49 For example, Ross's ladder of production specifies the following steps:

(1)  assembly of arms.
(2)  licensed production of components.
(3)  production of complete systems under license.
(4)  reverse engineering, or indigenous modification of foreign designs.
(5)  indigenous design and production.
Ross, *Arms Production in Developing Countries*, 4–5.

50 Andrew Pierre, *The Global Politics of Arms Sales* (Princeton: Princeton University Press, 1982), 125. Katz, 'Understanding arms production', 8; Ron Ayres, 'Arms production as a form of import-substituting industrialization: the Turkish case', *World Development*, 11 (1983), 814. See also Evans, 102.

51 Neuman, 'Arms transfers', 142; Herbert Wulf, 'Arms production in the Third World', *World Armaments and Disarmament: SIPRI Yearbook 1985* (Stockholm: Stockholm International Peace Research Institute, 1985), 330. Less explicitly, but none the less making the same assumption, Andrew Ross argues that 'military import substitution is a process that assumes different forms as it progresses through five distinct developmental stages'. Ross, 'Military import substitution', 3.

52 See Boutin, passim, for a detailed examination of the level of production achieved (and its evolution) in Brazil, Egypt and South Korea.

53 Boutin, passim.

54 Ibid., 52.

55 *International Herald Tribune* (25 July 1986); *Jerusalem Post* (international edition) (12 September 1987), *Financial Times* (13 January 1987). For an excellent presentation of the Lavi saga, see Perras in Haglund, 189–233.

56 *Jane's Defence Weekly* (5 August 1989); R. G. Matthews, 'The development of India's defence-industrial base', *Journal of Strategic Studies*, 12:4 (December 1989), 423.

57 Matthews, 424; Perras in Haglund, 221–2. For particular cases see the chapters on Brazil, India and Israel in Brzoska and Ohlson (eds.), *Arms Production*, and in Katz (ed.), *Arms Production*.

58 *International Defense Review* (October 1983), 1376; *Air International* (October 1983), 160; *Jane's Defence Weekly* (30 April 1988), 858.

59 Egypt's missile programmes have been equally unsuccessful, with cancellation of the Condor II project (to have been jointly developed with Iraq and Argentina). The Condor II would have involved independent R&D and production of an unsophisticated rocket artillery system. *Jane's Defence Weekly* (20 February 1988), 297; (1 April 1989), 553; *Le Monde* (31 May 1991).

60 *Air International* (September 1977), 109; *International Defense Review* (August 1979), 1281.

61 Figures from table 9 suggest that the third tier accounts for 1.6 per cent of world military R&D, although several states are not included.

62 The early heights were reached with the 1960–9 programme for licensed production of Spanish jet trainers (with the Egyptian name Al Kahira), and with production of the Walid armoured personnel carrier (based on West German and Soviet designs). *Air International*, 22:6 (1982), 279; Christopher Foss, *Jane's AFV Recognition Handbook* (London: Jane's, 1987), 213.

63 The omission of India from the top six (it scores eighth) appears to be a

statistical artifact. These figures correspond reasonably well with SIPRI data: of the 51 states identified as producing some arms in the early 1980s, 15 produced aircraft, 11 armoured vehicles, 7 missiles, and 5 tanks; the remainder were restricted to small arms and ammunition and ship-building. Brzoska and Ohlson (eds.), *Arms Production*, 16, 23.

64 Neuman, 'International stratification', 178, excludes Taiwan from her list.

65 Peleg, 226. This appears to be the conclusion of Michael Brzoska too, albeit with several caveats. Brzoska, 'Impact', 519–24.

66 Ross, 'Military import substitution', 15. This appears to be the same distinction Louscher and Salomone make between product and process transfers. David Louscher and Michael Salomone, 'Brazil and South Korea: two cases of security assistance and indigenous production development', in David Louscher and Michael Salomone (eds.), *Marketing Security Assistance* (Lexington, Mass.: D. C. Heath, 1987), 131.

67 Jacques Fontanel and José Drumont-Saraiva, 'Les Industries d'armements comme vecteur du développement économique des pays du tiers-monde', *Etudes polémologiques*, 40 (1986), 27. See also the exhaustive list of similar conclusions presented in Ross, 'Military import substitution', 13–14 and Stephanie Neuman, 'Arms and superpower influence: lessons from recent wars', *Orbis*, 30–4 (Winter 1987), 711–29.

68 Peter Lock and Herbert Wulf, 'The economic consequences of the transfer of military-oriented technology', in Mary Kaldor and Asbjørn Eide (eds.), *The World Military Order: The Impact of Military Technology on the Third World* (London: Macmillan Press, 1979), 226.

69 This is the problem with, for example, Anne Naylor Schwarz's otherwise suggestive method for calculating and comparing the level of dependence of 'second-level' arms industries. Anne Naylor Schwarz, 'Arms transfers and the development of second level industries', in Louscher and Salomone (eds.), *Marketing Security Assistance*, 109–15. This distinction between reliance and dependence is based upon Robert Keohane and Joseph Nye's distinction between 'sensitivity' and 'vulnerability' interdependence. Robert Keohane and Joseph Nye, *Power and Interdependence* (Boston: Little, Brown and Company, 1977), 12–13.

70 Brzoska and Ohlson (eds.), *Arms Production*, 306–49.

71 For a clear example of the military application of dual-use technologies see Gary Milhollin, 'India's missiles – with a little help from our friends', *Bulletin of the Atomic Scientists*, 45:9 (November 1989), 31–5.

72 Brzoska, 'Impact', 521, offers the example of a few bags of microfiche containing submarine designs being supplied by a West German firm to South Africa, which only became known when component delivery was also attempted.

73 This is essentially Ross's conclusion. Ross, 'Military import substitution', 14–15. For example, the ill-fated Indian Marut aircraft attempted to use engines from three different sources. Matthews, 424. The burgeoning 'retrofit' market, which installs more advanced weapons, power plants or electronics on existing platforms, is another strong indication of this trend. Two publications that deal with this periodically are the *International Defense Review* and the *World Retrofit and Modernization Letter*.

74 *Jane's Defence Weekly* (1 October 1988).
75 For example, Anthony Cordesman's conclusion that the Saudi Arabian air force throughout the 1980s 'could not sustain air defense operations ... by more than 45–60 aircraft for even a few days' without direct American assistance would clearly be changed by the development of even rudimentary depots and servicing capabilities. Anthony Cordesman, *The Gulf and the Search for Strategic Stability* (London: Mansell Publishing, 1984), 948.
76 For the argument that influence is not declining see Stephanie Neuman, 'The arms market: who's on top?', *Orbis*, 33:4 (Fall 1989), 509–29.
77 Franko-Jones, 'The Brazilian defense industry in crisis', 11. Difficulties in advancing South Korean defence production are discussed in Nolan, *Military Industry in Taiwan and South Korea*, 63–70, 81–3.
78 For examples of this dichotomy (cast in terms of political/security versus economic motives) see Evans, passim; Deger, 152–5.
79 As Stephanie Neuman points out, 'today's leading LDC arms producers ... are unlikely to be followed by a second tier of LDC competitors ... [and] the number of LDC producers of major weapons is likely to remain limited'. Neuman, 'International stratification', 192.
80 Wulf in Ball and Leitenberg, 311.
81 Edward Kolodziej, *Making and Marketing Arms: The French Experience and its Implications for the International System* (Princeton: Princeton University Press, 1987), 405–6 argues (wrongly, I think) that 'current research and experience suggests ... every state, whether wittingly or not, [is emulating] the French example' of arms production. See also Lock and Wulf, passim, for the argument that arms production militarises domestic economic relations.

## 8 The subordinate role of arms recipients

1 I have addressed these issues in a partial fashion elsewhere. See Keith Krause, 'Military statecraft: power and influence in Soviet and American arms transfer relationships', *International Studies Quarterly*, 35:3 (September 1991, 313–36); Keith Krause, 'Arms imports, arms production and the quest for security in the Third World', in Brian Job (ed.), *The Insecurity Dilemma: National Security of Third World States* (Boulder: Lynne Rienner, 1992), 121–42.
2 Amos Jordan, 'Military assistance and national policy', *Orbis*, 2:2 (1958), 237; Harold Hovey, *United States Military Assistance* (New York: Frederick A. Praeger, 1966), 184. Estimates of the value of arms transferred from the United States to Nationalist China range from a few hundred million dollars up to a thousand million. Jordan, 239.
3 Much of the 'disarmament and development' debate is conducted with such generalisations. See, for example, Richard Jolly (ed.), *Disarmament and World Development* (Oxford: Pergamon Press, 1978); United Nations, *Economic and Social Consequences of the Arms Race and of Military Expenditures* (New York: United Nations, 1978); United Nations, *The Relationship between Disarmament and Development* (New York: United Nations, 1982).

4 United States, Arms Control and Disarmament Agency, *World Military Expenditures and Arms Transfers* (Washington: ACDA, various years).

5 Edward Kolodziej, *Making and Marketing Arms: The French Experience and its Implications for the International System* (Princeton: Princeton University Press, 1987), 405–6, concludes that 'the quest for cooperation among states to slow the militarization of international relations . . . will be . . . daunting – if not utopian'.

6 Jacques Gansler, *The Defense Industry* (Cambridge, Mass.: MIT Press, 1980), 204, 208, 312n; Gu Guan-fu, 'Soviet arms sales and military aid policy to the Third World', *Osteuropa Wirtschaft*, 29:1 (March 1984), 52. India and Syria received the MiG-29, as it entered service with Soviet forces. *Flight International* (28 March–3 April 1990); *Air International* (May 1990).

7 See John Stanley and Maurice Pearton, *The International Trade in Arms* (London: Chatto & Windus, 1972), 210–21.

8 The concept of a security complex comes from Barry Buzan, *People, States and Fear* (Brighton: Wheatsheaf, 1983), 115.

9 Martin Navias, 'Ballistic missile proliferation in the Third World', *Adelphi Paper*, 252 (London: International Institute for Strategic Studies, 1990), 8, 29–31, estimates the number of states with ballistic missiles at 22. Aaron Karp, 'Ballistic missile proliferation', Stockholm International Peace Research Institute (SIPRI), *SIPRI Yearbook of World Armaments and Disarmament, 1990* (Oxford: Oxford University Press, 1990), 369–91, places it at 26. See also Thomas Mahnken and Timothy Hoyt, 'The spread of missile technology to the Third World', *Comparative Strategy*, 9:3 (1990), 245–64; Arthur Manfredi et al., *Ballistic Missile Proliferation Potential of Non-Major Military Powers*, Congressional Research Service, report for Congress, 6 August 1987.

10 Earlier estimates of up to fifteen producers (made, among others, by the Director of the CIA) have been revised downward, in part because of the success of the Missile Technology Control Regime. See Aaron Karp, 'Controlling Missile Proliferation in the New World Order', paper presented to a conference on Supply-Side Control of Weapons Proliferation, Ottawa, 21 June 1991, 3. See also Janne Nolan, *Trappings of Power: Ballistic Missiles in the Third World* (Washington: The Brookings Institution, 1991).

11 K. Subrahmanyam, 'The meaning of Agni', *Hindustan Times* (2 June 1989), cited in Mahnken and Hoyt, 246. See also Navias, 9–13.

12 The seven original members are the United States, Britain, France, Germany, Italy, Canada and Japan. Nine additional states have subsequently joined.

13 Its guidelines include only systems with a range of more than 300 kilometres and a payload greater than 500 kilograms. For evidence on the success of the MTCR, see Karp, 'Ballistic missile proliferation', 376–80.

14 Information in this paragraph is from International Institute for Strategic Studies, *The Military Balance 1990–1991* (London: IISS, 1990). See also Leonard Spector, 'Foreign-supplied combat aircraft: will they drop the Third World bomb?', *Journal of International Affairs*, 40:1 (Summer 1986), 143–58.

15 On the NPT and London suppliers' group see John Simpson, 'The nuclear

non-proliferation regime as a model for conventional armament restraint', in Thomas Ohlson (ed.), *Arms Transfer Limitations* (Oxford: Oxford University Press, 1988), 227–40; SIPRI, *Yearbook 1990*, 553–86. On the activities of the Australia group and the chemical and biological weapons convention negotiations, see SIPRI, *Yearbook 1990*, 107–38, 521–43; *Christian Science Monitor*, world edition (2–8 January 1989).

16 See Leonard Spector, *The Undeclared Bomb* (Cambridge, Mass.: Ballinger, 1988).

17 For varied estimates see SIPRI, *Yearbook 1988*, 101–25; *Globe and Mail* (17 October 1987); SIPRI, *Yearbook 1990*, 111–12.

18 Robert Rothstein, 'National security, domestic resource constraints and elite choices in the Third World', in Saadet Deger and Robert West (eds.), *Defense, Security and Development* (New York: St Martin's Press, 1987), 141.

19 These motivations have been dealt with differently by many authors concerned with explaining not only arms acquisitions but also military expenditures. For a general account see Andrew Pierre, *The Global Politics of Arms Sales* (Princeton: Princeton University Press, 1982), 131–5, 136–271; Stockholm International Peace Research Institute, *The Arms Trade with the Third World* (Stockholm: Almqvist and Wiksell, 1971), 41–85. For a detailed statistical correlative analysis see Robert McKinlay, *Third World Military Expenditure: Determinants and Implications* (London: Pinter, 1989).

20 See McKinlay, passim. There are, however, several conceptual and methodological problems with such macro-statistical approaches.

21 For good overviews of the 'military as moderniser' theory see Nicole Ball, *Security and Economy in the Third World* (Princeton: Princeton University Press, 1988), 5–18; Tae Dong Chung, 'Soldiers in politics: a comparative overview of the military as a social force in developing countries', *Asian Perspective*, 6:1 (1982), 66–87; Henry Bienen, *Armies and Parties in Africa* (London: Africana Publishing, 1978).

22 See Ball, *Security and Economy*, 266–94, for a discussion of American security assistance policies.

23 For a good overview of this problem see Mohammed Ayoob, 'Security in the Third World: the worm about to turn?', *International Affairs* (London), 60:1 (Winter 1983–4), 41–51. See also the contributions to Edward Azar and Chung-in Moon (eds.), *National Security in the Third World* (Aldershot: Edward Elgar, 1988); Cynthia Enloe, *Ethnic Soldiers: State Security in Divided Societies* (Athens, Georgia: University of Georgia Press, 1980).

24 See, for an overview, Steve Chan, 'The impact of defense spending on economic performance: a survey of evidence and problems', *Orbis*, 29:2 (Summer 1985), 403–34; Saadet Deger, *Military Expenditure in Third World Countries: The Economic Effects* (London: Routledge & Kegan Paul, 1986), passim; Ball, *Security and Economy*, passim.

25 See, for a discussion of the concept of militarism, Andrew Ross, 'Dimensions of militarization in the Third World', *Armed Forces and Society*, 13:4 (Summer 1987), 561–78. For an analysis of the link between militarism and arms transfers, see Michael Brzoska, 'Current trends in arms transfers', in Deger and West, 164. 'Militarism' has been defined by Alfred Vagts as 'an undue preponderance of military demands, and emphasis on military

considerations, spirits, ideals, and scales of value, in the life of states'. Alfred Vagts, *A History of Militarism*, revised edition (New York: Free Press, 1957), 14.

26 Ball, *Security and Economy*, 107.

27 Ibid., 396–402. Prominent exceptions to this pattern from among those states for which reliable information is available were Iran (31 per cent) and Nigeria (46 per cent).

28 See Mohammed Ayoob, 'Regional security and the Third World', in Mohammed Ayoob (ed.), *Regional Security in the Third World* (Boulder: Westview Press, 1986), 3–27.

29 United States, Committee on Foreign Relations, *U.S. Military Sales to Iran* (Washington: Government Printing Office, 1976). Iran purchased more than 14,000 million (constant 1979) dollars worth of weapons between 1970 and 1977. ACDA, *WMEAT 1977*.

30 Gary Sick, *All Fall Down* (New York: Random House, 1985), 14.

31 Bruce Arlinghaus, *Military Development in Africa* (London: Westview Press, 1984), 42.

32 See Stephanie Neuman, *Military Assistance in Recent Wars* (Washington: Center for International and Strategic Studies, 1986) for a discussion of how such resupply efforts have been manipulated by major arms suppliers.

33 Figures from *The Military Balance 1990–1991; Aviation Week and Space Technology* (13 February 1984).

34 For a good discussion of African military spending see Robin Luckham, 'Militarization in Africa', in SIPRI, *Yearbook 1985*, 295–324.

35 *The Military Balance 1989–1990* and *1986–1987*. See also *Strategic Survey 1987–1988* (London: IISS, 1988), 187–8 for an analysis of the conduct of the Chad war. Libyan aircraft are also reportedly flown frequently by North Korean pilots.

36 United States, Senate Committee on Foreign Relations, *Proposed Sale of F-16s to Venezuela* (Washington: Government Printing Office, 1982). Cuban MiG-23s have a range of 600 miles; Venezuela is at least 610 miles distant.

37 See the discussion in, for example, Raju Thomas, *Indian Security Policy* (Princeton: Princeton University Press, 1986), 246–53; William Staudenmaier, 'Defense planning in Iraq: an alternate perspective', in Stephanie Neuman (ed.), *Defense Planning in Less-Industrialized States* (Lexington, Mass.: D. C. Heath, 1984), 53–66; Anne Schulz, *Buying Security: Iran under the Monarchy* (Boulder: Westview, 1989), 13–30. In some cases, such as Iran under the Shah, the possible adverse consequences of dependence were simply ignored.

38 See, for example, Avi Beker, 'The arms–oil connection: fueling the arms race', *Armed Forces and Society*, 8:3 (Spring 1982), 419–42; Steve Chan, 'The consequences of expensive oil on arms transfers', *Journal of Peace Research*, 17:2 (1980), 235–46; Anthony Sampson, *The Arms Bazaar* (London: Hodder & Stoughton, 1977), 238–56, 295.

39 Marek Thee, 'Militarism and militarisation in contemporary international relations', in Asbjørn Eide and Marek Thee (eds.), *Problems of Contemporary Militarism* (London: Croom Helm, 1980), 30.

40 Michael Barnett and Alexander Wendt, 'Nowhere to run, nowhere to hide:

the systemic sources of dependent militarization', unpublished paper (March 1990), 15–16.

41 For a comprehensive discussion of the way in which influence is exercised in arms transfer relationships see Krause, 'Military statecraft', passim.

42 Ariel Levite and Athanassios Platias, 'Evaluating small states' dependence on arms imports: an alternate perspective', occasional paper 16 (Cornell: Cornell University Peace Studies Program, 1983), 30–1, their italics. See also Andrew Ross, 'Arms acquisition and national security: the irony of military strength', in Azar and Moon, 152–87.

43 For details of how such strategies have been implemented by various Middle Eastern states see Keith Krause, 'Arms transfers, conflict management and the Arab–Israeli conflict', in Gabriel Ben-Dor and David Dewitt (eds.), Conflict Management in the Middle East (Lexington, Mass.: D. C. Heath and Company, 1987), 224–6.

44 Roger Pajak, 'Soviet arms and Egypt', Survival, 17:4 (July/August 1975), 171; Staudenmaier in Neuman (ed.), Defense Planning, 59, 61; Jon Glassman, Arms for the Arabs (Baltimore: Johns Hopkins University Press, 1975), 134.

45 Pajak, 'Soviet arms', 171; International Herald Tribune (27 September 1982).

46 SIPRI, Yearbook 1984, 198. Unconfirmed reports claimed that Iraq also received 50 British Chieftain tanks from Kuwait and 30 Romanian-built T-55 tanks from Egypt (until the USSR halted the deliveries) in 1985, as well as some equipment from Egypt earlier. SIPRI, Yearbook 1985, 400.

47 Anthony Cordesman, The Gulf and the Search for Strategic Stability (London: Mansell, 1984), 133. The Saudis contributed $140 million, Kuwait $132 million and Libya $74 million. Egypt was cut off in 1970 after it agreed to the Rogers Plan ceasefire. Lawrence Whetten, 'The Arab–Israeli dispute: great power behaviour', Adelphi Paper, 128 (London: International Institute for Strategic Studies, 1977), 19.

48 Figures from United Nations Conference on Trade and Development, Financial Solidarity for Development, 1983 Review (New York: UNCTAD, 1984). An estimated $1,000 million annually was also provided as direct military assistance. Paul Jabber, 'Oil, arms and regional diplomacy', in Malcolm Kerr and El-Sayed Yassin, Rich and Poor States in the Middle East (Boulder: Westview Press, 1982), 429. The original decision was taken at the 1974 Rabat conference. Lewis Sorley, Arms Transfers under Nixon: A Policy Analysis (Lexington, Ky.: University Press of Kentucky, 1983), 72, 108.

49 Organisation for Economic Cooperation and Development, Aid from OPEC Countries (Paris: OECD, 1983), 24; The Military Balance 1985–1986, 85.

50 The Military Balance 1986–1987, 106.

51 Nadav Safran, Israel: The Embattled Ally (Cambridge, Mass.: Harvard University Press, 1981), 531.

52 Quoted in Sorley, 99. Responsiveness was further extended in the 1981 Memorandum of Strategic Cooperation, which committed both parties to cooperate in 'research and development and defense trade'. David Pollock, The Politics of Pressure: American Arms and Israeli Policy Since the Six-Day War (Westport, Conn.: Greenwood Press, 1982), 284–5.

53 As Bruce Arlinghaus argues, 'most African nations cannot afford arms purchases on anything less than a grant-aid basis, or ... on extremely concessional terms ... unlike the Middle East, where the buyers of weapons control the marketplace. The difference between dollars and defense is most often made up through concessions of political influence to suppliers.' Bruce Arlinghaus, 'Linkage and leverage in African arms transfers', in Bruce Arlinghaus (ed.), *Arms for Africa* (Lexington, Mass.: D. C. Heath, 1983), 4.

## Conclusion

1 Stephanie G. Neuman and Robert E. Harkavy (eds.), *Arms Transfers in the Modern World* (New York: Praeger Publishers, 1980), vii.
2 The only work directly addressing the historical dimension is Robert Harkavy, *The Arms Trade and International Systems* (Cambridge, Mass.: Ballinger, 1975). For an example of a work that addresses the structural dimension, albeit not in a historical fashion, see Michael Brzoska and Thomas Ohlson, *Arms Transfers to the Third World, 1971–1985* (Oxford: Oxford University Press, 1987), 125–36.
3 Brzoska and Ohlson, *Arms Transfers*, 127–32, discuss the evolution of the post-1945 system in similar terms and divide it into four phases:
    (a) 1945 to the mid-1960s: dominance of the system by the United States, Soviet Union and Britain.
    (b) 1970s: resurgence of Western European arms industries, shift from aid to sales, shift in sales to the developing world.
    (c) late 1970s to mid-1980s: dramatic expansion of transfers.
    (d) mid-1980s to today: shift towards a more competitive 'buyers' market'.
Their analysis does not, however, rest upon any broader historical generalisations or analysis of the structure of the system.
4 Harkavy, 41–7.
5 As noted in chapter 1, the term 'baroque' refers to 'perpetual improvements to weapons that fall within established traditions ... the hardware becomes more complex and sophisticated [and] results in dramatic increases in the cost of individual weapons. But it does not increase military effectiveness'. Mary Kaldor, *The Baroque Arsenal* (London: André Deutsch, 1981), 4–5.
6 William McNeill, *The Pursuit of Power* (Oxford: Basil Blackwell, 1983), 90–4, 171. The latter period refers to the French military under Gribeauval in 1765–76. McNeill and Maurice Pearton, *The Knowledgeable State* (London: Burnett Books, 1982), both present excellent analyses of this phenomenon.
7 Pearton, *Knowledgeable State*, 242.
8 Although, as noted above, the continued superpower status of the Soviet Union can be questioned. Some observers have even had the temerity to challenge the continued superpower status of the United States. See 'Y a-t-il encore un "Super-Grand"?', *Le Monde* (26 October 1990).
9 Aaron Karp, 'The trade in conventional weapons', in Stockholm International Peace Research Institute, *SIPRI Yearbook of World Armaments and Disarmament, 1988* (London: Oxford University Press, 1988), 197–8.

10 Exceptions that acknowledge the role of underlying factors include Stephanie Neuman, 'International stratification and Third World military industries', *International Organization*, 38:1 (Winter 1984), 167–98; and Lewis Snider, 'Do arms exports contribute to savings in defense spending?', in David Louscher and Michael Salomone (eds.), *Marketing Security Assistance* (Lexington, Mass.: D. C. Heath, 1987), 61n. For examples of *ad hoc* classifications into two tiers (with either developing world producers alone, or including smaller industrialised producers such as Belgium in the 'second tier'), see Michael Klare, 'The arms trade: changing patterns in the 1980s', *Third World Quarterly*, 9:4 (October 1987), 1257–81; and Anne Schwarz, 'Arms transfers and the development of second-level arms industries', in Louscher and Salomone (eds.), *Marketing Security Assistance*, 101–27. For a three-tier division see Frederic Pearson, 'Problems and prospects of arms transfer limitations among second-tier suppliers: the cases of France, the United Kingdom and the Federal Republic of Germany', in Thomas Ohlson (ed.), *Arms Transfer Limitations and Third World Security* (Oxford: Oxford University Press, 1988), 126–56.

11 See, for an example of this error, Michael Klare, 'The state of the trade: global arms transfer patterns in the 1980s', *Journal of International Affairs*, 40:1 (Summer 1986), 7–11.

12 See *Le Monde* (29 November 1986); *Christian Science Monitor* (15 May 1985). The same phenomenon manifested itself when British sales were boosted by the Saudi deal. *Financial Times* (5 March 1986); *The Economist* (4 July 1987).

13 Andrew Ross, 'The international arms market: a structural analysis', paper presented to the annual conference of the International Studies Association, Washington, 11 April 1990, 14.

14 See Ian Anthony, Agnès Courades Allebeck and Herbert Wulf, *Western European Arms Production* (Stockholm: Stockholm International Peace Research Institute, 1990).

15 Admittedly, this would not be true for low-technology items, with certain comparative advantages accruing to third-tier producers in low-level production such as transport and armoured vehicles or bombs and ammunition.

16 Trevor Taylor, 'Defence industries in international relations', *Review of International Studies*, 16 (1990), 59–73.

17 See, for Northrop's activities, Janne Nolan, *Military Industry in Taiwan and South Korea* (London: Macmillan, 1986), 53–6, 70–3. On American involvement in South Korea see United States, Office of Technology Assessment, *Arming Our Allies: Cooperation and Competition in Defense Technology* (Washington: Office of Technology Assessment, May 1990), 111–13. Details of the Brazilian–Italian AMX fighter can be found in *Jane's Defence Weekly* (30 March 1985). On Turkey see *Jane's Defence Weekly* (6 July 1985, 28 October 1989).

#### Appendix  Arms transfer data sources and problems

1 Arms are defined as 'weapons of war, parts thereof, ammunition, support equipment, and other commodities designed for military use', excluding (for the United States), 'construction, training and technical support'. United States Arms Control and Disarmament Agency, *World Military Expenditures and Arms Transfers, 1985* (Washington: Arms Control and Disarmament Agency, 1985), 142.

2 See Edward Laurance and Ronald Sherwin, 'Understanding arms transfers through data analysis', in Uri Ra'anan, Robert Pfaltzgraff and Geoffrey Kemp (eds.), *Arms Transfers to the Third World: The Military Buildup in Less Industrialized Countries* (Boulder: Westview Press, 1978), 97–9; David Louscher and Michael Salomone, 'The imperative for a new look at arms sales', in David Louscher and Michael Salomone (eds.), *Marketing Security Assistance* (Lexington, Mass.: D. C. Heath, 1987), 24–39.

3 Frank Blackaby and Thomas Ohlson, 'Military expenditure and the arms trade: problems of data', *Bulletin of Peace Proposals*, 13:4 (1982), 295.

4 Michael Brzoska, 'Arms transfer data sources', *Journal of Conflict Resolution*, 26:1 (March 1982), 89–90. SIPRI also uses its own weapons valuation system that determines the prices for individual weapons based on a complex set of calculations. For a brief explanation of this and other issues surrounding the SIPRI data see Michael Brzoska and Thomas Ohlson, *Arms Transfers to the Third World, 1971–1985* (Oxford: Oxford University Press, 1987), 352–69.

5 Central Intelligence Agency, *Arms Flows to LDCs: U.S.–Soviet Comparisons, 1974–77* (Washington: Central Intelligence Agency, 1978), 2.

6 Brzoska, 'Arms transfer data sources', 93.

7 United States Arms Control and Disarmament Agency, *World Military Expenditures and Arms Transfers 1987* (Washington: Arms Control and Disarmament Agency, 1987), 6.

8 Laurance and Sherwin in Ra'anan et al. (eds.), *Arms Transfers*, 92.

9 Edward Kolodziej, 'Measuring French arms transfers', *Journal of Conflict Resolution*, 23:2 (June 1979), 210. The annual range was from 1.5 to 5.76.

10 Lawrence Freedman, 'Britain and the arms trade', *International Affairs* (London), 54 (July 1978), 379. See also table 23.

11 Edward Fei, 'Understanding arms transfers and military expenditures: data problems', in Stephanie G. Neuman and Robert E. Harkavy (eds.), *Arms Transfers in the Modern World* (New York: Praeger Publishers, 1980), 44–6. Kolodziej, 'Measuring French arms transfers', 216, found that using French deflators, 'the rate of French arms sales is 20 percent higher each year [1965–75] . . . even on ACDA data!'.

12 See Edward Laurance and Joyce Mullen, 'Assessing and analyzing international arms trade data', in Louscher and Salomone (eds.), *Marketing Security Assistance*, 84–8.

# BIBLIOGRAPHY

## Books

Abrahamian, Ervand. *Iran Between Two Revolutions*. Princeton: Princeton University Press, 1982.

Anthony, Ian, Agnès Courades Allebeck and Herbert Wulf. *Western European Arms Production*. Stockholm: Stockholm International Peace Research Institute, 1990.

Arlinghaus, Bruce. *Military Development in Africa*. London: Westview Press, 1984.

Ashton, T. S. *The Industrial Revolution, 1760–1830*. Oxford: Oxford University Press, 1968.

Atwater, Elton. *American Regulation of Arms Exports*. Washington: Carnegie Endowment for International Peace, 1941.

Ayalon, David. *Gunpowder and Firearms in the Mamluk Kingdom*. London: Vallentine, Mitchell and Company, 1956.

Azar, Edward and Chung-in Moon (eds.), *National Security in the Third World*. Aldershot: Edward Elgar, 1988.

Bajusz, William and David Louscher. *Arms Sales and the U.S. Economy*. Boulder: Westview Press, 1988.

Ball, Nicole. *Security and Economy in the Third World*. Princeton: Princeton University Press, 1988.

Ball, Nicole and Milton Leitenberg (eds.), *The Structure of the Defense Industry*. London: Croom Helm, 1983.

Battistelli, Fabrizio. *Armi: nuovo modello di sviluppo?*. Turin: Giulio Einaudi Editore, 1980.

Beeler, John. *Warfare in Feudal Europe*. Ithaca: Cornell University Press, 1971.

Benoit, Emile. *Defense and Economic Growth in Developing Countries*. Lexington, Mass.: D. C. Heath, 1973.

Best, Geoffrey. *War and Society in Revolutionary Europe, 1770–1870*. Leicester: Leicester University Press, 1982.

Bienen, Henry. *Armies and Parties in Africa*. London: Africana Publishing, 1978.

Bond, Brian. *War and Society in Europe, 1870–1970*. London: Fontana, 1984.

Braudel, Fernand. *On History*. trans. Sarah Matthews. London: Weidenfeld & Nicolson, 1980.

  *The Mediterranean*, vol. I. trans. Siân Reynolds. London: Collins, 1973.

  *The Structures of Everyday Life*, vol. I, *Civilization and Capitalism*, trans. Siân Reynolds. London: Fontana Paperbacks, 1985.

Brockway, Fenner. *The Bloody Traffic*. London: Victor Gollancz, 1933.

Brzoska, Michael and Thomas Ohlson. *Arms Transfers to the Third World, 1971–1985*. Oxford: Oxford University Press, 1987.

(eds.), *Arms Production in the Third World*. London: Taylor and Francis, 1986.

Bull, Hedley and Adam Watson (eds.), *The Expansion of International Society*. Oxford: Oxford University Press, 1984.

Buzan, Barry. *People, States and Fear*. Brighton: Wheatsheaf, 1983.

Cahn, Anne, Joseph Kruzel, Peter Dawkins and Jacques Huntzinger. *Controlling Future Arms Trade*. New York: McGraw-Hill, 1977.

*Cambridge Economic History*, 2nd edn, vol. II. Cambridge: Cambridge University Press, 1987.

Cannizzo, Cindy (ed.), *The Gun Merchants: Politics and Policies of the Major Arms Suppliers*. New York: Pergamon Press, 1980.

Chan, Anthony. *Arming the Chinese: The Western Armaments Trade in Warlord China, 1920–1928*. Vancouver: University of British Columbia Press, 1982.

Cipolla, Carlo. *Before the Industrial Revolution*, 2nd edn. New York: Norton, 1980.

*Guns, Sails and Empires: Technological Innovation and the Early Phases of European Expansion, 1400–1700*. New York: Minerva Press, 1965.

Cochrane, Alfred. *The Early History of Elswick*. Newcastle upon Tyne: Mawson, Swann and Morgan, 1909.

Collier, Basil. *Arms and the Men: The Arms Trade and Governments*. London: Hamish Hamilton, 1980.

Cooling, Benjamin (ed.), *War, Business and World Military-Industrial Complexes*. Port Washington, New York: Kennikat Press, 1981.

Cordesman, Anthony. *The Gulf and the Search for Strategic Stability*. London: Mansell Publishing, 1984.

Creasey, Pauline and Simon May. *The European Armaments Market and Procurement Cooperation*. London: Macmillan Press, 1988.

Crowell, Benedict and Robert Wilson. *The Armies of Industry*, vol. I. New Haven: Yale University Press, 1921.

Dawisha, Karen. *Soviet Foreign Policy towards Egypt*. London: Macmillan Press, 1979.

Deger, Saadet. *Military Expenditure in Third World Countries: The Economic Effects*. London: Routledge & Kegan Paul, 1986.

Dougan, David. *The Great Gun-Maker: The Story of Lord Armstrong*. Newcastle upon Tyne: Frank Graham, n.d.

Dredge, James. *The Work of Messrs. Schneider and Company*. London: Bedford Press, 1900.

Drifte, Reinhard. *Arms Production in Japan*. Boulder: Westview Press, 1986.

Dussauge, Pierre. *L'Industrie française de l'armement*. Paris: Economica, 1985.

Efrat, Moshe and Peter Wiles. *The Economics of Soviet Arms*. London: Suntory-Toyota International Centre for Economics and Related Disciplines, London School of Economics, 1985.

Engelbrecht, Helmuth and F. C. Hanighen. *Merchants of Death: A Study of the International Armament Industry*. New York: Dodd, Mead and Company, 1934.

Enloe, Cynthia. *Ethnic Soldiers: State Security in Divided Societies*. Athens, Georgia: University of Georgia Press, 1980.

Ferrari, Paul, Jeffrey Knopf and Raul Madrid. *U.S. Arms Exports: Policies and Contractors*. Washington, D.C.: Investor Responsibility Research Center, 1987.

Ffoulkes, Charles. *The Gun Founders of England*. London: Arms and Armour Press, 1969.

Fisas, Vicenç. *Las armas de la democracia*. Barcelona: Editorial Critica, 1989.

Foss, Christopher. *Jane's AFV Recognition Handbook*. London: Jane's, 1987.

Franko-Jones, Patrice. *The Brazilian Defense Industry*. Boulder: Westview Press, forthcoming.

Freedman, Lawrence. *Arms Production in the United Kingdom: Problems and Prospects*. London: Royal Institute of International Affairs, 1978.

Gaier, Claude. *Four Centuries of Liège Gunmaking*. London: Sothebey, Parke Bernet, 1977.

  *L'Industrie et le commerce des armes dans les anciennes principautés belges du XIIIe à la fin du XVe siècle*. Paris: Société d'Edition 'Les Belles Lettres', 1973.

Gansler, Jacques. *Affording Defense*. Cambridge, Mass.: MIT Press, 1989.

  *The Defense Industry*. Cambridge, Mass.: MIT Press, 1980.

Garnsey, Peter et al. (eds.), *Trade in the Ancient Economy*. London: Chatto & Windus, 1983.

Gellner, Ernest. *Nations and Nationalism*. Oxford: Basil Blackwell, 1983.

Gerschenkron, Alexander. *Economic Backwardness in Historical Perspective*. Cambridge, Mass.: Harvard University Press, 1962.

Gilks, Anne and Gerard Segal. *China and the Arms Trade*. London: Croom Helm, 1985.

Gilpin, Robert. *War and Change in World Politics*. Cambridge: Cambridge University Press, 1981.

Glassman, Jon. *Arms for the Arabs*. Baltimore: Johns Hopkins University Press, 1975.

Good, David F. *The Economic Rise of the Habsburg Empire, 1750–1914*. Berkeley: University of California Press, 1984.

Goody, Jack. *Technology, Tradition and State in Africa*. London: Hutchinson, 1980.

Habaru, A. *Le Creusot: Terre féodale, Schneider et les marchands de canons*. Paris, 1934.

Hagelin, Björn. *Neutrality and Foreign Military Sales*. Boulder: Westview Press, 1990.

Haglund, David (ed.), *The Defence Industrial Base and the West*. London: Routledge, 1989.

Hale, John R. *War and Society in Renaissance Europe, 1450–1620*. London: Fontana Press, 1985.

Hamilton, F. E. Ian. *Industrialization in Developing and Peripheral Regions*. London: Croom Helm, 1986.

Hammond, Paul, David Louscher, Michael Salomone and Norman Graham. *The Reluctant Supplier: U.S. Decision Making for Arms Sales*. Cambridge, Mass.: Oelgeschlager, Gunn and Hain, 1983.

Harkavy, Robert. *The Arms Trade and International Systems*. Cambridge, Mass.: Ballinger, 1975.

al-Hassan, Ahmad and Donald Hill. *Islamic Technology*. Cambridge: Cambridge University Press, 1986.

Headrick, Daniel. *The Tentacles of Progress: Technology Transfer in the Age of Imperialism*. Oxford: Oxford University Press, 1988.

*The Tools of Empire: Technology and European Imperialism in the Nineteenth Century*. Oxford: Oxford University Press, 1981.

Hébert, Jean-Paul. *Les Ventes d'armes*. Paris: Syros/Alternatives, 1988.

Hellie, Richard. *Enserfment and Military Change in Muscovy*. Chicago: University of Chicago Press, 1971.

Hogg, O. F. G. *English Artillery, 1326–1716*. London: Royal Artillery Institution, 1963.

Holloway, David. *The Soviet Union and the Arms Race*, 2nd edn. London: Yale University Press, 1984.

Hovey, Harold. *United States Military Assistance*. New York: Frederick A. Praeger, 1966.

Howard, Michael. *War in European History*. Oxford: Oxford University Press, 1976.

International Institute for Strategic Studies. *Strategic Survey 1987–88*. London: IISS, 1988.

*The Military Balance*, annual. London: IISS, various years.

Jolly, Richard (ed.), *Disarmament and World Development*. Oxford: Pergamon Press, 1978.

Kahan, Arcadius. *The Plow, the Hammer and the Knout*. Chicago: University of Chicago Press, 1985.

Kaldor, Mary. *The Baroque Arsenal*. London: André Deutsch, 1981.

Katz, James Everett (ed.), *Arms Production in Developing Countries*. Lexington, Mass.: D. C. Heath, 1984.

Kennedy, Paul. *The Rise and Fall of the Great Powers*. New York: Random House, 1987.

Kennedy, Thomas. *The Arms of Kiangnan: Modernization in the Chinese Ordnance Industry, 1860–1895*. Boulder: Westview Press, 1978.

Kenwood, A. G. and A. L. Lougheed. *Technological Diffusion and Industrialization before 1914*. New York: St Martin's Press, 1982.

Keohane, Robert and Joseph Nye. *Power and Interdependence*. Boston: Little, Brown and Company, 1977.

Klare, Michael. *American Arms Supermarket*. Austin: University of Texas Press, 1984.

Klieman, Aaron. *Israel's Global Reach*. London: Pergamon-Brassey's, 1985.

Kobayashi, Ushisaburo. *Military Industries of Japan*. New York: Oxford University Press, 1922.

Kolodziej, Edward. *Economic Determinants of the Transfer of Arms and Military Technology under the French Fifth Republic*. Illinois: University of Illinois, Office of Arms Control, Disarmament and International Security, 1983.

*French Arms Transfers and the Military-Industrial Complex*. Chicago: Chicago Council on Foreign Relations, 1981.

*Making and Marketing Arms: The French Experience and its Implications for the International System*. Princeton: Princeton University Press, 1987.

272

Landgren, Signe. *Embargo Disimplemented: South Africa's Military Industry*. Oxford: Oxford University Press, 1989.

Lane, Frederic. *Navires et constructeurs à Venise pendant la Renaissance*. Paris: SEVPEN, 1965.

Lehmann-Russbüldt, Otto. *Der Blutige Internationale der Rüstingsindustrie*. Hamburg-Bergendorf: Fackelreiter-Verlag, 1929.

Leiss, Amelia C. et al. *Arms Transfers to Less-Developed Countries*. Cambridge, Mass.: Massachusetts Institute of Technology, Center for International Studies, 1970.

Leontief, Wassily and Faye Duchin. *Military Spending: Facts and Figures, Worldwide Implications and Future Outlook*. New York: Oxford University Press, 1983.

Lewinsohn, Richard. *The Profits of War through the Ages*. London: G. Routledge and Sons, 1936.

Looney, Robert. *Third-World Military Expenditure and Arms Production*. London: Macmillan Press, 1988.

Louscher, David and Michael Salomone. *Technology Transfer and U.S. Security Assistance: The Impact of Licensed Production*. Boulder: Westview Press, 1987.

Louscher, David and Michael Salomone (eds.), *Marketing Security Assistance*. Lexington, Mass.: D. C. Heath, 1987.

McKinlay, Robert. *Third World Military Expenditure: Determinants and Implications*. London: Pinter, 1989.

McNeill, William. *The Pursuit of Power*. Oxford: Basil Blackwell, 1983.

Manchester, William. *The Arms of Krupp*. Toronto: Little, Brown and Company, 1964.

Marsden, E. W. *Greek and Roman Artillery*. Oxford: Oxford University Press, 1969.

Menon, Rajan. *Soviet Power and the Third World*. London: Yale University Press, 1986.

Milward, Alan and S. B. Saul. *The Economic Development of Continental Europe, 1780–1870*. London: George Allen & Unwin, 1973.

Moodie, Michael. *Sovereignty, Security and Arms*. Beverly Hills: Sage Publications, 1979.

Nef, John. *War and Human Progress*. New York: Russell and Russell, 1950.

Neuman, Stephanie. *Military Assistance in Recent Wars*. Washington: Center for International and Strategic Studies, 1986.

Neuman, Stephanie G. and Robert E. Harkavy (eds.), *Arms Transfers in the Modern World*. New York: Praeger Publishers, 1980.

Noboru, Umetani. *The Role of Foreign Employees in the Meiji Era in Japan*. Tokyo: Institute of Developing Economies, 1971.

Nolan, Janne. *Military Industry in Taiwan and South Korea*. London: Macmillan Press, 1986.

*Trappings of Power: Ballistic Missiles in the Third World*. Washington: The Brookings Institution, 1991.

O'Connell, Robert. *Of Arms and Men*. Oxford: Oxford University Press, 1989.

Ohlson, Thomas (ed.), *Arms Transfer Limitations and Third World Security*. Oxford: Oxford University Press, 1988.

Owen, Roger. *The Middle East in the World Economy 1800–1914*. New York: Methuen, 1981.

Parker, Geoffrey. *The Military Revolution: Military Innovation and the Rise of the West, 1500–1800*. Cambridge: Cambridge University Press, 1988.

Partington, James R. *A History of Greek Fire and Gunpowder*. Cambridge: W. Heffer & Sons, 1960.

Pearton, Maurice. *Diplomacy, War and Technology since 1830*. Lawrence: University Press of Kansas, 1984.

*The Knowledgeable State*. London: Burnett Books, 1982.

Pierre, Andrew. *The Global Politics of Arms Sales*. Princeton: Princeton University Press, 1982.

(ed.), *Arms Transfers and American Foreign Policy*. New York: New York University Press, 1979.

Pollock, David. *The Politics of Pressure: American Arms and Israeli Policy Since the Six-Day War*. Westport, Conn.: Greenwood Press, 1982.

Qaisar, Ahsan Jan. *The Indian Response to European Culture and Technology (A.D. 1498–1707)*. Delhi: Oxford University Press, 1982.

Ra'anan, Uri. *The USSR Arms the Third World: Case Studies in Soviet Foreign Policy*. Cambridge, Mass.: MIT Press, 1969.

Ra'anan, Uri, Robert Pfaltzgraff and Geoffrey Kemp (eds.), *Arms Transfers to the Third World: The Military Buildup in Less Industrialized Countries*. Boulder: Westview Press, 1978.

Ralston, David. *Importing the European Army: The Introduction of European Military Techniques and Institutions into the Extra-European World, 1600–1914*. Chicago: University of Chicago Press, 1990.

Rapp, Richard. *Industry and Economic Decline in Seventeenth-Century Venice*. Cambridge, Mass.: Harvard University Press, 1976.

Rasler, Karen and William Thompson. *War and State Making*. Boston: Unwin Hyman, 1989.

Rawlinson, John. *China's Struggle for Naval Development, 1839–1895*. Cambridge, Mass.: Harvard University Press, 1967.

Regehr, Ernie. *Arms Canada*. Toronto: Lorimer, 1987.

Rosenberg, Nathan. *Inside the Black Box: Technology and Economics*. Cambridge: Cambridge University Press, 1982.

Rothenberg, Gunther. *The Art of Warfare in the Age of Napoleon*. London: B. T. Batsford, 1977.

Roy, Joseph. *Histoire de la famille Schneider et du Creusot*. Paris: Marcel Rivière et Cie, 1962.

Rudolph, Richard. *Banking and Industrialization in Austria–Hungary*. Cambridge: Cambridge University Press, 1976.

Safran, Nadav. *Israel: The Embattled Ally*. Cambridge, Mass.: Harvard University Press, 1981.

Sampson, Anthony. *The Arms Bazaar*. London: Hodder & Stoughton, 1977.

Savory, Roger. *Iran under the Safavids*. Cambridge: Cambridge University Press, 1980.

Schulz, Anne. *Buying Security: Iran under the Monarchy*. Boulder: Westview Press, 1989.

Schumpeter, Joseph. *Business Cycles*, vol. I. New York: McGraw-Hill, 1939.

Scott, John D. *Vickers: A History*. London: Weidenfeld & Nicolson, 1962.

Seldes, George. *Iron, Blood and Profits: An Exposure of the World-Wide Munitions Racket*. New York: Harper and Brothers Publishers, 1934.

Shaw, Martin (ed.), *War, State and Society*. London: Macmillan Press, 1984.

Shaw, Stanford and Ezel Shaw. *History of the Ottoman Empire and Modern Turkey*, vol. II. Cambridge: Cambridge University Press, 1977.

Sick, Gary. *All Fall Down*. New York: Random House, 1985.

Sloutzki, Nokhim. *The World Armaments Race, 1919–1939*. Geneva: Geneva Research Centre, 1941.

Smaldone, Joseph. *Warfare in the Sokoto Caliphate*. Cambridge: Cambridge University Press, 1977.

Snodgrass, Anthony. *Early Greek Armour and Weapons*. Edinburgh: Edinburgh University Press, 1964.

Söderberg, Marie. *Japan's Military Export Policy*. Stockholm: University of Stockholm, 1986.

Sorley, Lewis. *Arms Transfers under Nixon: A Policy Analysis*. Lexington, Ky.: University Press of Kentucky, 1983.

Spector, Leonard. *The Undeclared Bomb*. Cambridge, Mass.: Ballinger, 1988.

Spector, Stanley. *Li Hung-chang and the Huai Army*. Seattle: University of Washington Press, 1964.

Stanley, John and Maurice Pearton. *The International Trade in Arms*. London: Chatto & Windus, 1972.

Stockholm International Peace Research Institute. *SIPRI Yearbook of World Armaments and Disarmament*, annual. London: Oxford University Press, various years.

*The Arms Trade Registers*. London: MIT Press, 1975.

*The Arms Trade with the Third World*. Stockholm: Almqvist and Wiksell, 1971.

Taylor, Trevor and Keith Hayward. *The UK Defence Industrial Base: Development and Future Policy Options*. London: Brassey's, 1989.

Temple, Robert. *The Genius of China*. New York: Simon and Schuster, 1986.

Thomas, Raju. *Indian Security Policy*. Princeton: Princeton University Press, 1986.

Thompson, I. A. A. *War and Government in Habsburg Spain, 1560–1620*. London: Athlone Press, 1976.

Thompson, William. *On Global War: Historical-Structural Approaches to World Politics*. Columbia: University of South Carolina Press, 1988.

Thucydides. *The Peloponnesian War*. trans. Rex Warner. Harmondsworth: Penguin, 1972.

Tout, T. F. *Firearms in England in the Fourteenth Century*. London: Arms and Armour Press, 1968. Reprinted from *English Historical Review*, 26 (1911).

Trebilcock, Clive. *The Industrialization of the Continental Powers, 1780–1914*. London: Longman Group, 1981.

*The Vickers Brothers: Armaments and Enterprise 1854–1914*. London: Europa Publications, 1977.

Tuomi, Helena and Raimo Väyrynen (eds.), *Militarization and Arms Production*. London: Croom Helm, 1983.

Union of Democratic Control. *Patriotism Ltd.: An Exposure of the War Machine*. London: Union of Democratic Control, 1933.

Vagts, Alfred. *A History of Militarism*, revised edn. New York: Free Press, 1957.

Valkenier, Elizabeth Kridl. *The Soviet Union and the Third World: An Economic Bind*. New York: Praeger Publishers, 1983.

Van Creveld, Martin. *Technology and War*. New York: The Free Press, 1989.

Wallerstein, Immanuel. *The Modern World System*, vols I and II. New York: Academic Press, 1974, 1980.

Webster, R. A. *Industrial Imperialism in Italy 1906–1914*. Berkeley: University of California Press, 1975.

Wharton Associates. *Soviet Arms Trade with the Non-Communist Third World in the 1970s and 1980s*. Washington: Wharton Econometric Forecasting Associates, 1984.

White, Lynn. *Medieval Technology and Social Change*. Oxford: Oxford University Press, 1962.

Whynes, David. *The Economics of Third World Military Expenditure*. London: Macmillan Press, 1979.

Wiltz, John. *In Search of Peace: The Senate Munitions Inquiry, 1934–36*. Louisiana: Louisiana State University Press, 1963.

Winter, J. M. *War and Economic Development*. Cambridge: Cambridge University Press, 1975.

Yakemtchouk, Romain. *Les Transferts internationaux d'armes de guerre*. Paris: Pedone, 1980.

### Articles and theses

Aben, J. 'The French Socialists confronted with the problem of arms exports', *Defense Analysis*, 2:4 (December 1986), 307–18.

Albrecht, Ulrich. 'New strategies of mid-sized weapons exporters: the Federal Republic of Germany and Italy', *Journal of International Affairs*, 40 (Summer 1986), 129–42.

'Soviet arms exports', in Stockholm International Peace Research Institute. *World Armaments and Disarmaments: SIPRI Yearbook 1983*. Oxford: Oxford University Press, 1983, 361–70.

'The aborted UN study on the military use of research and development: an editorial essay', *Bulletin of Peace Proposals*, 19:3–4 (1988), 245–59.

Alexander, Arthur et al. *Modelling the Production and International Trade of Arms: An Economic Framework for Analyzing Policy Alternatives*. Rand report N–1555–FF/RC. Santa Monica: Rand Corporation, 1981.

Allebeck, Agnès Courades. 'Arms trade regulations', in Stockholm International Peace Research Institute. *SIPRI Yearbook of World Armaments and Disarmament, 1989*. Oxford: Oxford University Press, 1989, 319–38.

Arlinghaus, Bruce. 'Linkage and leverage in African arms transfers', in Bruce Arlinghaus (ed.), *Arms for Africa: Military Assistance and Foreign Policy in the Developing World*. Lexington, Mass.: D. C. Heath, 1983, 3–17.

'Arms and men', *Fortune Magazine*, 9 (March 1934), 52–7, 113–26.

Atmore, Anthony, J. M. Chirenje and S. I. Mudenge. 'Firearms in South Central Africa', *Journal of African History*, 12:4 (1971), 545–56.

Atwater, Elton. 'British control over the export of war materials', *American Journal of International Law*, 33 (April 1939), 292–317.

Awty, Brian. 'The continental origins of the Wealden ironworkers, 1451–1544', *Economic History Review*, 34 (1981), 525–39.

Ayoob, Mohammed. 'Regional security and the Third World', in Mohammed Ayoob (ed.), *Regional Security in the Third World: Case Studies from Southeast Asia and the Middle East*. Boulder: Westview Press, 1986, 3–27.

'Security in the Third World: the worm about turn?', *International Affairs* (London), 60:1 (Winter 1983–4), 41–51.

Ayres, Ron. 'Arms production as a form of import-substituting industrialization: the Turkish case', *World Development*, 11 (1983), 813–23.

Baek, Kwang-Il and Chung-in Moon. 'Technological dependence, supplier control and strategies for recipient autonomy: the case of South Korea', in Kwang-Il Baek, Ronald McLaurin and Chung-in Moon (eds.), *The Dilemma of Third World Defense Industries*. Inchon: Center for International Studies, Inha University, 1989, 153–84.

Ball, Nicole. 'Defence and development: a critique of the Benoit study', in Helena Tuomi and Raimo Väyryen (eds.), *Militarization and Arms Production*. London: Croom Helm, 1983, 39–56.

Barnett, Michael and Alexander Wendt. 'Nowhere to run, nowhere to hide: the systemic sources of dependent militarization', unpublished paper, March 1990.

Beachey, R. W. 'The arms trade in East Africa in the late nineteenth century', *Journal of African History*, 3:3 (1962), 451–67.

Bean, Richard. 'War and the birth of the nation state', *Journal of Economic History*, 33 (1973), 203–21.

Beker, Avi. 'The arms–oil connection: fueling the arms race', *Armed Forces and Society*, 8:3 (Spring 1982), 419–42.

Berg, Gerald. 'The sacred musket: tactics, technology and power in eighteenth-century Madagascar', *Comparative Studies in Society and History*, 27:2 (April 1985), 261–76.

Bittleston, Martyn. 'Co-operation or competition? Defence procurement options for the 1990s', *Adelphi Paper*, 250. London: International Institute for Strategic Studies, 1990.

Blackaby, Frank and Thomas Ohlson. 'Military expenditure and the arms trade: problems of data', *Bulletin of Peace Proposals*, 13:4 (1982), 291–308.

Borus, Joseph. 'The military industry in the War of Independence', in Béla Király (ed.), *East Central European Society and War in the Era of Revolutions, 1775–1856*. New York: Brooklyn College Press, 1984, 519–37.

Boutin, Kenneth. 'Import substitution or exports?: the determinants of arms production in developing countries'. Unpublished Master's thesis. York University, Toronto, 1990.

Brenner, Michael. 'Strategic interdependence and the politics of inertia', *World Politics*, 23:4 (July 1971), 635–64.

Brown, Delmer. 'The impact of firearms on Japanese warfare, 1543–98', *Far Eastern Quarterly*, 7 (1948), 236–53.

Brzoska, Michael. 'Arms transfer data sources', *Journal of Conflict Resolution*, 26:1 (March 1982), 77–108.

'Current trends in arms transfers', in Saadet Deger and Robert West (eds.),

277

*Defense, Security and Development*. New York: St Martin's Press, 1987, 161–79.

'The arms trade – can it be controlled?', *Journal of Peace Research*, 24:4 (December 1987), 327–31.

'The erosion of restraint in West German arms transfer policy', *Journal of Peace Research*, 26:2 (1989), 165–77.

'The impact of arms production in the Third World', *Armed Forces and Society*, 15:4 (Summer 1989), 507–30.

'The structure of arms production in Western Europe beyond 1992', occasional paper 26. Hamburg: Centre for the Study of Wars, Armaments and Development, 1989.

'Third World arms control: problems of verification', *Bulletin of Peace Proposals*, 14:2 (1983), 165–73.

Brzoska, Michael and Thomas Ohlson. 'The future of arms transfers: the changing pattern', *Bulletin of Peace Proposals*, 16 (1985), 129–37.

Cahn, Anne. 'Arms sales economics: the sellers' perspectives', *Stanford Journal of International Studies*, 14 (Spring 1979), 125–138.

Caldwell, David. 'The Royal Scottish Gun Foundry in the sixteenth century', in Anne O'Connor and D. V. Clarke (eds.), *From the Stone Age to the 'Forty-Five*. Edinburgh: John Donald Publishers, 1983, 427–49.

Chan, Steve. 'The consequences of expensive oil on arms transfers', *Journal of Peace Research*, 17:2 (1980), 235–46.

'The impact of defense spending on economic performance: a survey of evidence and problems', *Orbis*, 29:2 (Summer 1985), 403–34.

Checinski, Michael. 'An estimate of current Soviet military-industrial output and of the development of the Soviet arms industry', *Osteuropa Wirtschaft*, 29:2 (June 1984), 138–52.

'The costs of armament production and the profitability of armament exports in Comecon countries', *Osteuropa Wirtschaft*, 20:2 (1975), 117–42.

'The Warsaw Pact/Comecon and the Polish and Czechoslovak military-industrial complex', *Osteuropa Wirtschaft*, 33:1 (March 1988), 37–56.

'Warsaw Pact/CEMA military-economic trends', *Problems of Communism*, 36:2 (1987), 15–28.

Chipman, John. 'French military policy and African security', *Adelphi Paper*, 201. London: International Institute for Strategic Studies, 1985.

Chung, Tae Dong. 'Soldiers in politics: a comparative overview of the military as a social force in developing countries', *Asian Perspective*, 6:1 (1982), 66–87.

Cipolla, Carlo. 'The diffusion of innovations in early modern Europe', *Comparative Studies in Society and History*, 14 (1972), 46–52.

Clark, Ian. 'Soviet arms supplies and Indian Ocean diplomacy', in Larry Bowman and Ian Clark (eds.), *The Indian Ocean in Global Politics*. Boulder: Westview Press, 1981, 149–71.

Contamine, Philippe. 'Les Industries de guerre dans la France de la Renaissance: l'exemple de l'artillerie', *Revue historique*, 271 (April–June 1984), 249–80.

Cooper, Julian. 'Soviet arms exports and the conversion of the defence industry', paper presented to the United Nations, Department for Disarmament Affairs, Conference on Transparency in International Arms Transfers, Florence, 25–8 April 1990.

Cordesman, Anthony. 'U.S. and Soviet competition in arms exports and military assistance', *Armed Forces Journal International*, 118 (August 1981), 64–8.

Council on Economic Priorities. 'Weapons for the world: 1982 update', *Newsletter* (December/January 1981–2), 3–6.

Covington, Terrell et al. *A Review of European Arms Collaboration and Prospects for its Expansion under the Independent European Program Group*. Rand report N–2638–ACQ. Santa Monica: Rand Corporation, 1987.

Crouzet, François. 'Recherches sur la production d'armements en France (1815–1913)', *Revue historique*, 98:251 (January–March 1974), 45–84.

'Remarques sur l'industrie des armements en France (du milieu du XIXe siècle à 1914)', *Revue historique*, 98:251 (April–June 1974), 409–22.

Cutler, Robert, Lauré Després and Aaron Karp. 'The political economy of East–South military transfers', *International Studies Quarterly*, 31 (September 1987), 273–300.

Dagino, Renato Peixoto. 'A indústria de armamentos brasileira: uma tentativa de avaliação'. Unpublished doctoral thesis. University de Campinas, 1989.

De Andreis, Marco. 'Italian arms exports to Iran and Iraq', *Note & richerche*, 18. Rome: Centro studi di politica internazionale, 1988.

Deane, Phyllis. 'War and industrialization', in J. M. Winter (ed.), *War and Economic Development*. Cambridge: Cambridge University Press, 1975, 91–102.

Defense Marketing Services. *International Defense Intelligence*, 5 (December 1988).

Deger, Saadet. 'Soviet arms sales to developing countries: the economic forces', in Robert Cassen (ed.), *Soviet Interests in the Third World*. London: Sage Publications, 1985, 159–76.

Delbrück, Jost. 'International traffic in arms – legal and political aspects of a long neglected problem of arms control and disarmament', *German Yearbook of International Law*, 24 (1981), 114–43.

Dussauge, Pierre. 'La Baisse des exportations françaises d'armement et ses répercussions industrielles', *Défense nationale* (January 1988), 77–94.

Efrat, Moshe. 'Disentangling the economics of Soviet arms trade: are Western assessments really reliable?', *Osteuropa Wirtschaft*, 32:1 (March 1987), 38–59.

'The economics of Soviet arms transfers to the Third World – a case study: Egypt', *Soviet Studies*, 35 (October 1983), 437–56.

Esper, Thomas. 'Military self-sufficiency and weapons technology in Muscovite Russia', *Slavic Review*, 28 (1969), 185–208.

Evans, Carole. 'Reappraising Third-World arms production', *Survival*, 28 (March–April 1986), 98–118.

Farley, Philip. 'The control of United States arms sales', in Alan Platt and Lawrence Weiler (eds.), *Congress and Arms Control*. Boulder: Westview Press, 1978, 111–33.

Feazal, Michael. 'New liberal arms export rules force review of German policy', *Aviation Week and Space Technology* (2 December 1985), 27–8.

Fisher, Humphrey and Virginia Rowland. 'Firearms in the Central Sudan', *Journal of African History*, 12:2 (1971), 215–39.

Fontanel, Jacques and José Drumont-Saraiva. 'Les Industries d'armements comme vecteur du développement économique des pays du tiers-monde', *Etudes polémologiques*, 40 (1986), 27–42.

Franko, Lawrence. 'Restraining arms exports to the Third World: will Europe agree?', *Survival*, 21:1 (1979), 14–25.

Franko-Jones, Patrice. 'The Brazilian defense industry in crisis', paper presented to the annual conference of the International Studies Association, Washington, 13 April 1990.

'"Public private partnership": lessons from the Brazilian armaments industry', *Journal of Interamerican Studies and World Affairs*, 29:4 (Winter 1987–8), 41–68.

Freedman, Lawrence. 'Britain and the arms trade', *International Affairs* (London), 54 (July 1978), 377–92.

Freeman, Christopher. 'Technological innovation, diffusion, and long cycles of economic development', in Tibor Vasko (ed.), *The Long Wave Debate*. London: Springer-Verlag, 1987, 295–309.

Gaier, Claude. 'Le Commerce des armes en Europe au XVe siècle', in *Armi e Cultura Nel Bresciano 1420–1870*. Brescia: Ateneo di Brescia, 1981, 155–68.

Gambles, Ian. 'Prospects for West European security co-operation', *Adelphi Paper*, 244. London: International Institute for Strategic Studies, 1989.

Gibert, Stephen. 'Implications of the Nixon Doctrine for military aid policy', *Orbis*, 16:3 (Fall 1972), 661–81.

Goodrich, L. C. 'Early cannon in China', *Isis*, 55:2 (August 1964), 193–5.

Group de Recherches et d'Information sur la Paix. *Dossier*, 127 (November 1988).

Gu Guan-fu. 'Soviet arms sales and military aid policy to the Third World', *Osteuropa Wirtschaft*, 29:1 (March 1984), 49–60.

Guy, J. J. 'A note on firearms in the Zulu kingdom with special reference to the Anglo-Zulu War, 1879', *Journal of African History*, 12:4 (1971), 557–70.

Hacker, Barton. 'Greek catapults and catapult technology', *Technology and Culture*, 9:1 (January 1968), 34–50.

'The weapons of the West: military technology and modernization in 19th-century China and Japan', *Technology and Culture*, 8:1 (January 1977), 43–55.

Hagelin, Björn. 'At arms' length or arm in arm? Sweden and West European military production', paper presented at the International Studies Association annual meeting, London, March 1989.

Hall, A. Rupert. 'Early modern technology, to 1600', in Melvin Kranzberg and Carroll Pursell, Jr. (eds.), *Technology in Western Civilization*, vol. I. Oxford: Oxford University Press, 1967, 79–103.

'Military technology', in Charles Singer et al. (eds.), *A History of Technology*, vol. III. London: Oxford University Press, 1957, 347–76.

Harrison, R. J. 'British armaments and European industrialization, 1890–1914: the Spanish case re-examined', *Economic History Review*, 2nd series, 27:4 (1974), 620–31.

Heckenast, Gusztáv. 'Equipment and supply of Ferenc II Rákóczi's army', in János Bak and Béla Király (eds.), *From Hunyadi to Rákóczi: War and Society in Late Medieval and Early Modern Hungary*. New York: Brooklyn College Press, 1982, 421–31.

Hellie, Richard. 'The Petrine army: continuity, change, and impact', *Canadian–American Slavic Studies*, 8:2 (Summer 1974), 237–53.

Henderson, W. O. 'The rise of the metal and armament industries in Berlin and Brandenburg 1712–1795', *Business History*, 3:1 (December 1960), 63–74.

Hertz, A. Z. 'Armament and supply inventory of Ottoman Ada Kale, 1753', *Archivum Ottomanicum*, 4 (1972), 95–115.

Hess, A. C. 'Firearms and the decline of Ibn Khaldun's military elite', *Archivum Ottomanicum*, 4 (1972), 173–99.

Hilbert, Lother. 'Der zunehmende Waffenexport seit den 1890er Jahrens', in Fritz Klein and Karl Otmar von Aretin (eds.), *Europa um 1900*. Berlin: Akademie Verlag, 1989, 59–72.

'Waffenexport. Aspekte des internationalen Waffenhandels nach dem Ersten Weltkrieg', in Jürgen Hedeking et al. (eds.), *Wege in die Zeitgeschichte*. Berlin: De Gruyter, 1989, 415–32.

Holloway, David. 'Western technology and Soviet military power', in Mark Schaffer (ed.), *Technology Transfer and East–West Relations*. New York: St Martin's Press, 1985, 170–87.

Holzman, Franklyn. 'Politics and guesswork: CIA and DIA estimates of Soviet military spending', *International Security*, 14:2 (Fall 1989), 101–31.

Hug, Peter. 'Rüstungsproduktion der Schweiz', n.d.

Inalcik, Halil. 'The socio-political effects of the diffusion of fire-arms in the Middle East', in Vernon Parry and M. E. Rapp (eds.), *War, Technology and Society in the Middle East*. London: Oxford University Press, 1975, 195–217.

Inikori, J. E. 'The import of firearms into West Africa 1750–1807', *Journal of African History*, 18:2 (1977), 339–68.

Isnard, Jacques. 'Marketing weapons systems: an analysis of France's export apparatus', *Defence & Armament*, 20 (June 1983), 32–43.

Jabber, Paul. 'Oil, arms and regional diplomacy', in Malcolm Kerr and El-Sayed Yassin, *Rich and Poor States in the Middle East*. Boulder: Westview Press, 1982, 415–47.

John, A. H. 'War and the English economy, 1700–1763', *Economic History Review*, 2nd series, 7 (1954–5), 319–45.

Jordan, Amos. 'Military assistance and national policy', *Orbis*, 2:2 (1958), 236–53.

Karp, Aaron. 'Ballistic missile proliferation', in Stockholm International Peace Research Institute. *SIPRI Yearbook of World Armaments and Disarmament, 1990*. Oxford: Oxford University Press, 1990, 369–91.

'Controlling missile proliferation in the new world order', paper presented to a conference on supply-side control of weapons proliferation, Ottawa, 21 June 1991.

'The trade in conventional weapons', in Stockholm International Peace Research Institute, *SIPRI Yearbook of World Armaments and Disarmament, 1988*. (Oxford: Oxford University Press, 1988, 175–201.

Karasapan, Ömer. 'Turkey's armaments industries', Middle East Report, 17:1 (January–February 1987), 27–31.

Kea, R. A. 'Firearms and warfare on the Gold and Slave Coasts from the sixteenth to the nineteenth centuries', Journal of African History, 12:2 (1971), 185–213.

Kemp, Geoffrey. 'The international arms trade: supplier, recipient and arms control perspectives', Political Quarterly, 42 (1971), 376–89.

Khan, Iqtidar Alam. 'Early use of cannon and musket in India, A.D. 1442–1526', Journal of the Economic and Social History of the Orient, 24:2 (May 1981), 146–64.

Klare, Michael. 'Soviet arms transfers to the Third World', Bulletin of Atomic Scientists, 40:5 (May 1984), 26–31.

'The arms trade: changing patterns in the 1980s', Third World Quarterly, 9:4 (October 1987), 1257–81.

'The state of the trade: global arms transfer patterns in the 1980s', Journal of International Affairs, 40:1 (Summer 1986), 1–21.

Kolodziej, Edward. 'Determinants of French arms sales: security implications', in Patrick McGowan and Charles Kegley (eds.), Threats, Weapons and Foreign Policy. Beverly Hills: Sage Publications, 1980, 137–76.

'France and the arms trade', International Affairs (London), 56 (January 1980), 54–72.

'Measuring French arms transfers', Journal of Conflict Resolution, 23:2 (June 1979), 195–227.

Kramer, Mark. 'Soviet arms transfers to the Third World', Problems of Communism, 36:5 (September/October 1987), 52–68.

Kranzberg, Melvin. 'The technical elements in international technology transfer: historical perspectives', in John McIntyre and Daniel Papp (eds.), The Political Economy of International Technology Transfer. New York: Quorum Books, 1986, 31–45.

Krause, Keith. 'Arms transfers, conflict management and the Arab–Israeli conflict', in Gabriel Ben-Dor and David Dewitt (eds.), Conflict Management in the Middle East. Lexington, Mass.: D. C. Heath and Company, 1987, 209–38.

'Constructing regional security regimes and the control of arms transfers', International Journal, 45:2 (Spring 1990), 386–423.

'Military statecraft: power and influence in Soviet and American arms transfer relationships', International Studies Quarterly, 35:3 (September 1991), 313–36.

'Arms imports, arms production and the quest for security in the Third World', in Brian Job (ed.), The Insecurity Dilemma: National Security of Third World States (Boulder: Lynne Reinner, 1992), 121–42.

Kurth, James. 'The political consequences of the product cycle: industrial history and political outcomes', International Organization, 33:1 (Winter 1979), 1–35.

Lamb, John. 'Canada, arms transfers and arms control', unpublished paper, 1987.

Landgren-Backstrom, Signe. 'The transfer of military technology to Third World countries', in Helena Tuomi and Raimo Väyrynen (eds.), Militarization and Arms Production. London: Croom Helm, 1983, 193–204.

Levite, Ariel and Athanassios Platias. 'Evaluating small states' dependence on arms imports: an alternative perspective', occasional paper 16. Cornell: Cornell University Peace Studies Program, 1983.

Lock, Peter. 'Towards a European arms industry?', occasional paper 27. Hamburg: Centre for the Study of Wars, Armaments and Development, 1989.

Lock, Peter and Herbert Wulf. 'The economic consequences of the transfer of military-oriented technology', in Mary Kaldor and Asbjørn Eide (eds.), *The World Military Order: The Impact of Military Technology on the Third World*. London: Macmillan Press, 1979, 210–31.

Looney, Robert and P. C. Frederiksen. 'Profile of current Latin American arms producers', *International Organization*, 40 (Spring 1986), 746–52.

Loose-Weintraub, Evamaria. 'Spain's new defence policy: arms production and exports', in Stockholm International Peace Research Institute. *World Armaments and Disarmament: SIPRI Yearbook 1984*. Oxford: Oxford University Press, 1984, 137–49.

Louscher, David. 'The rise of military sales as a U.S. foreign policy instrument', *Orbis*, 20 (Winter 1977), 933–64.

Luckham, Robin. 'Militarization in Africa', in Stockholm International Peace Research Institute. *World Armaments and Disarmament: SIPRI Yearbook 1985*. Oxford: Oxford University Press, 1985, 295–328.

'Soviet arms and African militarization', in Robert Cassen (ed.), *Soviet Interests in the Third World*. London: Sage Publications, 1985, 89–113.

Mahnken, Thomas and Timothy Hoyt. 'The spread of missile technology to the Third World', *Comparative Strategy*, 9:3 (1990), 245–64.

Mallmann, Wolfgang. 'Arms transfers to the Third World: trends and changing patterns in the 1970s', *Bulletin of Peace Proposals*, 10 (1979), 301–7.

Marks, Shula and Anthony Atmore. 'Firearms in Southern Africa: a survey', *Journal of African History*, 12:4 (1971), 517–30.

Martin, Tom and Rachel Schmidt. *A Case Study of the F-20 Tigershark*. Rand report P–7495–RGS. Santa Monica: Rand Corporation, 1987.

Matousek, Jirí. 'Complex attitude [*sic*] to conventional arms trade control – reduction of forces/arms, conversion and deep reduction of weapons sales: the example of Czechoslovakia', paper presented to the United Nations Department for Disarmament Affairs, conference on Transparency in International Arms Transfers, Florence, 25 8 April 1990.

Matthews, R. G. 'The development of India's defence industrial base', *Journal of Strategic Studies*, 12:4 (December 1989), 405–30.

Menon, Rajan. 'The Soviet Union, the arms trade and the Third World', *Soviet Studies*, 24 (July 1982), 377–96.

Miers, Sue. 'Notes on the arms trade and government policy in Southern Africa between 1870 and 1890', *Journal of African History*, 12:4 (1971), 571–7.

Milhollin, Gary. 'India's missiles – with a little help from our friends', *Bulletin of the Atomic Scientists*, 45:9 (November 1989), 31–5.

Miller, Steven. 'Arms for the third world: indigenous weapons production', occasional paper 3. Geneva: Geneva Programme for Strategic and International Security Studies, 1980.

Mintz, Alex, '"Guns vs. butter": a disaggregated analysis', paper presented at the International Studies Association annual meeting, London, 28 March–1 April 1989.

Modelski, George. 'The long cycle of global politics and the nation-state', *Comparative Studies in Society and History*, 20:2 (April 1978), 214–35.

Moravcsik, Andrew. 'The European armaments industry at the crossroads', *Survival*, 32:1 (January/February 1990), 65–85.

Nadvi, Syed Abu Zafar. 'The use of cannon in Muslim India', *Islamic Culture*, 12:4 (October 1938), 405–18.

Navias, Martin. 'Ballistic missile proliferation in the Third World', *Adelphi Paper*, 252. London: International Institute for Strategic Studies, 1990.

Needham, Joseph. 'The guns of Khaifêng-fu', *Times Literary Supplement* (11 January 1980), 39–42.

Neuman, Stephanie. 'Arms and superpower influence: lessons from recent wars', *Orbis*, 30:4 (Winter 1987), 711–29.

'Arms transfers, indigenous defence production and dependency: the case of Iran', in Hossein Amirsadeghi, *The Security of the Persian Gulf*. London: Croom Helm, 1981, 131–50.

'Coproduction, barter and countertrade: offsets in the international arms market', *Orbis*, 29:1 (Spring 1985), 183–213.

'International stratification and Third World military industries', *International Organization*, 38:1 (Winter 1984), 167–97.

'The arms market: who's on top?', *Orbis*, 33:4 (Fall 1989), 509–29.

Nolan, Janne. 'The conventional arms trade: prospects for control', working paper 42. Canberra: National University of Australia, 1988.

Nowak, Tadeusz. 'Wpłw Rozwoju Nauki i Techniki na Wojskowość Polską XVI-XVII w', *Kwartalnik Historii Nauki i Techniki*, 26 (1981), 39–56.

Ofer, Gur. 'Economic aspects of Soviet involvement in the Middle East', in Ya'acov Ro'i (ed.), *The Limits to Power*. London: Croom Helm, 1979, 67–93.

Ohlson, Thomas. 'Third World arms exporters: a new facet of the global arms race', *Bulletin of Peace Proposals*, 13:3 (1982), 211–20.

Pajak, Roger. 'Soviet arms and Egypt', *Survival*, 17:4 (July/August 1975), 165–73.

'West European and Soviet arms transfer policies in the Middle East', in Milton Leitenberg and Gabriel Sheffer (eds.), *Great Power Intervention in the Middle East*. New York: Pergamon Press, 1979, 134–64.

Papp, Daniel. 'Soviet military assistance to Eastern Europe', in John Copper and Daniel Papp (eds.), *Communist Nations' Military Assistance*. Boulder: Westview Press, 1983, 13–38.

Paul, Jim. 'The Egyptian arms industry', *Merip Reports*, 13:2 (February 1983), 26–8.

Pearson, Frederic. '"Necessary evil": Perspectives on West German arms transfer policies', *Armed Forces and Society*, 12:4 (Summer 1986), 525–52.

'Of leopards and cheetahs: West Germany's role as a mid-sized arms supplier', *Orbis*, 29 (Spring 1985), 165–81.

'The question of control in British defence sales policy', *International Affairs* (London), 59:2 (Spring 1983), 211–38.

Pearson, Frederic and Edward Kolodziej. 'The political economy of making and marketing arms: a test for the systemic imperatives of order and welfare', occasional paper 8904. St Louis: Center for International Studies, University of Missouri–St Louis, April 1989.

Peleg, Ilan. 'Military production in Third World countries: a political study,' in Patrick McGowan and Charles Kegley (eds.), *Threats, Weapons and Foreign Policy*. Beverly Hills: Sage Publications, 1980, 209–30.

Petrović, Djurdjica. 'Fire-arms in the Balkans on the eve of and after the Ottoman conquests of the fourteenth and fifteenth centuries', in Vernon Parry and M. E. Rapp (eds.), *War, Technology and Society in the Middle East*. London: Oxford University Press, 1975, 164–94.

Pierre, Andrew. 'Arms sales: the new diplomacy', *Foreign Affairs*, 60 (Winter 1981–2), 266–304.

Potter, William and Adam Stulberg. 'The Soviet Union and ballistic missile proliferation', unpublished paper, 1990.

Pratt, Erik. 'Trading guns for butter: net-export earnings from the arms trade', paper presented at the International Studies Association annual meeting, London, 28 March 1989.

Quiggan, Tom. 'Production, dependence and appropriate technologies: arms production in the lesser developed countries'. Unpublished Master's thesis. York University, Toronto, 1990.

Richards, W. A. 'The import of firearms into West Africa in the eighteenth century', *Journal of African History*, 21:1 (1980), 43–59.

Rilling, Rainer. 'Military R&D in the Federal Republic of Germany', *Bulletin of Peace Proposals*, 19 (1988), 317–42.

Roberts, Michael. 'The military revolution, 1560–1660', reprinted in *Essays in Swedish History*. London: Weidenfeld & Nicolson, 1967, 195–225.

Rollins, Patrick. 'Soviet arms transfers to the Third World, 1980–84', in David Jones (ed.), *Soviet Armed Forces Review Annual, 1985–86*. Gulf Breeze: Academic International Press, 1987, 202–12.

Ross, Andrew. 'Arms acquisition and national security: the irony of military strength', in Edward Azar and Chung-in Moon (eds.), *National Security in the Third World*. Aldershot: Edward Elgar, 1988, 152–87.

*Arms Production in Developing Countries: The Continuing Proliferation of Conventional Weapons*. Rand Report N–1615–AF. Santa Monica: Rand Corporation, 1981.

'Dimensions of militarization in the Third World', *Armed Forces and Society*, 13:4 (Summer 1987), 561–78.

'Military import substitution in the developing world: the market, industrialization, the state and dependency', paper presented at the annual conference of the International Studies Association, London, March 1989.

'Security and self-reliance: military dependence and conventional arms production in developing countries'. Unpublished doctoral thesis, Cornell University, 1984.

'The international arms market: a structural analysis', unpublished paper presented at the annual meeting of the International Studies Association, Washington, 12 April 1990.

Rossi, Sergio. 'The Italian defence industry with respect to international competition', *Defence Today*, 77–8 (1984), 406–8.

Rothstein, Robert. 'National security, domestic resource constraints and elite choices in the Third World', in Saadet Deger and Robert West (eds.), *Defense, Security and Development*. New York: St Martin's Press, 1987, 140–57.

Royal United Services Institute. *Newsbrief* (January 1990).

*RUSI*, 124 (June 1979).

Schubert, H. 'The first cast-iron cannon made in England', *Journal of the Iron and Steel Institute*, 146 (1942), 131–40.

Schubert, H. R. 'The superiority of English cast-iron cannon at the close of the sixteenth century', *Journal of the Iron and Steel Institute*, 161 (February 1949), 85–6.

Scott-Morrison, S. 'The Arms Export Control Act: an evaluation of the role of Congress in policing arms sales', *Stanford Journal of International Studies*, 14 (Spring 1979), 105–24.

Shichor, Yitzhak. 'Unfolded arms: Beijing's recent military sales offensive', *The Pacific Review*, 1:3 (1988), 320–30.

Shuey, Robert, 'U.S. legislative responses to missile proliferation', paper presented at the International Studies Association annual meeting, Washington, 13 April 1990.

Simpson, John. 'The nuclear non-proliferation regime as a model for commercial armament restraint', in Thomas Ohlson (ed.), *Arms Transfer Limitations and Third World Security*. Oxford: Oxford University Press, 1988, 227–40.

Singh, Bilveer, 'ASEAN's arms industries: potential and limits', *Comparative Strategy*, 8:2 (1989), 249–67.

Snitch, Thomas. 'East European involvement in the world's arms market', in Arms Control and Disarmament Agency, *World Military Expenditures and Arms Transfers, 1972–1982*. Washington: Arms Control and Disarmament Agency, 1984, 117–21.

Spector, Leonard. 'Foreign-supplied combat aircraft: will they drop the Third World bomb?', *Journal of International Affairs*, 40:1 (Summer 1986), 143–58.

Staudenmaier, William. 'Defense planning in Iraq: an alternative perspective', in Stephanie Neuman (ed.), *Defense Planning in Less-Industrialized States*. Lexington, Mass.: D. C. Heath, 1984, 53–66.

Stork, Joe. 'Arms industries of the Middle East', *Middle East Report*, 17:1 (January–February 1987), 12–16.

Taylor, Trevor. 'Defence industries in international relations', *Review of International Studies*, 16 (1990), 59–73.

Thee, Marek. 'Militarism and militarization in contemporary international relations', in Asbjørn Eide and Marek Thee (eds.), *Problems of Contemporary Militarism*. London: Croom Helm, 1980, 15–35.

Thomas, Raju. 'India: the politics of weapons procurement', in James Katz (ed.), *The Implications of Third World Military Industrialization: Sowing the Serpent's Teeth*. Lexington, Mass.: D. C. Heath, 1986, 151–63.

Trebilcock, Clive. 'British armaments and European industrialization, 1890–1914', *Economic History Review*, 2nd series, 26 (1973), 254–72.

'Legends of the British armaments industry: a revision', *Journal of Contemporary History*, 5:4 (1970), 3–19.

'"Spin-off" in British economic history: armaments and industry, 1760–1914', *Economic History Review*, 22:3 (1969), 474–90.

Treddenick, John. 'The economic significance of the Canadian defence industrial base', in David Haglund (ed.), *Canada's Defence Industrial Base: The Political Economy of Preparedness and Procurement*. Kingston: Ronald Frye, 1988, 15–48.

Van Steenburg, Robert. 'An analysis of Canadian–American defence economic cooperation: the history and current issues', in David Haglund (ed.), *Canada's Defence Industrial Base: The Political Economy of Preparedness and Procurement*. Kingston: Ronald Frye, 1988, 189–219.

Vincent, John. 'Change and international relations', *Review of International Studies*, 9:1 (January 1983), 63–70.

Walker, William and Philip Gummett. 'Britain and the European armaments market', *International Affairs* (London), 65:3 (1989), 419–42.

Wallerstein, Immanuel. 'The future of the world economy', in Terence Hopkins and Immanuel Wallerstein (eds.), *Processes of the World-System*. Beverly Hills: Sage Publishing, 1980, 167–80.

Wang Ling. 'On the invention and use of gunpowder and firearms in China', *Isis*, 37:109–10 (July 1947), 160–78.

Westney, D. Eleanor. 'The military', in Marius Jansen and Gilbert Rozman (eds.), *Japan in Transition: From Tokugawa to Meiji*. Princeton: Princeton University Press, 1986, 168–94.

Whetten, Lawrence. 'The Arab–Israeli dispute: great power behaviour', *Adelphi Paper*, 128. London: International Institute for Strategic Studies, 1977.

Whittaker, C. R. 'Late Roman trade and traders', in Peter Garnsey et al. *Trade in the Ancient Economy*. London: Chatto & Windus, 1983, 163–80.

Wulf, Herbert. 'Arms production in the Third World', in Stockholm International Peace Research Institute. *World Armaments and Disarmament: SIPRI Yearbook 1985*. Stockholm: Stockholm International Peace Research Institute, 1985, 329–43.

'Arms production in Third World countries: effects on industrialization', unpublished paper.

'Recent trends of arms transfers and possible multilateral action for control', paper presented to the United Nations conference on Transparency in International Arms Transfers, Florence, 25–8 April 1990.

'The West German arms industry and arms exports', *Alternatives*, 13:3 (July 1988), 319–35.

Zukrowska, Katarzyna. 'East European international arms transfers and prospects for limitation', paper presented to the United Nations conference on Transparency in International Arms Transfers, Florence, 25–8 April 1990.

## Government documents

Assembly of Western European Union. *Defence Industry in Spain and Portugal.* Paris: WEU, 1988.

*Konversiya – Conversion in Soviet Military Industry.* Paris: WEU, 1990.

Canada, Department of External Affairs. *Task Force on Europe 1992: Report of the Working Group on Defence Products.* Ottawa: External Affairs, 1989.

Grimmett, Richard. *Trends in Conventional Arms Transfers to the Third World by Major Supplier,* various years. Washington: Congressional Research Service, various years.

Independent European Programme Group. *Towards a Stronger Europe,* vols. I and II (2 vols.). Brussels: Independent European Programme Group, 1986.

International Labour Office. *Year Book of Labour Statistics.* Geneva: International Labour Office, various years.

League of Nations. *Statistical Yearbook of the Trade in Arms and Ammunition.* Geneva: League of Nations, annual, 1924–38.

Manfredi, Arthur et al. 'Ballistic Missile Proliferation Potential of Non-Major Military Powers', Congressional Research Service Report for Congress, 6 August 1987.

Organization for Economic Cooperation and Development. *Aid from OPEC Countries.* Paris: OECD, 1983.

*Science and Technology Indicators: Basic Statistical Series, Recent Results. Selected S&T Indicators 1981–86.* Paris: OECD, 1986.

Shuey, Robert. 'Missile proliferation: a discussion of U.S. objectives and policy options', Congressional Research Service Report for Congress, 90–120, 21 February 1990.

United Kingdom. *Foreign Policy Aspects of Overseas Arms Sales.* Memorandum submitted by the Foreign and Commonwealth Office to the House of Commons, Foreign Affairs Committee, 4 March 1981.

United Nations. *Economic and Social Consequences of the Arms Race and of Military Expenditures.* New York: United Nations, 1978.

*National Accounts Statistics: Main Aggregates and Detailed Tables, 1985.* New York: United Nations, 1987.

*The Relationship between Disarmament and Development.* New York: United Nations, 1982.

United Nations Conference on Trade and Development. *Financial Solidarity for Development, 1983 Review.* New York: UNCTAD, 1984.

United States, Arms Control and Disarmament Agency. *World Military Expenditures and Arms Transfers,* annual. Washington: Arms Control and Disarmament Agency, various years.

United States, Central Intelligence Agency. *Arms Flows to LDCs: U.S.–Soviet Comparisons, 1974–77.* Washington: Central Intelligence Agency, 1978.

*Communist Aid Activities in Non-Communist Less-Developed Countries, 1979 and 1954–1979.* Washington: Central Intelligence Agency, 1980.

United States, Committee on Foreign Relations. *U.S. Military Sales to Iran.* Washington: Government Printing Office, 1976.

United States, Congress, House of Representatives. *Arms Sales in North Africa and the Conflict in the Western Sahara*. Hearing before the Subcommittees on International Security and Scientific Affairs and on Africa, Committee on Foreign Affairs, 98th Congress, 1st session. Washington: Government Printing Office, 1981.

'Munitions Control Newsletter 47', reprinted in *Review of the President's Conventional Arms Transfer Policy*. Hearing before the Subcommittee on International Security and Scientific Affairs, Committee on International Relations, 95th Congress, 2nd session. Washington: Government Printing Office, 1978.

*Proposed Arms Transfers to the Yemen Arab Republic*. Hearing before the Subcommittee on Europe and the Middle East, Committee on Foreign Affairs, 96th Congress, 1st session. Washington: Government Printing Office, 1979.

United States, Congress, Senate. *Arms Transfer Policy*. Hearing before the Committee on Foreign Relations, 95th Congress, 1st session. Washington: Government Printing Office, 1977.

*Conventional Arms Sales*. Hearing before the Committee on Foreign Relations, 97th Congress, 1st session. Washington: Government Printing Office, 1981.

*Proposed Sale of F-16s to Venezuela*. Hearing before the Committee on Foreign Relations, 97th Congress, 2nd session. Washington: Government Printing Office, 1982.

United States, Congressional Budget Office. *Budgetary Cost Savings to the Department of Defense Resulting from Foreign Military Sales*. Staff working paper, 24 May 1976. Washington: Congressional Budget Office, 1976.

*The Effect of Foreign Military Sales on the U.S. Economy*. Staff working paper, 23 July 1976. Washington: Congressional Budget Office, 1976.

United States, Congressional Research Service. *Changing Perspectives on U.S. Arms Transfer Policy*. Report prepared for the Subcommittee on International Security and Scientific Affairs, Committee on Foreign Affairs, House of Representatives, 97th Congress, 1st session. Washington: Government Printing Office, 1981.

*Implications of President Carter's Conventional Arms Trade Policy*. Report prepared for the Committee on Foreign Relations, Senate. Washington: Government Printing Office, 1977.

United States, Department of Defense, Defense Security Assistance Agency. *Fiscal Year Series 1989*. Washington: Department of Defense, 1990.

*Foreign Military Sales, Foreign Military Construction Sales and Military Assistance Facts*. Washington: Department of Defense, 1983 and 1989.

United States, Department of State. *International Security and Development Cooperation Program*, Special Report 108, April 1983. Washington: Department of State, 1983.

*International Security and Development Cooperation Program*, Special Report 116, April 1984. Washington: Department of State, 1984.

'U.S. foreign military affairs', *Current Policy* (July 1975).

United States, General Accounting Office, Comptroller General. *Arms Sales Ceiling Based on Inconsistent and Erroneous Data*. Washington: General Accounting Office, 12 April 1978.

United States, Office of Technology Assessment. *Arming Our Allies: Cooperation and Competition in Defense Technology*. Washington: Office of Technology Assessment, May 1990.

## Other sources

*Afrique défense*
*Air International*
*Armed Forces Journal International*
*Aviation Week and Space Technology*
*Christian Science Monitor*
*Damoclès*
*Defence*
*Defence and Foreign Affairs Weekly*
*Defence Today*
*Défense & armement Héraclès*
*Defense News*
*The Economist*
*Far Eastern Economic Review*
*Financial Times*
*Flight International*
*Globe and Mail*
*Guardian*
*The Independent*
*Interavia*
*International Defense Review*
*International Herald Tribune*
*Izvestia*
*Jane's Defence Weekly*
*Jerusalem Post*
*Le Monde*
*Middle East Economic Digest*
*Military Technology*
*New York Times*
*Pravda*
*Technologia militar*
*The Times* (London)
Warnke, Paul. Personal interview, 25 September 1984.

# INDEX